This is the first full-length account of the county court, which in contemporary English life has become the main forum for most civil disputes. It began as the 'poor man's court', largely concerned with the pursuit of working-class debtors; but, as this book shows, it has expanded far beyond its origins as an agency 'for the more easy recovery of small debts' and now includes in its jurisdiction a diverse range of matters, including housing, accidents and consumer goods.

Drawing on a wide range of sources, the author traces the history of the county court from its creation in 1846 through to the reconstruction of the court system in 1971. He describes its organisation and officers, from judges to bailiffs, and discusses the roles of judges, practising lawyers and lay persons.

Given the current controversy over access to justice, this is a timely new history.

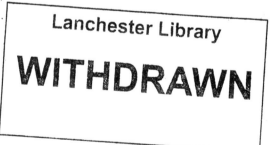

# CAMBRIDGE STUDIES IN ENGLISH LEGAL HISTORY

Edited by
J. H. BAKER
*Fellow of St Catharine's College, Cambridge*

*Recent series titles include*

Sir William Scott, Lord Stowell
Judge of the High Court of Admiralty: 1798–1828
HENRY J. BOURGUIGNON

Sir Henry Maine
A Study in Victorian Jurisprudence
R. C. J. COCKS

Roman Canon Law in Reformation England
R. H. HELMHOLZ

Fundamental Authority in Late Medieval English Law
NORMAN DOE

Law, Politics and the Church of England
The Career of Stephen Lushington 1782–1873
S. M. WADDAMS

The Early History of the Law of Bills and Notes
A Study of the Origins of Anglo-American Commercial Law
JAMES STEVEN ROGERS

The Law of Evidence in Victorian England
CHRISTOPHER ALLEN

John Scott, Lord Eldon, 1751–1838
ROSE MELIKAN

Literary Copyright Reform in Early Victorian England
CATHERINE SEVILLE

# A HISTORY OF THE COUNTY COURT, 1846–1971

PATRICK POLDEN

PUBLISHED BY THE PRESS SYNDICATE OF THE UNIVERSITY OF CAMBRIDGE
The Pitt Building, Trumpington Street, Cambridge CB2 1RP

CAMBRIDGE UNIVERSITY PRESS
The Edinburgh Building, Cambridge CB2 2RU, UK
http://www.cup.cam.ac.uk
40 West 20th Street, New York, NY 10011–4211, USA
http://www.cup.org
10 Stamford Road, Oakleigh, Melbourne 3166, Australia



First published 1999

Printed in the United Kingdom at the University Press, Cambridge

Typeset in Imprint 10/12 [CE]

*A catalogue record for this book is available from the British Library*

*Library of Congress cataloguing in publication data*

Polden, Patrick.
A history of the county court, 1846–1971 / Patrick Polden.
p. cm. – (Cambridge studies in English legal history)
ISBN 0 521 62232 8 (hb)
1. County courts – Great Britain – History. I. Title. II. Series.
KD7228.P65 1999
347.41'02 – dc21 98–43621 CIP

ISBN 0 521 62232 8 hardback

TO MY MOTHER

AND

THE MEMORY OF MY FATHER

# CONTENTS

# ACKNOWLEDGEMENTS

Many people have helped me in the writing and production of this book. Several members of the Lord Chancellor's Department, particularly the former Departmental Records Officer, Mrs Enid Smith, gave me valuable assistance. Thanks are also due to the staff at various libraries and repositories, notably the Public Record Office, the Bodleian Law Library, the British Library and the Guildhall Library. Professor K. J. M. Smith provided helpful and acute comments upon several chapters. My frequently ill-tempered and often ineffectual struggles with the most basic features of modern technology have called for and received both forbearance and practical assistance from Brunel Law Department's secretarial staff; Angela Duncan and Amanda Crew, especially, tendered help well beyond the call of duty. I am indebted also to Professor John Baker and the staff of the Cambridge University Press.

The chief sufferer throughout has been my wife, who has heroically refrained from pointing out how much more straightforward is the study of modern courts than her own field of medieval landowners. She has earned thanks, and a break.

# ABBREVIATIONS

| | |
|---|---|
| *AALR* | *Anglo-American Law Review* |
| *Al. Cant.* | J. and J. A. Venn, *Alumni Cantabrigienses* |
| *Austin Jones Report* | *Final Report of the Committee on County Courts, 1949, PP* 1948–9 [Cmd 7668] XIII |
| *Beeching Report* | *Report of the Royal Commission on Assizes and Quarter Sessions, PP* 1968–9 [Cmnd 4153] XXVIII |
| *Boase* | F. R. Boase, *Modern English Biography* |
| *CCC* | *County Courts Chronicle* |
| *CCO* | *County Court Officer* |
| *Childers Report* | *Report from the Select Committee on Civil Service Expenditure, 1873, PP* 1873 (248) VII |
| *CLJ* | *Cambridge Law Journal* |
| *CLP* | *Current Legal Problems* |
| *Conv.* | *Conveyancer and Property Lawyer* |
| *DNB* | L. Stephen and S. Lee (eds.), *Dictionary of National Biography* |
| *Fifth Report* | *Fifth Report of the Commissioners on Courts of Common Law, 1833, PP* 1833 [247] XXII |
| *Foster* | J. Foster, *Men at the Bar* |
| *Hansard* | *Parliamentary Debates* |
| *HCJ* | *House of Commons Journals* |
| *HEL* | Sir W. S. Holdsworth, *A History of English Law* |
| *HLJ* | *House of Lords Journals* |
| *HLSP* | *House of Lords Sessional Papers* |
| *JLH* | *Journal of Legal History* |

| | |
|---|---|
| *Jur.* | *Jurist* |
| *Lisgar Commission* | *Second Report of the Royal Commission on the Legal Departments, PP* 1874 (C 1107) XXIV |
| *Lisgar Evidence* | *Evidence to the Royal Commission on the Legal Departments, PP* 1875 (C 1245) XXX |
| *LJ* | *Law Journal* |
| *LJ(CCR)* | *Law Journal County Court Reporter* |
| *LM* | *Law Magazine* |
| *LM & LR* | *Law Magazine and Law Review* |
| *LM & R* | *Law Magazine and Review* |
| *LN* | *Law Notes* |
| *LO* | *Legal Observer* |
| *LQR* | *Law Quarterly Review* |
| *LR* | *Law Review* |
| *LSG* | *Law Society's Gazette* |
| *LT* | *Law Times* |
| *MacDonnell Commission* | *Sixth Report of the Royal Commission on the Civil Service, 1915, PP* 1914–16 [Cd 7832] XII |
| *MacDonnell Evidence* | *Evidence to the Royal Comission on the Civil Service, PP* 1914–16 [Cd 8130] XII |
| *MacNaghten Report* | *Report of the Committee on County Court Fees, 1923, PP* 1923 [Cmd 1856] X |
| *MLR* | *Modern Law Review* |
| *NLJ* | *New Law Journal* |
| *Payne Report* | *Report of the Royal Commission on the Enforcement of Judgment Debts, 1969, PP* 1969 [Cmnd 3909] XXXVI |
| *PP* | *Parliamentary Papers (House of Commons)* |
| *Radcliffe Report* | *Report of the Committee on County Courts, 1919, PP* 1919 [Cmd 431] XIIIa |
| *Romilly Report* | *Report of the Royal Commission on County Courts, 1855, PP* 1854–5 [1914] XVIII |
| *Second Report* | *Second Report of the Judicature Commissioners, 1872, PP* 1872 [C631] XX |
| *Select Committee, 1878* | *Report of the Select Committee on the* |

| | |
|---|---|
| | *County Courts (no. 2) Bill, PP* 1878 (267) XI |
| *SJ* | *Solicitors' Journal* |
| *Swift Evidence* | *Evidence to the Committee on County Court Staff* |
| *Swift Report* | *Report of the Committee on County Court Staff, PP* [Cmd 1049] XIII |
| *TNAPSS* | *Transactions of the National Association for the Promotion of Social Science* |
| *WW* | *Who's Who* |
| *WWW* | *Who Was Who* |

# TABLE OF CASES

# TABLE OF STATUTES

*Statutory instruments*

| | | | |
|---|---|---|---|
| 1955 | 1799 (L14) | County Court (Amendment) Rules | 225 |
| 1956 | 501 (L4) | County Court Fees Order | 163, 231 |
| 1957 | 1136 (L8) | County Court (Amendment) (no. 2) Rules | 222 |
| 1958 | 2154 (L16) | County Court Fees Order | 232 |
| 1960 | 1275 (L14) | County Court (Amendment) Rules | 224 |
| 1961 | 355 | County Court Fees Order | 232 |
| | 1526 | County Court (Amendment) Rules | 173, 222 |
| 1963 | 403 (L1) | County Court (Amendment) Rules | 225 |
| 1968 | 219 (L4) | Matrimonial Causes Rules | 193 |
| 1970 | 30 (L3) | County Court (Amendment) Rules | 226 |
| | 228 (L9) | County Court Funds (Amendment) Rules | 239 |

# INTRODUCTION

To inflict one more book upon a world already awash with information demands some justification beyond the need to propitiate that modern Moloch the Research Assessment Exercise. Nor is it enough to offer the familiar incantation that this is 'an unjustly neglected subject', for readers will have learned from grim experience that all too often such subjects have been very properly neglected by more discriminating scholars as being insignificant, abstruse or plain dull. So what justifies a book on the history of the county courts?

Aside from obtaining a grant of probate or letters of administration, a citizen's most likely involvement with the civil courts is through divorce or separation, or being subjected to (or much more rarely, initiating) claims for debt. These proceedings are nowadays overwhelmingly most likely to be conducted through the county court, so what was, for most of its 150 years, often described as 'the poor man's court' remains the court of law most frequently encountered by the people in civil disputes. Throughout its history many defendants, if not most, never actually attended the court, or at least got no further than the court office, but their perceptions of the legal system in its civil garb will certainly have been influenced, and perhaps shaped or reshaped, by that experience.

Those perceptions in turn help to shape society's conception of the law as it is and as it ought to be. Individual experiences feed into the collective consciousness of communities, helping to mould their views of law's legitimacy and its perceived effectiveness in action. This in turn subtly affects how, and how well, the law operates within a community – how well it lives up to its pretensions in fact. For that reason, if no other, we should know something of these courts, for if the superior courts gave out the law, the county courts put it into practice, not always as its makers envisaged.

That would, I think, justify a book on county courts, and there is certainly no existing work to supersede or displace, though a few scholars have produced interesting and valuable studies on which I have drawn freely, gratefully and, I hope, accurately.[1] But there are as many possible 'histories' of an institution as there are historians and the fashioning of the story needs justification as well as the subject.

In view of what is said above, the most enlightening approach would perhaps be to examine the experience of the litigants and those others (such as debtors' families and friends) directly touched by court proceedings. This however presents formidable difficulties. Litigants, especially those 'one shotters' made famous by Marc Galanter, are notoriously elusive. In most courts of common law their own narrative, if given at all (as it is only in a minority of cases), will have been oral and will have perished in the absence of the shorthand writer. In the inferior courts laymen's accounts are unlikely to have survived even in the distorted shape of a judge's summation, and, even if they have, will have been subjected to the court's own ritualised reshaping. And the difficulties are compounded in the case of county courts by the destruction of court records[2] and by the fact, much commented upon by contemporaries, that with nearly 500 courts, local variations in practice were so great that generalisation is to be undertaken only with great caution.

Nevertheless, I do not believe that the difficulties are insuperable and I do believe that local studies using sources such as local newspapers, trade journals and official statistics would reveal some very interesting things. One of my aims in writing this book has been to encourage such studies by providing an accessible outline of the national picture which will, I hope, suggest topics for study and give non-lawyers the confidence to undertake it.

My other objective has been to fill in (perhaps with polyfilla) one of the many gaps in our knowledge of the operations of civil

1 In particular Gerry Rubin, whose two contributions on county courts in D. Sugarman and G. R. Rubin (eds), *Law, Economy and Society, 1750–1914* (Abingdon, 1984) (see bibliography) suggested that this was a subject which warranted more investigation.

2 G. R. Rubin, Debtors, Creditors and County Courts, *JLH* 17 (1996), 74–82.

law in the last two centuries. An extraordinary amount of filling remains to be done. Some parts of the history of the legal professions, for example, have been admirably illuminated[3] but large tracts remain in darkness. Former *terra incognita* such as insolvency and property law have been mapped[4] but there are many more voyages of discovery to be made. We still lack a full account of the making of the Judicature Acts, for example and our knowledge of the courts remains woefully inadequate, with the important, but limited exceptions of the House of Lords and the Privy Council.[5] Where, for instance, is the history of the King's Bench and the Chancery over the last two centuries?

When these and other subjects have found their historian the story of the county courts may look very different from that presented here, but all histories are provisional and this one may assist the writing of others. The aims of the book, then, are modest and traditional and they became more so in the writing. It was originally intended that its narrative should extend to the 150th anniversary, but the past twenty-five years have involved very extensive changes: to the jurisdiction – notably in family matters; to the courts' internal structure – the small claims court in particular; and to the whole court system – with the creation of circuit judges, the court service, etc.; and the pace of change shows no sign of abating. As a result, any adequate treatment of the modern era would have required more space than was available and would have unbalanced the narrative.

Fortunately, a stopping point was easily chosen. The Courts Act 1971 was a real watershed in the civil justice system, both symbolically with the abolition of the assizes and practically, for while it stopped short of bringing about that unification of high and county courts that had so long been urged, it did bring both within the embrace of an overarching judicial and administrative structure; indeed the creation of the small claims procedure in

[3] See e.g. the works by D. Sugarman, R. Cocks, D. Duman and R. Abel cited in the bibliography.

[4] J. S. Anderson, *Lawyers and the Making of English Land Law* (Oxford, 1992) and V. M. Lester, *Victorian Insolvency* (Oxford, 1995).

[5] R. Stevens, *Law and Politics: The House of Lords as a Judicial Body, 1800–1976* (London, 1979) and D. B. Swinfen, *Imperial Appeal: The Debate on the Appeal to the Privy Council 1813–1986* (Manchester, 1987).

1973 went some way towards creating the three-tier structure which had been mooted in the 1870s.

However, even thus reduced, my original plan was too ambitious. I have had to jettison much of the material on the enforcement of judgments, and the sections dealing with staff have been severely pruned. I regret particularly that those central figures the registrars have not received their due and I hope that the overall effect is not to place too much emphasis on the narrative of changes proposed and sometimes achieved as against the description of the everyday workings of what, after all, was a court whose principal function throughout was the collection of debts.

As this suggests, the shape and contents of this book are the outcome of deliberate choices on my part. They are also, no doubt, influenced by my prejudices and background. I claim no special qualifications for writing it. My professional appearances in the county courts of East Kent in the 1970s were few, brief and usually inglorious and my grasp of the Green Book is little less tenuous now than it was then. Furthermore, since I am not a member of that 'gentleman's club ... of white, male Britons, all formerly students of, and currently staff at, the Oxbridge–London nexus of legal education',[6] I am presumably excluded from the 'phallocracy' they are said to have imposed on English legal history. Even in this neutered state, however, I expect I still pipe in the 'voice of the white, middle-class patriarch'.[7] Critical readers will doubtless make appropriate allowances for distortions of class, race and sex as well as those brought about by an ignorance and carelessness which are all my own.

[6] W. P. McNeile, Living on Borderlines, *Law and Criticism* 6 (1995), 167–91 at 182.

[7] *Ibid.*, at 180.

1

# THE MAKING OF THE NEW COUNTY COURTS

## THE DEFICIENCIES OF THE COURTS

England in 1820 was on the verge of becoming 'the first industrial nation'.[1] Population was growing fast, from about 10 million in 1801 to 14 million by 1821 and more people were living in towns.[2] Most towns were still small but some were growing at a tremendous rate and a few were already very large: Manchester had 90,000 people, Liverpool 83,000 and Leeds 53,000.

Apart from ports like Liverpool most towns were still what towns had always been, centres for the supply and exchange of produce for the surrounding countryside; but there were new ones whose primary function was making goods – the factory and the mill were becoming familiar features of the northern townscape.[3] London was still a city apart: a home of industry, commerce, government and culture – the biggest and most diverse city in the western world.[4] It still dwarfed all rivals at home, yet such was the rate of growth in provincial towns that London's share of the urban population of England fell from nearly three-fifths to barely one-third.

England had long been a commercial country but internal trade, facilitated by improvements in communications,[5] became ever more intensive. Townsmen always had to be supplied with food and as more and more became wage-earners they had to buy

1 The title of Peter Mathias' book (London, 1969).

2 Mathias, *The First Industrial Nation* (2nd edn, London 1983), fig. 6, p. 227; P. Corfield, *The Impact of English Towns* (Oxford, 1982), p. 9.

3 Corfield, *Impact of English Towns*, ch. 2.

4 *Ibid.*, p. 10. Peking and Tokyo were bigger.

5 Mathias, *First Industrial Nation*, pp. 97–107. The improvements, however, should not be exaggerated.

almost everything they wanted, while in the countryside the march of enclosures was steadily eroding the possibility of even partial self-sufficiency for labourers; there was no peasantry worth the name in England by now.[6]

More crowded cities increased the potential for accidents. In the streets vehicles collided with pedestrians and with each other. Now and then houses collapsed or caught fire. In the factories, docks and mines the hands were killed or injured by machinery, for the workshop of the world was a dangerous place. Where accidents could be attributed to a breach of the duty of man to man, whether under the common law or some particular statute, there was the possibility of a law suit.[7]

Such actions, however, never formed more than a small proportion of the work of the courts of law. For centuries past their principal source of business (apart from their role in enforcing the criminal law) had been the breach of contractual obligations and in particular the obligation to pay money.[8] Here too, industrialisation promised to expand the courts' workload. A consumer society was developing with an ever-widening range of goods offered more pressingly to an enlarging class of potential purchasers; for however harshly the transition to industrialisation pressed on the lower orders, it was steadily swelling the ranks of the better off.[9]

Consumer credit was expanding. Credit purchases had long been a matter of course for the upper classes; now they were becoming a temptation for the middle classes as well, though many restrained themselves owing to a well-grounded apprehension of the draconian remedies available to their creditors should

6 *Ibid.*, pp. 55–9. One estimate for 1821 puts 24.8 per cent of the labour force in agriculture, forestry and fishing; 38.4 per cent in manufacturing and industry; 12.1 per cent in trade and transport; 12.7 per cent in domestic and personal service; 8.5 per cent in public, professional and other categories: P. Deane and W. A. Cole, *British Economic Growth, 1688–1959* (2nd edn, Cambridge, 1962), table 30.

7 W. R. Cornish and G. de N. Clark, *Law and Society in England, 1750–1950* (London, 1989), pp. 483–512, summarise the leading developments in tort law.

8 C. W. Brooks, Interpersonal Conflict and Social Tension: Civil Litigation in England, 1640–1830, in A. L. Beier (ed.), *The First Modern Society* (Cambridge, 1989), pp. 357–99 at 390.

9 N. McKendrick, The Consumer Revolution of 18th Century England, in N. McKendrick, J. Brewer and J. H. Plumb, *The Birth of a Consumer Society* (London, 1982), pp. 9–33.

they default.[10] Imprisonment for debt was routine, even on mesne process, with bankruptcy a refuge open only to traders, and humanitarian efforts to procure the release of hopeless debtors encountered resistance from many who felt it a wholesome discipline against improvidence.[11]

The poor often had little choice but to buy on credit, which sometimes took particularly pernicious forms in the tommy-shop and truck dealing.[12] Dependent upon inadequate earnings, forced to rent housing, and – a sinister new development – at the mercy of sudden slumps in trade which became the hallmark of a capitalist society[13] – many were regularly in debt. Others, who need not have been, fell victim to the blandishments of travelling pedlars and salesmen inveigling their wives into the purchase of fripperies to brighten drab and anxious lives.[14]

Credit underpinned the whole economy and the obverse of credit was debt and the coercive force of the law. Courts of law are seldom popular with those who have to use them. Debtors are apt to see them as merely an extension of the arm of the creditor and to resent the extra burden of legal costs, while creditors feel they have been deprived of their due unless the recovery of the debt is expeditious and complete. Where the debt is comparatively small it is difficult to devise an economical system which combines proper safeguards for the debtor and rapid recovery for the creditor, and Regency England had not managed to do so.

Among the features of the courts which most irritated suitors in the provinces was the striking concentration of judicial facilities in London, for though common law trials at nisi prius might take place at the assizes, every action had to start and finish in London.[15] The assizes in any case were far from satisfactory. The judges only went on their circuits twice a year – for a total of about

[10] *Ibid.*, pp. 203–30 (J. Brewer, Commercialization and Politics); J. C. Beckett, *The Aristocracy in England, 1660–1914* (Oxford, 1986), pp. 295–315.

[11] The realities of bankruptcy and its fictional treatments are examined in B. Weiss, *The Hell of the English* (Lewisburg, 1986), and there is a thorough recent treatment by V. M. Lester, *Victorian Insolvency* (Oxford, 1995).

[12] These practices were not wholly eradicated by the Truck Acts of 1831 and 1887.

[13] Mathias, *First Industrial Nation*, pp. 206–17. Sharp fluctuations due to the state of the harvest, wars and political crises were, of course, already endemic.

[14] D. Alexander, *Retailing in England during the Industrial Revolution* (London, 1970), pp. 63–86.

[15] *HEL* vol. I (5th edn, 1931), p. 188.

seventy days – and the location of the assize towns exhibited, though less outrageously, the idiosyncracies of the unreformed House of Commons. Admittedly there were no Grampounds and Old Sarums among the assize towns, but many sleepy market towns welcomed the red judge while major industrial centres never saw him: Sheffield did not receive an assize until 1955.[16] Criminal business always took precedence, so witnesses in civil suits had to be kept in hotels at the parties' expense, often many miles from their homes and businesses.[17] However valuable as a training ground for barristers, the assizes were an inefficient way of bringing justice to the people.

The same inconvenience to witnesses was even greater at trials in Westminster Hall and was one substantial element in the expense of going to law. There were several others. The courts had developed an adversarial pattern of operation and a highly elaborate and technical body of procedural rules and practice which made it foolhardy to attempt even the simplest action without professional assistance, generally involving both attorney and barrister. Lawyers revelled in this 'natural environment for technical objections and procedural stratagems: those choking, fee-sucking devices were the bane of 18th century litigation'.[18] Not surprisingly, although the common law courts had engaged in competitive strategies designed to win clients from their rivals,[19] they had not been able to make small actions economical and it was not easy to see how they could do so without far more drastic changes than even reformist lawyers were willing to contemplate.

Almost as frustrating as the cost of going to law were the law's delays. Some were the product of the traditional organisation of the legal year; no courts sat during the long summer vacation, and the four terms, outside which only interlocutory business was done, lasted only three weeks each.[20] Within this framework the

[16] *First Report of the Common Law Commissioners*, *PP* 1829 (46) V, pp. 17, 42 ff. and table 9; Sir B. Nield, *Farewell to the Assizes* (London, 1972).

[17] Brougham's speech, *Hansard* 1830 3rd s., vol. 1, cols. 711–58.

[18] Cornish and Clark, *Law and Society*, p. 25.

[19] C. W. Francis, Practice, Strategy and Institution: Debt Collection in the English Common Law Courts, 1740–1840, *North-Western University Law Review* 80 (1986), 808–954 at 847–52. Despite the competition, 'the overall cost of litigation in the central courts doubled between 1680 and 1750': Brooks, Interpersonal Conflict, pp. 381–2.

[20] *First Report*, pp. 12–16.

courts could not handle any substantial growth in business without more judges, but the judges were reluctant to add to their number lest the quality and consistency of judge-made law be impaired; moreover judges were remunerated in part from suitors' fees.[21]

Despite all these disincentives, however, recourse to the courts increased along with the expansion of commerce, and by the 1820s the King's Bench, which had drawn well ahead of its rivals in the popularity stakes, was struggling to cope with its workload.[22] Expense, delay and complexity made the courts at Westminster unsuitable for the hearing of claims for small amounts of money, for which they had never been the intended forum. There was, after all, a national network of local courts – for the county, the hundred and the borough – to provide that service, and in the sixteenth century attempts, seemingly ineffectual, had been made to exclude small debts from the royal courts.[23]

Unfortunately for suitors these local courts were for the most part very unattractive. For one thing a perverse interpretation of the Statute of Gloucester limited the jurisdiction of the county and hundred courts to claims not exceeding 40s, which became progressively more inconvenient as the value of money fell.[24] Even within these limits, however, their sometimes inconvenient location, archaic procedures and vulnerability to corruption and partiality, plus the fact that by writ of pone a suit could be removed into the superior courts, ensured that both the county and the hundred court were unpopular and largely moribund institutions.[25] A few of the hundred courts which were private franchises were still active and a handful were really busy, notably the Salford Hundred Court, serving a great town of recent growth and which therefore lacked the institutions of a borough.[26]

Borough courts were more varied in the extent of their jurisdiction and some retained their local importance longer than was

21 They became fully salaried by 6 Geo. IV c. 84.

22 *First Report*, p. 17 and table 4.

23 *HEL*, vol. I, p. 74.

24 Ibid., vol. I, p. 72; J. H. Baker, *An Introduction to English Legal History* (3rd edn, London, 1990), p. 27.

25 *HEL*, vol. I, pp. 72–5; *Fifth Report of the Common Law Commissioners*, *PP* 1833 (247) XXII, pp. 6–10.

26 *HEL*, vol. I, p. 134.

formerly assumed.[27] Even so, by 1820 few were really active. In Kent, for instance, returns to the House of Commons noted courts 'not held very often' (Canterbury), 'not held for many years' (Folkestone), 'discontinued' (Queenborough) and 'not held since 1747' (Sandwich). Even the Maidstone Court of Pleas, established by charter in the reign of George II with unlimited monetary jurisdiction, was 'not used, being as expensive as the courts of Westminster Hall'.[28]

Legal writers were generally complacent about the decline of local courts, extolling the superior quality of justice in Westminster Hall and maintaining that only through confining litigation of any substance to this narrow channel could the coherence and certainty of the common law be sustained and the need for lawsuits be restricted.[29] The high-water mark in the centralisation of justice was reached as late as 1830, when the Great Sessions for Wales, exercising a parallel jurisdiction to the superior courts, were abolished.[30]

Laymen had always been less easily persuaded of the transcendent merits of a system which required suitors to travel to London or await the assize, paying a high price for the best justice because the alternatives, where they existed at all, were so bad as to be unacceptable. Demands for change had been insistently made during the Interregnum and found their most imposing and plausible expression in the elaborate proposals of the Hale Commission.[31] In the eighteenth century potential litigants voted with their feet and stayed away from the courts – almost all courts – in great numbers.[32]

Dissatisfaction with the existing courts led to the creation of new institutions to operate alongside them, small claims courts

[27] C. W. Brooks and M. Lobban (eds.), *Communities and Courts in Britain, 1150–1900* (London, 1997), pp. xxi–xxii.

[28] *HCJ* 78 (1823), 1026.

[29] A view popularised by Sir W. Blackstone (*Commentaries on the Laws of England*, vol. III, (1979 edn, Chicago) p. 82), which became received wisdom at the bar, repeated *ad nauseam* in e.g. the *Legal Observer* and the *Law Magazine*.

[30] 11 Geo. IV & 1 Will. IV c. 70, based on recommendations by the Common Law Commissioners (*First Report*, pp. 35–52).

[31] D. Veall, *The Popular Movement for Law Reform, 1640–1660* (Oxford, 1970), pp. 167–78.

[32] Brooks, Interpersonal Conflict, pp. 360–7, 381–4; W. Prest, Law Reform in Eighteenth Century England, in P. Birks (ed.), *The Life of the Law* (London, 1993), pp. 113–24.

known initially as 'courts of conscience', a title gradually displaced by 'courts of requests'.[33] Perhaps inspired by the City of London's court of conscience, Bristol and Gloucester (jointly), Newcastle upon Tyne and Norwich obtained their courts at the end of the seventeenth century, but had few followers until the second half of the eighteenth century when towns became so eager that by 1830 some 250 courts had been established.[34]

In typically English fashion, the new courts sat alongside the old, adding to the confusion of the juridical landscape.[35] Usually however, they effectively annihilated their older rivals. In Kent in 1830 the county court had only 166 suits, and while the courts of record in Dover and Gravesend had just six and five respectively, their courts of requests could show 273 and 513. Some courts of requests were far more popular than those, Tower Hamlets having 28,624 suits, Halifax 22,864 and Liverpool 21,334.[36] In that year over 200,000 suits were brought in courts of requests, and about 300,000 in local courts of all kinds, dwarfing the 90,000 writs issued for the superior courts and justifying the claim that 'for most Englishmen, civil justice was the justice of courts of requests (and other local courts), not the justice of the common law and the superior courts'.[37]

The courts of requests gradually began to conform to a common pattern.[38] Their jurisdiction was geographically confined and limited in amount, usually to 40s but increasingly to £5; parties were allowed to give evidence, something which legal purists regarded with horror as a direct incitement to perjury; payment in instalments might be ordered, a facility the superior courts did not acquire until much later; there was no jury, and the judge, one of several commissioners appointed by the corporation, often lacked any legal qualifications. From 1747 most of the local Acts were entitled 'for the more easy and speedy recovery of small debts' and

33 W. H. D. Winder, The Courts of Requests, *LQR* 52 (1936), 369–94; M. Slatter, The Norwich Court of Requests – a Tradition Continued, *JLH* 5 (1984), 97–107.

34 *Fourth Report of the Common Law Commissioners, PP* 1831–2 (239) XXV, pt II.

35 For the profusion of courts *c.* 1600 see L. Knafla, *Kent at Law* (London, 1994).

36 *Fourth Report*, app. 1, reproduced in part in H. W. Arthurs, 'Without the Law': Courts of Local and Special Jurisdiction in Nineteenth Century England, *JLH* 5 (1984), 130–49 at 132.

37 Arthurs, 'Without the Law', 132.

38 Winder, Courts of Requests, 376.

the courts seem to have achieved that aim, providing 'a much speedier and cheaper debt collecting agency than any [the creditor] enjoys at the present day'.[39]

In the view of their leading contemporary champion, the Birmingham commissioner William Hutton, 'if the commissioners cannot decide against the law, they can decide without it'[40] and although some later Acts expressly required the court to adhere to the common law, their own lack of legal knowledge, the rarity of legal representation in the court and the want of an effective appeal meant that the commissioners had a pretty free hand.

It is not surprising that most lawyers affected either disdain or downright hostility to courts of this sort, with their potential for oppression and inconsistency. Even suitors, overwhelmingly traders, did not regard them as entirely satisfactory, for while they did possess coercive powers – in 1830 Greenwich issued 367 executions against goods and 379 against the body – their limitations were frustrating.[41] First there was a range of actions, roughly between £5 and £20, outside the jurisdiction of the courts of requests but still uneconomical to take to the superior courts. Second, there were still towns with no court of requests and no viable borough court either. Third, the problem with almost all local courts was that they were essentially fora for disputes between inhabitants of the borough, lacking effective jurisdiction over outsiders; for the increasing number of traders who operated on a regional or even a national scale, they were inadequate.

The concerns of retail traders however were not a central issue in the politics of the age. Humanitarians began to agitate for the reform of the 'bloody code' of the criminal law and the relief of insolvent debtors, and property owners became restless under Lord Eldon's costive regime in the court of Chancery, but until 1820 no prominent politician championed the cause of more effective local justice.[42]

39 *Ibid.*, 391.
40 Quoted in H. W. Arthurs, *'Without the Law': Administrative Justice and Legal Pluralism in Nineteenth Century England* (Toronto, 1985) at p. 29. This book supplements the article referred to above.
41 *Fourth Report.*
42 *HEL*, vol. XIII (1952), pp. 259–307.

## THE ORIGINS OF THE NEW COUNTY COURTS

Lord Althorp was a rising man among the opposition Whigs who, having recently succeeded in putting through Parliament a bill to reform insolvency proceedings,[43] next turned his attention to the related problem of pursuing small debts through the courts. Like Mackintosh and Romilly before him, Althorp had already found that law reform was 'a topic of no party interest, and leading to no political results';[44] hence he could expect little support from his political associates. In fact some of the most vehement opposition would come from leading Whig lawyers, while his staunchest supporter in the Lords was Lord Redesdale, an arch-reactionary in politics.[45]

Althorp presented his first bill in March 1821. He proposed to revitalise the county courts by raising their jurisdiction to £15 and giving the sheriff an 'assessor' with legal training. Each assessor would make a quarterly circuit of towns nominated by the justices at quarter sessions, holding jury trials with attorneys addressing the court only on points of law.[46] The response was discouraging, the Attorney-General pronouncing it 'extremely objectionable' and shrewdly playing on the fears of the county members by predicting that it would result in a heavy charge on the county rate.[47] It was evident to Althorp that he would need influential backing if he was to make headway, so when he tried again in 1823 he had the bill sent to a select committee, having taken steps to procure convincing evidence of the deficiencies of the courts and the great volume of credit trading which they were failing to support.[48]

The committee pronounced that 'every witness ... agrees in stating, that no prudent tradesman ever thinks it for his interest to

43 Sir D. Le Marchant, *A Memoir of John Charles, Viscount Althorp* (London, 1876), pp. 182–90.

44 *Ibid.*, p. 188.

45 Redesdale had in fact presented a bill of his own in 1820: *HLSP* CXIV, nos. 18, 97; *Hansard* 1820 2nd s., vol. 1, cols. 742–6.

46 *PP* 1821 (85, 233) I.

47 *Hansard* 1821 2nd s., vol. 4, col. 1264.

48 Althorp asked the radical William Hone to collect data for him: E. A. Watson, *Whig Renaissance: Lord Althorp and the Whig Party, 1782–1845* (New York and London, 1987), pp. 111–12. The many petitions in support of the Bills of 1824 and 1825 (*HCJ* 79 and 80, with at least fifty in the latter) may also have been engineered.

sue for any debt below [£15]'.[49] Nor was the injustice confined to creditors, because in the superior courts and at the assizes 'the expense of these proceedings ... puts it into the power of unprincipled men to harass the poor, and to compel them to pay money, which according to justice they ought not'.[50] While giving a broadly favourable verdict on courts of requests, the committee did not feel that they could safely be expanded beyond the bigger towns where 'it is very easy to find intelligent and respectable men, well qualified to perform the duties of commissioners'.[51] Nor could the limit of their jurisdiction safely be enlarged to £10 or more since (and the committee's logic is rather questionable here) many cases might then arise which called for greater legal knowledge than even intelligent laymen were likely to possess.

Two popular courts were rejected as possible models: the Clerk of the Middlesex county court volunteered that its process was too summary for cases above 40s,[52] while the county court of Lancaster, despite possessing advantages over other county courts, was nevertheless, through 'the necessity of adopting all the modes of proceeding in the superior courts ... an inconvenient and expensive system of trial for small debts'.[53]

The committee therefore proposed to revitalise the old county court. It was to have a legally qualified assessor as judge and, since 'they would have felt great objection to such an increase to the influence of the crown',[54] the committee altered Althorp's proposal, giving the appointment instead to the *Custos Rotulorum.* Jurisdiction was to be raised to £10 and, though there was to be a full twelve-man jury, procedure was to be greatly simplified. The court was to have the power to direct payment by instalments and, since 'it is quite obvious that if a power to appeal is given in courts such as those ... all hopes of establishing a cheap jurisdiction must be given up',[55] the assessor was given instead a power to order a new trial if the jury returned a verdict contrary to law or evidence.

Althorp was concerned lest the lack of effective remedies should

49 *PP* 1823 (386) IV, p. 1. 50 *Ibid.*, p. 2. 51 *Ibid.*, p. 3.

52 *Ibid.*, pp. 4–5. The court under Serjeant Heath and his son was later severely criticised in Parliament: *Hansard*, 1841–2 3rd s., vol. 65, cols. 1184–6.

53 *PP* 1823 (386) IV, p. 5. Whereas in the rest of the country, county courts could hear cases above 40s only if the plaintiff obtained the writ *Justicies* from the King's Bench, in the Duchy it was available from the Chancery 'at a much smaller expense'.

54 *Ibid.*, p. 7. 55 *Ibid.*, p. 9.

curtail the supply of credit to the urban poor, but many on the committee shared the common fear that better remedies might make traders too lax in giving credit; to prevent this they recommended that there should be a two-year limitation period for debts sought to be recovered in the county courts.[56] On the vexed question of emoluments the committee came down decisively in favour of a salaried assessor, though his staff might be paid by fees. Salaries, to come from suitors' fees, would vary from one county to another, being set by the justices at quarter sessions; any shortfall was to be made up from the county rate.[57]

Althorp quoted extensively from the report when reintroducing his bill in February 1824 and it made good progress despite predictable differences over patronage and salaries and City objections to the shorter limitation period.[58] Loudest in opposition were the lawyers; the Attorney-General averred it would be useless unless advocates were barred from appearing and the assessor was empowered to cross-examine witnesses himself, while others maintained that the bar would be corrupted by the lure of these judicial posts.[59] What proved to be the most intractable objection however had nothing to do with the merits of the bill.

The superior courts had certain 'patent officers', some of whom were perfect sinecurists like Lord Ellenborough (chief clerk of the court of King's Bench, worth £9,000 a year),[60] while others performed functions of a largely formal nature. All extracted fees from suitors and most had either purchased the office themselves or had it purchased for them. Though public opinion was growing less tolerant of sinecures it was generally accepted that an office-holder was entitled to compensation if his office were abolished or if reform of the institution seriously diminished its value. These patent officers, however, had a novel complaint: they claimed compensation for the diversion of business – estimated at one quarter – from the superior courts to a reinvigorated county

56 Le Marchant, *Viscount Althorp*, pp. 189–90; *PP* 1823 (386) IV, p. 9.

57 *PP* 1823 (386) IV, p. 10.

58 *Hansard* 1824 2nd s., vol. 10, cols. 210–12, 303–4, 728–9, 1425–42; vol. 11, cols. 852–6.

59 *Ibid.*, vol. 10, col. 1441.

60 The son of the former Lord Chief Justice, he launched an intemperate attack on the Bill: *Hansard* 1824 2nd s., vol. 10, col. 1315. As shown in J. Wade, *The Extraordinary Black Book* (London, edn of 1830) at p. 485, he was also joint *custos brevium* of the same court.

court.[61] Such a claim was almost unprecedented and posed a threat to future reforms of the public service if it were admitted. Nevertheless it furnished a convenient excuse to resist a measure which even Eldon acknowledged was probably necessary,[62] and in a House of Lords with an elevated conception of the sanctity of property rights it was fatal to the bill's chances.

The 1825 session proved equally frustrating even though Althorp reluctantly gave way on compensation. He erred in trying to placate concerns about patronage by substituting for his new assessors the existing commissioners of the Insolvency Court, augmented by four; this failed to win over opponents and worried supporters, who were doubtful whether the judges could take on the extra volume of work.[63] Realising that only the government could carry the measure, Althorp besought the Home Secretary, Sir Robert Peel, to take it over. Peel's record had already, in the despondent view of one Whig leader, established him in the public mind as 'the only reformer'[64] and he agreed to add local courts to the queue of reforms he had in hand, though he would not adopt Althorp's bill unaltered.

Peel was a reformer indeed, but was a cautious and pragmatic one, devoted to shoring up institutions by judicious modernisation, not to root-and-branch reconstruction. His introduction to the Small Debts Recovery Bill in June 1827 affords a good illustration of his outlook:

> We find ... in existence at present, a court of very ancient institution, familiar therefore to the people, founded upon good principles and of known and defined powers and constitution. It appears to me a wise course to retain and to improve this institution; to enlarge the sphere of its operation and to infuse into it new energy and vigour, rather than to supersede it by the establishment of a novel jurisdiction, resting on no foundation of antiquity, with no prescription to plead in its favour, and in the constitution of which, in every step, an experiment of doubtful issue must be made.[65]

[61] *Hansard* 1824 2nd s., vol. 10, cols. 1426–30. The Attorney-General put the compensation at £5–6,000 p.a., diminishing as the sinecurists died.

[62] *Ibid.*, vol. 11, col. 1316.

[63] Le Marchant, *Viscount Althorp*, pp. 193–5; *Hansard* 1825 2nd s., vol. 12, col. 152; vol. 13, cols. 599–601; *HCJ* 80 (1825–6) and *HLJ* 57 (1825). Evidence of the office-holders to the select committee is in *PP* 1825 (276) V.

[64] George Tierney, quoted in N. Gash, *Mr Secretary Peel* (London, 1961), p. 337.

[65] *Hansard* 1827 2nd s., vol. 17, cols. 1350–8.

Most of Althorp's bill was retained by Peel. The main difference was in the judges. The sheriff or his deputy would preside and though the sheriff might appoint an assessor *ad hoc*, he would not be permanent, so avoiding any claim to a pension. The jury was to be only of five; execution against goods was to be the principal sanction – there was no right to imprison a debtor – and to meet recent complaints about abuses by bailiffs of local courts, the sheriff was empowered to dismiss county court bailiffs for misconduct and to award damages against them for extortion.[66]

It was a typical measure of Liberal Toryism, conservative and inexpensive, and since Althorp generously hailed it as an improvement on his own it seemed to have a fair wind behind it.[67] But the claims of the patent officers continued to obstruct progress.[68] Anxious for an end to 'compensation in instalments',[69] Peel referred the whole question of the patent officers to the Common Law Commissioners and by the time this 'most rank and unweeded garden of lucrative offices without employment'[70] had been purged of its sinecures Peel had resigned for the second time and the old order was engulfed in a turmoil which threatened to blow it away.

The Whigs were in office at last, among them their great champion of law reform Henry Brougham, who had presented his credentials in a six-hour *tour de force* in the Commons in 1828.[71]

66 *Ibid.*, cols. 297–8, 1350–6; *PP* 1826–7 (535) II.

67 *Hansard* 1827 2nd s., vol. 17, col. 1360. It was also welcomed by the Attorney-General, Sir James Scarlett.

68 The Bill went through its committee stage but the report was shelved on 22 June: *HCJ* 82, 595.

69 *Hansard* 1828 2nd s., vol. 19, col. 1475; Gash, *Mr Secretary Peel*, p. 477.

70 Wade, *Extraordinary Black Book*, p. 485; *Hansard* 1829 2nd s., vol. 21, col. 1165. The Act abolishing the patent offices (11 Geo. IV & 1 Will. IV c. 58) is described in S. Walpole, *A History of England from 1815*, vol. III (London, 1880), pp. 48–50.

71 Brougham has proved a daunting subject for biographers. Lord Campbell, *Lives of Lord Lyndhurst and Lord Brougham* (vol. VIII of *Lives of the Lord Chancellors*, London, 1869) is entertaining, well informed and relishably malicious, while his more balanced modern biographers, e.g. C. New (1961), R. Stewart (1985) and F. Hawes (1957) do not examine his contribution to law reform in detail. The omission is being repaired by T. H. Ford, first through several articles and then in *Henry Brougham and his World* (Chichester, 1995), which goes down to 1830. R. K. Huch, *Henry, Lord Brougham, the Later Years, 1830–1868* (Lewiston, 1993), despite the title, is mostly on the 1830s. Brougham's own *Life and Times* (3 vols., London, 1871) has useful correspondence but is not a reliable narrative.

Though local courts had figured in it only briefly,[72] Brougham aspired to bring about the reforms which had eluded Althorp and Peel through a bill presented to the Commons in 1830.[73] Before the year was out he found himself bringing it forward again, this time in the other House and from the Woolsack, prudence, as much as fitness, having suggested him for the great office of Lord Chancellor which removed him from the Commons.[74]

Brougham was one of the wonders of the age and seemed the embodiment of the 'march of intellect'. He brought to law reform a daring and confidence which knew no bounds, an arrogance which scouted opposition and obstacles and a fecundity in producing bills matched only by an airy irresponsibility when it came to the niceties of draftsmanship.[75] When such a man turned his mind to local courts the result was unlikely to resemble the productions of less adventurous spirits. Indeed, so ambitious was the scope of Brougham's proposals that even their author felt it prudent to confine them in the first instance to two diverse counties, Kent and Northumberland, by way of an experiment.

Introducing his measure in the Lords, Brougham began by demonstrating that a large proportion of the business of the superior courts of common law concerned claims for less than £100 – 'he took that sum as a natural limit for those actions which ought not to be removed'[76] – and that even when the trial of small actions took place at the assizes they were unacceptably expensive, 'out of all keeping, in fact, to the value of the thing litigated'.[77] This, of course, was conventional wisdom. The natural home for small claims was in local courts and Brougham extolled the courts of the Sheriff Depute in his native Scotland.[78] His solution to

[72] *Hansard* 1828 2nd s., vol. 18, cols. 190–1.

[73] *Hansard* 1830 2nd s., vol. 24, cols. 243–74.

[74] R. Stewart, *Henry Brougham, 1778–1868* (London, 1985), pp. 248–52.

[75] Sir John Eardley Wilmot, an admirer who became a county court judge, listed 112 bills he claimed were produced or inspired by Brougham: A. H. Manchester, *A Modern Legal History of England and Wales, 1750–1950* (London, 1979), p. 16.

[76] *Hansard* 1830 3rd s., vol. 1, col. 719. Returns to the Commons in 1827 showed 64,000 of 93,000 affidavits for debt filed in the common law courts to be for sums under £50; only 15,000 exceeded Brougham's 'natural limit'.

[77] *Ibid.*, col. 720. Brougham had been particularly influenced by his own experience at the spring assizes of 1826, when the average award in fifty-two verdicts at Lancaster was £14 15s.

[78] *Ibid.*, col. 716.

England's problems, however, lay in 'forming a Court, new in its kind, but modelled upon ancient principles' since 'it was evident, from all the attempts which had been made to recall the ancient County Courts into existence ... [and] from the opposition which had been made to such plans ... that they must abandon the ancient County Courts as incapable of being now (*sic*,?new) modelled to suit the wants of the country'.[79]

The new courts, courts of record, were to be styled 'Courts of Local or Ordinary Jurisdiction'. Each county would have one, its resident judge sitting in towns of his choosing, holding court in each at least once a month except for his vacation in August. His jurisdiction would be impressively wide; personal torts up to £50; debts, contracts, trespass to goods, trover and small legacies up to £100. Ultimately the jurisdiction would also be an exclusive one but at the outset the superior courts would have cognisance of cases within these limits if they involved titles to land or complex questions of law; the other inferior courts would eventually be abolished to leave the new courts masters of the field in their locality.[80]

Not content with this, Brougham conferred on his protégés the power to sit as arbitrators and in 'courts of reconcilement'. He had been deeply impressed by the success of such courts in Denmark and expounded their virtues:

> if the suitors who daily thronged the Courts of Common Law had, instead of consulting a counsel or an attorney, or any other person equally interested in the actual existence of an action, the advantage of a previous conference with a conciliatory judge, he would not say that nine cases out of ten, but certainly two out of three, would never be brought to trial.[81]

Courts of reconcilement became a sort of King Charles' head with Brougham, who tried unwearyingly for the rest of his active life to persuade the invincibly insular English of their merits. Under Brougham's scheme the local judges would therefore be required to act in a bewildering variety of capacities- as 'conciliatory judge', arbitrator, small claims judge, judge in ordinary and also as magistrate. Different rules as to juries, pleadings and costs would govern each role, and such was Brougham's impatience

79 *Ibid.*, col. 727.

80 The Bill, concerted with M. A. Taylor, a veteran law reformer, and Thomas Denman, is in *HLSP* 1830–1 CCLXXXIII (17) and *PP* 1830 (568, 569) I.

81 *Hansard* 1830 3rd s., vol. 1, col. 735.

with fine detail that acute critics could find plenty in the way of inconsistencies, contradictions and omissions;[82] even the experienced attorney entrusted with the task of drawing up the schedule of costs was said to have found it impossible to create a workable scheme.[83] Since the judges would need to be men of considerable ability the rewards would have to be attractive. They were to receive £1,500 plus up to £500 out of the fees, and would be assisted by registrars on £400 plus up to £300 from the fees.

By the sheer ambition of his proposals Brougham had raised the stakes in the debate about local courts. Previous proposals would have taken a quantity of small business away from Westminster Hall and, in the case of Althorp's bills, would have created a cadre of junior provincial judges; but their impact on the legal profession and the administration of justice would have been trivial compared with what was now put forward. Brougham had already made himself thoroughly unpopular with attorneys on the northern circuit[84] and the profession resented his imputation that they did not give disinterested advice.[85] Furthermore the vested interests of the bar and big London agency firms of solicitors were sure to oppose his plans as a threat to their prosperity.[86] And for diehard Tory peers here was radicalism indeed. They would take their cue from Eldon and from Lyndhurst, who gave the bill an ominously chilly reception.[87]

One attack came from the opposite quarter, from a viewpoint which denounced the bill vehemently as a feeble thing, a shoring up of 'matchless constitution' and a betrayal of true, logical reform. This was the line taken by Jeremy Bentham and robustly pressed in the *Westminster Review*:[88] sorely wounding to Brougham's vanity, it was highly amusing to his many enemies. Bentham,

[82] E.g. *LM* 5 (1831), 1–49; *LO* 1 (1830–1), *passim*.
[83] *LO* 1 (1830–1), 170–3.
[84] T. H. Ford, Henry Brougham on the Northern Circuit: Even His Own Solicitor: paper to the Tenth British Legal History Conference, Oxford, 1991.
[85] *Hansard* 1830 3rd s., vol. 1, col. 735.
[86] The first issues of the journal the *Legal Observer* have leaders, letters and reviews of pamphlets, almost all of them hostile.
[87] *Hansard* 1830 3rd s., vol. 1, cols. 739–40. According to E. Myers, *Lord Althorp* (London, 1890), p. 39n, Lyndhurst had abandoned his support for Althorp's bill when he found that Eldon had become opposed and with 'unscrupulous effrontery' spoke and voted against it.
[88] Mr Brougham and Local Judicatories, vol. 13 (1830), 420–57. This followed a denunciation of his law reform views in vol. 11 (1829), 447–71.

who had 'an extreme detestation of jobbery',[89] seems to have taken violent exception to the patronage which would accrue to the Lord Chancellor under this scheme, but his own ideas, characteristically stark and uncompromising, were not practical politics and his disciples, though eloquent, were few and not in a position to mount an effective opposition.

It was evident that the bill would not make headway in the Lords unless it could be presented as more than the wild project of an erratic radical politician. With even his energies fully taxed in trying at once to fulfil his boast that he would rapidly clear off the accumulated arrears in Chancery and to participate vigorously in the intense political activity surrounding the Reform Bill, Brougham was probably not sorry to buy time by sending the local courts issue away to the Common Law Commissioners for more dispassionate examination. These Commissioners had been appointed in 1827 and now their terms of reference were extended 'to inquire into the practice and proceedings of provincial courts ... for the recovery of small debts'.[90] They were all barristers[91] and the conservative tone of their first three reports encouraged lawyers to suppose that they would find little to commend in Brougham's extravagant scheme and would, at worst, recommend something along the lines Peel had brought forward.

In fact, however, the Commissioners formed a most unfavourable view of existing arrangements for justice in the provinces and began their report with a devastating indictment:[92]

It appears to us that the present inferior courts are more or less open to some or all of the following objections:

[89] A. Aspinall, *Lord Brougham and the Whig Party* (Manchester, 1927), pp. 230–1. For Bentham's reaction to Brougham's great speech see J. F. Dillon, Bentham's Influence on the Reforms of the Nineteenth Century, in *Select Essays in Anglo-American Legal History*, vol. I (London, 1907), pp. 492–515, at 502–3. Brougham's old vehicle, *The Edinburgh Review*, was more sympathetic: vol. 51 (1830), 478–95.

[90] *Fifth Report*, *PP* 1833 (247) XX. On the role of commissions in nineteenth century law reform see A. H. Manchester, Law Reform in England and Wales, 1840–1880, *Acta Juridica* (1977), 189–202.

[91] J. F. Pollock, H. J. Stephen, J. Evans, T. Starkie and W. Wightman. Pollock and Wightman later became judges, Starkie a county court judge. Those commissioners who were judges already did not participate in this report: J. M. Collinge (ed.), *Officials of Royal Commissions of Inquiry* (London, 1984), pp. 14–15.

[92] *Fifth Report*, p. 1.

That their jurisdiction is in general too limited in point of amount and local extent.
That frequently suits are removable into the higher courts without security.
The want of competent Judges and Juries.
The want of efficient inferior ministers to serve and execute process.
The use of complicated and expensive pleadings.
The distance of the place of trial from the residences of the parties and witnesses.
The want of sufficient means to compel the attendance of witnesses.
Delay.
The facility of evading execution.
The abuses occasioned by entrusting the execution of process to improper agents, for whose misconduct no superior is responsible.
The want of appeal.
The expense of the proceedings as compared with the amount of the demand.

Institutions were reviewed in turn and none escaped condemnation. County courts were 'inefficient for the administration of justice, and the subject of general complaint'. As for hundred courts, 'incompetent juries, an ill-regulated course of pleading, and the practice of allowing costs wholly disproportioned to the action ... render these courts inoperative for any useful purpose'.[93] One or two local courts were singled out for praise, notably the Palace Court of Whitehall,[94] but most of the borough courts were condemned for their arbitrary and sometimes exorbitant costs and the narrowness of their geographical jurisdiction.[95]

The select committee of 1823, composed mostly of laymen, had been quite favourable to the courts of requests, but the Commissioners were severe. As lawyers they were naturally predisposed to share Blackstone's suspicions of courts 'with methods of proceeding entirely in a derogation of the common law, and whose large discretionary powers make a petty tyranny in a set of standing commissioners'.[96] In fact there was little evidence before them of 'petty tyranny' and the 'suspicion ... that their decisions are often wanting in impartiality' was just

93 *Ibid.*, pp. 6, 9.
94 *Ibid.*, p. 10. The Palace Court, however, gave exclusive audience to six attorneys and four counsel and, following damning criticism, was abolished in 1849: T. Mathew, The Mayor's Court, the Sheriffs' Courts and the Palace Court, *Juridical Review* 31 (1919), 139–51.
95 *Fifth Report*, pp. 10–11.
96 Quoted by the Commissioners on p. 11.

that, a suspicion.[97] The main objection to courts of requests was that since 'so much is left to the discretion of those who decide the cause' (necessarily so if they were to be cheap enough to fulfil their function), the judges needed to be 'persons of considerable ability and learning'; yet in fact 'they consist in general, of commissioners whose pursuits in life can give no assurance of their possessing these qualities'.[98] Lay magistrates, it would seem, might safely be entrusted with an immense range of important functions but decisions about a 40s debt needed legal training.

When taxed with the inadequacies of local courts, defenders of the *status quo* were given to retort that their decay was the result of consumer preference for the superior justice developed at Westminster and that if there were deficiencies in its delivery the remedy lay in improving the superior courts, though they were usually rather vague about how this might be done.[99] The Commissioners, however, did not share the view that nothing else should be attempted until every avenue had been explored to make Westminster Hall cheap enough for bringing a small claim to be worthwhile. Admitting that 'the extent to which the jurisdiction of the inferior courts ought to be carried must depend much on the question how far the delay and expense attending suits in the superior courts are capable of reduction, which has not yet been sufficiently ascertained', they nevertheless felt that the latter 'are far too costly and dilatory for the decision of suits of small importance as to amount'[100] and for the very small they could never be otherwise.

Concluding that 'the inadequacy of the present Courts, in causes of action from 40s to at least £20, amounts almost to a denial of justice',[101] the Commissioners recommended a national network of small claims courts. No-one should need to travel more than twenty or twenty-five miles to one and each market town of 20,000 persons should have its court. They would handle

[97] *Ibid.*, p. 12. Arthurs, 'Without the Law', pp. 33–4, forcefully points out that the evidence before the Commissioners hardly justified their doubts on this score.

[98] *Fifth Report*, p. 12.

[99] See e.g. *LM* 10 (1833) at 179; *LO* 1 (1830–1), *passim*, and the speeches of the Attorney-General (*Hansard* 1830 3rd s., vol. 1, cols. 274–6) and Lyndhurst (*Hansard* 1833 3rd s., vol. 18, cols. 883–4).

[100] *Fifth Report*, p. 17.

[101] *Ibid.*

personal claims up to £20, small legacies and ejectments relating to tenements with an annual value not above £20. About twenty judges were envisaged, chosen from barristers of ten years' standing, salaried and resident in their district and assisted by a registrar for each court. Court forms would be simple; all process would be served by the court; there would be no special pleading; and except where he wished to raise certain technical defences the defendant would need to hand in only a notice that he intended to defend. Juries would be six strong and although lawyers would be allowed, they would receive no costs where less than £5 was claimed or recovered; above that amount attorneys should receive 'a fair remuneration' – which was rather begging the question.[102]

Though much less ambitious than Brougham's proposals in some ways – the much lower money limit of jurisdiction and the omission of reconcilement for instance – the Commissioners went beyond him in wanting the new courts to supersede the existing local courts immediately rather than run alongside them. Overall, however, there was a surprising degree of consistency between the two – surprising because Lyndhurst's subsequent charge that Brougham had packed the Commission with his supporters was nonsense.[103]

The Commission's report dismayed opponents of reform and, because it soon came to be regarded as authoritative, provided supporters with a strong and non-partisan endorsement. To Brougham's great indignation, it also enabled Conservatives to claim that bills to establish local courts were based on the Commission's ideas and not his. As with all the law reforms of Brougham's time, 'he himself claimed credit for nearly all of it, and his enemies – who were many – denied him any credit at all'.[104]

The report was not published until the spring of 1833 but Brougham reintroduced his Local Courts Bill, somewhat modified to meet the Commissioners' views and no longer confined initially

102 *Ibid.*, pp. 18–30.

103 *Hansard* 1833 3rd s., vol. 18, cols. 868–9, 889–90; *LO* 7 (1833–4), 35. Starkie, Evans and Wightman were appointed by Brougham but none of them was known for liberal or radical views.

104 G. R. Y. Radcliffe and G. Cross, *The English Legal System* (6th edn, by G. J. Hand and D. J. Bentley, London, 1977), p. 263. For an example of a disparaging overview of Brougham's contribution see *Quarterly Review*, 105 (1859), 504–26.

to two counties, before publication.[105] He still claimed that it was not a government measure, but it was generally regarded as such and in an unguarded moment in debate Brougham admitted it.[106]

The Bill came before a House of Lords unsure of its place in the constitution after the trauma of being coerced into passing the reform bill. One of the first acts of aristocratic defiance against the reformed House of Commons was against the Local Courts Bill.[107] The instigator was the former Lord Chancellor Lyndhurst, the once dominant Eldon being now a woebegone and ineffective figure. Lyndhurst's 'whole cast of mind was critical rather than constructive'. As he said himself: 'the Duke [of Wellington] comes down every day, and tries to make Bills better; if I could make them worse I should come too'.[108] There was no party line on local courts and in 1830 Peel had welcomed Brougham's bill in principle; to the objection that it would foment 'a spirit of litigation' he had retorted that a worse evil 'was that spirit of discontent which was engendered by being told that the injured had no protection, and no alternative but to acquiesce in injustice'.[109] Peel would presumably have tried to purge Brougham's bill of its wilder and more extravagant elements, but Lyndhurst, who disliked the very idea of local courts, had no scruple in engaging in a wholly destructive opposition.[110]

In this Lyndhurst was also acting as the spokesman for the big London agency firms, who provided him with the briefing on foreign jurisdictions which enabled him to meet Brougham on his own ground.[111] On the second reading, 'lounging down to the House with a handsome woman on his arm, looking more like a Colonel of cavalry than a Chief Baron',[112] Lyndhurst fluffed his attack through insufficient preparation. He exaggerated the cost of the proposals and the volume of business the superior courts

[105] *HLSP* 1833 CCXIV, bills 16, 79, 86, 95, 100. The Bills of 1830 and 1833 are compared in *LO* 5 (1833), 452–62, 472–6 and *LM* 9 (1833), 392–413.

[106] *Hansard* 1833 3rd s., vol. 18, col. 1123.

[107] A. S. Turberville, *The House of Lords in the Age of Reform, 1784–1837* (London, 1958), pp. 215–16.

[108] *Ibid.*, pp. 218, 334.

[109] *Hansard* 1830 2nd s., vol. 24, col. 870.

[110] In 1835 Peel's and Lyndhurst's opposing views on the role of a parliamentary opposition brought them into open conflict: Turberville, *House of Lords*, pp. 356–9. For a more favourable view of Lyndhurst's approach see D. Lee, *Lyndhurst: the Flexible Tory* (1994).

[111] *Quarterly Review* 126 (1860), 1–61 at 27.

[112] *Ibid.*

would lose and offered the bleak and unappealing proposition that 'hardship and inconvenience were almost inseparable from any system which could be devised'.[113] He failed to rouse much support among the Tory peers and the Bill went into committee without a vote.[114]

Lyndhurst resolved to rescue his reputation on the third reading and word went round that there would be an all-out contest between two of the greatest orators of the day. The government called another eloquent speaker, Thomas Plunket, over from Ireland to second their champion[115] and Brougham foolishly made unsuccessful and counterproductive attempts to foment an outdoor agitation in support of the bill.[116] Though ministers were more concerned with the fate of their Irish Church Bill, they were well aware that a Tory success against local courts would embolden the Lords to further truculence.[117]

Lyndhurst triumphed both in his personal duel with Brougham and in the vote which followed.[118] Now fully master of his brief, he could effectively exploit the strong vein of Podsnappery in the House by a well-informed attack on the 'foreign' elements in Brougham's scheme and also make good use of its other vulnerable features. The scheme would be costly – more costly than the whole apparatus of Westminster Hall if Lyndhurst was to be believed. It would encourage litigation, which the law should try to reduce by providing such a degree of certainty that lawyers could confidently advise clients on the outcome of a dispute. It was not so much a 'Poor Man's Court' which would be created as a court in which the poor would be at risk from their creditors. It would further increase the already immense patronage of the Lord Chancellor by an unknown number of judges – a telling point this, for there were few even on his own side who trusted Brougham to

[113] *Hansard* 1833 3rd s., vol. 18, col. 870.

[114] *Ibid.*, cols. 857–902; Turberville, *House of Lords*, pp. 215–16. However, a motion to recommit the Bill was carried against Brougham by 52 votes to 38 a few days later.

[115] *Blackwood's Magazine* 35 (1834), 577.

[116] *LO* 7 (1833–4), 26.

[117] See Brougham's correspondence with the King's private secretary, Sir Herbert Taylor, in his *Life and Times*, pp. 295–302.

[118] *Hansard* 1833 3rd s.,vol. 19, cols. 307–74. There is a pungent, partisan account by Samuel Warren in *Blackwood's Magazine* 35 (1834), 562–86, on which Campbell drew for his *Lives of Lyndhurst and Brougham.* Voting among the peers present was tied at 82 each and proxies carried the day by 53 to 41.

exercise patronage responsibly.[119] And not least, it would degrade and imperil the bar, on whose behalf Lyndhurst found his most eloquent voice.

Lyndhurst's attack was wholly destructive, utterly unscrupulous and dreadfully effective. Plunket was disappointing in reply and when it came to Brougham's turn he failed lamentably, seeming bitterly aware that the day was lost. For one whose oratory sometimes 'puts you in mind of Demosthenes or those fellows you used to read about in school',[120] his was an unworthy speech in which he directed his fire not so much at Lyndhurst as at his blundering ally Lord Wynford.[121] The venom of Brougham's attack destroyed any lingering compunction opposition peers may have felt in voting down the Bill and by 134 votes to 122 it was, in the terse phrase of *Hansard*, 'thrown out'.[122]

## THE EMERGENCE OF THE NEW COURTS

Brougham was fast becoming almost as unpopular with his colleagues as with the Tory peers and within a year of this humiliation his intolerable behaviour forced Grey to dismiss him from the government, never again to hold high office in the rest of his long life.[123] Soon afterwards Grey himself retired and Lord Melbourne became Prime Minister.

Melbourne's administrations have been unfairly disparaged and their law reforms at any rate were by no means negligible.[124] But with no-one in the cabinet having any real enthusiasm for local courts, bills and promises of bills made only fleeting appearances, never working their way to the top of the legislative programme.[125] Progress would, in any event, have been difficult, for

119 Brougham was perhaps unwise to ask rhetorically, 'could the Lord Chancellor appoint an unfit judge?' (col. 362).

120 Le Marchant, *Viscount Althorp*, p. 289.

121 The former Chief Justice Best, see *LR* 2 (1845), 168–76.

122 1833 3rd s., vol. 19, contents page.

123 R. Stewart, *Henry Brougham 1778–1868*, pp. 285–302.

124 D. Southgate, *The Passing of the Whigs* (London, 1965), pp. 63 ff. Measures included the Wills Act 1837, Small Tenements Recovery Act 1838, Metropolitan Police Act 1839 and several criminal law reform Acts of 1837.

125 Petitions are in *HCJ* vols. 93, 94. For proposals and bills see *LO* 9 (1834–5), 401; *LO* 10 (1835), 1–117; *LO* 13 (1836–7), 273 ('all is rumour and conjecture'), and the summary in *LO* 17 (1838–9), 401.

there was no disposition among the Tories to co-operate and most of the swarm of barristers in the Commons were implacably hostile.[126] Even so, Lord John Russell made matters worse by seeking to combine local courts with something much more contentious, the reform of the quarter and petty sessions.[127] Country gentlemen were stubbornly attached to these institutions, which remained in their hands, as a bulwark of 'legitimate' local influence against the encroachment of boards and commissioners,[128] so it was unwise to link the provision of local civil justice with the reform of the criminal courts. Even when the two were uncoupled, however, proceedings in a select committee exposed sharp differences over patronage, powers of imprisonment and the future of existing local courts.[129] Russell grew despondent and was grateful when the Lord Chancellor, Cottenham, demanded a further delay while he grappled with the twin-headed monster of insolvency and bankruptcy.[130]

While the government dithered, others acted. Clauses in the Municipal Corporations Act encouraged boroughs to revive their own courts of record[131] and all the while the number of courts of requests continued to rise,[132] leading some opponents of decentralised justice to realise that the choice lay only between a haphazard proliferation of municipal courts and a coherent set of small claims

[126] There were eighty lawyers in the Commons in 1837, 12 per cent of the House: D. Duman, *The English and Colonial Bars in the Nineteenth Century* (London, 1983), table 6.1.

[127] *Hansard* 1837–8 3rd s., vol. 41, cols. 332–44; *Jur.* 1 (1837), 665 ff.; *Jur.* 2 (1838), 332, 553; *LO* 15 (1837–8), 353.

[128] O. MacDonagh, *Early Victorian Government, 1830–1870* (1977), pp. 162–77; *Monthly Law Magazine* 2 (1838), 215–31.

[129] *PP* 1839 (387–II) XIII; *Hansard* 1838–9 3rd s., vol. 45, cols. 221 ff.; vol. 46, cols. 873–5; vol. 47, cols. 1214–16; *LO* 17 (1838–9), 401 ff.; *LO* 18 (1839), 208, 213, 272.

[130] *Hansard* 1838–9 3rd s., vol. 47, col. 519; 1839–40 3rd s., vol. 52, col. 1080.

[131] Russell's draft bill proposed to give every municipal borough a court of requests, R. Russell (ed.), *The Early Correspondence of Lord John Russell, 1805–40* (London, 1913), vol. II, p. 110, cl. 17. Sir William Follett moved the revised clause: *LO* 10 (1835), 225. Ss. 98–9 extended the jurisdiction of these courts to £20; rules made by their judges were to be confirmed by three or more judges of the superior courts.

[132] *LO* 17 (1838–9), 291–2; on p. 401 Russell is quoted as noting that twenty-five were in progress. A full list of the courts active in 1840 is reproduced in *HEL*, vol. I (5th edn, 1931), appendix 28.

courts which at least approximated to the lawyers' idea of a judicial forum.[133]

The Whigs' Small Debts Courts Bill finally made its appearance in February 1841, along with another dose of bankruptcy reform. The two were necessarily linked because it was proposed to give the judges of the local courts bankruptcy and insolvency jurisdiction as well.[134] The Bill was a combination of Brougham's, shorn of its more extravagant and innovative elements, and the Commissioners' proposals, but with infusions from the existing Irish Civil Bill Courts about whose value opinions differed sharply.[135]

There were to be twenty-five judges, appointed by the Lord Chancellor from barristers of seven years' standing or attorneys of ten. Paid between £800 and £1,500 a year, barred from practice and resident in their district, they would handle tort, contract and debt claims up to £20 and would also deal with ejectments where the value of the tenement did not exceed £20 a year. Only in larger cases, and then only if the parties requested it, would there be a jury. Only rudimentary pleadings would be required, pleas being determined 'in a summary way'. Examination of the parties would be allowed but legal representation would need the judge's leave and in claims below 40s an attorney would have no entitlement to costs. The venue would be the defendant's home court unless the parties lived more than twenty miles apart or the cause of action had arisen elsewhere. The judge would make 'such orders and decrees as shall appear to him to be just and agreeable to equity and good conscience' and these might include payment in instalments. Appeals were limited to suits for £5 or more. The courts of requests were to be abolished and plaintiffs bringing in one of the superior courts actions which were potentially within the local courts' limits would not be awarded costs unless they recovered at least £20 or the judge certified that they had had cause to think they would do so.

It is questionable whether the government could have got the bill through Parliament, but before the summer was over it had

133 *LO* 17 (1838–9), 401.

134 *PP* 1841 (43), (153) I; *Hansard* 1840–1 3rd s., vol. 56, cols. 472–81. It was said to be based on the bill of 1839 as amended in committee. The bill to give county courts bankruptcy, insolvency and lunacy jurisdiction is *PP* 1841 (44) I.

135 *LM* 25 (1841), 310–44. For a proposal for courts modelled explicitly on the Irish ones see *Jur.* 7 (1843), 169.

tottered to its fall.[136] The Whig bill was altogether too drastic for the Conservatives. While acknowledging 'the necessity of a universal arrangement with regard to facilities for the recovery of small debts', they disliked the 'democratic tendencies'[137] inherent in new institutions which Wellington felt to be 'branches of a plan for ... destroying the influence of the landed gentry'.[138] Instead the Home Secretary, Sir James Graham, almost as reluctant a convert to the need to do something as Lyndhurst, found himself in charge of a bill which drew explicitly on the constitution of courts of requests as they were now being approved; so far from abolishing them, it gave the Crown the power to create new ones wherever there was a need.[139] Judges, with the same qualifications and tenure as in the Whig bill, would not be resident; rather they would live in London and go regularly on circuit round their district. The jurisdiction, procedure and powers of the courts would not differ much from the Whig proposals and Brougham and Cottenham, while lamenting how far short they came of their own proposals, were prepared to support these.[140] Unfortunately, however, shortage of time forced the government to prune its programme and bankruptcy was given priority once again.[141]

Just how low a priority local courts had became apparent over the next two sessions. In 1843 the government reduced both the jurisdiction (to £10) and the number of courts envisaged, then the appearance of a rival scheme gave Graham a pretext to withdraw his own in order to study it.[142] This plan, promoted by Sir John Jervis, was in fact not so much a different version of local courts as an attempt to head them off, first by giving the justices jurisdiction

136 The second reading showed strong opposition to the patronage which would accrue under the two Acts: *Hansard* 1840–1 3rd s., vol. 57, cols. 172–93.

137 Peel to Graham, 12 Oct. 1842, C. S. Parker, *The Life and Letters of Sir James Graham* (London, 1907), vol. I, p. 333.

138 Wellington to Graham, 22 Nov. 1842, *ibid.*, p. 335.

139 *HLSP* 1842 II, (139, 215); *PP* 1842 (498) (531) (550) I. For its progress see *Hansard* 1841–2 3rd s., vol. 63 col. 2 and vol. 65. Discussions are in *LO* 23 (1841–2) and 24 (1842).

140 *Hansard* 1841–2 3rd s., vol. 65, cols. 224–41.

141 *Ibid.*, col. 1182. On the background to the Bankruptcy Act see C. S. Bowen, Progress in the Administration of Justice in the Victorian Period, in *Select Essays in Anglo-American Legal History*, Vol. I (London, 1907), pp. 516–57 at 543–8 and Lester, *Victorian Insolvency*, pp. 61–3.

142 *PP* 1843 (198) I; *Hansard* 1842–3 3rd s., vol. 68, col. 973. On the government's indecisiveness see *LO* 26 (1843), 18.

over debts up to £5 and second, in a separate bill, reviving the old idea of sheriffs' assessors to take bigger cases remitted from the superior courts.[143] These two bills reappeared in 1844[144] and, though Graham agreed that 'he could not conceive a worse tribunal for that purpose'[145] than the justices, he sought to combine the other proposal with the government bill, which had made a belated appearance just before Easter.[146]

Once again there was no time, and evidently very little determination, to pass a bill, and once again the need to repair the weaknesses in the arrangements for bankruptcy so recently put into place was held to be paramount.[147] Ironically, however, the consuming passion for tinkering with the affairs of bankrupts and insolvent debtors which had regularly elbowed aside the demand for local courts at last set in motion the chain of events which swept them into existence.

With the Bankruptcy Act 1842 acknowledged to need amendment in any case, Cottenham prepared a more ambitious bill to put an end to the dual system of bankruptcy and insolvency.[148] Not to be upstaged, Brougham promptly brought out a plan of his own[149] and since the two men were personal enemies neither would give way. Lyndhurst, cynically enjoying the spectacle, contributed by his detached attitude to a highly unsatisfactory piece of lawmaking. After rancorous debates, Cottenham's bigger measure lost out to Brougham's more modest Execution Bill, which was chiefly concerned with tidying up the uncertainties surrounding the power to imprison debtors,[150] and with the House almost deserted as the session wound down, the Bill was given a radical twist by humanitarian (some said sentimental) concern for the plight of those in debtors prisons.[151]

The movement to abolish imprisonment for debt was growing in strength, encouraged by the Common Law Commissioners' recommendation that it should be confined to cases of fraud,

143 *PP* 1843 (214) II; (232) IV.

144 *PP* 1844 (8) IV; (9) I.

145 *Hansard* 1844 3rd s., vol. 72, col. 683.

146 *Ibid.*, vol. 73, col. 1672–4; vol. 74, cols. 192–5.

147 *LO* 27 (1843–4), 257, 461; 28 (1844), 67.

148 *Hansard* 1844 3rd s., vol. 74, cols. 442–57.

149 *Hansard* 1844 3rd s., vol. 75, cols. 173–82.

150 *Ibid.*, cols. 1173–204, 1387–411.

151 The deplorable state of local prisons used by the courts of requests as revealed by the Prison Commissioners was influential in this: *LT* 5 (1845), 420.

deliberate removal of property and refusal to surrender assets after judgment.[152] Imprisonment on mesne process had gone in 1838[153] and, despite objections from traders, there were now moves afoot to restrict post-judgment imprisonment more narrowly, as Cottenham's bill had proposed. Cottenham and others were especially concerned at the use of committals by the courts of requests and other local courts, though both the Whig and Conservative bills had proposed to give this power to their new creations. Before the Execution Bill left the Lords it had acquired almost unnoticed a clause abolishing imprisonment for debts up to £20 except in cases of fraud, and with this clause it went through the Commons without serious debate.[154]

The change so casually effected was greeted with disbelief by the trading community and the attorneys who collected their debts, the *Law Magazine* claiming wildly that 'those unadvised measures . . . have virtually absolved a majority of the debtors of this country from any legal obligation to pay their debts'.[155] When Parliament reassembled for the next session the Lords' table was covered in petitions and a well-orchestrated campaign had ensured that the peers were well aware that they had made a serious blunder, a view rapidly confirmed by their own select committee.[156]

No-one would take the blame. Brougham blamed Cottenham, Cottenham disclaimed parentage of the Bill which had been preferred to his own and Lyndhurst denied that it had been a government measure.[157] In the end Brougham came forward with a short amending bill which restored the power of imprisonment in certain situations, among them:

> fraud in contracting the debt, or of having wilfully contracted it without reasonable prospect of being able to pay it . . . or if he appears to have the means of paying the same by instalments or otherwise, and shall not pay

[152] *Fourth Report*: *PP* 1831–2 (239) XXV-1; Lester, *Victorian Insolvency*, pp. 111–22.

[153] 1 & 2 Vict. c. 100; B. Kerchner, The Transformation of Imprisonment for Debt in England, 1828–38, *Australian Journal of Law and Society* 2 (1984), 61–109.

[154] *Hansard* 1844 3rd s., vol. 74, col. 459 (Duke of Richmond); vol. 76, cols. 1489, 1623–41, 1706–13, 1847; 7 & 8 Vict. c. 96; *LT* 5 (1845), 420, 447; *LO* 28 (1844), 67.

[155] *LM* 34 (1845), 309.

[156] *HLSP* 1845 XIX (153) 1; *HLJ* 77 (1845), 189, 239, 282.

[157] There is a good account in *LR* 3 (1845–6), 49–65.

the same at such times as the commissioner or court shall order, or as the court shall have ordered.[158]

Because of these attempts at pass the parcel, the Bill reached the Commons late in the session. The Solicitor-General, Fitzroy Kelly, urged the need for it to be taken at speed and so it was.[159] But the Bill which whistled through all its stages so quickly was not at all the Bill that had come down from the Lords.[160] Kelly had transformed it completely, the key provision being that the Privy Council might enlarge the jurisdiction of any inferior court to £20 if it was willing to appoint a legally qualified judge.[161]

No satisfactory account of this remarkable episode has yet been given, but according to one source the initiative came from officials in the many courts of requests which lacked a legally qualified judge and which were therefore denied the power to imprison debtors. Conceiving that if they were given a wider jurisdiction, they could afford a paid judge and also turn in a handsome profit in fees, they lobbied the government for a general statute to bring this about.[162] Ministers were receptive because they still had the Local Courts Bill on the stocks, having already stalled it for two sessions on the pretext of the great changes being made in the law of debtor and creditor, and probably saw this as a way of meeting the demand for local justice at minimal cost and with minimal impact on the bar and the superior courts. After all, the new model of courts of requests had already been endorsed in their own plans[163] and there was less objection to giving such courts the power to commit debtors when they had a lawyer-judge presiding rather than a lay commissioner.

Whatever the motive, it resulted in a striking instance of the sort of legislative incompetence the law journals regularly denounced. The Bill returned too late to the Lords for any effective scrutiny. Lyndhurst apologetically acknowledged that it had followed a course quite inconsistent with established procedures but disin-

[158] See the commentary in *LM* 24 (1845), 309–15.

[159] *Hansard* 1845 3rd s., vol. 82, col. 671 (18 July).

[160] *LT* 5 (1845), 361. Twenty-one new clauses were added. One MP protested at the haste on the second reading (22 July, cols. 890 ff.); the third reading was on the 29th.

[161] Kelly (1796–1880) became Solicitor-General on 29 June. An 'ardent law reformer' (*DNB*, vol. XXX, p. 347; he joined Bentinck in the revolt against Peel and later became Chief Baron of the Exchequer).

[162] *LM* 36 (1846), 189 at 201–2.

[163] *Hansard* 1844 3rd s., vol. 73, col. 1673.

genuously disclaimed it as a government measure on the flimsy ground that Kelly had introduced it a few days before he became Solicitor-General.[164] Campbell acridly criticised their use of Brougham 'as the organ of the government this session' but since no-one could countenance leaving small debtors free of the threat of jail for another year the peers gulped down the whole Bill.[165]

This time it was the legal profession that professed outrage. A local courts bill had been sneaked through in disguise while no-one was looking; no-one knew how many courts were likely to emerge with the enlarged jurisdiction; attorneys were dismayed that they did not have a monopoly of representation and must compete with 'sham lawyers' and 'accountants'; traditionalists lamented that there would be no juries.[166]

Even the government seems to have been disconcerted by its own creation, for it allowed applications for the new powers to lie on the Council table for months.[167] In the end the Act so recently passed was jettisoned with scarcely an explanation in favour of the revival of a full-blown local courts scheme.

And so in 1846 a local courts bill yet again made an appearance near the end of the session. Appearing in the midst of a political crisis, its chances seemed poor when Peel was voted out of office, but the Whigs picked it up, made it their own and hustled it on.[168]

There is a perfunctory quality about the debates on the Bill 'for the more easy recovery of small debts' which partly reflects the anti-climax following the excitements of so momentous a session but also the weariness of overfamiliarity.[169] Local courts had been before Parliament in session after session and Cottenham took

164 *Hansard* 1845 3rd s., vol. 82, cols. 1424–8, 1430. According to an interesting eyewitness account given by 'Old Attorney' (*CCC* 24 (1873)), 19, Lyndhurst demolished the arguments presented by deputations which pressed him to support the Bill, then cynically gave it his backing.

165 *Hansard* 1845 3rd s., vol. 82, cols. 1428–30. They passed it on 5 August, the session ending on the 9th.

166 E.g. *LT* 5 (1845), 420 ('an imposture upon the Profession and the public'), 447. The Commons' cavalier mode of legislating was severely criticised in the *Quarterly Review* 77 (1845–6), 215–20.

167 *LM & R* 36 (1846), 189 at 204.

168 *PP* 1846 (Bills 587, 609, 644, 678) IV. It was read for the first time on 15 June, the ministry fell in July and Cottenham, resuming as Lord Chancellor, presented it in revised form for its second reading on 28 July.

169 *Hansard* 1845–6 3rd s., vol., 88, cols. 109–13, 227–8, 279–81, 349; in the Lords, 909–25, 947–8, 977, 1020.

advantage of this by stressing the continuity between his Bill and those of the early 1840s.[170] Even lawyers who opposed the principle were by now reconciled to the eventuality and sought no more than to lower the limit from £20 and to make other changes of detail.[171]

One novel feature was set out in the preamble and first clause, which recited the passage of the Acts of 1844 and 1845 and asserted that it was 'expedient that the provisions of such Acts should be amended, and that one rule and manner of proceeding for the recovery of small debts and demands should prevail throughout England'. This was to be achieved by annexing small debts courts to the ancient county court; however, by order in council any county might be divided into districts and an order issued 'that the County Court shall be holden for the recovery of debts and demands under this Act in each of such districts'.

The preamble is of course a wholly and deliberately misleading version of what was being done. What was really the abolition of all the courts of requests (but not all of the older local courts) and the substitution of a network of new courts, was dressed up as the refurbishment of a hallowed institution, the medieval county court. In the immediate aftermath of the Bill's passage lawyers devoted a good deal of time and ink to puzzling out what survived of the old court and how it fitted into the new, but it was largely learning thrown away:[172] the old county courts and the new shared nothing but a name which was artfully chosen to confer a spurious pedigree on the latter and to clothe their principal role as debt collection agencies with a cloak of dignity.[173]

It was left to the lawyers in committee to tidy up the Bill, since in the debates attention was given almost exclusively to the question of judges. In contrast to most earlier bills and presumably as a sop to the bar, this one made attorneys ineligible for judgeships and the government beat off strong representations on

170 *Ibid.*, cols. 109–10.

171 As suggested in *LM & R* 36 (1846), 156–7.

172 E.g. J. Moseley, *A Treatise on the New County Courts* (London, 1846) and H. Udall, *The New County Courts* (London, 1846)

173 '[The old county court's] end was abrupt and ignominious. Shorn of all its remaining functions in the nineteenth century, on 17 October 1977 the old county court ceased to exist.': Baker *Introduction to English Legal History*, p. 28. This was the result of Administration of Justice Act 1977 s. 23 and schedule 4, via SI 1977/1589.

their behalf.[174] It was patronage which exercised MPs and, allegedly, excited the bar.[175] This had always been the most embarrassing question, since no minister wanted to be seen to be clutching greedily at new places under government yet no satisfactory alternative could be found. The Conservative Bill had reverted to the discredited idea of letting the lord-lieutenant make the appointments, but the Whigs went boldly for giving them to the Lord Chancellor and, though Lord George Bentinck with characteristic exaggeration deplored a decision 'which will make the government of the day almost despotic at the next election',[176] it was reluctantly accepted that the Chancellor was the least bad choice;[177] whether it would have been equally acceptable had Brougham held the Great Seal is more open to question.

The Bill embodied elements about which a consensus had gradually evolved through successive proposals; instalment orders; a jury which would be optional, and then only in larger actions; examination of the parties and very abbreviated pleadings. The lawyers had won their right to preserve the concurrent jurisdiction of the superior courts, subject to the plaintiff putting himself at risk of losing his costs if he brought a small claim there without justification.[178] They had also won the right to appear in the new courts by right, whereas the 'accountants', 'agents' and other rivals to provincial attorneys would need the leave of the judge; their costs however were set at a discouragingly low level.[179] The new county courts would be courts of law as lawyers understood them but stripped of most of the rococo ornament that encrusted the superior courts.

The Bill for the More Easy Recovery of Small Debts received the royal assent on 28 August 1846 as the 95th Act of 9 & 10 Victoria.[180] It was more than twenty-five years, and almost as many bills, since Althorp's first effort and the story of those bills

174 *Hansard* 1845–6 3rd s., vol. 88, cols. 919 ff., 1056–7; 9 & 10 Vict. c. 95 ss. 9–10. For an indignant reaction see *LO* 32 (1846), 401, 497.

175 *Hansard* 1845–6 3rd s., vol. 88 cols. 912 and discussion at 913–19.

176 *Ibid.*, col. 909.

177 *LM* 5 (1846), 157–8 suggested the chief justices of the common law courts.

178 Ss. 92, 69–73, 58–9, 74–90, 128–9; *LO* 32 (1846), 305 ff.

179 S. 91.

180 Commons amendments were extensive but mostly technical or verbal (*HCJ* 101 pt 2, 1253, 1278); they can be followed best in *LO* 32 (1846). There is a thorough analysis by DDK[eane] in *LM* 5 (1846), 189–255; he attributes the drafting to F. K. Eagle, who became one of the new judges.

is profoundly unedifying. The long delay in passing a measure which from the beginning commanded a wide degree of support in principle was partly due to the determined rearguard action fought by those members of the legal profession whose practice lay in the superior courts, among them almost all of the most influential men at the bar and among the attorneys. It also owes something to the haphazard way in which legislation was made. Since these bills were never a high priority they all too often made their appearance too late and then were not pressed energetically. Furthermore creditors, the principal beneficiaries, had no Anti-Corn Law League to advance their cause and never lobbied with real persistence, perhaps because they found that the more productive course was to organise the promotion of bills for local courts of requests. Finally, from the mid-1830s onwards, the waters were persistently muddied by the interaction between local courts for small debts and the reform of the insolvency and bankruptcy laws. The former were several times held up by yet a further reconsideration of the latter; even when putting through the 1846 Bill, Cottenham restrained himself with difficulty from trying to deal with insolvency at the same time.[181] Nevertheless, a local courts bill had been enacted at last and it was perhaps fitting that it was the Whigs who gained the right to exercise the patronage, since it was a Whig who had begun the campaign so long before.

181 *Hansard* 1845–6 3rd s., vol. 88, col. 112.

2

# AN AGE OF EXPANSION, 1847–1870

## THE NEW COURTS AND THE NEW JUDGES

The government moved to implement the Small Debts Act with unexpected speed and thoroughness. Instead of the gradual and piecemeal creation of courts which opponents claimed the Act envisaged, the Lord Chancellor instructed Drinkwater Bethune to draw up a nationwide scheme for immediate operation and within months it was ready to be put into place.[1]

There were to be sixty districts and no fewer than 491 courts. Even in a rural county like Suffolk no-one would be far from a county court town, since they included Beccles, Bury St Edmunds, Eye, Framlingham, Halesworth, Haverhill, Ipswich, Lowestoft, Mildenhall, Stowmarket, Sudbury and Woodbridge.

In contrast to the courts of requests, each of which had its own part-time judge, the county courts were to share a judge who was appointed for the whole district and who would arrange his own pattern of work,[2] sitting in each of his courts at least once a month; in the metropolitan area and in Liverpool, however, the judge had only a single court in his district and would sit there as often as he felt necessary.

Restrictions on the judges' outside activities were originally confined to those which might put into question their impartiality,[3] but the spectacle of a metropolitan judge practising at Westminster Hall and the announcement that another intended to stand for Parliament soon obliged the government to extend

[1] See pp. 210–12 below.

[2] County Courts Act 1846 s. 56, interpreted in *R v. Parham* (1849) 13 QB 858.

[3] County Courts Act 1846 s. 17.

them.[4] Even so, for some years judges could supplement their income by arbitrations and were allowed to retain recorderships.

This substantial addition to the nation's public institutions was not intended to burden the taxpayer very much. Central administration was to be undertaken by the clerks in the Home Office and Treasury, while the chief officers of the court would be responsible for employing and paying such assistants as they needed; since court staff would not be civil servants there would be no burden of pensions on the state. Suitors' fees were to cover the costs of judges and registrars, the fixing of salaries being deferred until the yield became clear; meanwhile, contrary to the emerging canons of public administration, they would be remunerated directly from fees.[5]

As for the courtrooms, since there were few places where the judge would be sitting very frequently, it would be left to the district treasurers to arrange the hire or use of suitable accommodation.[6] New courts did have to be built in London and other big towns but the scale and cost (eighteen, at £42,668, in the first eight years) were modest. Since disagreements predictably arose over the use of town halls and other municipal buildings, it was soon enacted that they must be made available free of charge, which in turn tended to create friction over the fixing of court days and the condition of the building.[7]

Questions of economy also affected the selection of the judges. To the disappointment of the bar – for rumour had it that applications from serjeants and silks as well as juniors, had come flooding in – the Lord Chancellor announced that he would give priority to suitably qualified judges of the defunct courts of requests when filling vacancies in their locality.[8] A few of these judges would have been strong candidates anyway, and several

4 County Courts Extension Act 1850 s. 3. *LT* 16 (1850–1), 248; *LT* 9 (1847), 337, 381.The aspiring MP was George Clive, later Home Office under-secretary. The Home Secretary refused to rule on whether the judge at Nottingham might practise at the East Midland assizes (PRO HO 86/1, f. 314: H. Waddington to R. Wildman, 4 Jul. 1848).

5 County Courts Act 1846 ss. 37, 39; HLSP 1851 (176) XI. Only eighteen judges were gainers when they became salaried at £1,200.

6 County Courts Act 1846 s. 48; PRO HO 86/1.

7 *PP* 1854–5 (350) XLIII and see pp. 316–17 below.

8 *Hansard* 1845–6 3rd s., vol. 87 cols. 113, 279. There were said to have been 750 applicants in all, including all but four of the serjeants, but that was probably a joke: *LT* 8 (1846–7), 380.

others gave great satisfaction, but it was widely felt that the transferred judges were an incubus on the new courts, tarnishing their prestige and devaluing their decisions.[9]

Not all of the new appointments met with approval either. Some were distinguished scholars: Andrew Amos had been Professor of English Law at London University, a member of the first Criminal Law Commission and of the Supreme Council of India and Thomas Starkie, well known for his writings on evidence, was sometime Downing Professor at Cambridge, Lecturer to the Inner Temple and a Common Law Commissioner. Others, such as Serjeant Manning, were well known as law reporters.[10] But political considerations had naturally entered into the process; David Leahy was eminent as a political journalist as well as a barrister and W. M. Praed was the son of a Whig politician.[11] By any standard some of the appointments were uninspiring and grievous to the practising bar – retired practitioners of comfortable means 'who do not want the gift, and have not earned it'.[12] They went unnamed but probably included Robert Wharton and Robert Temple.[13]

The judges were given a generous latitude both in the organisation of their courts and in the conduct of suits. The fifteen judges in the common law courts practised before a small and close-knit bar. Puisne judges, even on circuit, had very limited freedom in interpreting the law (the ready availability of appeals saw to that) and that elusive but powerful 'opinion of the profession' ensured a high degree of conformity in the administration of justice as well as consistency in its substance.

In the county courts much of this would be lacking. Whereas one judge's experience in any of the common law courts was very much like another's, the life of a county court judge in a metropolitan court, monotonously exposed to a thronging press of suitors, would be very different from his rural brother's, jolting around his district by carriage, or (increasingly) by railway, often

9 Sir T. W. Snagge, *The Evolution of the County Court* (London, 1904), p. 12.

10 All of these are in the *DNB*.

11 *LT* 8 (1846–7), 484; *Boase*, vol. II, p. 1619. According to his entry in A. W. B. Simpson (ed.), *A Biographical Dictionary of the Common Law* (London, 1984), p. 413, Cottenham 'packed the county courts with Whigs'.

12 *LT* 8 (1846–7), 484. The *Legal Observer* had been able to find among the juniors appointed only three who had been engaged in reported cases in the previous year: 33 (1846–7), 529–31.

13 *Boase*, vol. III, p. 909 (Temple); *Al. Cant.*, vol. VI, p. 420 (Wharton).

to find little or no business waiting for him in the next sleepy market town.[14] These 'circuits' had none of the pomp of the real thing; no trumpeters greeted the judge and no white gloves were presented if suitors were not in evidence. Small wonder that some of the judges tried to curtail their statutory visits (a practice which soon had to be regularised), or to fit in two courts on the same day (a habit which, to their indignation, was outlawed by rule).[15]

## THE NEW COURTS IN ACTION

It was the fate of the county courts to be born into the age of the Blue Book. Like so many Gradgrinds, Victorian legislators and the more serious minded of their constituents possessed a ferocious appetite for information, and the county courts from the outset performed in the spotlight.

Well before the regular series of judicial statistics was begun in 1857, it was possible to learn a great deal about their workings. In addition to the annual series,[16] as it quickly became, which showed the business done in each court and district in considerable detail, Parliament probed into the background of judges and the use they made of deputies and the way in which the other officers performed their duties; there was particular interest in where the suitors' fees went.

Of course, statistics did not tell the whole story, but what they missed the press often picked up. With the abolition of the stamp on newspapers in 1855 a steady and unspectacular rise in the number of local newspapers became a rush.[17] They were hungry for local news and they could usually find something newsworthy in the county court. The routine misfortunes of the poor were hardly worth reporting but interspersed among the acres of small debts were 'human interest' stories: the Duke of Newcastle sued

[14] On three occasions when Martineau arrived at East Grinstead the bailiff came to report that there was 'no case to try': *PP* 1878 (267) XI, q. 1859. A Midlands judge who learned that there was only one case in his list paid the disputed sum himself to save the trouble of attending.

[15] PRO HO 86/1–3, especially circular of 23 July 1857 in 86/3; *LT* 17 (1851), 153 ('Constant Reader').

[16] Beginning in April 1848 (*PP* 1848 (271) LI) and continuing with some variations in form and content.

[17] M. Jones, *Justice and Journalism* (London, 1974), pp. 38–9.

by his wine merchant, Lord St Leonards in dispute with his neighbour; Judge Hulton in an unseemly family wrangle with his sister.[18] There was also the chance that an incautious or exasperated judge would give vent to incendiary *obiter dicta* on the state of the country, the habits of the labouring poor or the iniquities of the law. Even better, he might quarrel with one of the advocates.

The regular presence of the reporter in courts was a very important development. If the Blue Books inform us about the quantity of the justice they meted out, the newspapers enable us to make an appraisal of its quality. Moreover, extracts from the local press found their way regularly into the weekly legal journals, all of which took a keen and critical interest in the new courts and one of which, the *County Courts Chronicle*, was devoted exclusively to their doings.[19] Some judges basked in the limelight the newspapers offered them and used it to propagate their views on matters of the day and to puff their own achievements; others resented their independent and often critical stance and a few of the more intolerant rashly tried to curtail their activities; in Judge Ramshay's case this led directly to his downfall.[20]

These sources complement one another. The annual returns told how many days Judge Dowling sat, the press that he started the day annoyingly late;[21] the returns show how seldom juries were to be found in Judge J. W. Smith's courts, but the newspapers report verbatim his determination not to have them.[22] Naturally the most colourful judges and the courts of the metropolis, always in session and teeming with Dickensian city life, received the fullest press coverage. A judge like Cantrell, quietly doing his duty in Derbyshire, or Francillon in Cheltenham, made the news only if obliged to decide an awkward point and when he retired or died.[23]

18 *Parkyns v. Duke of Newcastle LT* 23 (1854), 155; *Wyatt v. St Leonards LT* 24 (1854–5), 66; *Davies v. Lord Cockburn SJ* 1 (1857–8), 379 (action for a cab fare); *Hulton v. Hulton LT* 33 (1859), 311. The *CCC* ran a series under the heading 'remarkable cases'.

19 It ran from 1847 to 1920. Other weeklies included its parent organ, the *Law Times* (from 1843), the *Legal Observer* (1830–56), the *Solicitors' Journal* (1857 on), the *Law Journal* (from 1866) and the *Jurist* (1838–66).

20 See below, p. 50.

21 *LT* 34 (1859–60), 54.

22 E.g. *LT* 57 (1874), 10 (*Page v. Halsted*).

23 See their obituaries in *LT* 37 (1861–2), 378 and *CCC* 19 (1866), 227 respectively.

But all the judges, whether modest or flamboyant, had to make decisions about procedure and evidence which were of importance to suitors and to the lawyers of the district, and such decisions were more significant for the administration of justice than any points of law that came before them. Among these points none was more important to lawyers than the question of audience. One of the lawyers' objections to the courts of requests was that many barred legal representation while others made it impracticable by not allowing costs, so that 'from the point of view of the profession ... it was imperative that the county courts should be established on a basis that would give lawyers access to a lucrative new area of practice'.[24] But for the business community, in whose interests 'the more easy recovery of small debts and demands' was to be facilitated, the new courts had to be cheap. Of the two outlays a plaintiff might have to make – and might fail to recover in full even if he won – court fees would have to be relatively high if the courts were to be self-financing, so it was lawyers' costs which had to be kept down or, better still, eliminated if the courts were to be popular.

To prohibit legal representation, or even to make each party pay for his lawyers regardless of the outcome of the suit, was considered too drastic: instead it was sought to make it so unprofitable to lawyers that they would not normally be willing to undertake business in the courts. Thus the Act allowed no costs at all in the smallest actions, for 40s or less, limiting attorneys' costs to 10s in actions not above £5, and to 15s in the others; counsel's services might only be charged if the plaintiff recovered £5 or more, or by the judge's order if the defendant won.[25]

Such meagre pickings ensured that practitioners on both sides of the profession would shun the new courts entirely unless appearing as a service to a valued client. Moreover, barristers were not to have audience unless instructed by an attorney, giving statutory force to what was as yet only a weak convention, one that Brougham had flouted when the attorneys combined against him and that Lord Campbell would shortly rule unenforceable.[26]

Such was the condition of the profession, however, that even

[24] Arthurs, '*Without the Law*', p. 43.

[25] *LR* 7 (1847–8), 246–58 compares costs with the superior courts.

[26] *Doe d. Bennett v. Hales* (1850) 15 QB 171; Duman, *English and Colonial Bars*, pp. 43–4; Ford, Henry Brougham on the Northern Circuit.

these scraps were destined to be fought over with unexpected vigour. For many lawyers, these were 'the hungry forties', when a falling off in business at Westminster and assizes, coupled in the case of the bar with an embarrassing increase in the number of potential practitioners, brought about a crisis.[27] The inception of the new courts dismayed the junior bar, for they threatened to draw business from courts in which they had a monopoly of advocacy.

The county courts, then, were always likely to set attorneys and barristers at each others' throats, though their rivalry was initially blunted because the leaders of each branch could afford to stand aloof from the struggles of briefless barristers and grubbing attorneys. But events soon combined to sharpen the antagonism. The new courts attracted so much business that while a single suit might not be worthwhile, a day in court was, still more so once the jurisdiction was extended to £50 in 1850 and costs, though still ungenerous, became worth having.[28]

Barristers had lobbied unsuccessfully against the extension and when a bill giving yet further business to county courts swiftly followed, the Attorney-General made a fruitless attempt to give the bar exclusive audience in the bigger cases. The attorneys' satisfaction at his failure was short-lived: when the bill reached the Lords at the end of the session it mysteriously emerged with two new elements – the repeal of the prohibition on direct access by barristers to clients and a ban on 'attorney-advocates'; attorneys, that is, who undertook representation on behalf of other attorneys' clients.[29] A number of attorneys had built up a practice of this sort, which was profitable because in their day in court they could handle both their own cases and those of their fellows. Given the way most courts operated it was a practice which benefited suitors as well as attorneys, but their interests were surreptitiously sacrificed on the altar of the bar.[30]

Apart from C. Rann Kennedy and other independent spirits in

[27] Duman, *English and Colonial Bars*, pp. 1–32; R. Cocks, *Foundations of the Modern Bar* (London, 1983), esp. pp. 83–8. For contrasting contemporary views of the situation see *LM* 15 (1851), 276–80.

[28] Sheffield attorneys set their own scale and prohibited undercutting: *LT* 16 (1850–1), 12–13.

[29] W. W. Pue, Rebels at the Bar, *AALR* 16 (1987), 303–52.

[30] *Ibid.* There was angry reaction, the *Law Times* attributing these last-minute changes to a 'secret enemy': 19 (1852), 30, 117. The *Jurist* (16 (1852), 205)

the big cities however, few barristers made use of their new-found freedom;[31] nor did the attorney-advocate disappear, for unless there were barristers present who raised objection it was a matter for the judge himself and many judges were more concerned to have adequate legal assistance than to uphold the privileges of the bar.[32]

For attorneys who practised regularly in the new courts these demarcation disputes with the bar were much less momentous than their rivalry with 'agents' and 'accountants' from outside the profession. Some were charlatans who sold their doubtful services to the unwary and naïve, touting for business outside the court itself and, in Whitechapel at least, sometimes ending up in the neighbouring police court for fighting over clients.[33] Few judges were likely to grant them audience if the attorneys were vigilant enough to challenge their credentials. Others however had a better claim. These were the men acting for big creditors who brought numerous suits *en bloc* in the same court. Since the mass of these were small debts – one of the firms which supported a deputation to the Lord Chancellor claimed to have 3,130 accounts, of which 2,755 were below £50[34] – it was essential to make their collection economical and, as most would be undefended, all that was needed in court was proof of the debt and perhaps of the debtor's means; for this a regular, local agent would be cheaper and probably better than an attorney. In many courts of requests the agents were familiar figures and it quickly became clear that they did not intend to be kept out of the county courts.

The decision whether to grant them audience lay wholly with the judge and each judge's verdict was anxiously awaited and diligently reported, beginning, curiously enough, with Kekewich's in distant Cornwall.[35] It was hardly to be expected that they would all follow the same line. On the whole the new judges tended to be hostile to agents, at least initially, while at least some

contended that the county courts had been 'intended to be . . . thoroughly open, free trade courts'.

31 Pue, Rebels at the Bar, 344–5.

32 In order to encourage advocates the judges had mostly construed the rather loosely drawn costs provisions liberally, but the superior courts gave conflicting interpretations. This led to an interesting debate among the law lords: *Hansard* 1852 3rd s., vol. 119, cols. 754–62.

33 *SJ* 11 (1868), 888; *CCC* 3 (1850), 48; *LT* 48 (1869–70), 404.

34 *LT* 15 (1850), 193.

35 *LT* 8 (1846–7), 25.

of those from the courts of requests were unwilling to turn out men who had expedited the handling of business. Thus Arthur Palmer in Bristol refused to bar them, but when he was succeeded by Sir John Eardley Wilmot the attorneys renewed their attack and Wilmot, having sought advice from the Lord Chancellor, restricted their appearance.[36] It was in the big northern cities that the agents proved most tenacious; in Sheffield for instance, where the judge found them indispensable.[37] This was less a battle than a hundred years' war, with hostilities breaking out spasmodically in different places; as late as the 1940s the Austin Jones Committee found that there was still a great divide between courts which would not hear agents and those in which they had an institutionalised role.[38]

Even in those courts which were most liberal in granting audience the judge would still be confronted with a host of litigants in person. The procedures of the county court were designed to be usable by laymen and many of the great landmarks of Westminster Hall were unrecognisable. Thus the whole forbidding jungle of pleadings through which Baron Surrebutter and his ilk zestfully rampaged was cut down: the plaintiff had only to disclose 'the substance of the action' in the plaint and summons while the defendant, unless he wished to raise certain specified defences, need not disclose any defence at all in advance of the hearing.[39] There, from a confused and contradictory mass of allegation and refutation, the judge, often without the benefit of counsel and almost invariably without the advantage of time to reflect, had to extract the legal issues and, with the aid of such store of learning as was in his head and a scanty stock of law books, apply it to the facts. He was also the sole judge of fact in the overwhelming mass of cases. A jury (of five) might be demanded in cases above £20 and requested in smaller cases, but

[36] *LT* 23 (1854), 197; *LT* 28 (1856–7), 101; *SJ* 3 (1858–9), 249.

[37] *LT* 17 (1850–1), 74.

[38] While the internal demarcation disputes of the two branches of the legal profession are well documented, the equally important challenge to solicitors by the newer accountancy profession is not. For an overview see D. Sugarman, Who Colonized Whom?, in Y. Dezalay and D. Sugarman (eds.), *Professional Competition and Professional Power* (London, 1995), pp. 227–36.

[39] County Courts Act 1846 s. 76, strongly criticised e.g. in *LT* 6 (1845–6), 385; *Legal Practitioner* (1846–7), 121–7. For a more favourable view see *LR* 7 (1847–8), 248 ff.

few suitors proved to want one: of 267,445 causes heard in the first eight months just 800 were jury trials.[40]

There were practically no pleadings, practically no jury and, to complete the disregard for common law traditions, a latitude towards rules of evidence that shocked traditionalists. In the county courts the parties to the suit were allowed to give evidence and availed themselves freely of the opportunity. Rampant perjury was the predicted outcome and there is no doubt that it occurred;[41] but distasteful as the spectacle of blatant lying was, the judges found that it was far outweighed by the greater opportunity it gave them of getting at the truth. When after a few years' experience, they were asked about the operation of the rule they were almost unanimous in its favour and it was not long before it was introduced into the superior courts.[42]

Other parts of the Act and the rules gave the judge a wide discretion to accept proof which would not be admissible according to the strict rules of evidence on matters such as the existence of a debt, service of documents and a defendant's means. Some judges made very free use of their discretion, especially where it avoided the necessity for adjourning the case; outside London they did not sit in one court from day to day, so an adjournment might well put the case back for a month or more.[43]

There is no doubt that some judges were cavalier in admitting evidence[44] and that others were unjust in excluding it where they had already made their mind up or were in haste to get through the list. E. W. Landor experienced an example of the latter sort of injustice when he rashly allowed a disgruntled plumber to take a dispute over a trivial amount to 'the legal threshing machine at Romford in Boeotian Essex',[45] where the judge found against him without allowing him to call his three witnesses. On the other hand some were impressively vigilant, especially on behalf of the

40 *PP* 1847–8 (265) VI.

41 See e.g. the views of judges Birch, Burnaby and Palmer in *HLSP* 1851 (21) I and C. J. W. Allen, *The Law of Evidence in Victorian England* (Cambridge, 1997), pp. 115–17.

42 *Ibid.* One judge, Amos, wrote a pamphlet extolling its virtues: *On the Expediency of Admitting the Testimony of Parties to Suits* ... (Cambridge and London, 1850).

43 *LM* ns 15 (1851), 141–6.

44 *Romilly Report* at q. 1110 (T. Kennedy); J. Moseley, *A Treatise on the New County Courts, Part II* (London, 1847), p. 232.

45 *SJ* 2 (1857–8), 1022.

unrepresented; Cyrus Jay, having heard one judge do justice successively in favour of a printer's boy suing over a bad shilling and a servant girl brutally beaten by her master, wrote that 'the decision in each of them nearly approaches the wisdom of Solomon'.[46]

But as well as the wisdom of Solomon some of the judges needed the patience of Job. Even the highest judges in the land had often to work in deplorable conditions, not only in the smaller assize towns but in Westminster, where the courts were often far removed from the decorum which nowadays prevails.[47] In county courts however, things were often much worse. The scene in one busy court was graphically described by 'Regular Practitioner':

> How is it possible to restrain within limits the tempers, and the legal hostility of marine-storekeepers, Jew-brokers, horse-dealers, cab-drivers, tinkers, cobblers, journeymen tailors, scavengers, publicans, and sinners of every kind, and, worst than all, their wives and their daughters, when they are called upon to perform their several parts in their new capacity of counsel and witnesses. Sometimes they roar at each other like bull-calves, while the judge in vain commands silence; at other times they will shake their fists in a way that threatens pugnacity even across the court; abusive names and personal threats are often bandied between them, careless of the judicial censure; and witnesses are nudged and prompted, malgre the sternest rebuke and menaces from the bench that would be formidable to anybody that understood them.[48]

Small wonder that Jay encountered one gentleman who 'declares that he is tired of comedies and farces at a theatre, and that to his mind there is nothing in the shape of amusement and fun equal to the proceedings of a County Court'.[49] If the courts of requests had been beargardens some of the county courts were clearly no better and it is not surprising that a President of the Law Society (E. F. Burton) declared some thirty years later, when they had become a good deal more respectable, that 'a man of position cannot go into the county court'.[50] It was the lack of social segregation that was so objectionable, albeit almost inevitable given the buildings which had to be used and the caseload to be disposed of.

Burton's view, like that of 'Regular Practitioner', was formed by

46 *The Law* (London, 1868), pp. 113–15.

47 J. R. Lewis, *The Victorian Bar* (London, 1982), p. 18 ff.

48 *LT* 19 (1852), 218.

49 Jay, *The Law*, p. 78.

50 *Select Committee, 1878*, qq. 4216–491. His ignorance of county court procedure shows that he practised what he preached.

metropolitan and other big city courts. Most of the others were quite different: places like Canterbury where the soft-hearted Charles Harwood sat and 'it was not unusual for him to spend half an hour in sifting a disputed baker's account of a few shillings'.[51] Even in country towns, however, the extent to which dignity and decorum prevailed depended largely on the personality of the judge. Some judges felt it would be enhanced by adopting the trappings of the superior courts, put on robes themselves and encouraged advocates to do likewise. James Espinasse went further than most, dressing up in silk gown and wig and being preceded into court by his officers bearing wands; this was felt to be affecting the majesty of the law a little too much, but when Amos held court muffled up in his greatcoat he was considered to be lowering the dignity of the court.[52]

Amos was a sick man, which goes far to explaining why the Brompton court and that at Marylebone were sharply criticised for the fewness of the sittings and the disorder which attended them.[53] Elderly barristers suddenly pitched into London courts were always likely to find it a struggle, though Moylan at Westminster earned good opinions as a dignified and humane judge.[54] Others found their new authority intoxicating and, freed of the restraint that a regular bar imposed in the higher courts, became autocratic and overbearing. Chilton was one such: 'his bearing is said to be imperious, his tone harsh, his language inconsiderate ... He is ... too impatient of contradiction; interrupts the advocates too much; tries to play too prominent a part in the drama of the Court, and evidently mistakes pomp for dignity.'[55]

There was not much to be done about judges like Chilton. Complaints might be made to the Home Secretary, who passed them to the Lord Chancellor, but the only sanction he possessed was the extreme one of dismissal for 'inability or misbehaviour'.[56]

[51] *LT* 41 (1865–6), 819. [52] *CCC* 5 (1852), 59, 77–8; *LT* 14 (1849–50), 297.

[53] *CCC* 4 (1851), 21; *LT* 16 (1850–1), 472; *LT* 14 (1849–50), 297, 303.

[54] *LT* 14 (1849–50), 297. Moylan refused to commit a judgment debtor to a prison where cholera was raging even though his creditor was implacable in wishing it: *LT* 13 (1849), 408.

[55] *LT* 10 (1847–8), 121; 11 (1848), 362. George Chilton succeeded to the first county court vacancy, at Greenwich and Lambeth, in July 1847.

[56] County Courts Act 1846 s. 18; PRO T 10/2 f. 22. The surviving papers do not record the outcomes of complaints.

One judge became so outrageous that he actually was dismissed, not in fact by the Lord Chancellor but by the Chancellor of the Duchy of Lancaster, who stood in his place for appointments and dismissals in those courts situated within the Duchy. In William Ramshay's case the misbehaviour was palpable and probably indicative of mental illness; feeling himself persecuted on all sides he struck out against a newspaper editor, incarcerating him for contempt and thereby raising such a storm of protest among the citizens of Liverpool that his retention in office would have discredited the court completely.[57] No other judge of a county court was publicly dismissed until 1984.

Short of such flagrant misconduct the county court judges were more or less free to do as they chose. At the outset there was no appeal from their decisions, and although some of the superior court judges did their best to exert restraints through the liberal use of the prerogative writs, these did not always produce the desired effect: one judge 'when he received the prohibition signed by Mr. Justice Paterson ... exclaimed "Oh I don't mind that; Mr Justice Paterson does not half know what my powers are." '[58]

Critics complained both of errors in their judgments and of contradictory decisions on the same point of law.[59] The latter were inevitable and unfortunate but probably grew less frequent once the law journals began to report county court decisions on points of wider interest. Mistakes of law were sometimes excusable given the pressure to deliver verdicts immediately and the lack of good quality argument, but some were egregious even so. The *Globe* gave to the world 'My Aunt's Case', which was for years the stock in trade of those who would sneer at county court justice: 'In a rural court, not far from the Metropolis ... a defendant having lost his cause, declared that he had no money to pay the debt; but added that he believed his aunt would pay it. "Oh" said the Judge "then I will make an order upon your aunt".' The *Legal Observer*,

[57] *Ex p. Ramshay* (1852) 18 QB 174; P. Polden, Judicial Selkirks: the County Court Judges and the Press, 1847–1880, in Brooks and Lobban, *Communities and Courts*, pp. 245–62.

[58] *LM* ns 15 (1863), 145. Exchequer judges freely granted *certiorari* and *prohibition*: *LT* 16 (1850–1), 348 and returns in *HLSP* 1851 (25) I and (161) XI, but Amos, *Testimony of Parties*, wrote that most county court judges were unimpressed by the threat of *prohibitions* and one county court judge hit back in print: *LR* 15 (1851–2), 313–26 (A. J. Johnes).

[59] A good selection is in *LM* ns 7 (1847), 4–14.

giving the story wider currency, claimed that 'we have heard of twenty judgments pronounced in these courts quite as absurd, which we refrain from publishing'[60] and all the law weeklies told tales of disquieting verdicts, shameful ignorance and disregard for all canons of evidence.[61] Most would admit, however, 'that after allowing for all these defects, a vast deal of rough justice is done in these courts'.[62] And none could deny the one great fact: the county courts were getting a tremendous amount of business.

## THE COURTS UNDER SCRUTINY

By December 1847, after just nine months in operation, 429,215 plaints had been issued: the annual total in the common law courts of Westminster was barely 100,000. Westminster county court alone issued almost 14,000, Clerkenwell close on 12,000, Liverpool nearly 10,000. In 1849 there were 395,191 plaints and 226,403 trials (the majority trials only in the most technical sense – courts were breezing through sixty or seventy plaints an hour since few defendants showed up and fewer still contested the plaintiff's claim); almost £1.2 million was claimed and judgment given for £628,000.[63] The journals attributed much of the activity to an inrush of suits dammed up for want of a suitable forum.[64]

This threatened 'almost a revolution in legal economy'.[65] The *Legal Observer*, which had 'ventured to predict that the whole experiment will end in disappointment and injustice', still railed at this 'ruinous piece of experimental quackery'[66] but now stressed its ill effects on the bar and the superior courts, though it would have found few laymen to agree that the latter 'have not in any respect forfeited the respect and confidence of the public'.[67] Laymen appreciated 'justice without any unnecessary legal technicalities'[68] and resorted freely to a forum that seemed to offer it.

That is not to say that county court justice always came up to litigants' expectations. Creditors, whose views would ultimately

[60] 35 (1847–8), 50–1.
[61] E.g. *Tottenham v. Barwell*, *LT* 16 (1850), 180.
[62] *LM* ns 7 (1847), 8.
[63] *PP* 1847–8 (271) LI; *PP* 1850 (561) XLVI.
[64] *LM* ns 7 (1847), 1–2; *cf.* 13 (1850), 71–82.
[65] The phrase occurs both in *LT* 11 (1848), 502 and *LM* ns 7 (1847), 1.
[66] 33 (1846–7), 484; 34 (1847), 557.
[67] 39 (1849–50), 73.
[68] *LR* 13 (1850–1), 115.

determine their success, had plenty of complaints. Judges were said to be too willing to use their novel power to order repayment by instalments;[69] the requirement that the defendant be sued in his local court was 'a nuisance so perfectly intolerable that it is idle to suppose it can be suffered long to exist';[70] the want of judgment by default was a great inconvenience.[71] The universal outcry however was that the fees charged to suitors were 'monstrous'.[72]

This was a direct and unavoidable consequence of the decision that the courts must be self-financing, and precisely because they were *small* debt courts – in 1851 the average amount per plaint at Westminster was £5 16s, at Bow only £2 2s[73] – there was little scope for tapering the fees so that they bore least hardly on the smallest suits. Paradoxically, in undefended causes it was actually cheaper to use the superior courts, whose sheriffs' officers were also considered more zealous in enforcing judgments than the county court bailiffs.[74] It was alleged in Parliament that fees were 50 per cent of the sum claimed[75] and there was a great clamour for an immediate reduction, which the high yield made quite feasible.

What many lawyers found even more alarming than the success of the county courts in fulfilling their immediate purpose as small debt courts was the strong current of opinion in favour of giving them a much more extensive jurisdiction. *The Times* and other newspapers insistently contrasted their straightforward procedures with the labyrinthine subtleties which had enmeshed the 'new Pleading Rules' of the common law courts, while the appearance of the first number of *Bleak House* put Chancery in the dock again.[76] Competition from the new courts gave a fresh impetus to the movement for reforms to the central courts, however reluctant many eminent lawyers were to embrace change.[77]

The threat did not come from the government, since the Home

[69] *LO* 40 (1850), 41–4; *LO* 43 (1851–2), 451; *CCC* 1 (1847–8), 361; *Jur.* 18 (1854), 143, 151.

[70] *LR* 7 (1847–8), 248.

[71] *LT* 15 (1850), 93; *CCC* 2 (1849), 41.

[72] *LR* 7 (1847–8), 248; *CCC* 2 (1849), 273. There was a public meeting in Sheffield: *LT* 9 (1847–8), 541; *LT* 10 (1848), 8.

[73] *PP* 1851 (545) XLII.

[74] *LR* 7 (1847–8), 248.

[75] *Hansard* 1847–8 3rd s., vol. 96, col. 429. According to *HLSP* 1852–3 (257) XVIII, the percentage of costs to the sum for which judgment was given was 26.

[76] The first instalment appeared in March 1852. W. S. Holdsworth, *Charles Dickens as a Legal Historian* (Yale, 1928), pp. 79–115.

[77] Cornish and Clark, *Law and Society*, pp. 38–43.

Secretary, the Lord Chancellor and the Attorney-General were all opposed to the onward march of the county courts. However, in the strange political situation following Peel's death, ministries could not keep a grip on the Commons, while a cluster of Chancellors, past and future, dominated legal debates in the Lords, seldom in agreement on anything and often maliciously eager to discomfort each other.[78]

It was a situation made for Brougham's own brand of mischief. 'His thirst for legislation knew no slaking'[79] and the fecundity of his lawmaking was matched only by its irresponsibility. Brougham took to flying as many kites as he could fashion at the opening of a session in the hope that some would catch a passing breeze; brazen and insouciant, he airily invited an exasperated Lord Chancellor to take charge of bills which did not yet exist in any presentable form and was provokingly indifferent to the mess created by his scattergun approach.[80]

In any case, ministers were the architects of their own misfortune over Henry Fitzroy's County Courts Extension Bill of 1850.[81] A serious misreading of the temper of the Commons led them to oppose it outright without having a decent argument to offer, and Fitzroy Kelly made things worse by his lawyerly evasiveness on the question insistently posed – would he advise a client to try to recover a £50 debt in the superior courts?[82]

Humiliatingly beaten on the second reading by more than two to one, the government had to concede that the central proposal, to raise the jurisdiction to £50 in tort and contract, had too much momentum to be stopped, and their further incompetence at the committee stage[83] meant that the Bill reached the Lords late in the session and in an unsatisfactory shape. Ironically it was Brougham

78 Stevens, *The House of Lords as a Judicial Body* pp. 37–44; T. H. Ford, Truro, Brougham and Law Reform during Russell's Administration, *Revue Historique de Droit*, 52 (1984), 1–43.

79 J. B. Atlay, *The Victorian Chancellors* (London, 1908), vol. I, p. 365.

80 For contemporary criticism of his approach see *LO* 41 (1850–1), 445. Ford, Truro, Brougham and Law Reform, is more favourable.

81 Fitzroy was MP for Lewes from 1837 to 1859, the year he died. A Lord of the Admiralty under Peel and ultimately a Liberal; under-secretary at the Home Office in the Aberdeen ministry, Dec. 1852 to Feb. 1855.

82 *Hansard* 1849–50 3rd s., vol. 109, cols. 59–68; vol. 131, cols. 131–53.

83 *Ibid.*, vol. 131, cols. 1108–31, 1162–74. There was particular confusion over appeals, the 'costs sanction' and venue, not helped by farcical conditions which rendered some speakers quite inaudible. It was also marked by disgracefully

who came to the rescue, pressing it 'at railroad speed'[84] through a hastily convened select committee, cobbling together an acceptable compromise on the important question of appeals and diminishing its adverse effect on the superior courts by preserving a concurrent jurisdiction, unfettered by costs sanctions, in claims above £20.[85]

Though Fitzroy was bewildered at some of the modifications and one disgusted county courts partisan wrote that it 'had not preserved a single redeeming feature',[86] others, *The Times* among them, felt that Westminster Hall had received a body blow.[87] All shades of opinion concurred that 'everything tends to enhance the importance of the county courts',[88] and while the profession was still grappling with the implications of Fitzroy's Act, Brougham's cornucopia spilled out offers of equity, bankruptcy, tithes, unlimited arbitrations and the inevitable 'courts of reconcilement'.[89]

The only one of Brougham's bills to get anywhere was the Further Extension Bill which, intended primarily to give county court judges the powers of Chancery masters, was transformed first by a savage onslaught from Lord Chancellor Cranworth and then by the untrammelled inventiveness of the Commons[90] into a 'remarkable example of legislative versatility'[91] which finally reached the statute book in 1852 as a hotchpotch of mostly innocuous provisions, notable chiefly for a deftly insinuated protection for the bar in the matter of audience.[92] Brougham naturally had no intention of abandoning his more ambitious schemes and Cranworth, pessimistic of his ability to control the progress and shape of these grand designs, sought to disarm him

rowdy lobbying by barristers, who almost pulled Roebuck's coat off his back (col. 1114).

84 *LO* 40 (1850), 214. The select committee sat for just three hours, taking evidence from Judge J. H. Koe. Its proceedings are only briefly reported in the *HLJ*.

85 *Hansard* 1849–50 3rd s., vol. 112, cols. 1059–63, 1286–9, 1337–9.

86 *CCC* 3 (1850), 157, 183.

87 See e.g. the discussion in *LM* ns 13 (1850), 69–74.

88 *LM* ns 15 (1851), 141.

89 *Hansard* 1850–1 3rd s., vol. 114, cols. 170–3, 502, 1100–19. For the bills see *PP* 1851 (257) (304) (461) (636) II.

90 *Hansard* 3rd s., vol. 114, cols. 958–67, 1208–26; *LT* 17 (1850–1), 1, 34, 173.

91 *LO* 42 (1851), 191–4.

92 *HLJ* 83, 84 (1851, 1852). Debates are in *Hansard* 1851–2 3rd s., vols. 118–20. Mullings' verdict that it was 'a complete mass of confusion' (*Hansard* 1852–3 3rd s., vol. 120, col. 796) is justified.

by a device not yet become the hackneyed resort of harassed ministers: he announced a royal commission on county courts.[93]

The Commission was chaired by the Master of the Rolls, Sir John Romilly, and comprised two common law judges (Erle and Crompton), three county court judges (J. H. Koe, A. S. Dowling and J. Pitt Taylor), a barrister (H. S. Keating), a progressive attorney (J. R. Mullings) and Fitzroy. Their remit included court fees and lawyers' costs; more generally they were 'to consider whether any improvements can be made for the better administration of justice' and whether 'any further business can be profitably transferred' to the county courts.[94] Romilly wisely refused a later request to suggest a basis for differentials in the judges' salaries.[95]

The Commission took eighteen months to produce a report which hardly seems to have needed so long. Less than a score of witnesses were invited, little written evidence received, and as with so many inquiries into the courts, lay opinions were scarcely sought.[96]

The Report is a lacklustre affair which does not adequately justify some of its conclusions. Supporters of the county courts could take pleasure from the verdict that 'the experiment has been eminently successful, and benefits have been conferred on the community by means of these courts, which it is perhaps difficult to exaggerate', and that their procedure was 'simple, prompt and inexpensive'.[97] Despite these virtues, however, 'the consideration which we have bestowed upon the subject has not induced us to recommend any considerable extension of the court'.[98] The Report dealt only with the common law jurisdiction, 'leaving other branches ... to be hereafter considered';[99] thus the forceful plea by Judge Graham Willmore for an equity jurisdiction (he claimed there was a 'universal outcry upon the subject')[100] was put

93 At the beginning of the session Brougham brought in his County Courts Equitable Jurisdiction, County Courts Further Extension and District Courts of Bankruptcy Abolition Bills (*Hansard* 1852–3 3rd s., vol. 123, col. 164). On the first reading of yet another, the Arbitration Law Amendment Bill (28 July), Cranworth announced the royal commission (vol. 129, col. 849).

94 *Romilly Report*, instructions.

95 *Hansard* 1855–6, 3rd s., vol. 141, cols. 295 ff.

96 Of eighteen witnesses, five were county court judges, two were registrars, two were high bailiffs and one was a treasurer. The others were mostly attorneys.

97 *Romilly Report*, pp. 25, 37. 98 *Ibid.*, p. 25. 99 *Ibid.*, p. 24.

100 *Ibid.*, q. 1469. Willmore's evidence received the fullest press coverage.

by for a second report. All that was offered in the way of extension was malicious prosecution, ejectment actions by mortgagees, an almost unlimited expansion of the jurisdiction by consent and better facilities for interpleader and replevin.[101]

Suggested improvements to procedure were also mostly of a modest character. Judgment by default should become available where more than £20 was at stake and such substantial awards should not be the subject of instalment orders; the venue rules should not be changed except to allow a judgment creditor, with the judge's leave, to summon the debtor to the court where judgment was given; the use of *certiorari* and *prohibition* should be curtailed.[102]

Rather curiously, the Report concluded with a fierce onslaught on the surviving local courts and proposed to reduce their attractiveness to attorneys by limiting costs.[103] This was tantamount to an acknowledgement that, as was expressly conceded in small suits, county court costs were still too low. However, it hardly took a royal commission to pronounce that costs in the bigger suits should afford 'a reasonable compensation', nor was it helpful to avoid becoming entangled in the costs dispute by doubting 'whether the language of the statute was sufficiently explicit to enable [the superior court judges] to dispose of the subject in a satisfactory way'.[104]

The most valuable part of the Report dealt with fees. It repudiated the notion that the fees should cover the full costs of the courts and drew up detailed proposals which would reduce their yield by nearly £125,000 a year, restructuring the fees to give the defendant more incentive to admit the claim.[105]

Pitt Taylor insisted on writing separate 'observations' which were severely critical of several points in the Report.[106] His view that the consent jurisdiction was an utter failure was more convincing; he wanted the plaintiff to be able to sue in the county court of his choice subject to safeguards for the defendant, and because there were already too many speculative tort actions in the superior courts he would deprive the plaintiff of costs in any such action for under £20.[107]

101 *Ibid.*, pp. 25–9. 102 *Ibid.*, pp. 29–31, 35–7. 103 *Ibid.*, pp. 50–1.
104 *Ibid.*, p. 47. 105 *Ibid.*, pp. 38–44.
106 *Ibid.*, unpaginated at the end of the report.
107 Pitt Taylor (1811–88) succeeded Chilton at Greenwich and Lambeth in 1852

Pitt Taylor was on close terms with the Lord Chancellor and may have had something to do with the decision not to invite Romilly to continue with the Commission's work. Indeed, when Cranworth introduced a bill to implement some of the Romilly Report, Lord Campbell accused him of taking more note of Pitt Taylor's views than the Commission's. There was some truth in that,[108] but the bill was altogether less radical than Pitt Taylor would have wished; in particular it adopted the timid 'costs sanction' proposals of the Report – limited to awards of not more than £5 in tort and excluding default actions from its scope – in preference to his.[109]

Though the legal profession predictably disapproved of any curtailment on their choice of forum, there was almost universal approval (except on the part of doctrinaire Liberals like Gladstone)[110] for the government's acceptance of the principle that the state ought to bear the cost of providing the courtrooms and the judges.[111] This was gained at a price however, for the Treasury insisted on a scheme of differential salaries for judges which aroused more interest among MPs than all the other clauses of an otherwise unexciting bill put together.[112]

## COUNTY COURTS ASCENDANT

Pitt Taylor was one of many who supported the disarmingly plausible proposal that in common law business the county courts should have an unrestricted concurrent jurisdiction with the superior courts, but with the defendant able to remove a suit into the latter, either without restriction or, as the bolder souls preferred, on showing cause.[113] For a hundred years, however, governments were to shrink from that course, preferring instead to

and remained there until 1885. An authority on evidence, he drafted the Documentary Evidence Act 1845. *Boase*, vol. III, p. 897.

108 *Hansard* 1855–6 3rd s., vol. 142, col. 5. In vol. 141 at col. 1906 Cranworth says that he has asked Taylor to draft a clause.

109 County Courts Amendment Bill, *PP* 1856 (179, 252) II.

110 *Hansard* 1855–6 3rd s., vol. 143, col. 688.

111 *Ibid.*, vol. 142, cols. 1–5 (Cranworth LC).

112 *Ibid.*, vol. 141, cols. 279–309; vol. 143, cols. 692–708, 995–7. See p. 251 below.

113 This course was urged in the *Westminster Review* ns 34 (1868), 313–34 and *TNAPSS* (1868), 205–16 (A. J. Williams).

tinker with the costs sanction whenever they wished to push more small matters into the county court, avoiding the accusation that they were depriving suitors of their sacrosanct right of resort to the superior courts.

This was the approach adopted in the Amendment Act of 1867, which raised the figure for the so-called 'exclusive jurisdiction' in torts to £10; another clause entitled the defendant in a superior court action in contract for not more than £50 to have it transferred to the county court unless the plaintiff could show good cause.[114] This seems mild enough but alarmists calculated that between them these provisions could deprive Westminster Hall of up to half its business, making 'not a reform but almost a revolution'[115] and causing something of a panic in the profession – which seems to have been rather easily panicked if the journals are to be believed.[116]

The rest of the Act was unremarkable, going some way to aid creditors by introducing judgment by default, though only for goods sold and delivered for use in trade etc., and enabling them by leave of the judge to sue in the district where the cause of action arose. It also prised loose from the grip of the self-appointed guardians of the sacred rights attached to land small causes involving disputes over title. Coming in the session dominated by the Reform Bill, the measure received only perfunctory scrutiny, so that its 'lamentably bad' drafting was not much improved.[117] Twenty years after Fitzroy's Act had substantially enlarged it, the county courts' bread and butter jurisdiction had scarcely been pushed any further, the ceiling of £50 remaining in place except for remitted and consent actions. But by 1870 it had become a court of remarkably wide jurisdiction, capable of taking, *inter alia*, probate, bankruptcy, equity and admiralty.

With the exception of small probates, which came their way in 1858 when Doctor's Commons received its *quietus*,[118] each was strongly fought by an influential specialist bar and by the London agency firms, but they were unable to halt the seemingly irresistible progress of this upstart court.

Bankruptcy came first, in 1861, when the antique and anom-

114 County Courts Act 1867 s. 5.
115 *CCC* 20 (1867), 249.
116 *LM* 24 (1867–8), 218–65.
117 *Ibid.*, 23 (1867), 322.
118 Court of Probate Act 1857 s. 10; *HEL*, vol. XV (1965), pp. 203–5.

alous co-existence of separate regimes for traders and other insolvent debtors was finally ended.[119] Since 1847 the county courts had exercised some jurisdiction over the latter,[120] and now the powers of the commissioners in bankruptcy outside London were given to county court judges and registrars in selected towns. Bankruptcy and insolvency engaged Victorian legislators and lawyers with striking frequency and, though most agreed that the commissioners were highly unsatisfactory, there was no consensus that county court judges would be any better, the clause giving them jurisdiction barely scraping through the Lords.[121] The acquisition of bankruptcy was of considerable importance, for there was no upper limit on the size of the estate which might be handled, and with even registrars dealing with estates worth several thousands of pounds it was difficult to contend that their judges could not be entrusted with torts and contracts of a few hundred.[122]

Equity finally arrived in 1865. Brougham's repeated bills in the early 1850s were passionately opposed by leading Chancery men, notably Lord St Leonards, but although there were good grounds for doubting whether the elaborate machinery of Chancery could be replicated in county courts, critics were insistent that small estates could not be economically handled in Chancery and Lord Westbury at length offered jurisdiction up to £500.[123] Commentators anticipated that there would be a great influx of suitors hitherto deterred by Chancery's sinister reputation[124] and so confident was this expectation that the judges, grumbling about the imposition of this on top of the bankruptcy work, were able to wring an extra £300 a year from the Treasury.[125]

119 Lester, *Victorian Insolvency*, pp. 124–46.

120 P. W. J. Bartrip, County Court and Superior Court Registrars, 1820–1875: the Making of a Judicial Official, in Sugarman and Rubin, *Law, Economy and Society*, pp. 349–79 at 349–50, 359–61.

121 *Hansard* 1860 3rd s., vol. 158, cols. 1565 ff.; 1861 3rd s., vol. 161, col. 507; *LT* 36 (1860–1), 380. According to the *County Courts Chronicle*, the issue split the legal profession: 14 (1861), 33, 65–6, 74–6. The Walpole Committee of 1854 had come out against this change: *PP* 1854 [1770] XXIII.

122 Bartrip, Registrars, at p. 361, citing a case in which the Walsall registrar made an order for nearly £3,000.

123 County Courts (Equitable Jurisdiction) Act 1865.

124 The *County Courts Chronicle* promised a regular section on equity: 18 (1865), 239.

125 *Hansard* 1864–5 3rd s., vol. 180, col. 527.

The last and least acquisition was admiralty, for which several big ports had petitioned. Admiralty Court officers and practitioners lobbied effectively to have the scope of the proposals narrowed and the jurisdiction was given only to twenty-two courts in coastal towns.[126]

Divorce apart, the county courts were now practically courts of complete jurisdiction in civil matters, Judge Daniel claiming that in his courts there was a practical fusion of law and equity which caused very little difficulty.[127] There were those who felt that some county court judges had been mingling the streams of these waters for many years and without the benefit of any authority.[128]

These accretions radically altered the image of the county courts. Critics who still insisted that they were just small debt courts – which 'furnish a mere machinery for the recovery of trumpery debts, indeed, are a kind of collecting agency for the tallyman and other small dealers'[129] – carried no conviction, whereas *The Law Magazine's* prediction that 'we shall find it rise into the one universal court of First Instance in Law and Equity throughout England'[130] seemed highly plausible.

Statistically, however, the added jurisdictions had little impact; indeed in some of the rural backwaters they probably made no difference at all. For all the fuss and striving to bring equity to the people, the people proved perplexingly indifferent to the boon: between 1867 and 1873 the number of equity suits ranged between 613 and 767 a year, the property at stake never much more in aggregate than £100,000 and the yield to attorneys (*c.* £5,000) and the Exchequer (*c.* £3,700) equally meagre.[131] Such an ignominious outcome to all that lobbying led to puzzlement in the press and to sarcastic comment from a Treasury representative sore at having paid the judges extra for so little work.[132] Admiralty business, confined to a handful of courts, was never expected to

[126] *HLJ* 100 (1867–8), *passim.* Liverpool petitioned against (p. 277); County Courts (Admiralty Jurisdiction) Act 1868 (c. 71), esp. s. 52.

[127] *TNAPSS* (1868), 225–37.

[128] E.g. Judge J. W. Smith: Polden, Judicial Selkirks, pp. 25–51.

[129] *LJ* 2 (1867), 515.

[130] *LM & LR* 27 (1869), 351.

[131] *Civil Judicial Statistics.* Equitable causes are fully analysed by type.

[132] *Childers Report*, qq. 2069–76: H. C. E. Childers to H. Nicol. As early as 1867 the *County Courts Chronicle* was inviting readers to suggest explanations: 20, p. 16.

generate much work but bankruptcies made a mark in the larger courts; in 1869 there were 4,931 suits, with £70,013 at stake.[133]

Even so, beside the work of debt collection this was insignificant. In terms of the sheer volume of business this period falls into two distinct halves: about ten years of rapid and more or less continuous growth, reflecting in part the enlargements in jurisdiction, followed by a slowdown which at times went into reverse.[134] Thus, between 1852 and 1861 plaints rose from 474,149 to 903,875; in 1871 they were 918,503. The figures for judgment summonses show this pattern even more strikingly: 47,704 in 1853, 130,254 in 1861, 123,928 in 1871. By contrast execution warrants against goods were still rising remorselessly, from 59,702 in 1851, to 129,140 in 1861 and 181,123 in 1871.

The great mass of these actions were for very small sums: plaints claiming above £20 actually fell in the 1850s, and in 1871 still numbered only 14,503. Just how small many of these were can be seen from the statistics for judgments in 1865:[135]

| | | |
|---|---|---|
| not exceeding | 40s | 300,158 |
| 40s to | £5 | 88,309 |
| £5 to | £10 | 30,257 |
| £10 to | £20 | 11,760 |
| £20 to | £50 | 3,486 |
| above | £50 | 13 |
| by consent above | £5 | 13 |
| TOTAL | | 434,036 |

This was still the ‘poor man's court’ – the court in which the poor man was sued – and lost, almost always lost; something like 96 per cent of actions ended with judgment for the plaintiff, more often than not without a fight.[136]

For most judges outside the big commercial centres an equity or

[133] *PP* 1870 (224) LVII: *Civil Judicial Statistics* at p. 54.

[134] *LT* 53 (1872), 301. P. Johnson, Small Debts and Economic Distress in England and Wales, 1857–1913, *Economic History Review*, 46 (1993), 67–87, concludes that the fluctuations were ‘strongly related to specific short-term fluctuations in the labour market and labour income’ (p. 86); he tacitly assumes that changes in fees, costs and procedure were statistically insignificant.

[135] *PP* 1866 (456) LVIII.

[136] *LJ* 6 (1871), 657. Johnson, Small Debts and Economic Distress, 67, suggests that over the period 1857–1913 defendants in small debt cases had an even worse chance, never better than 2 per cent.

bankruptcy suit was a rare diversion from their daily routine. But though comparatively few in number, these matters, like those remitted from the superior courts, were usually more complex and time consuming than the run of county court business.[137] In the busier county courts it was customary to fill the lists to bursting in the expectation that few cases would take more than a few minutes; in one day at York, for instance, Dowling got through 237 plaints, 11 adjourned plaints and 22 judgment summonses after three o'clock.[138] In most courts there was no possibility of going on with the hearing on the next day and since even a single jury trial could disrupt the programme quite badly, the hostility of certain judges to juries is readily explicable.[139] Bankruptcy and equity matters likewise had a disproportionate impact on the court's timetable.

In the early 1870s some of the metropolitan courts were becoming very congested,[140] even though county court business overall was more or less stagnant and the annual returns disclosed that some of the provincial judges seemed to be enjoying a leisurely existence.[141] This naturally led to demands for a review of the overall distribution of judges and courts. Devotees of economy and efficiency in the House of Commons and in an increasingly intrusive Treasury sought a reduction in the number of judges or at least a major redistribution to equalise their work-loads and improve the suitor's lot in busy courts.[142]

The only changes hitherto had been minor ones – a few of the sleepiest courts were shut, a couple of districts were absorbed, a second judge was given to Liverpool and some flexibility was arranged to facilitate business in the industrial West Riding.

137 Examples from *PP* 1868–9 (241) LI include a breach of promise for £1,000; £408 for goods sold and delivered; £2,000 for an assault; £1,000 for negligence.

138 *LJ* 2 (1867), 548. See also *LT* 50 (1870–1), 124–5. At West Hartlepool in 1910 hearings averaged 85 seconds: Johnson, Small Debts and Economic Distress, 70.

139 According to B. L. Moseley, *LM & LR* ns 4 (1879), 364–5, it was common knowledge that some judges browbeat suitors out of having a jury.

140 *LT* 49 (1870), 142.

141 See e.g. *HLSP* 1873 XVIII (277) at p. 67, showing the structure of the judge's day in each of his courts: e.g. in Canterbury he sat once a month, listed between 71 and 110 plaints, heard and disposed of between three and nine contested suits, sitting between one and four hours; of the rest 40 per cent were either 'admitted' or 'not appeared'. The judges' sitting days ranged from 104 to 174, their average of causes heard from 25 to 132.

142 See pp. 212–13 below.

There were plausible reasons for inaction, some administrative, others political. It had quickly been learned, for instance, that town councils regarded a county court as an asset and would resist its removal as tenaciously as the small assize towns would fight for the red judge and his trumpeters. As ministers had no wish to seek trouble, they had shelved more ambitious schemes and as a result the geography of the county courts looked much the same in 1870 as it had in 1850.[143]

Their internal arrangements however had undergone substantial changes, the most significant being the transformation of the clerk into the registrar, the change of style indicating a change in role from clerical and managerial to judicial as well.[144] On the administrative side his authority was enhanced, and his workload slightly increased, by the abolition of the district treasurers in 1866, while the gradual absorption of the office of high bailiff began in the same year. No-one regretted the demise of the treasurers, who had only been included in the first place to avoid compensation claims, but the abolition of separate high bailiffs was carried as an economy measure against the opposition of many judges.[145]

These changes put the registrar more firmly in charge of the everyday running of his court. It was almost invariably a single court now, for the pluralism which had initially been allowed had been restricted after some bad publicity,[146] but some needed so little attention that part-time registrars had to be allowed despite the awkwardness which their dual role as court officer and local practitioner now and then caused.

In addition the registrar had set off on the road which led by slow stages to his destination as an exclusively judicial officer, styled a District Judge. Two milestones stand out. In 1861 registrars in the courts nominated for bankruptcy business acquired the extensive judicial and administrative powers belonging to their counterparts in the now defunct district courts of bankruptcy; in places like Birmingham, Leeds and Liverpool this work

143 *Select Committee, 1878*, q. 5055: evidence of Nicol.

144 Bartrip, Registrars, pp. 354–64.

145 County Courts Act 1866; Judicature Commission, *Second Report*, replies to q. 22.

146 It was restricted to exceptional cases by County Courts Act 1852: see pp. 281–2 below.

was demanding and prestigious, greatly enhancing the registrar's standing.[147]

The second milestone was more relevant to those with smaller courts. The County Courts Amendment Act of 1867 gave the registrar the power to hear undefended causes and enter judgment, including settling the terms of payment by instalments. With the leave of the judge – and few judges were not willing to delegate – he might similarly hear cases where the defendant did appear and admitted the claim.[148] In fact, as the Judicature Commissioners were told, 'many of them now help the judges with the contentious business, and without their aid it could not often be disposed of'.[149] This was of the utmost importance, for it freed the judge to deal with defended suits and spared litigants and lawyers the frustration of waiting around while the judge first disposed of the undefendeds; no wonder Pitt Taylor was unpopular in Lambeth for insisting on keeping them for himself.[150] It did however create practical difficulties where the layout of the court building meant that both judge and registrar had to hold court simultaneously at either end of the room, 'the noise at either end being so great as to obstruct the business at the other'.[151]

Most judges were thankful to off load the humdrum undefendeds and most probably welcomed the advent of some variety in their diet, even though it was sometimes strong meat. Bankruptcy was not always a favourite; one journal described it as 'the most tedious, the most repulsive and not the least difficult department of legal administration'.[152] Equity too could be embarrassing for those whose practice had been at common law, but they did their best and the best of some was very good indeed; Daniel was as good a bankruptcy judge as any on the bench and Stonor was graciously complimented by Stuart VC on one of his equity decisions.[153]

As the range and complexity of the judges' responsibilities widened, better men were needed, but although there was never a shortage of well-qualified candidates, and some appointees – men such as Daniel and Stonor, Pitt Taylor, Petersdorff and

147 Bartrip, Registrars, p. 361.

148 *Ibid.*, pp. 363–4. The provisions are in ss. 16–17.

149 *Ibid.*, p. 364.

150 Judge Stonor at q. 965, *Select Committee, 1878.*

151 *LT* 50 (1870–1), 124. Similar difficulties arose at Llanelli: *LT* 49 (1870), 368.

152 *LJ* 4 (1869), 333.

153 *Phillips v. Burrows*, *LT* 45 (1868), 169.

Wheeler[154] – would have graced the superior court benches, the lack of pensions meant that many of the original incumbents clung to office far too long[155] (several, like some more illustrious judges, until they were very deaf[156]).Worse, the county court bench was perceived by governments of every hue as a suitable reward for political services, for old connexions who had failed to make their way at the bar, for decent barristers worn out by the strains of practice and for the private secretaries of Lord Chancellors.

The really unjustifiable appointments were a small minority, but they tainted the image of the entire bench. Cranworth forfeited the good opinions he had earned by choosing Eardley Wilmot when he followed it up with Christopher Temple, 'utterly unknown to the public, scarcely known even by name to the profession'.[157] There was despair and exasperation from the friends of county courts who had urged that Chelmsford be given the benefit of the doubt on the charge of appointing his friends when his very next vacancy was filled with C. F. D. Caillard, a man nobody knew, thereby raising 'another storm of reproach'.[158] And there was an explosion of anger when the radical politician Edmond Beales was chosen by Hatherley, quite openly in compensation for having been deprived of his revising barristership for his part in the rally that led to a riot in Hyde Park.[159] It was not that all these appointments turned out badly, but they implied that the county courts did not need good judges and that the incumbents often got there without merit.[160]

154 W. T. S. Daniel (1806–92) was the author of the *History and Origin of the Law Reports* (London, 1884) and instrumental in the creation of the Council of Law Reporting; a member of the Digest Commission in 1866, he was judge in West Yorkshire from 1867 to 1884 (*Foster*, p. 113). H. J. Stonor (1820–1908) was Chief Commissioner of West Indian Encumbered Estates 1858–65, then a judge until 1905. His mother was a daughter of the famous conveyancer Charles Butler (*ibid.*, p. 450). C. E. Petersdorff (1800–86) was counsel to the Admiralty, an industrious legal author and judge from 1865 to 1886 (*DNB*, vol. XV, p. 965). Thomas Wheeler (1805–83) was a former Manchester solicitor, judge of the Salford Hundred Court in 1860 and a county court judge from 1862 until retirement in 1883 (*Al. Cant.*, vol. VI, p. 424).

155 In 1870 twenty of the original judges were still in office.

156 E.g. the suburban judge who had to have a bailiff standing next to him to bellow the utterances of advocates and witnesses into his ear: *LT* 45 (1868), 114.

157 *Jur.* ns 1 (1855), 75; *CCC* 7 (1854–5), 26.

158 *LT* 33 (1859), 93; *SJ* 3 (1858–9), 492.

159 Duman, *English and Colonial Bars*, p. 97; *SJ* 14 (1869–70), 910, 918.

160 Duman, *English and Colonial Bars*, p. 102.

Nor was the bad impression created by these appointments countered by promotions from the ranks of county court judges. Pitt Taylor had a promise but the Lord Chancellor who gave it went out of office before he could carry it out;[161] otherwise none seems even to have been thought of. Judges did what they could to bolster their status by imposing strict rules about dress on lawyers and sometimes laymen too and by dressing up themselves.[162] They at length got official permission to style themselves 'judge'[163] and the more ambitious took every opportunity to publicise their decisions and to keep their names before the public by writing and speaking on the legal issues of the day.[164] Some of their number, however, undermined every attempt to present the county courts as a fit repository for bigger suits by wayward practice and idiosyncratic decisions; J. W. Smith on the Welsh Marches was probably the most embarrassing,[165] but W. H. Cooke in East Anglia drove suitors into the neighbouring district courts by his unpleasant ways, and one London judge had to suspend sittings because he was in gaol for debt.[166]

The impression that county court justice was still rough justice and often arbitrary justice was fostered by a critical and in some cases hostile legal press. All the journals were London based and since their readership was the bar and the better class of attorney they ran no risk in attacking county courts in harsh terms: 'No class of English tribunal is so costly, either to the state or to suitors, so ill-conducted or so unsatisfactory, as are these county courts',[167] opined one, while 'the establishment of the county courts has been a gross blunder'[168] was the verdict of another. These organs delighted in ferreting out the latest examples of gross blunders, like Herbert's decision in *Hinckley v. Williams*, which bade fair to rival 'My Aunt's Case'.[169]

Of course the abuses and defects were real and some were

161 *Select Committee, 1878*, at q. 517.
162 Judge Lonsdale threatened to deny costs to persons not dressed smartly: *SJ* 12 (1867–8), 71.
163 Pp. 255–6 below. Pitt Taylor would neither do that, nor sit robed.
164 P. Polden, Judicial Independence and Executive Responsibilities, part two, *AALR* 25 (1996), 153–61.
165 Polden, Judicial Selkirks, pp. 249–53.
166 *CCC* 21 (1868–9), 139; Polden, Judicial Independence, part one, 10.
167 *SJ* 6 (1861–2), 483.
168 *Jur.* ns 11 (1865), 496.
169 *SJ* 10 (1865–6), 481, 489.

serious. Defenders of the county courts argued that the small number of appeals were testimony to the soundness of most judges, but that was disingenuous; most of them knew full well that appeals lay only in the larger cases and then only on questions of law; that some judges were so affronted at the questioning of their judgment that they did their best to make appeals impossible and that the form of appeal – by case stated – was all against the appellant.[170]

The regular presence of lawyers was probably a more effective curb on judicial waywardness and, although the scales of costs were still not generous, attorneys and, in the bigger courts, barristers were becoming more common.[171] Since the latter were usually young and inexperienced they often found it a trying experience to appear before judges with their own peculiar ways of doing things. Edward Parry, later to become the best-known county court judge of his day, had to confront Crompton Hutton, 'a man of cantankerous character and rude, overbearing manner [whose] methods were irregular [though] they did not lack common sense'. Parry had been warned that Hutton sat unrobed and disliked lawyers who wore theirs, but he had not yet discovered other 'rules of the court', such as not standing between the judge and the fire.[172] Parry had the self-assurance (and the legal pedigree) to handle such men but few novices were Parrys.

Barristers were generally birds of passage, but local attorneys had to adapt to their judge's peculiarities. They sometimes acted collectively, as when J. H. Koe rashly tried to give the bar pre-

170 Polden, Judicial Independence, part one, 31–2.

171 This is one feature of the courts where statistics are in short supply. However, Judge Pollock gave the Romilly Commission (q. 1042) these figures for Liverpool:

| | |
|---|---|
| barrister for plaintiff only | 8 |
| barrister for defendant only | 5 |
| barrister for one party, attorney for the other | 42 |
| attorney on both sides | 401 |
| attorney for plaintiff only | 730 |
| attorney for defendant only | 381 |
| TOTAL with some representation | 1,578 |

Pollock's figures excluded insolvency, and it needs to be borne in mind that Liverpool was atypical in the volume of substantial suits.

172 *My Own Way*, (London, 1932) pp. 119–21. Hutton's manner changed immediately Parry told him that he was the son of a well-known serjeant.

audience,[173] but more often it was a determined, sometimes wrongheaded, individual who made a stand. The 'loud shop boy manner'[174] which offended more delicate sensibilities was much in evidence, and if attorneys found some of the judges autocratic, judges needed all their patience and firmness in training uncouth attorneys in the rudiments of advocacy.[175]

## DEBTORS AND CREDITORS

Many attorneys still advised their clients to sue in the superior courts rather than in the county court, and not always because of the better quality of justice. The sort of attorney who depended upon small cases for his livelihood could not afford to be entirely disinterested in the matter of costs and it was convenient to portray the costs sanction as an infringement of the Englishman's birthright of justice in the royal courts even if, as laymen were not slow to observe, the spectacle of the Lord Chief Justice 'engaged for the greater part of two days [at the Surrey assizes] in trying, with a jury, whether a stack of hay was worth £100 or £120'[176] hardly showed that principle in a good light.

None the less, though attorneys had it in their power to influence the choice of forum, the success of the county courts in their primary role in enforcing debts would be determined by traders. What they wanted was a process that was speedy, ruthless, economical and effective and it was soon claimed that the county courts failed on all four counts.

First of all there were delays in getting process served because, it was plausibly alleged, bailiffs lacked incentive and determination; service by the parties or their agents ought therefore to become the rule.[177]

Far worse, many judges were said to be soft on debtors. Some

173 *SJ* 2 (1857–8), 566, 584, 625.

174 H. Kirk, *Portrait of a Profession*, (London, 1976) p. 157, quoting *LM & LR* ns 4 (1875), 89.

175 E.g. *LM* 7 (1847), 6.

176 *Westminster Review*, ns 34 (1868), 313–34 at 321.

177 The Attorney-General had put such a clause forward in 1850 but withdrew it without debate: *Hansard* 1850 3rd s., vol. 111, col. 1163. According to *PP* 1860 (322) LVII, 10–15 per cent of summonses were returned as 'not served' in Manchester and Liverpool.

unquestionably were. Charles Harwood was notorious for it and John Worlledge owed much of his local popularity to a reluctance to be too severe, while F. K. Eagle apparently combined deafness and advancing years with gullibility.[178] But complaints on this score must be treated with caution since the creditors' voices, especially when orchestrated by their trade associations, were always loud, while harshly treated debtors often suffered in silence and ignorance.[179] Even so, there is no doubt that some insolvents rather quickly learned which provincial judges would most readily absolve them of their financial sins and 'White Washertons' (as such courts were styled by the popular press) became notorious for a few years.[180]

A particular source of indignation was the readiness and flexibility with which indulgent judges availed themselves of their power to order repayment by instalments. No such thing existed in the superior courts and there were those who argued that it was a denial of a creditor's fundamental right to recover his money – indeed instalments were sometimes ordered which had precisely that effect when a judge felt that the creditor was especially undeserving. But such instances were comparatively rare and it was at least as common for a judge to overestimate a debtor's available resources as to let him escape too lightly. There was a legitimate complaint that some judges did not differentiate between consumer debts and trade debts and Judge Rupert Kettle, a shrewd and knowledgeable observer, criticised the making of instalment orders for traders.[181] But whether creditors acknowledged it or not, instalment orders proved to have real advantages when it came to coercing the lower-class debtor and it seems likely, as was claimed, that they actually encouraged credit selling.[182]

Since creditors wanted a streamlined process they objected to the protections debtors were supposed to enjoy, protections which

[178] *LT* 41 (1865–6), 819; *Public Men of Ipswich etc.*, 237–41; *LT* 26 (1855–6), 272.

[179] For a disputed allegation of this sort, about R. G. Temple, see *LT* 27 (1856), 217, 242, 254.

[180] Publicised in articles in *Household Words*, see *LT* 26 (1855–6), 249, 259; *LT* 27 (1856), 16; *CCC* 13 (1860), 73; *LT* 31 (1858), 150.

[181] Select Committee on Tribunals of Commerce, *PP* 1871 (409) XII: qq. 1608–10. Kettle admitted that he occasionally stretched the law to do justice.

[182] G. R. Rubin, Law, Poverty and Imprisonment for Debt, 1869–1914, in Sugarman and Rubin, *Law, Economy and Society*, at pp. 341–4.

also contributed to making the process expensive. They resented the judges' reluctance to order transfers of venue, wanting all cases to be brought in the creditor's home court; with the growth of mail orders and large credit sales firms in Leeds, Manchester and elsewhere, this would effectively mean that few debtors would have the means or the time to appear in court. Creditors also resented the insistence of some judges on strict proof that the debtor had the means to pay and the reluctance of many to allow debt collectors to handle suits in court; all these hindrances increased their costs, so it is unsurprising that many sold their debts to professional collectors.[183]

Through trade associations and MPs, creditors lobbied hard for the introduction of more favourable procedures, especially for the default summons that the superior courts dispensed and which spared a plaintiff the need to attend armed with evidence to prove his claim in case the defendant unexpectedly put in an appearance. They extolled the virtues of the Salford Hundred Court and the Mayor's Court where defendants had a harder time, opposed attempts to reduce the limitation period for debts and insisted that as a body they were socially responsible and entitled to a better service.[184]

Their loudest complaints, however, concerned the difficulty and expense of actually extracting the money from the debtor once they had judgment. Some wished to be able to bypass altogether the so-called 'banking system' whereby all payments were channelled through the court; this, however, was perceived as an integral part of the instalment order facility and Parliament was not willing to risk the inevitable disputes over payments which direct collection would create.

Creditors lamented the ineffectiveness of the threat of execution against goods.[185] It may have been true that the bailiffs were less zealous both in chasing up overdue instalments and in levying warrants against goods than the sheriff's officers of the superior

[183] *Ibid.*, pp. 327–30, 338–40. For criticism of the Cornwall judge's strictness see *LT* 41 (1865–6), 2. Judge Gale (of *Easements* fame) ruled that Trade Protection Societies which enforced debt claims were guilty of maintenance, leading to a deputation to the Lord Chancellor: *SJ* 8 (1863–4), 627–8.

[184] Figures demonstrating the cheapness of the Salford Court are in *Jur.* ns 2 (1856), 255.

[185] Rubin, Law, Poverty and Imprisonment, pp. 341–4.

courts who were paid by results, but there were real difficulties in seizing goods when they exposed the officers to the risk of interpleader actions,[186] and towards the end of the 1860s a new menace appeared in the shape of the first hire purchase agreements; more than ever, what little saleable property was to be found in the homes of the poor was likely to belong to someone other than the debtor.[187] The manifest ineffectiveness of other remedies drove judgment creditors to increasing reliance on coercion through the threat of imprisonment and this embroiled the courts in a public controversy of mounting importance.

Parliament had come very close to abolishing imprisonment for debt in the 1840s but creditor pressure had made them timidly withdraw, retaining the prison where the debt was small and had been incurred without reasonable expectation of being able to pay. In one important respect, moreover, the small debtor's position was worsened, for imprisonment was no longer to operate in satisfaction of the debt: instead of being punitive, it became coercive.[188] At first no-one seems to have taken much notice, even though it was apparent that imprisonment was occurring on quite a large scale. In 1852 870 men were gaoled in London alone, 512 for less than £5; forty-five of them were gaoled twice, six three times and three hardy, stubborn or unlucky men four times.[189] What is more the figures crept upwards; when national statistics came out in 1859 they showed that not less than 30,756 committal orders had been made and 10,748 enforced.[190]

Letters by J. A. Busfield to *The Times* in February 1859 brought the phenomenon before a wider public and Brougham drew attention to another disquieting feature – that the national figures concealed very marked discrepancies between comparable courts; the judges, it seemed, had no common approach.[191] A vigorous

[186] On interpleader actions see the *Romilly Report* at pp. 28–9.

[187] *SJ* 12 (1867–8), 748: *Moore v. Moore and Bradford*, concerning a pianoforte. There is a useful brief account of its early history in the Crowther Report: *PP* 1970–1 (Cmnd 4596) IX, pp. 42–6.

[188] Cornish and Clark, *Law and Society*, pp. 226–30; Kerchner, Transformation of Imprisonment for Debt, 61–109; Rubin, Law, Poverty and Imprisonment, pp. 244–6.

[189] *PP* 1857 (90 s. 1) XIV.

[190] There are very detailed returns in *HLSP* 1856 (85) III and *PP* 1859 (195) XXII(I).

[191] *SJ* 3 (1858–9), 390, 413, 449. *Hansard* 1859 3rd s., vol. 155, col. 140. Rubin, Law, Poverty and Imprisonment, 261–5. Busfield was treasurer at Bradford.

debate followed. The progressive Law Amendment Society, the Chief Baron of the Exchequer and many writers attacked committals, as did one rash county court judge, Serjeant Storks, who blamed Parliament for cowardice and drew down upon himself so scathing a rebuke from the dreaded 'slashers' of the *Saturday Review* that he hastily retracted his threatened refusal to make committals and resigned soon after.[192] Storks was one of a small minority, for when the judges' views were sought by the Lord Chancellor they were strong for retention of the sanction, leading the *Solicitors' Journal* to comment acidly that 'it used to be supposed that the tenacious defence of recognised abuses was confined to old institutions, grown stagnant from partial disuse'.[193]

Though that attack on committals failed, it was sure to be renewed. Once bankruptcy had at last become available to others besides traders the 'class nature' of the insolvency legislation was embarrassingly exposed: in the same county court a man could be whitewashed of debts of many thousands, irresponsibly incurred, while a wretched workman was pursued relentlessly for a couple of pounds.

It was not only humanitarians who were affronted: the spectacle of tallymen using the prisons at the public expense to recover debts into which they had lured working men (or more often their wives) for pathetic luxuries exasperated the economy minded.[194] Many judges had no love for the tallyman, some making their animosity plain and boasting of their success in keeping him away from their district.[195] Almost all judges insisted that they only made committals when they were fully satisfied that they were justified and their committee opposed

> any interference with the transactions of travelling drapers and such persons, because we think that the judges of the courts, by carefully weeding from the accounts of these persons all sums charged for goods supplied to a wife on the credit of her husband not befitting her station, or which he has not sanctioned, can prevent any ill effect which would

[192] Rubin, Law, Poverty and Imprisonment, p. 246.

[193] *SJ* 3 (1858–9), 598. The report (*ibid.*, 777) was not published as a parliamentary paper until 1867 (*PP* (209) LVII).

[194] Rubin, Law, Poverty and Imprisonment, pp. 275–6, 332–4; P. Johnson, Class Law in Victorian England, *Past and Present* 141 (1993), 147–69.

[195] Examples are Everett (*LT* 44 (1867–8), 173) and Eardley Wilmot (*SJ* 8 (1863–4), 655).

otherwise arise from this system of trading, and because we think that when so restrained the system is not disadvantageous to the labouring classes.[196]

These judges would have agreed with Lord Westbury, who 'looked upon the working classes as little better than children in these matters', but while he said 'they must be taken care of and laws made for them accordingly',[197] the judges regarded themselves as well able to balance the interests of suppliers and consumers.

Although creditors scouted the substitution of attachment of earnings[198] and no other remedy promised to be effective, Gladstone's administration made a determined onslaught on committals in 1868, by which time they were approaching 10,000 a year. The Debtors Act 1869 put a stop to the use of prison in all but a few circumstances. Most of the exceptions were insignificant, but s. 5 preserved it for cases where an order for payment had been made and the debtor defaulted, either having, or having had, the means to satisfy the judgment at some point since it was made. The section was presumably aimed at the unscrupulous debtor who thumbed his nose at a court order, but it proved to have a much wider reach and an enormous significance for the county courts.

Henry Brougham died in 1868. The idea of courts of reconcilement died with him, but much of the rest of his plan for a network of local courts dispensing speedy and cheap justice had become a reality; indeed they had already far outgrown their origins. While reforms to the superior courts, though considerable, had proceeded piecemeal, leaving untouched many inconveniences and the whole of the outmoded assize system, the county courts had advanced remorselessly.

In 1868 964,146 plaints were issued, including more than 11,000 above £20; 117,528 judgment summonses were issued, plus 178,894 execution warrants; and there were orders for costs to the amount of £1,323,006.[199] The future role of the county court was widely discussed amid apprehension at the bar that it would become ever more expansive, and when the government set up a royal commission to investigate the organisation of civil justice there seemed every likelihood that those fears would prove well grounded.

196 *PP* 1867 (209) LVII. 197 *SJ* 8 (1863–4), 569. 198 *Ibid.*, 627–8.
199 *PP* 1868–9 (241) LI.

3

# AN AGE OF FRUSTRATION, 1871–1914

## THE TURNING POINT

The work of the Judicature Commission recast the courts of law in a shape which endured substantially unaltered for almost a hundred years. From the various common law, equity and civilian courts, which were collectively the 'superior courts', was created the Supreme Court of Judicature (SCJ), whose judges possessed the jurisdiction of all the old courts and the power to administer their doctrines and remedies in the same action; in addition the procedure in the divisions of the new high court was to be largely governed by a common set of rules. Although the provisions for appeals, already complicated by the retention of divisional courts, were further elaborated when political considerations led to the preservation of the House of Lords, the SCJ was an excellent foundation for a durable structure of civil justice.[1]

A foundation, however, is all it was. What should have been the first stage in a complete reconstruction remained the only one, 'a terminus rather than a staging post'.[2] The other stages should have been the re-ordering of justice in the provinces and of the relationship between the high court and the inferior courts, in particular the county courts. This had been outside the remit of the original commissioners and only Ayrton had disturbed their impressive unanimity by urging his colleagues to consider whether all actions should be started in the county courts.[3]

[1] The best concise account of the reforms is Radcliffe and Cross, *English Legal System*, ch. 17.

[2] Cornish and Clark, *Law and Society*, p. 93.

[3] First Report, *PP* 1868–9 [4130] XXV at 26. Acton Ayrton, a barrister MP, was Financial Secretary to the Treasury, but soon afterwards he was sidelined to the Office of Works because his tactless zeal for cost-cutting had upset too many

A few months after the first report, the Commission, augmented by a county court judge, C. S. Whitmore, was given a wider brief. It is clear from the questionnaire they circulated that big changes were under consideration, for in addition to all the defects in the county courts to which creditors' organisations and law societies had repeatedly drawn attention, respondents' views were sought about the desirability of a large-scale consolidation of districts with business divided into two classes, the small debts being handled by registrars and the rest, possibly considerably extended in scope, by judges at major trial centres.[4]

The Commission finished taking evidence in June 1870 but it was August 1872 before its second report appeared and this long interval, ominously suggestive of stubborn differences of opinion, had a significant effect on the reform programme.[5] Hatherley's ill-starred bill to implement the first report was withdrawn in May 1870 and, had the second report appeared in good time, a comprehensive measure covering both might have been put together; as it was, Selborne had the revised Judicature Bill ready for the new session before the second report came out.[6] The Second Report may have been 'potentially a revolutionary document',[7] but its potential was fatally undermined by the trail of dissents, absences and reservations with which it concludes;[8] the *Solicitors' Journal* was prophetic in damning it as 'a death blow to law reform for the present generation'.[9]

The Commission identified three classes of business in the civil courts:

there are two classes at least of the subject matter of litigation – those which can bear the expense of being tried before an elaborate and central

people: M. Wright, *Treasury Control of the Civil Service, 1854–74* (Oxford, 1969), pp. 46 n. 1, 336.

4 *Second Report*, appendix. One judge (Christopher Temple) did not reply, probably because of ill-health (he died in January 1871). Another answered one of the questions so impertinently that it was censored (Sir J. Hollams, *Jottings of an Old Solicitor* (London, 1906), p. 99).

5 Of forty-three witnesses seen in connection with county courts, forty were either court officers or lawyers.

6 Cocks, *Foundations of the Bar*, pp. 138–43. Selborne's account is in *Memorials, Part II: Personal and Political* (London, 1898), vol. I, pp. 298–315.

7 Bartrip, Registrars, at p. 366.

8 There were reservations from Ayrton, Cairns, Collier, Blackburn, Penzance, Coleridge and Erle.

9 *SJ* 16 (1871–2), 798.

tribunal, and those which require a cheap, simple and local procedure and trial. But there is a third or intermediate class of cases, which frequently involve questions of complexity, and of serious importance to the parties interested, yet the expense of taking the parties and witnesses to any considerable distance from the place where the cause of action arose, and they probably dwell, is generally wholly disproportionate to the value of the matter in dispute.[10]

It was this third category which was to be catered for by the creation of 'central courts', where a county court judge would ordinarily be found and which would be serviced by a resident registrar. At least one other registrar would cover the rest of the district and the judge would continue to hold court at less important centres when business required it. Since, however, it was proposed to give registrars jurisdiction over defended actions up to £5 and to discontinue the least-used courts, the number of districts and judges could be progressively reduced. The judges who remained would have a more extensive jurisdiction, for it was proposed to allow common law actions to any value (including the excluded torts) to be brought in the county court, the defendant having the absolute right to remove them into the high court. The costs sanction for bringing small actions in the high court would remain in a simplified form and all the surviving local courts would be abolished.[11]

Since 'the existing system is too costly and elaborate',[12] it was to be radically simplified. The banking function must go; service of process by the parties (and on the parties) would be the normal mode and default judgment would be possible, with some protection for defendants in small debt cases. The county courts would form constituent parts or branches of the new high court and the separate rules of procedure for equity, bankruptcy and so forth would become largely otiose. Procedure would be kept simple, fees be set at a level lower than the high court and registrars be salaried; differential salaries would reflect the actual responsibilities undertaken by each judge and registrar.[13]

There was something here to offend almost everyone with a vested interest in the legal system, and whereas the inconvenient structure of the old superior courts could hardly be defended, lawyers and judges might hope for lay support in fighting some of

[10] *Second Report*, p. 10. [11] *Ibid.*, pp. 11–17. [12] *Ibid.*, p. 14.
[13] *Ibid.*, pp. 16–21.

these proposals, which were, moreover, singularly lacking in detail despite their long gestation.[14] For instance, the whole area of sheriffs and bailiffs would need 'consideration and revision'[15] but neither there, nor on the number of districts and judges, the level of fees and salaries or any number of key issues were the reforms worked through. And on one crucial question – audience – there was silence.

The Commission rather casually acknowledged that the proposed abolition of local courts might meet with opposition from the cities concerned,[16] but since it also admitted that the proposals 'will necessarily cause a considerable diminution in the civil business at the assizes'[17] it was abundantly clear that it would not be from that quarter that the main opposition would come. Selborne had signed the Report without reservations, though whether he would have tried to implement it is not clear, but the Liberals went out of office before he had to decide. Cairns, the Conservatives' Chancellor, had refused to sign, though he had expressed his agreement with its general tenor and was believed to have ambitious plans for local justice.[18] Even so, it would have been a brave or foolhardy Chancellor who put the Commissioners' package forward in anything like its full form and Cairns gave no indication that he would do so. When no proposals of any sort emerged the proponents of reform grew impatient and forced the issue by putting up bills of their own.[19]

Two bills were before Parliament in 1877. One was drafted by T. J. C. Bradshaw, once secretary to the Judicial Commission and now a county court judge in Newcastle. Designed to appeal to the big cities by offering them 'principal county courts' staffed by an elite of judges on £3,000 p. a., it was claimed to be along the lines suggested by the Commission and to have the backing of Selborne and many county court judges, although it stopped short of making the county courts part of

[14] As the *Solicitors' Journal* noted: 16 (1871–2), 785, 798.

[15] *Second Report*, p. 16. [16] *Ibid.*, p. 18. [17] *Ibid.*, p. 21.

[18] *LT* 56 (1873–4), 302. He refused to sign until more adequate arrangements were proposed for business in Lancashire and Yorkshire and he did not approve the immediate abolition of the Duchy courts.

[19] A government bill introduced in 1874 and passed the next session *inter alia* made changes to the appeals process, introduced a limited equivalent of judgment by default and enabled judges to appoint assessors. No wider measure was promised: *LT* 19 (1874–5), 193, 346.

the high court.[20] The other bill was Eardley Wilmot's, giving unlimited concurrent jurisdiction with the defendant able to remove a suit to the high court if he gave security for costs.[21] When this bill was debated the Attorney-General (Sir John Holker) showed himself hostile to all ambitious plans[22] and Charles Norwood, taking the hint, came forward next session with a more modest measure. All three bills were then sent off to a Commons select committee.[23]

With the ample evidence of the Judicature Commission readily to hand it is difficult to see why the committee found it necessary to traverse the same ground, sometimes with the same witnesses, but so they did.[24] The atmosphere was quite different however, with witnesses summoned not so much to provide information as to support members' entrenched positions. Wilmot was a partisan chairman who tried to lead witnesses in the direction of his own ideas, while Morgan Lloyd and Gregory, opposed to all the bills, were frequently rude and openly hostile. At times the examination degenerated into mere point scoring and when the hearings were over there was no pretence of trying to reach a consensus.[25]

Though voting on the key issues was close, Wilmot's optimistic draft report was humiliatingly mangled.[26] The central proposal of his own bill scraped by, but with the important deletion of the requirement to give security for costs; there was to be no increase in the costs-protected jurisdiction, and though registrars were to be given contested actions in contract up to 40s, only those not practising as solicitors were to act in a judicial capacity. Judges' salaries were to be raised to £2,000 and a pension scheme

20 *PP* 1877 (71) I. Its main sponsor was the radical MP Joseph Cowen and it owed something to a very elaborate scheme published by Judge Harington: *LT* 61 (1876), 212 ff.; 62 (1876–7), 275 ff.

21 *PP* 1877 (110) I. For Wilmot see p. 260 below.

22 *Hansard* 1877 3rd s., vol. 234, cols. 586–99 at 597–8.

23 *PP* 1878 (100) I; *Hansard* 1878 3rd s., vol. 238, cols. 439, 1478–80.

24 Ten judges, several registrars, eight solicitors and representatives of several trades bodies were seen, as well as Henry Nicol. Baron Bramwell was again interviewed and breezily confessed to having forgotten the details of the Judicature Commission's report.

25 *Select Committee, 1878.* See e.g. the questioning of Edmund Newman (qq. 4026–38) and M. D. Osbaldeston (5573–870).

26 *Ibid.*, pp. vi–xii. The clause giving unlimited jurisdiction passed by seven votes to five, then one member changed his mind and the chairman had to use his casting vote. Raising the protected jurisdiction to £200 was only carried by five votes to four.

established, while fees on the plaint note or summons were to be reduced.[27]

As one journal immediately predicted, the Treasury vetoed any rise in salaries or reduction in fee income, and with the Eastern Question engrossing everyone's attention the report fell rather flat.[28] Nevertheless the reformers sank their differences and started out again with the Norwood bill (as amended by the select committee) as their platform. Rather to their surprise, they found themselves outflanked by the government, for Cairns produced a County Courts Bill in the Lords which was considerably more ambitious. There was a serious blockage in the Queen's Bench and this Bill combined several current suggestions for diverting business downwards; unlimited concurrent jurisdiction at common law and raised monetary limits in equity; an increase in the costs-protected limit to £200, and better facilities for remitting actions. Cairns also hit hard at the local courts by limiting their solicitors' costs to the county court scales and he made a few minor changes on audience and default actions.[29]

The fate of this Bill is perplexing. It was not debated on the floor of the House, but was emasculated in a select committee including Selborne and Hatherley. Out went the enhanced equity jurisdiction and the costs sanction in cases where more than £50 was claimed; the unlimited jurisdiction was to be available only in metropolitan courts and those with bankruptcy; remitting cases was not to be facilitated and the local courts regained most of their freedom over costs. Brought before the Commons in May, it was withdrawn in July with no announcement as to its future, the last government measure of its kind for many years.[30] When Norwood's bill reappeared next session the Solicitor-General, Sir Hardinge Giffard, was unenthusiastic, describing the extension as an experiment and any threat to the future of the assizes as a calamity; the government would promise only a consolidation bill.[31]

27 *Ibid.*, pp. iii–iv.

28 *SJ* 22 (1877–8), 758; *LT* 65 (1878), 25. Watkin Williams, a member of the select committee who wanted 'free trade in law' (q. 5834), introduced a bill supported by Cowen.

29 *PP* 1878–9 (40, 191) I; *HCJ* vol. 134.

30 *LT* 67 (1878–9), 23–4; *SJ* 23 (1878–9), 539; *Hansard* 1878–9 3rd s., vol. 245, cols. 258, 1239; *HLJ* vol. 111, esp. 139, 146.

31 *PP* 1880 (6) I; *Hansard* 1880 3rd s., vol. 250, cols. 1385–411.

Selborne returned to office in 1880 in the wake of Gladstone's triumph at the polls but offered no encouragement either to Norwood's persistence or to other bills of a more or less ambitious character.[32] In 1882 the Royal Courts of Justice opened in the Strand, symbolising the triumph of London over the provinces and marking, as it turned out, the end of the era of reform in legal administration. There would be no Ministry of Justice, no provincial branches of the high court and no unified structure embracing high and county courts. After thirty years of advance the county courts steam engine had finally run out of puff.

Explanations for this outcome can be sought at various levels. The attitude of Selborne and Cairns and their cabinet colleagues was clearly very important,[33] and the reluctance of the Treasury to sanction increases in salaries and reductions in fees was a constant obstacle, perhaps not impossible to overcome. But it is clear that the opposition to the decentralisation of justice had grown more formidable and that the most effective resistance came from the bar. The Victorian bar was fragmented, disorganised and, to judge from the laments which filled the pages of the legal journals, demoralised. The butt of *Punch's* wearisome facetiousness and a favourite target for *The Times*' sententious leaders, barristers felt themselves unappreciated and misunderstood.[34]

From the outset the junior bar had regarded the county courts as a potent threat to their livelihood and had lobbied vociferously against every extension to their powers, sometimes to the embarrassment of the leaders of the profession. The clamour had won some notable concessions, particularly the ban on attorney-advocates, but the encroachment of the county courts was nevertheless remorseless. Confronted also with schemes to reform the Inns and to promote effective training, to remodel the circuits and to challenge restrictive practices, by all political logic a profession so lacking in organisation and unity ought to have fallen an easy prey to Victorian modernisers, yet the bar saw off most of the threats

32 *PP* 1881 (34) II; *PP* 1882 (146) I; *PP* 1883 (103) II.

33 Neither Selborne's *Memoirs* nor the biographies of these Chancellors throw light on this point.

34 R. Abel-Smith and R. Stevens, *Lawyers and the Courts* (London, 1967), pp. 53–7, 63–79, 211–35; Cocks, *Foundations of the Bar*, pp. 83–162; Duman, *English and Colonial Bars* pp. 50–77.

and emerged with privileges intact and dauntingly capable of resisting further attacks, a dreadnought of legal conservatism.

One reason for its success was its remarkable strength in the House of Commons, where some 16 per cent of members in the House elected in 1874 were barristers, though not all practised.[35] Though they did not vote as a bloc even on issues directly concerning the profession, they could always muster a strong turnout, included among their number a disproportionate share of capable speakers and were adept at quizzing witnesses before select committees. In addition they always had access to, and often the support of, the Attorney-General, whose acknowledged role as 'head of the bar' sometimes sat uneasily with his duty to present the Lord Chancellor's measures in the Commons.[36]

The bar had other important allies in the judges. Judges remained members of their Inns and many convinced themselves that the prosperity of the 'great central bar of England' was inseparably bound up with the public interest. Though not all judges endorsed this convenient view,[37] it permeated every inquiry into the defects of the judicial system. Moreover, from 1883 onwards the Bar Committee and its successor the Bar Council could ensure that it was wheeled out in good time to meet any new threat. The bar might be affronted to be seen as a trade union,[38] but few trade unions managed to promote their members' interests so effectively.

The resistance of the bar would not have been nearly so effective had it not been echoed by the Incorporated Law Society (ILS). By comparison with the bar (though only by comparison with the bar) the solicitors were well organised, despite being more numerous and more scattered. Most big cities had an active and vigilant law society and all spoke loudly, if not with one voice. In most cases the voice was that of the richer and more reputable practitioners who formed the bulk of their membership and nowhere was this more apparent than the ILS. An essentially

35 Duman, *English and Colonial Bars*, p. 170.

36 *Ibid.*, pp. 169–98; J. Ll. Edwards, *The Law Officers of the Crown* (London, 1964), pp. 276–82.

37 Bramwell took a very robust line on the bar's future in his evidence to the select committee of 1878: 'if there is any disparagement or injury to the Bar for the benefit of the public, the Bar must undergo it, that is all' (q. 3485).

38 Cocks, *Foundations of the Bar*, pp. 127–30.

metropolitan body, it was widely perceived as concerned mainly to represent big London firms. Attorneys of the less prosperous sort regularly filled the columns of the more sympathetic newspapers with complaints that their interests were sacrificed – though many of the complainers had not bothered to join the ILS or any other law society.[39]

These divisions among solicitors were very evident in relation to county courts. For instance, to give evidence to the Judicature Commission the ILS chose J. Young, solicitor to the GWR, and W. Ford, who had some little experience of county courts, but also E. W. Williamson and E. F. Burton, who never went near them.[40] Ignorance did not always equate with hostility – John Hollams blithely admitted that he had never been in a county court but still advocated giving them broad powers[41] – but it is clear that these men were primarily there to serve the interests of the London agency firms who made their living out of the Westminster courts and stood to lose from decentralisation. Both professionally and now socially as well, they had more in common with the bar than with the men who grubbed about for small fees in the county courts.[42]

It is no surprise therefore to find that the ILS was generally opposed to county court expansion, while the most influential provincial societies were keener on bringing the judges from Westminster to be permanently in their town, or at least to have the souped-up county courts envisaged by the Judicature Commission, than on extension generally. It was envisaged that big firms in Leeds and Manchester would then become agents for their own legal hinterlands, undertaking the interlocutory work they thought would be needed by the provincial courts.[43]

39 Kirk, *Portrait of a Profession*, pp. 37–9, 157–8; J. S. Anderson, *Lawyers and the Making of English Land Law* (Oxford, 1992), pp. 125–7.

40 *Second Report*, qq. 6106–254.

41 *Ibid.*, p. 132 and *Select Committee, 1878*, q. 3266.

42 Even within the Law Society, unrepresentative of solicitors as it was, there were complaints that the Council was 'a close corporation of London solicitors and their friends': quoted in D. Sugarman, Bourgeois Collectivism, Professional Power and the Boundaries of the State. The Private and Public Life of the Law Society, 1825 to 1914, *International Journal of the Legal Profession* 3 (1996), 81–135 at 106.

43 This was the gist of the evidence given by representatives of the law societies of Birmingham, Manchester, Leeds, Newcastle and Liverpool (*Second Report*, qq. 5922–6105) and their replies to the questionnaire.

As a result of these divisions, the antagonism about audience in the county courts, which prejudiced all discussion at the bar, was muted. Instead of lawyers being divided along professional lines, the division tended rather to be on regional or practice lines, with a few whose altruism, usually coupled with prosperity, led them to take up a position independent of their own professional interests.

Outside the confines of the legal professions, opposition in principle to a wider role for the county courts was mostly confined to those with an interest in discouraging litigation in which they would be cast as defendants, notably railway companies with bitter experience of the generosity of county court juries and some of their judges too.[44] On the whole, though, most large trading concerns were likelier to view themselves as plaintiffs and they tended to favour local justice in principle while judging it in practice according to the facilities it afforded for getting in their debts. By that yardstick their trade bodies, and the organisations for assessing creditworthiness and collecting bad debts to which traders subscribed, judged that the county courts were sadly wanting and would support extended jurisdiction only if it were accompanied by the changes in practice and procedure for which they endlessly pressed.[45]

As this suggests, the county courts were vulnerable to criticisms which cast doubts upon their suitability for an enhanced role. Not all of the criticisms were just, and after all courts are made to serve defendants as well as plaintiffs; still, the unashamedly paternalist approach embodied in their original constitution was generally acknowledged to be inappropriate for the larger cases they were being asked to handle,[46] and there was legitimate opposition to measures which failed to address the need to adapt the county courts for a dual role as small claims courts and subordinate branches of the high court.

It was also legitimate to question the calibre of judges and registrars to handle more complex actions. With the expansion of the bar there was no shortage of potentially suitable judges but, as Nicol testified, the rewards did not tempt them until they were

44 Young was particularly critical of the way judges sabotaged appeals: *ibid.*, qq. 6247 ff.

45 See e.g. evidence of V. Pococke (*ibid.*, qq. 768–971) and memorandum by the Association of Trade Protection Societies (*ibid.*, appendix).

46 *LT* 66 (1878–9), 203–4.

past their prime;[47] G. L. Russell, for instance, admitted that he became a judge 'because I had got old, and found the labour and wear and tear of the Bar very heavy';[48] at sixty-three, he was one of eight men over sixty appointed in the 1860s. But proposals to make the judgeships more attractive would meet Treasury resistance and not everyone wanted to pay more to judges who were (rightly in some cases) thought to be underworked and lazy.[49]

In fact, many of those who sat least often spent much of their lives travelling and prospective judges who tried out the life as a deputy often found, as Serjeant Pulling did, that 'it was very much the life of a bagman'.[50] Recruitment was made no easier when the Treasury high-handedly sought to reduce their travelling expenses, treating them 'with a distrustful meanness that would be resented by a third rate commercial traveller'.[51]

Even when good men were available, however, they were not always preferred. In 1878 the *Solicitors' Journal* exploded:

> having come to the conclusion that of late the preponderance of appointments of county court judges is so greatly on the side of those which, like the present, it is impossible to approve, we think it best to give up the attempt to estimate the merits of such appointments, and to reserve any comments until they come to be made in accordance with some standard which the profession can recognise or at least understand.[52]

Furthermore some judges continued to furnish endless ammunition to the critics. In the 1870s J. W. Smith and T. E. P. Lefroy made repeated appearances in the legal press and every disclosure about their antics was a blow to advocates of extended powers,[53] while even a less notorious figure, J. B. Dasent, attracted the headline 'buffoonery on the bench'.[54] Such men were perhaps adequate for what a high court judge condescendingly described as 'usefully administering summary imperfect justice',[55] but it could not be pretended that they might safely be entrusted with

[47] *Select Committee, 1878*, qq. 4940, 4968. [48] *Ibid.*, q. 915.

[49] *Ibid.*, q. 5187 (Nicol). Henry Fowler MP was a particularly persistent critic of lazy judges, e.g. *CCC* 29 (1884), 427.

[50] *Second Report*, q. 7145.

[51] *LJ* 8 (1873), 144. For the row over travelling expenses see *Hansard* 1871–2, 3rd s., vol. 213, cols. 47–9; *Childers Report*: examination of Nicol and Hon.W. E. Baxter; also *LT* 53 (1872); *SJ* 16 (1871–2).

[52] *SJ* 23 (1878–9), 293. [53] Polden, Judicial Selkirks.

[54] *LT* 62 (1876–7), 264. Dasent is described in T. E. Crispe, *Reminiscences of a KC* (2nd edn, London, 1909), pp. 111–12.

[55] *SJ* 20 (1875–6), 641–2 (Grove J).

wider powers, and what was true of judges was also true of registrars, where there was the added complication that their interests as practitioners might conflict with their judicial duties.[56]

To some extent these concerns could be met by providing a more effective system of appeal, and an Act of 1875 attempted to do just that.[57] First experiences with the new procedure, however, suggested that it was still vulnerable to manipulation by the judge[58] and the indignant response of judges like Falconer when their decisions were overturned indicated that they did not take kindly to curbs on their independence.[59]

The county court judges also remained vulnerable to criticism of their use of imprisonment for debt. The Debtors Act 1869 had preserved the power to imprison defaulting judgment debtors, but the basis of the committal power was highly uncertain – it was not properly for contempt of court because the imprisonment did not operate to extinguish the debt, yet it could not strictly be imprisonment for debt *simpliciter* either. Such niceties did not prevent most judges from using it as a matter of routine though,[60] and when they came under attack for doing so, most of them insisted that it was an indispensable safeguard for the supply of cheap credit to the lower class. Even the minority who favoured its abolition mostly agreed with that proposition, holding, however, that such credit was itself a social evil which ought to be discouraged by depriving the creditor of his most potent weapon of enforcement.[61]

A renewed attack on committals was led by the brewer MP Michael Bass and culminated in the recommendation of a Commons select committee in 1873 for abolition.[62] But the

56 This had worried the Judicature Commissioners and it is evident from replies to questions on this topic that some judges shared their concern: *Second Report*, app. 1.

57 County Courts Act 1875 s. 6.

58 See e.g. *LT* 86 (1879–80), 76; *LJ* 14 (1879), 691–2.

59 *LT* 59 (1875), 140. He published a pamphlet seeking to vindicate his judgment, overturned by Malins VC in *Williams v. Evans*.

60 Rubin, Law, Poverty and Imprisonment, pp. 241–99.

61 *PP* 1867 (209) LVII. These are the judges' answers to questions put to them in 1859, but there is no reason to suppose that the views expressed would have changed ten years on.

62 *PP* 1873 (348) XV. Nicol, R. M. Kerr (Judge of the City of London Court), two registrars, four judges and two high bailiffs were among those who gave evidence.

Walpole Committee was not representative of parliamentary opinion and a bill (not the first of its kind) to give its report effect was soundly defeated.[63] Throughout the 1870s the bill was revived and every session Bass called for a return of committals; but the judges had the backing of trade organisations and many commentators acknowledged that committals were justified in principle. Still, there were well-publicised instances of seemingly cruel and heartless jailings – the case of William Smallbones at Farnham and the 'Matilda incident' at Grantham both caused outrage[64] – and the returns, as well as appeal cases such as *Evans v. Wills* and *Horsnail v. Bruce*, exposed awkward inconsistencies both in the judges' interpretation of the statute and the frequency with which they invoked it.[65]

As a result, the county courts were identified in the public mind with a system condemned by a strong current of humanitarian opinion. Even some who were generally in favour of decentralised justice may well have hesitated in giving more powers to judges who resorted so readily to punitive measures against debtors, especially if it went along with other changes designed to reduce the safeguards built into the system for the benefit of the poor and ignorant.

The final factor which was significant in the fate of the reform proposals was the division among those who espoused the decentralisation of justice. The preference of influential opinion in the great cities for provincial sittings of the high court was one manifestation of this, and another was the strong current of commercial opinion supporting so-called 'Tribunals of Commerce', in which judges, preferably businessmen themselves, would deal with commercial disputes through the application of commercial norms and flexible, informal procedures. The tribunals had been commended by a select committee in 1871 and though the Judicature Commission decisively rejected them, the strong movement for their establishment had drawn support away at a crucial time from those who sought to strengthen the county courts.[66]

63 *Hansard* 1874 3rd s., vol. 218, cols. 548–73. Essentially the same bill (156 of 1872) was presented in every session from 1874 to 1877.

64 *Hansard* 1874–5 3rd s., vol. 225, col. 1818; vol. 226, cols. 55, 215–16, 291–2; *CCC* 26 (1878), 339, 352.

65 *Evans v. Wills* (1875–6) 1 CPD 229; *Horsnail v. Bruce* (1872–73) 8 CP 378.

66 Arthurs, '*Without the Law*', pp. 58–62.

## THE HALSBURY ERA

### *A measure of consolidation*

On 24 June 1885 Lord Halsbury received the Great Seal. He relinquished it for the last time on 11 December 1905, having held it for a total of seventeen years and two months in all, his tenure interrupted by two short periods of Liberal government in which Farrer Herschell was Chancellor.

As he made plain in a speech at the opening of a new court in Derby in their golden jubilee year, Halsbury was strongly opposed to giving the county courts any further common law jurisdiction.[67] Vague promises of government measures were made if support for such changes reached dangerous levels, but they were never meant to materialise and, since the Conservative cabinets were indifferent on this question, Halsbury had only to fear backbench initiatives. Even out of office, a dominating figure in a Conservative upper house, he was able to exert a powerful negative influence.

The last fruit of the co-operation between Selborne and Cairns was a long overdue reorganisation of the curious collection of officers who were attached to the Lord Chancellor. The first Permanent Secretary was Kenneth Muir McKenzie, a radical barrister who loyally suppressed his reforming instincts but gained the reputation for exercising considerable influence behind the scenes.[68] However, the Treasury's county courts department continued to be responsible for day-to-day administration and Nicol continued in effective charge until he retired in 1892.

In Halsbury's time there seems to have been a distinct slackening in Treasury pressure for modernisation and economies in legal administration. The county courts had been a favourite target and within the space of five years Nicol had been quizzed by the Judicature Commission, the Select Committee on Civil Service Expenditure and the Royal Commission on the Legal Departments, all posing uncomfortable questions about the distribution of courts, the workload of judges and the remuneration

[67] *LT* 102 (1896–7), 558–60. Muir McKenzie sought his views on this when Halsbury took office (25 Sep. 1885, BL Add. Mss. 56, 370, f. 18), but the reply does not survive.

[68] P. Polden, *A Guide to the Records of the Lord Chancellor's Department* (London, 1988), pp. 13–21.

of registrars.[69] It would be forty years before the MacDonnell Commission made a similar inquiry and, though there was still sporadic criticism of lazy judges and underused courts, it did not translate either into demands to reduce the gap between fee income and public expenditure on the courts, now well over £100,000, or to leave vacant judgeships unfilled.

It rather looks as though there was a tacit bargain. On its side the Treasury would accept the deficit and the extravagant provision of local justice, while the Lord Chancellor for his part would abstain from pressing for pensions and higher salaries for the judges, civil service status for registrars and staff and bigger spending on new courtrooms.

Not surprisingly, therefore, the basic features of these courts remained more or less unchanged for thirty years. There was a small reduction in the number of judges (fifty-five in fifty-three districts in 1914) and a handful of small courts were abolished, but far fewer than the sixty on Nicol's 'hit list'. Muir McKenzie and a Treasury official did start to wrestle with a comprehensive reorganisation aimed at producing drastic cuts but quickly concluded that it would be politically unacceptable.[70]

A similar outlook characterised the approach to the status and rewards of staff. Halsbury never fought hard for his judges and they fared no better under his successors, who followed the line taken in 1906 that 'it is impossible for [the Lord Chancellor] to close his eyes to the fact that a county court judgeship with its present salary and work is regarded as a very desirable office by a large number of most competent men at the Bar'.[71] Likewise, though there was statutory authority to put registrars on a wholly salaried and full-time footing in the busier courts, there were only eighteen of those out of 476 in 1919, while an internal report on the question of putting the clerks and bailiffs on the civil service establishment was allowed to sit around for two years and was finally sent to the Treasury without any strong recommendation.[72]

It is easy to see why Halsbury did not want to touch the county courts even to make desirable improvements. He feared that any

[69] *Second Report*; *Childers Report*; *Lisgar Commission*.

[70] *MacDonnell Commission*, qq. 55, 472.

[71] K. Muir McKenzie to Judge W. H. Roberts, 26 Feb. 1906, PRO LCO 2/204.

[72] *MacDonnell Commission*, B. J. Bridgman at q. 51, 882; A. G. C. Liddell, *Notes from the Life of an Ordinary Mortal* (London, 1911), pp. 318–19.

legislation put before Parliament would be hijacked in the Commons and returned to the Lords laden with all sorts of unpalatable additions; that, after all, was what had happened to his Consolidation Bill in 1888.

Consolidation was badly needed and the Judicature Commission had prepared a bill as long ago as 1870.[73] A measure was finally brought out in 1886, almost unnoticed because on the same day the ministry was beaten in the Commons and it resigned. It was accompanied by the promise of an amending bill to follow, a promise significantly absent when it came forward again in 1888.[74] Halsbury's stern warning against any attempts to tack on changes of substance[75] had no effect in the lower house and the Attorney-General (Sir Richard Webster) was sorely beset in standing committee, where Reid's amendment to raise the common law jurisdiction from £50 to £150 was beaten by just three votes and would have come closer still had not some MPs accepted Webster's assertion that it was beyond the proper scope of the Bill. Fowler's rehash of the time-honoured proposal for unlimited jurisdiction subject to the defendant's right to remove the suit to the high court also came close to success and Webster barely scraped together the votes to render harmless a threat to expand the costs sanction in contract from £20 to £50.[76]

Once it was out of committee the whips allowed the Bill to languish until the end of the session drew near, then it was hustled on 'with indecent haste'.[77] Left with no time to undo several minor but unpalatable changes, Halsbury had to content himself with an angry rebuke to those responsible; he would not readily court a repetition.[78]

73 *SJ* 14 (1869–70), 792–3.

74 *SJ* 30 (1885–6), 546; F. K. Munton, *LQR* 5 (1889), at 139. Muir McKenzie had a bill 'dealing with various small matters' ready: to Halsbury, 25 Sep. 1885, BL Add. Mss. 56, 370, f. 18.

75 *Hansard* 1888 3rd s., vol. 322, cols. 1596–7.

76 *Ibid.*, vol. 324, col. 373; vol. 330, cols. 359 ff.; *PP* 1888 (172) X; *LJ* 23 (1888), 235–6, 262–3; *CCC* 31 (1888), 407, 412–13; *SJ* 32 (1887–8), 416, 432, 468. There is a very good review of the Act by M. D. Chalmers in *LQR* 5 (1889), 1–10.

77 *SJ* 33 (1888–9), 177.

78 *Hansard* 1888 3rd s., vol. 330, col. 383. The special procedure for consolidation bills which ensured they could not be turned into amending legislation had not then been introduced and the Commons changed its title by adding 'And Amendment': *HCJ* 120, 407–9.

Despite Halsbury's annoyance, the changes embodied in this Act, the basis of county court law for the next forty-six years, were not very substantial.[79] Registrars at last got the right to decide defended cases but only up to £2 and only in contract. Two separate provisions entitled the Chancellor to require registrars in busy courts to abandon their private practice[80] but he was not saddled with Fowler's clause, which would have salaried all of them at their average income over the past five years.[81] Most of them therefore remained on a hideously complicated pay structure linked to the fee receipts of their courts. Most of the ILS 'shopping list' of changes were ignored[82] and the only section which really alarmed the self-appointed defenders of the high court was the badly drafted s. 65, which now required contract actions in which not more than £100 was claimed to be remitted to the county court 'unless good cause is shown to the contrary'; since one writer calculated that 30 per cent of the non-default actions in the Queen's Bench Division (QBD) were already being remitted, the new clause was felt to have the potential to make serious inroads into its business.[83]

### *Torts and workmen's compensation*

The number of remitted actions climbed to 1,638 at the turn of the century,[84] but many were the sort of trivial tort actions some judges detested and, apart from the remitted cases, torts were many fewer than might have been expected.

Some torts were deliberately excluded from the county courts because of the feeling among their betters that the poor should be discouraged from pursuing their 'pothouse slanders' etc. through

[79] Curiously, however, it omitted the admiralty jurisdiction, and though its drafting was praised by Chalmers (*LQR* 5 (1889), 1–10), and in *SJ* 32 (1887–8), 533–6, it was not universally admired: see e.g. T. W. Wheeler in *LJ* 23 (1888), 288–9 and G. Pitt-Lewis, *The County Courts Act 1888* (London, 1888).

[80] Ss. 25, 45; *Swift Report*, pp. 4–5.

[81] M. D. Chalmers, *LQR* 5 (1889), at 7. For the earnings of registrars see *PP* 1888 (148) LXXXIII.

[82] *SJ* 32 (1887–8), 470.

[83] F. K. Munton *LQR* 5 (1889), 135. See also *LJ* 23 (1888), 309.

[84] Snagge, *Evolution of the County Court*, p. 22. Remitted actions are described in detail in the annual county court returns.

the courts,[85] but the very fact that this litigious spirit was thought to exist makes it surprising that it was not more readily indulged in matters where the poor man's court was open. Indeed, it sometimes was, as Sir Rupert Kettle testified:

> people go to law about trespasses by poultry scratching up a few seeds in a neighbour's garden. They go to law for breaking windows by accident; trespass by pigs; and when we talk of torts it is often the veriest trifle, perhaps a neighbour's quarrel about the use of some outbuilding to which they claim a just right, or some quarrel of a trivial nature, just as magistrates at petty sessions are called upon to dispose of.[86]

Kettle was a judge in the industrial West Midlands, yet this account is reminiscent of a pre-industrial society. In that same decade there was an annual average of 1,200 deaths and 4,000 injuries on the railways; perhaps 100,000 road accidents with 1,000 fatalities; probably 1,000 deaths and 5,000 injuries in the coal mines; several hundreds killed and an unknown number injured in factories. In addition to this carnage was massive damage to property by collision, fire and industrial pollution.[87] It is no wonder then, that the law of torts, particularly nuisance and negligence, underwent momentous developments, yet there is remarkably little reflection of all this judicial and legislative activity in the controversies about the role and performance of the county courts.[88]

There are, to be sure, some generalised allegations that the new courts fostered a litigious spirit and that there were plenty of Dodsons and Foggs to get up speculative actions,[89] but there are few allegations that such opportunism was rife in the county courts and little criticism of their failure to attract genuine torts.[90]

85 Successive inquiries had come out against removing this restriction, most recently in 1878: *Select Committee, 1878*, p. 8.

86 *Second Report*, q. 3404, and cf. replies to the questionnaire in app. 1.

87 H. Smith, The Resurgent County Court in Victorian Britain, *AJLH* (1969), 126–37; P. W. J. Bartrip and S. B. Burman, *The Wounded Soldiers of Industry* (1983), pp. 43–53.

88 For a brief account of the major developments see Cornish and Clark, *Law and Society*, pp. 486–520.

89 *Romilly Report*, q. 1413 (Judge Willmore), and *Select Committee, 1878*, q. 3867 (H. Owston).

90 Note, for example, the absence of any question relating to torts in the list circulated by the Judicature Commissioners (*Second Report*, app. 1) and any reference to county courts in the proceedings of the Select Committee on Employers' Liability: *PP* 1876 (371) IX; 1877 (285) XX.

Judges and commentators occasionally disputed the ability of the county courts to handle torts without the superior courts' apparatus of pleadings and interlocutories,[91] but even these exchanges are few in comparison with the endless debates about the best forum for equity and bankruptcy.

Several possible explanations have been advanced for this phenomenon. The rarity of juries is one, but even in districts where the judge did not discourage juries litigants seem not to have wanted them.[92] The upper limit of £50 on damages claimed is another, but the author of that suggestion acknowledged that £50 was a not inconsiderable sum, greater perhaps (to judge from the testimony of a high court master in 1878) than the average damages awarded in the QBD.[93] However, it was solicitors, not plaintiffs who usually chose the forum and since most tort plaintiffs, unlike many suing in debt, were novices in litigation they were unlikely to question their choice. And for lawyers the superior courts always were superior because of their greater generosity with costs, scarcely hampered by the 'costs sanction'.[94]

There were also unimpeachable reasons to prefer the courts in the Strand. The county court venue rules worked in favour of defendants, so a railway company or carrier would usually have to be sued in their home court; furthermore such defendants, professionally advised and often concerned not to be thought a soft touch, were all too ready to appeal, a discouraging prospect for the poor litigant.[95] Far more than contract, tort actions were a gamble and the high court was the best place for gambling.

The situation began to change a little in the 1880s. Personal injury claims under the Employers Liability Act 1880 had to be started in the county court even though the amount (limited to three years' wages) exceeded £50, and though they might be removed by *certiorari* if a high court judge felt a difficult or

[91] Compare the opinions of Bramwell with those of Judges Adolphus and Furner (*Romilly Report* at qq. 1206, 1200, 179).

[92] Smith, Resurgent County Court, 131.

[93] *Ibid.*, 132; *Select Committee, 1878*, q. 4862 (H. J. Hodgson).

[94] Smith, Resurgent County Court, 130. It was not raised from £5 to £10 until 1867.

[95] See e.g. Judge Martineau on the London and Brighton Railway, *CCC* 27 (1879), 86. Both the Lord Chief Justice and Chief Baron Pollock were critical of the railway companies' attempts routinely to have their cases removed into the superior courts.

important point of law was involved, judges were said to be hard to persuade.[96] But as with several other statutory torts, the Pollution of Rivers Act for example,[97] the expected volume of business never really materialised. There was some improvement after a slow start: in 1882 the number of cases more than doubled to 320, the success rate for plaintiffs rose to about 23 per cent and the average sum recovered was nearly £100.[98] Nevertheless the Act was generally deemed a failure and the burst of reported cases in the *County Courts Chronicle* soon dwindled to a trickle.[99] The failure was not set down to any defect in the county courts though. Employers knew that some judges were biased against them and could instance 'wrong decisions', though some of these owed more to ignorance of factory conditions than bias;[100] nevertheless they thought county court judges much preferable to the juries of the higher courts. When the workman failed, as he did more often than not, it was usually due to the narrow drafting of the Act rather than the failings of the county court.[101]

Ironically, while this Act, which encouraged the injured workman to seek redress in the county courts, brought them little business, one which was designed to provide compensation without involving the courts was to bring them a great deal. Joseph Chamberlain intended his Workmen's Compensation Act to cut through the protective thicket which the common law judges had planted around the employer by imposing strict liability for accidental injuries received by workmen in the course of their employment, and although frustrated in his wish to deny the courts any place in this scheme, he was sanguine that they would be relegated to the margins. Events quickly proved him

96 Bartrip and Burman, *Wounded Soldiers*, pp. 158–89; *Report on the Employers' Liability Amendment Bill*, *PP* 1886 (192) VIII, session 1, A. H. Ruegg at qq. 562–3.

97 *Select Committee, 1878*, q. 2076 (Judge Motteram).

98 Bartrip and Burman, *Wounded Soldiers*, p. 178.

99 By 1882 the *CCC* (28, p. 187) was already seeking explanations for the paucity of cases.

100 *Report on the Employers' Liability Amendment Bill*, qq. 562–3 (Ruegg) and 4759, 4701 (John Robinson).

101 Bartrip and Burman, *Wounded Soldiers*, p. 169 quote the TUC's Parliamentary Committee view that 'the Act would seem to have received a liberal interpretation from the county courts'. In the crucial case of *Griffith v. Earl Dudley* (1882) 8 QBD 357, Kettle's decision that contracting out was contrary to public policy was overturned.

dreadfully wrong and his 'simple, immediate and effective' compensation scheme became a playground for lawyers and judges.[102] Judges blamed the draftsman, but their own decisions were marked by inconsistencies of approach that often seemed grounded in ideology or prejudice, and the disillusion which set in as appeal followed appeal was to have a big influence on the form of later welfare legislation.[103]

The county courts came into this picture rather indirectly. Their judges were among the arbitrators available under the Act in case of dispute and in practice it was to them that by far the greatest number of the depressingly frequent disputes were referred. As reports sought by the Home Office in 1900 and 1903 reveal, most were sympathetic to the aims of the Act, and the Court of Appeal, which seemed not to be, frequently reversed them in the early years.[104]

Judges like Gye were soon alive to the unscrupulous ways of insurers, and several, such as Greenhow and Steavenson, wanted the power to impose a paternalist regime on the improvident and incompetent in which the court would dole out weekly sums.[105] A Home Office committee under Sir Kenelm Digby (a former county court judge) and including Judge Lumley Smith was also troubled by some of the tactics employers had evolved and the fecklessness of some workmen, but none the less recommended a major expansion of the scheme, enacted in 1906, without any notable extension of the courts' powers.[106]

The 1906 Act brought most trades within its compass and made workmen's compensation an important part of county court business. Cases heard by the judges rose from 1,046 in 1900 to 5,289 in 1913 and the total of actions started rose from 1,552 to 7,586.[107] But despite attempts to simplify key concepts in the legislation its interpretation continued to give rise to conflict and judges found themselves confronted with a 'library of litigation'.[108] They had to

[102] P. W. J. Bartrip, *Workmen's Compensation in Twentieth Century Britain* (Aldershot, 1987), pp. 1–17.
[103] *Ibid.*, pp. 22–7.
[104] *Ibid.*, p. 20, table 1; replies of the judges to circular of November 1900 and further comments of 1903, PRO PIN 12/1.
[105] PRO PIN 12/1.
[106] Bartrip, *Workmen's Compensation*, pp. 38–45; *PP* 1904 (743) LXXXVIII.
[107] Bartrip, *Workmen's Compensation*, pp. 58–74, esp. table 4.1.
[108] *Ibid.*, p. 59, quoting T. F. Lister.

be more thorough too, for whereas in general they faced few appeals, in workmen's compensation the insurers who stood behind employers and the trade unions who often backed workmen had the means and the will to appeal and had lawyers in court to ensure that points of law were duly discussed and noted. Appeals ran at 6 per cent in the early years and, though they fell back to 1.4 per cent in 1904, rose again to almost 3 per cent (150 cases) in 1913.[109]

Even legal commentators deplored the way the system piled up costs and decisions without bringing the certainty it had promised, but few blamed the county court judges for failing to get decisions right. Indeed it would have been hard to find better judges than some of those who had passed their judicial lives in the industrial districts, let alone Ruegg and Parsons, who wrote leading books on the subject.[110] In fact workmen's compensation cases probably helped to improve the quality of their judgments by bringing them into more regular contact with good class counsel, at the same time raising the reputation of those who demonstrated their competence.

Registrars also had a role in workmen's compensation, in appraising the adequacy of settlements brought before the court for approval, and in looking after the fund if it was lodged in court. For many of them this was the most satisfying part of their work and they took great pains with it.[111]

## *The renewed campaign for wider powers*

The year that brought the first Workmen's Compensation Act was the county courts' golden jubilee and they had something to celebrate, for business was booming. Introducing the first issue of the revamped *Civil Judicial Statistics*, Sir John MacDonnell had remarked that 'the drift of business is distinctly towards the county courts'[112] and one of his tables clearly shows it:

109 *Ibid.*, p. 70, table 4.3.

110 A. H. Ruegg, *The Law Regulating the Relations of Employers and Workmen in England* (London, 1905); A. Parsons and R. Allen, *The Workmen's Compensation Act 1906* (London, 1906). Parry wrote an interesting critical account in *The Gospel and the Law* (London, 1928), pp. 11–52.

111 Sir A. Wilson and H. Levy, *Workmen's Compensation* (Oxford, 1941), vol. I, pp. 115–16; *MacDonnell Evidence* and *Swift Evidence*, *passim*.

112 *PP* 1896 [C 8263] XCIV, p. 20 and table on p. 63.

*Proceedings commenced*

| Quinquennial period | % increase/decrease High court | % increase/decrease County court | % of total preceding quinquennial average High court | % of total preceding quinquennial average County court |
|---|---|---|---|---|
| 1862–6 | 13.76 | 2.71 | 12.4 | 82.9 |
| 1867–71 | −23.14 | 17.06 | 8.6 | 87.7 |
| 1872–6 | −16.10 | −3.75 | 7.6 | 88.9 |
| 1877–81 | 29.35 | 18.66 | 8.2 | 88.0 |
| 1882–6 | −10.04 | −6.49 | 7.8 | 88.2 |
| 1887–91 | −8.72 | 3.92 | 7.0 | 89.3 |
| 1892–6 | −1.33 | 6.80 | 6.5 | 90.1 |

As this table suggests, the trend was not unbroken but it was unmistakable, although with marked geographical variations which would repay closer investigation.[113] What struck observers most forcefully were the increases in the bigger actions, for while the amounts at stake in most suits remained trivial – the average claim actually dipped below the £3 mark[114] – the number above £50, negligible until the mid-1870s, had leapt from 32 to 420 between 1875 and 1878 and, after briefly falling back, grew again from 683 in 1883 to 1,129 in 1897. These were cases the court could only hear if both parties signified their consent, and it had been the universal verdict of judges and lawyers that they hardly ever would agree.[115] That piece of conventional wisdom seemed no longer to hold good, and with the dramatic rise in remitted actions as well, the amount of 'high court' business in the county courts was becoming rather impressive.

Almost all these cases came from the sphere of the Queen's Bench and MacDonnell's figures vividly demonstrate the decline in that division. A sudden fall from 127,000 to 83,000 actions commenced in the single year 1867–8 could be put down to the paralysis in the business world following the crash of Overend Gurney and to the strengthening of the costs sanction, but

113 *Ibid.* at p. 64 and cf. *PP* 1898 [C 8838] CIV at pp. 63 ff.

114 In 1889 it was £2 16s 10d as against £3 2s in 1885: *PP* 1890 [C 6104] LXXX.

115 Snagge, *Evolution of the County Court*, p. 20. The conventional wisdom was well expressed by the solicitor Ebenezer Tillyard: 'my experience is, that litigants do that which they think will most annoy the other, and the longest purse has the biggest advantage': *Select Committee, 1878*, q. 3620.

recovery was incomplete and a long slow fall set in down to as low as 68,000 in 1897. The cases actually tried fell in proportion: the average for 1891–5 was only 5,098 and for 1897–1901 just 3,623. Yet even this was more than the division could cope with: arrears were so heavy that the Law Society and Bar Council were calling for an extra judge and the rise in remitted cases was a clear admission that the Queen's Bench judges could not handle their business.[116]

This paradoxical situation had several causes. With actions now increasingly heard in London (trials at assizes fell from an average of 1,200 in 1886–90 to 819 in 1896–1900) it made less sense than ever to have some judges traipsing round sleepy market towns touting for business while their colleagues struggled to keep abreast of the London caseload. Perhaps even more important was the slowdown in the speed at which litigation was conducted, with the increasing resort to interlocutories and a marked lack of will on the bench and in chambers to drive things purposefully along; and as cases were drawn out longer so were bills of costs.[117]

Businessmen grew so exasperated that they resorted increasingly to arbitration, triggering off the only effective judicial initiative, the institution of the commercial list in 1894. Otherwise the judges proved incapable of concerted action and a demarcation dispute between the Lord Chancellor and the Lord Chief Justice was a further obstacle. At the root of the trouble however lay the assizes and no-one in authority was willing to tackle that question. Halsbury rejected repeated calls for a royal commission and seemed content to let things drift.[118]

Suitors voted with their feet and some drifted into the county courts. Calls for an extended jurisdiction grew in strength, though for some very much as a *pis aller*; even the *Law Times* gave up the QBD in disgust.[119] Campaigners did not cease to point out the defects of the county courts however, and made it clear that reforms should accompany any extension. The litany of familiar

116 Snagge, *Evolution of the County Court*, pp. 25–33.

117 Abel-Smith and Stevens, *Lawyers and the Courts*, pp. 85–90. There is some material in the *Gorell Report* (*PP* 1909 (71) LXXII) and the *Royal Commission Report on Delays in the KBD* (*PP* 1913 [Cd 6761] XXX), but this phenomenon deserves further investigation.

118 Abel-Smith and Stevens, *Lawyers and the Courts*, p. 90. Lord Esher had called for a royal commission in 1890: PRO LCO 2/47.

119 *LT* 102 (1896–7), 453.

criticisms was best expressed in the 'shopping lists' frequently presented by the Law Society and other groups of solicitors and their remedies were just as familiar and in some cases (like the insistent demand for greatly reduced fees) quite unrealistic.[120]

Certain defects were a direct consequence of the influx of bigger suits. Judges had to arrange their lists more carefully, and while some were praised for their consideration,[121] others were too selfish or incompetent to give satisfaction.[122] Judges who prided themselves on not inconveniencing litigants by adjourning their cases found it increasingly difficult when remitted cases were sprung on them; Emden was one among many who disliked these cuckoos in his nest, but was more outspoken than most about it, saying that 'the present procedure amounts to nothing less than a system for the robbery of poor people'.[123] Metropolitan judges naturally attracted most attention, and while the Wandsworth judge was attacked for rising too early, Bacon displeased lawyers by sitting unrelentingly through the day without a lunch break. Congestion in the London courts always got more than its fair share of attention but things were just as bad in some other places, in South Wales for example.[124]

The courtrooms themselves came in for increasing criticism. The Bar Council protested at the state of some[125] (a sign of their growing importance to the bar) and one was described in *The Law Times* where

> as things stand on a busy day, in the morning it is practically impossible to pass in or out of the court; to get a seat is out of the question; counsel and solicitors are huddled together on a small bench capable of holding about one tenth of those who want to sit thereon. No proper waiting rooms or lavatories exist, and the only safe place for a consultation is the open street.[126]

Elsewhere things were worse: the court at Oldham was said to have been the death of Judge Jones.[127]

There were minor scandals too. Some bailiffs proved

120 *CCC* 29 (1883), 113–14; *LT* 73 (1881–2), 162–3; *SJ* 35 (1890–1), 80; *SJ* 45 (1897–8), 320.

121 *LT* 86 (1888–9), 156–7.

122 *LJ* 37 (1902), 273 ('City Solicitor'); *SJ* 33 (1888–9), 639; *LT* 96 (1893–4), 235; 109 (1900), 193.

123 *LJ* 38 (1903), 42.

124 *LT* 98 (1894–5), 46; 114 (1902–3), 143.

125 *LT* 96 (1893–4), 235.

126 *LT* 108 (1899–1900), 360.

127 *LT* 109 (1900), 411–12.

corrupt,[128] registrars were accused of appointing their sons or nephews 'joint registrars' with them[129] and some judges defied the bar's etiquette by allowing their sons to practise before them.[130] There were judges who were deaf, and probably senile,[131] and one had to be quietly removed for financial misconduct.[132]

Like his high court appointments, Halsbury's choice of county court judges also drew some strong criticism.[133] Some were men of little repute: according to the *Law Journal*, of his first twenty-one, scarcely half a dozen 'ever enjoyed anything approaching to a large practice at the Bar'[134] and one or two, Ellicott in particular, were so obscure that they seemed an insult to the profession.[135] Yet Halsbury was adept at disarming criticism by following a doubtful appointment with an impeccable one, and won praise by choosing political opponents like Willis and Waddy. Still, there were undoubtedly too many indifferent judges and far too many veterans; T. H. Ingham, the last of the original judges, clung on until 1891 and Bayley was nearly ninety when he was induced to retire.

What is more some of the judges painted unflattering pictures of their own courts, and in particular were disgusted at the torrent of perjury they encountered and which they lacked the means to stem. Homersham Cox was abruptly transferred from a Welsh district for saying what was widely acknowledged about the lying propensities of Welsh witnesses,[136] while Bacon and French were

128 *LT* 98 (1894–5), 139–40; 106 (1898–9), 15, 39. There are several instances in the PRO T 10 series.

129 *LT* 98 (1894–5), 527. See also the complaint against one of Bedwell's registrars in PRO LCO 1/39.

130 E.g. *LT* 92 (1891–2), 300. In reply to a parliamentary question in 1893 the Attorney-General said 'it is a question of good taste': *Hansard* 1893–4, 4th s., vol. 8, col. 835.

131 See the criticism of Abdy and Bayley in *Law Gazette* 6 (1892–3), and *CCC* 29 (1884), 314 on *Green v. Gould*, where an eighty-year-old judge 'really could not be brought to give his attention to the matter'.

132 Judge P. M. Leonard. Muir McKenzie to Halsbury, 7 Apr. 1898, BL Add. Mss. 56, 370 f. 158.

133 R. F. V. Heuston, *Lives of the Lord Chancellors, 1885–1940*, (Oxford, 1964) pp. 40–66.

134 *LJ* 27 (1892), 491.

135 *Law Gazette* 4 (1892), 327. Presumably he was one of the 'specimens of the Chancellor's frolicsome fancy' referred to by E. Bowen Rowlands, County Court Judges and their Jurisdiction, *LQR* 18 (1902), 237–46.

136 *CCC* 29 (1883–4), 188, 292, 315. Judge Lloyd said much the same in 1886 but escaped censure; he was, of course, Welsh: *CCC* 30 (1886), 359.

openly cynical about their Jewish litigants – in one case French charged the jury: 'Gentlemen, if you can believe either the plaintiff or the defendant, or any of the witnesses for either . . . you will find accordingly'. Elsewhere in London, Judge Edge fumed that 'these aliens did not come into court as honest men, and [he] felt sure they had some sort of secret meeting where the general lines of defence were mapped out'.[137] Chalmers, describing Birmingham as worse than India for perjury, hardly improved the reputation of the county courts.[138] Despite all these defects however, the pressure grew for an extension of the county court's powers.

The campaign opened[139] with a bill presented by C. J. Monk for the northern chambers of commerce. It was quite ambitious, giving common law jurisdiction up to £1,000, with actions above £100 removable to the high court on the defendant showing good cause; on nineteen circuits 'special courts' were to be designated, with better paid judges and with full-time registrars holding their own courts to hear actions up to £20.[140] Four times Monk's bill was presented, always to be met by the objection that the county courts were already overcrowded and that the special courts scheme was impracticable,[141] but in 1899, when there seemed a danger of it making headway, the Attorney-General begged for time and let it be known that the government would consider 'the schemes of practical men'. Judge Selfe mistook this Parliamentary manoeuvre for a serious invitation and drafted a bill that met the prescription, but it was soon apparent that nothing would be done.[142]

Then in 1902 Sir Albert Rollit took up the standard. As a former county court registrar Rollit could not be so easily dismissed as 'impractical'. He persuaded the Law Society and the

137 *CCC* 34 (1894), 662–3; 38 (1901–2), 569; 39 (1903), 317.

138 *LQR* 11 (1895), 217–22; evidence to the Lords Select Committee on the Perjury Bill, *Hansard* 1893–4 4th s., vol. 9, col. 669.

139 The Association of British Chambers of Commerce had been pressing this issue for some years (A. R. Ilersic and P. F. B. Liddle, *The Parliament of Commerce* (London, 1960), pp. 86–90) and was now joined by *The Times*: *LT* 101 (1896), 482–3.

140 *PP* 1897 (42) I.

141 *HCJ* vols. 152, 153; *Hansard* 1899 4th s., vol. 67, cols. 834–55; 1900 4th s., vol. 81, col. 1174.

142 *Hansard* 1899 4th s., vol. 67, col. 846; PRO LCO 2/111.

chambers of commerce to throw their weight behind a compromise measure which would raise the common law jurisdiction to just £100, give registrars jurisdiction up to £5 and make various changes to procedure which had figured regularly in the bills of the past thirty years and were thought unlikely to be contentious; furthering the particular interests of his Hull constituents, he also proposed raising the admiralty jurisdiction to £1,000.[143]

When this County Courts Bill also got nowhere Rollit made an important concession: actions above £50 were to be heard only in courts named in an order in council (in effect allowing the Lord Chancellor to select those with the facilities and the arrangements in place to handle them). The Association of County Court Registrars (ACCR) thought this betrayed tactical naïvety,[144] but Rollit's was a shrewd decision for the Commons had lost patience with the government's stalling tactics and he had to restrain the bolder souls in committee from raising the bidding. At the report stage arguments about the lack of 'machinery' to implement the proposals were met with impatient scorn and the vote in its favour – 197 to 53 – was emphatic. Foolishly persisting in its opposition on the third reading, the government mustered just ten votes against 160, the announcement being greeted with derisive laughter.[145]

Rightly fearing that it would precipitate a clamour from the judges for a pay rise, the Treasury had urged Halsbury to defeat the Bill, but that was not practical politics, especially as the Lord Chancellor's Office (LCO) had found by enquiry that the argument that the county courts could not cope with the extra business was not sustainable.[146] With characteristic rudeness Halsbury denounced the 'marvellous ignorance' which had produced the Bill and with equally characteristic effrontery said it should have been left to such a bill of his own 'as has been in contempla-

143 *LJ* 36 (1901), 464; *PP* 1902 (26) I. Monk's bill (Bill 82) was reintroduced by Sir William Holland but made no progress: *HCJ* vol. 157.

144 *SJ* 47 (1902–3), 550–1.

145 *Report of Standing Committee*: *PP* 1903 (97) V; *Hansard* 1903 4th s., vol. 118, cols. 1016–26, 1460–71; vol. 124, cols. 665–84; *LT* 115 (1903), 216; *LJ* 38 (1903), 339, 376.

146 E. Hamilton to Halsbury, 9 Mar. 1903; Muir McKenzie to Treasury, 13 Mar. 1903; judges' memorandum, Apr. 1903; A. J. Elliot to Halsbury, 2 Jul. 1903, PRO LCO 2/153; *LT* 115 (1903), 275; judges' replies, PRO LCO 2/154, 155; Halsbury to Chancellor of the Exchequer, 11 May 1904, 2/157.

tion'.[147] He accepted the unwanted offering gracelessly, altering the order in council provision to specify 'any court, where His Majesty is satisfied that due provision has been made for carrying on the business of the court without interference with the ordinary jurisdiction of the court'.[148]

Unfortunately, having declared Rollit's Act unworkable the LCO took so long to produce the amending bill which they insisted was necessary that it was unable to pass except as an agreed measure.[149] The main difficulty was that the Treasury would not give all the judges a pay rise for the extra work, while most judges were furiously hostile to any scheme that confined the wider jurisdiction to a few of them and reintroduced salary differentials.[150] Since the bill which eventually emerged in 1904 empowered the Chancellor to pay £1,800 to up to twenty judges, in whose 'principal courts' (chosen by the Chancellor) the extended jurisdiction might alone be exercised, while also reducing the impact of the costs sanction contained in Rollit's Act, it had no chance of passing.[151]

Rollit was so angered by this transparent attempt to limit the scope of his Act that he brought out his own amending bill, overlapping with the government's in a number of uncontentious changes, but neither found a foothold in the next session's timetable, with the result that the LCO had to produce a scheme to implement Rollit's Act after all.[152] It was not based on any obvious principle and while the bigger actions were restricted to a very few towns on some circuits – to just one on circuit 19 for example – on others all or nearly all the courts could hear them.[153] Meanwhile the procedural reforms which were badly wanted were again lost.

147 *Hansard* 1903 4th s., vol. 126, cols. 826–8.

148 County Courts Act 1903 (c. 42) s. 5.

149 *PP* 1904 (291) I; *HLJ* vol. 136. Presented on 7 July, it did not pass the Lords until 1 August.

150 Some metropolitan judges later broke ranks: A. Woodfall to Loreburn, 6 Feb. 1906, PRO LCO 2/204.

151 Drafts of the Bill are in PRO LCO 2/156–8. On the financial aspect see Halsbury to Chancellor of the Exchequer, 11 May 1904, 2/157.

152 Selfe took it upon himself to negotiate with Rollit and Brynmor Jones in an attempt to save the bill: note to Muir McKenzie, 6 Aug. 1904, PRO LCO 2/158. See also *Hansard* 1904 4th s., vol. 139, cols. 550–79.

153 *PP* 1905 (150, 180) I; *LJ* (1905), 436–7; PRO LCO 2/159–60; *Radcliffe Report*, p. 2.

LIBERAL GOVERNMENTS

Lord Loreburn was unusual among Lord Chancellors in his genuine desire to promote the county courts, but he was also outspoken in his opposition to their continuing reliance on imprisonment for debtors.[154] Controversy over committals flared up at regular intervals and in the early 1890s had led to a Lords' select committee, the *Law Gazette* confidently predicting that 'its days are numbered'.[155] The committee however found little evidence of widespread dissatisfaction[156] and the 'relic of barbarism' not only lingered on but flourished; from a low of 4,064 in 1875, committals climbed to an all-time peak of 12,014 in 1906.[157]

Loreburn set up another committee, hoping that it would decisively recommend abolition, but with the credit traders well organised to fight their corner and organised labour indifferent,[158] humanitarian opinion alone was unlikely to prevail so long as most judges and registrars remained adamant that it was a necessary sanction. As the Pickersgill Committee's report[159] shows, the arguments had hardly changed in the forty years since the Walpole Report.[160]

It was, unfortunately, undeniable that other sanctions were ineffective, with execution against goods claimed to be less and less so as hire purchase spread its temptations. Much had been hoped of the 'poor man's bankruptcy' introduced by Chamberlain (assisted by Judge Motteram) in s. 122 of the Bankruptcy Act 1883, but to the bafflement of Nicol and other well-wishers it proved a complete failure.[161] From the outset administration

154 Circular to judges, 30 Nov. 1906, PRO LCO 2/211.

155 *Law Gazette* 6 (1893), 146.

156 *HLJ* vol. 125, 260; *HLSP* 1893–4 (156), esp. p. 6. The witnesses included six county court judges, a registrar and the recently retired Nicol, who disclosed his antipathy to committals at q. 61.

157 Rubin, Law, Poverty and Imprisonment, table B on p. 292. The quotation, from Mr Justice Joyce, was used as a chapter heading by J. A. Rentoul, judge of the City of London Court, in his book *Stray Thoughts and Memories* (London, 1921).

158 Rubin, Law, Poverty and Imprisonment, pp. 281–5.

159 *PP* 1909 (344) VII. The judges' replies to Loreburn's earlier letter, in PRO LCO 2/211–13, foreshadow the evidence they gave to the Pickersgill Committee; 2/213 contains an excellent summary of their differences.

160 *PP* 1873 (348) XV.

161 *HLSP* 1893–4 (156), q. 98 (Nicol). Judge Daniel had predicted its failure: *SJ* 28 (1883–4), 199–200, 278, 789.

orders under the section were almost unknown in most courts and after a few years a small committee of experts concluded that they would remain a rarity so long as creditors still had the power to seek a committal instead.[162] Some judges argued for the rule committee to encourage its use by rule changes but were met with well-grounded scepticism.[163]

The judges who wanted an end to committals were often strenuous in their public denunciations and a few, notably Parry, won a wider audience through their eloquence and passion.[164] In their own courts they used the prison as sparingly as possible; Emden, for instance, would not commit a defendant unless he had an income of more than 5s a week for each member of his family, while Amphlett found that he was able drastically to reduce committals in Birmingham without any seeming loss in the effectiveness of judgment orders.[165] Others were ruthlessly selective, Edge shocking the venerable draftsman Sir Henry Thring by openly admitting that he discriminated among creditors according to their deserts.[166]

Among the retentionist majority were men like Bedwell, who asserted that the county court was 'one of the most perfect systems ... that was ever built up'[167] and claimed a quasi-scientific basis for his practices. Others carefully adapted theirs to the characteristics of each district; thus Cadman found that leniency was misplaced in Dewsbury, where 1,160 out of 1,242 men against whom warrants were issued paid up immediately, and promptly adjusted his thinking.[168]

These deliberate strategies contributed to remarkable discrepancies between districts which the commentary on the judicial statistics pointedly underlined. In 1913 just five districts out of fifty-four accounted for more than one-third of all committals,

162 *PP* 1887 [C 5139] XXVII. The Committee comprised Chalmers, Muir McKenzie, Nicol and T. H. Farrer of the Board of Trade. For variations between circuits see *PP* 1884–5 (290) LXIV.

163 Paper by judges Smyly, Selfe, Harington and Martineau, PRO LCO 2/114.

164 Parry's attacks were published in various places at various times; see e.g. The Insolvent Poor, *Fortnightly Review*, os 69 (1898), 797–804 and *The Gospel and the Law* (1928). Snagge was another fierce critic: *SJ* 56 (1911–12), 2.

165 *SJ* 54 (1910–11), 300; 57 (1912–13), 182. Amphlett called it 'thoroughly loathsome work': *LJ* 46 (1911), 11. For other strategies see Rubin, Law, Poverty and Imprisonment.

166 *HLSP* 1893–4 (156) II at qq. 1435–6.

167 *Ibid.*, at q. 1018.

168 *CCC* 36 (1897), 35.

while a few years earlier circuit 18 (Nottingham and surrounds), long notorious among abolitionists, gaoled more than all the metropolitan courts together.[169] It is unlikely that much greater consistency would have resulted even if the judges had met together more frequently and in greater numbers than they did,[170] for not all of them agreed that consistency was important. Retentionists felt that they were performing a valuable function in sustaining a supply of cheap credit to a class for whom it was indispensable and that it was essential and just to coerce men who had, or had had, the means to pay even if the money was actually found by their family and friends; in other words they operated what Chalmers dubbed 'the screw theory'.[171] But even such judges felt distaste when they became the instruments not of tradesmen but of parasitic tallymen, rapacious moneylenders and remorseless assignees of debts. Many were attracted to the notion that prison should be reserved for cases of 'involuntary credit' or confined to 'necessaries' – the class of goods for which a wife had the common law right to pledge her husband's credit.[172]

This was the recommendation of the Pickersgill Committee, carried by the slenderest majority against the abolitionist draft of the chairman,[173] but though it found some favour at the Home Office, the Board of Trade was disparaging[174] and, faced with a hopeless lack of consensus, Loreburn knew that there was no chance of doing anything. Moreover, perhaps sensing the trend of public opinion, the judges began to use the prison more sparingly; committals plunged to 5,820 in 1913, which helped blunt the force of the abolitionist case.[175]

Loreburn's decision was a realistic one, for when he and his successor Lord Haldane did try to legislate for the county courts they experienced only frustration. Appearing before the MacDonnell Commission in 1915, Muir McKenzie ascribed the melancholy situation that the bills 'continued to be slaughtered year

169 Rubin, Law, Poverty and Imprisonment, pp. 261–5; *CCC* 41 (1907), 80–1.

170 As the Lords select committee had urged: *HLSP* 1893–4 (156) II, p. 14.

171 Rubin, Law, Poverty and Imprisonment, pp. 249–52.

172 G. R. Rubin, The County Courts and the Tally Trade, 1846–1914, in Sugarman and Rubin, *Law, Economy and Society*, pp. 321–48; *PP* 1908 (344) VII: report, p. ix.

173 *Ibid.*; Judge Graham's memo, PRO LCO 2/213.

174 PRO BT 37/22.

175 *Civil Judicial Statistics*, *PP* 1914–16 [Cd 7807] LXXXII.

after year down to the present time'[176] to the fact that, lacking its own minister in the Commons, the LCO had to entrust its bills to the law officers who preferred to see that their own bills advanced; he might have added that the *ex officio* head of the bar was not the best person to act as midwife to a county courts bill.

There was some truth in this explanation but other factors were at least as important. The Liberal programme was exceptionally heavy and little time was left over for legal matters. Law reform was gradually slipping towards the margins of the political stage, and with pressing reforms to the law of property, bankruptcy and the codification of branches of the criminal law in train it became almost impossible to get any other law bill onto the floor of the Commons unless it could be guaranteed non-contentious. The bar's self-interested suspicion of any measure to improve the county courts' efficiency, let alone widen their powers, ruled out any such assurance.

The period of the Liberal administrations falls into three parts. In the first Loreburn set up inquiries, the Pickersgill Committee and the Gorell Committee, the latter to examine the interface between high court and county court jurisdiction. Meanwhile he brought forward a modest bill incorporating a few of the reforms that had featured in Rollit's and Halsbury's bills, but even this ran out of time.[177]

The second phase began with the publication of the Gorell Report in March 1909 and ended with the presentation of a bill embodying some of its recommendations in 1911. The Report was a disappointment to those who had hoped that from this 'strong and influential' body 'a great and memorable change in our legal system may arise'.[178] The Report deflated such hopes immediately by emphasising that 'we have endeavoured to recommend that which may reasonably be expected to be capable of being carried out when we have to start with an existing order of affairs rather than to attempt to suggest alterations based on theories of perfection beyond the reasonable possibility of attainment'. Its conclu-

176 *MacDonnell Evidence*, qq. 44, 234–5.

177 PRO LCO 2/205–6. The Bar Council, however, opposed even such a bill because, *inter alia*, it widened registrars' powers (report of 9 May 1907 in PRO LCO 2/205). *Hansard* 1907 4th s., vol. 171, cols. 175–9; vol. 175, col. 1239, and (in 1908) vol. 184, col. 445; vol. 186, col. 1178; vol. 187, cols. 636, 1293–4.

178 *LJ* 47 (1908), 669.

sion was that 'notwithstanding the defects in our system which undoubtedly exist ... the fact remains that the administration of justice in civil cases as well as in criminal is more satisfactory than in any other country in the world'.[179]

Permeating the Report is the conviction that the only real form of justice is high court justice and that people should not be encouraged to seek redress outside the high court except where it is plainly impracticable to make the high court available to them. The preferred solution to the unsatisfactory condition of the civil justice system therefore is a reform of the high court and especially the assizes, and on that premise proposals to make the county courts a branch of the high court, or even to extend their jurisdiction, are inappropriate.[180] However, faced with undeniable popular demand, the Committee was reluctantly prepared to concede that in all King's Bench actions it should be open to the plaintiff to issue his plaint in the county court, the defendant being entitled to remove it to the high court simply by entering an appearance there. These bigger actions should be tried only at special centres and sittings where it would probably be desirable to give the bar exclusive audience.[181] The strangest recommendation was that even this experiment should be deferred until the changes recommended for the King's Bench Division (KBD) had been put into effect. As was drily observed, it was curious to force litigants into a defective forum for now, offering them a choice only when the defects had been cured and it was no longer necessary;[182] the reason of course was that a haemorrhage of business from the KBD might imperil the all-important vitality of the bar.

In remarkable contrast to its conservatism in the arrangements for common law business however, the Committee, much impressed with the 'practical denial of justice' created by the existing arrangements for divorce hearings, boldly advocated transferring divorce for the relatively poor to the county courts, again with exclusive audience for the bar.[183] It was not the first time this had been suggested, for besides Isaac Butt's amendment to the 1857

[179] *Gorell Report*, 1, 35. Evidence was not printed and is not in the only LCO file on the subject (2/214).

[180] *Ibid.*, 15–21.

[181] *Ibid.*, 17. The bar's representative on the Committee, H. D. Bonsey, refused to sign it. He became a county court judge in 1911.

[182] *SJ* 53 (1908–9), 442–3.

[183] *Gorell Report*, pp. 23–6.

Divorce Bill, there had been a bill in 1884.[184] Still, it was a radical proposal to come from an official committee and predictably met a gale of protest. Gorell was asked to investigate further with a full-scale royal commission. This reported in 1912 in favour of allowing selected county court judges sitting as commissioners of assize rather than the county courts themselves to deal with the poorer petitioners. Both this and Gorell's proposed reforms in the grounds for divorce threatened to be a major vote loser for any party that took them up so they were left severely alone; it was to be thirty years and more before the Denning Committee resurrected the idea of the county court judges doing divorce in disguise and many years more before they came to do it in their own robes.[185]

Meanwhile Loreburn had gone ahead with a County Courts Bill combining much of the LCO's long-standing draft with some of the recommendations of the Gorell Committee. He boldly fronted it with a clause conferring unlimited common law jurisdiction, emphasising in his introductory speech its venerable and distinguished antecedents. Gorell gave him able support but the Liberals were weak in the Lords and Loreburn did not endear himself to the opposition by declaring that 'my profession has nearly always opposed reforms in the law'. Halsbury mustered thirty-seven votes to Loreburn's thirty-two on the first clause and rather than let the Bill go forward without its central plank the Chancellor withdrew it.[186]

Loreburn tried again in 1911, presumably hoping that in the highly charged atmosphere of constitutional crisis the Tory peers would be less uncompromising, but though it came in under the long shadow of the Parliament Bill Halsbury was not the least deterred. He made unscrupulous use of evidence presented by the divorce bar to the Gorell Commission in support of its opposition to county court divorce, studiously ignoring what Gorell himself pointed out, that many of the instances purporting to show that

184 *PP* 1884–5 (77) I; *SJ* 29 (1884–5), 450.

185 *PP* 1912–13 [Cd 6478], XVIII, paras. 52–7; *Hansard* 1909 5th s., vol. 2 (HL), cols. 473–507. There is useful material on the Commission in J. E. G. de Montmorency, *John Gorell Barnes, 1st Lord Gorell* (London, 1920).

186 *Hansard* 1909 5th s., vol. 2 (HL), cols. 239–50, 729–50 (the quotation is at col. 744). Muir McKenzie to the President of the Law Society, 28 July 1909, PRO LCO 2/207.

the county courts were overloaded had been discredited.[187] In essence the whole argument was not about litigants at all but about the privileges of the bar, which eminent judges queued up to defend; among them was Robson, until recently the government's Attorney-General.[188]

Halsbury's delaying tactics reduced Loreburn, already dismayed and worn out by having to coerce his fellow peers over the Parliament Bill, to uncharacteristic irritability,[189] and though the Bill finally struggled through the Lords, it was by then August and too late for it to pass the Commons.

Loreburn resigned in June 1912 and Haldane had other priorities.[190] In this third phase the whips could not be induced to give the Bill time. The Attorney-General claimed that he had done his best, extending to an unauthorised offer to pass the uncontroversial clauses if the Conservatives would give them a clear passage, but he was probably not sorry that they did not respond and no one pressed them. After that, the Bill disappeared into limbo.[191]

For seventeen years the reform and expansion of the county courts had been regularly before Parliament, yet the only outcome was Rollit's Act. Changes generally agreed to be desirable were left undone because some wanted to extend the courts' role while others were adamant that they should not be expanded. Litigants suffered while lawyers took up entrenched positions, with the Law Society now firmly in favour of expansion, the Bar Council resolutely against it. And as in the great struggle to come, it was the defenders who had the easier task.

## *Envoi*

As the County Courts Bill struggled through the House of Lords in the dog days of 1911 even that most starchy of county court

187 *Hansard* 1911 5th s., vol. 7 (HL), cols. 1049–62; vol. 8, cols. 835–9; vol. 9, cols. 394–439, 544, 647–74.

188 *Hansard* 1911 5th s., vol. 9 (HL), cols. 396–439, 544, 647–70. Robson spoke for three-quarters of an hour on the report stage, which looks like a delaying tactic. The other leading opponent in the debate was Lord Alverstone, the Lord Chief Justice, with Lord Mersey also weighing in.

189 *Ibid.*, cols. 404–5, 544.

190 Heuston, *Lord Chancellors, 1885–1940*, pp. 165–7.

191 Hansard 1912 5th s., vol. 42 (HC), cols. 2566, 2583; vol. 46, col. 1681; 1913 5th s., vol. 53 (HC), cols. 55–7; Selfe's memo, June 1912, PRO LCO 2/285.

judges Sir George Sherston Baker held the court at Gainsborough under the shade of a plane tree.[192] This idyllic image of 'the long, hot summer' is at odds with the prosaic reality however, for Baker and many of his colleagues were disgruntled at the continuing rejection of their claims for better pay and a pension scheme. Some claimed to be overworked, though only a few metropolitan judges really were,[193] for the overall number of sitting days remained constant while business was falling from a peak of 1,308,849 plaints in 1910 to 1,179,132 in 1913; the larger actions declined in proportion and only workmen's compensation cases continued to rise.[194]

The discontents of the judges, however, were mild compared with those of the clerks and bailiffs. It was the lack of job security and pensions that vexed them and provoked them into forming associations to press for civil service status. In practice they were seldom dismissed when they became old or infirm, but they were seldom pensioned either. Instead their registrar usually kept them on the payroll, but this was compassion at the expense of efficiency and scarcely defensible in a public service.[195] No wonder some of them had remarkable records of long service: William Molesworth for instance had joined Birmingham county court as a boy of fourteen and in August 1914 was completing his sixtieth year of service; at least five others could claim over fifty years.[196] Although they made little impact at first the staff were becoming more militant and in 1914 two associations amalgamated and began a lobbying campaign which was intended to culminate in an ambush of the Estimates to publicise their grievances.[197] The County Court Judges Society was also planning a novel activity: with unfortunate timing they were to hold their first seaside conference at Great Yarmouth in September 1914.[198]

192 *CCC* 43 (1911–12), 210.

193 *LJ* 47 (1912), 744, 753. Giving evidence to the Royal Commission on Delays in the King's Bench, Loreburn said 'the statement that seemed to be generally accepted that these judges were already overworked did not appear to him to have any foundation in fact': *PP* 1914 [Cd 7178] XXXVII, q. 4308.

194 *Civil Judicial Statistics*, *PP* 1914–16 [Cd 7807] LXXXII, pp. 15–17, 26.

195 See p. 295 below.

196 *County Courts Gazette* 2 (1914), 29; *ibid.* 1 (1912–13), 205.

197 *Ibid.* 1 (1912–13), 185; 2 (1914), 33.

198 *CCC* 44 (1914), 370.

# 4

# WAR TO WAR

## THE GREAT WAR

Britain had not experienced war on such a scale and so close to home since Napoleon was on the rampage across Europe, and the immediate dislocation of international trade and finance found the government hopelessly underprepared. All was improvisation and expedients: the courts were kept closed for a few days while the first expedient, a moratorium on the enforcement of commercial debts above £5, was arranged and when they reopened the judges were without usable guidance in how to interpret it; in the county courts each made up his own directions and Selfe's attempt to bring consistency only made for more confusion.[1] Rules were promised but before they materialised the moratorium was largely superseded by the more wide-ranging Courts (Emergency Powers) Act and a torrent of rules flowed from that.[2]

Under this Act and its successors judges were 'endowed with a new and vast responsibility affecting the whole range of social and economic conditions throughout the country',[3] acquiring a broad discretion over the enforcement of all judgments where the debt or debts were caused by the war. The measure was not given the widest publicity however, and there were those who believed, or affected to believe, that the moratorium was a comprehensive and continuing absolution from liabilities.[4] Nevertheless applications

[1] *CCC* 44 (1914), 480–3, 504–6; *County Courts Gazette* 2 (1914), 34–45; *LJ* 45 (1914), 501, 511, 528. In a rare example of judicial comity, county court judges agreed to follow Judge Tindal Atkinson's interpretation of the moratorium in *Jupp v. Whittaker* (Romford CC).

[2] *CCC* 44 (1914), 523–9.

[3] *LJ* 49 (1914), 531.

[4] D. Englander, *Landlord and Tenant in Urban Britain, 1838–1918* (Oxford, 1983), pp. 196–7, 201–2.

flooded in at first – 270,121 orders were made in 1915[5] – and while the high court judges, accustomed to ordering payment in full without delay, found their new powers disturbing, they were nothing unfamiliar to county courts.[6] But all judges found that the quality of the legislation left much to be desired – 'slipshod and vague to a remarkable degree' commented one[7] – and since the Acts were not properly dovetailed into other legislation, the process of making rules was fraught and tiresome; after one endless round of efforts to reconcile contradictory provisions the Lord Chancellor wrote in exasperation, 'my advice is to burn all the rules and the people who drew them'.[8]

As the war became seemingly interminable and all-embracing the Emergency Powers Acts had to be revised and extended, but on the whole they served their purpose quite well.[9] In any case, credit became tighter and creditors, whether from humanity or realism, were less zealous in pursuing their debts through the courts, though some were still prepared to make full use of 'blue frighteners' and similarly dubious means of extra-legal recovery and an Islington grocer still found himself sued for 6d. In 1918 only 97,000 orders were made under the Acts.[10]

In one vital area, however, the emergency legislation proved seriously defective. Although landlords and tenants initially found some advantages in a statute which gave the tenant time to pay his arrears and the landlord some assurance that they would be paid, nothing in it prevented rents being raised to a level which the tenant could not meet.[11] Some landlords were out and out profiteers but others too were driven to raise rents by the pressure of tax increases, inflation and mortgagees seeking to match the returns they could get from war bonds.[12] The inevitable result was mass

5 *Civil Judicial Statistics*: *PP* 1920 [Cmd 831], L.

6 According to Judge Graham, almost all of the orders postponing repayments could have been made under County Courts Act 1888 s. 153 but for the very restrictive decision in *Attenborough v. Henschel* (1895) 1 QB 833: *LJ* 49 (1914), 563.

7 *Ibid.* The editor (at 558) agreed.

8 Buckmaster to Schuster, 24 Jan. 1916, PRO LCO 2/357. Rules under the Acts were made by the Lord Chancellor alone, but Selfe and the Birmingham registrar A. L. Lowe were always consulted.

9 There is a good summary in *CCC* 46 (1917–18), 127 ff.

10 *CCC* 45 (1915–16), 75; *LJCCR* 6 (1917), 46; *PP* 1920 [Cmd 831], L.

11 Englander, *Landlord and Tenant*, p. 204.

12 *Ibid.*, pp. 207–8, 213–14, 220–1; D. Rider, *Ten Years' Adventures among Landlords and Tenants* (London, 1927), pp. 54–60.

evictions, and the discontent those aroused, culminating in well-publicised rent strikes and public disorders on Clydeside, contributed to the imposition of the portentous Rent and Mortgage Interest Restriction Act 1915.[13]

By freezing rents as well as denying repossession except in a few particular circumstances,[14] the Rent Act interfered drastically with the tenancy agreement. Many property owners and probably most lawyers, imbued with the sanctity of that bargain, found it deeply shocking and judges were initially disposed to construe it restrictively, though they had been perfectly willing to use the Emergency Powers Act to postpone repossessions.[15]

A few judges remained of this mind, but most became reluctantly converted to the necessity for severe curbs on landlords' rights. Even a hostile critic acknowledges that 'the administration of justice in the county courts gradually improved and was certainly far superior to proceedings in the lower [magistrates'] courts',[16] and that judges were usually very ready to do justice according to the spirit as well as the letter of the Act. They were sometimes duped by cunning landlords and their agents and no doubt by crafty and manipulative tenants too.[17] They all too often lacked the time and the means to make adequate investigations and at least one, the always impulsive Mulligan, was unbalanced by the hysterical anti-German spirit which got abroad; he was roundly taken to task for behaving disgracefully towards a long-settled naturalised alien, but seems an isolated case.[18] Certainly the county court judges had no truck with landlords trying to keep the proceeds of illegal rent increases until the Court of Appeal, in *Sharp Brothers and Knight v. Chant*, forced their hand.[19]

Even the influx of Rent Act cases did not go far towards

13 Englander, *Landlord and Tenant*, pp. 205–33.

14 Chiefly, that premises were 'reasonably required' for occupation by the landlord or an employee. Given a very broad interpretation by the Court of Appeal in *Sharp v. Wakefield*, it offered great scope for evasion: Rider, *Landlords and Tenants*, pp. 80 ff.

15 *Ibid.*, pp. 83, 87–8. For the vigilance of judges under the earlier Act see pp. 47–9 (Smyly) and Englander, *Landlord and Tenant*, p. 203 (Mellor).

16 Englander, *Landlord and Tenant*, p. 255, and see the report quoted at p. 260.

17 Rider, *Landlords and Tenants*, pp. 89, 99–100, 117–18, 127, 132–3.

18 *R v. Judge Mulligan* (QBDC); *LJ* 50 (1915), 305; *SJ* 59 (1914–15), 558.

19 [1917] 1 KB 771. The case began before Judge Amphlett. On its impact see Englander, *Landlord and Tenant*, pp. 257–9 and Rider, *Landlords and Tenants*, p. 104.

offsetting a steep decline in the staple debt business, and this had grave consequences for registrars and their staffs. From nearly 1.2 million in 1913 plaints for small claims collapsed to just 300,000 in 1918; in 1913 nearly 400,000 judgments had been entered for plaintiffs, plus almost 400,000 by consent or admission and 300,000 by default; corresponding figures for 1918 were 98,000, 63,000 and 17,500. With judgment summonses plummeting from 240,000 to 56,000 it is no wonder one northern registrar said his court was 'moribund'.[20]

Registrars with emoluments geared to plaints were in some cases reduced to desperate straits, yet few would lay off loyal staff. Since many of the younger men had succumbed to the blandishments of recruiting propaganda, registrars were anxious to keep those of military age who possessed an 'indispensability certificate' protecting them from conscription, and could not turn away the more elderly and less useful without causing them real hardship.

When rising inflation forced the Treasury to grant 'war bonuses' to civil servants the anomalous situation of county court staff was further highlighted. Tortuous negotiations brought concessions replete with fine distinctions which, however justifiable by Treasury dogma and practice, caused more resentment.[21] A threatened clerks' strike in 1917 was only headed off by an emollient Lord Chancellor and some further concessions, too tardy and grudging to restore goodwill.[22] Registrars could not descend to similar threats but those who resigned were proving difficult to replace and the prospect of bankruptcies was very real. The judges were wholly in sympathy and Parry put himself at the head of a staff deputation to Stanley Baldwin and Bridgeman; the superintendent's unsympathetic stance only added to the odium in which he was held.[23] Whoever was doing well out of the war, it was not the staff of the county courts.

20 *PP* 1920 [Cmd 831] L; *LJCCR* 5 (1916), 81.
21 Summarised in the *Swift Report*, pp. 30–3.
22 *County Courts Gazette* 3 (1916–17), 47–9, 73, 111–12; *LJ* 52 (1917), 370–5; 53 (1918), 112–13; *LJCCR* 6 (1917–18), 30.
23 *LJCCR* 6 (1917–18), 81, 89.

## RECONSTRUCTION: COURTS FIT FOR HEROES

For the LCO, however, the crisis in county court finances was something which could be exploited, for the gap between fee income and expenditure could not be allowed to stay at half a million a year and any proposal to raise fees was bound to reopen other issues. For once the Treasury was vulnerable and in its new Permanent Secretary Claud Schuster, who succeeded Muir McKenzie in 1915, the LCO had just the man to seize the opportunity.[24] Energetic, combative and keenly intelligent, Schuster was the ideal man to transform the 'interesting little museum'[25] which had so bemused Haldane into a small department of state. During his thirty-year term he was seen by some as the epitome of the over-mighty civil servant, and he certainly exerted a powerful influence over the nine Chancellors he served.[26]

One of the first targets of that influence was Haldane's cherished project for a Ministry of Justice, essentially a remodelled Home Office, with full responsibility for the administration of the courts. Whatever chance of success Haldane's blueprint may have had, Schuster and Lord Chancellor Birkenhead between them ensured that it was pigeonholed.[27] It was part of their argument that the LCO could itself become both an effective agency for law reform and an efficient organiser of the judicial system[28] and in relation to the county courts that meant ending the existing division of responsibility which the Machinery of Government Committee had severely criticised.[29] The Swift Committee echoed this condemnation and, though there were those in the Treasury who felt the Lord Chancellor unsuitable to head an administrative department, the *status quo* was indefensible and they knew it.[30]

24 *DNB* 1951–60, pp. 867–9 (A. Napier) and *The Times*, 29 July 1956. By 1915, 'he had twelve years' experience of constructive administration and ... the machinery of government at his fingertips' (*DNB*).

25 R. M. Jackson, *The Machinery of Justice in England* (Cambridge, 1940), quoted in G. Drewry, Lord Haldane's Ministry of Justice – Stillborn or Strangled at Birth?, *Public Administration*, 61 (1983), 396–414 at 399.

26 R. Jackson, *The Chief* (London, 1957), pp. 258–70; R. Stevens, *The Independence of the Judiciary* (Oxford, 1993), pp. 33–9.

27 Drewry, Haldane's Ministry of Justice. The report is *PP* 1918 [Cd 9230], XII.

28 An achievement Schuster claimed when the Ministry of Justice project threatened to resurface in 1943: memo of 31 Jan. 1943, PRO LCO 2/3630.

29 *PP* 1918 [Cd 9230], XII, at p. 16.

30 Drewry, Haldane's Ministry of Justice, 406.

One obstacle remained – the immovable and impossible superintendent Bridgeman – and when he was finally persuaded to retire his branch was moved wholesale to the LCO in the House of Lords. The head was now responsible to the Lord Chancellor,[31] whose Permanent Secretary became the Accounting Officer for the County Court Vote, though Schuster devolved responsibility for county court business to the Assistant Secretary, Albert Napier.[32] Henceforth, 'relations between the Treasury and the [LCO] became ... similar to those between the Treasury and any other department of the Government'.[33]

In private Schuster was scathing about the blighting effect of the dead hand of the Treasury which 'conducted the whole organisation of the Courts with a complete ignorance of the work performed by the Courts and a complete absence of any policy except that of wilful blindness'. Within a year of the transfer he was claiming 'a great improvement in administrative efficiency and economy'; forms had been standardised and reduced in number and the accounting system was under revision, 'no examination in this matter having been made since the Courts were established'.[34]

There was chronic discontent among staff at all levels in the county courts but the judges were the easiest to deal with and were tackled first. While the LCO was generally sympathetic to their long-standing grievance over salaries, it was plainly hopeless to press their case while many of them had a reduced caseload and all had the war bonus. However, some things could be done to bolster their morale without expense. With the war over, they could dress up in their new purple robes[35] and by royal warrant might continue to use the style 'his honour'[36] after retirement. For the first time knighthoods were given for their judicial service, so the bench could now be seen as a pathway to honours.[37]

At last it could also be seen as a route, albeit an unusual one, to

[31] See ch. 6 below.

[32] A younger son of the Field Marshal, Napier came from the bar to the LCO in 1915 and took on the county courts in 1920. Succeeding Schuster in 1944, he retired in 1954 aged seventy-two.

[33] Memo of 31 Jan. 1943, PRO LCO 2/3630.

[34] Schuster's memo, 28 Jan. 1924, PRO LCO 2/938.

[35] See p. 256 below.

[36] *LJCCR* 8 (1919), 89. J. B. Edge was the moving spirit: PRO LCO 12/128.

[37] See p. 256 below.

the high court, for in 1919 Edward Acton was promoted to be a judge in the KBD. Schuster explained that there had been other worthy candidates but they had been too old when the vacancy occurred.[38] Acton was promoted after less than three years and, although it would be twenty-five years before another Cinderella went to the ball, his example kept hopes alive for some time.

Even so, something more tangible had to be done and if a pay rise could not be managed a pension scheme might. The existing power was seriously deficient, for since only an incapacitated judge who wanted to retire could benefit, it failed to remove the veterans who outstayed their powers. Though Muir McKenzie defended the arrangements as 'a most extraordinarily good bargain',[39] they could hardly survive the criticism they suffered when Judge Napier, resigning through ill-health after sitting just one day, received the two-thirds of his salary which convention had established as standard.[40] With a royal commission pressing for compulsory retirement of even high court judges at seventy-two, change was inevitable.[41]

For several years new county court judges had been required to give a morally binding undertaking to retire at seventy,[42] but the statutory scheme introduced in 1919 fixed the retirement age at seventy-two, giving the Lord Chancellor the power to extend a judge's service by up to three years if he felt it 'in the public interest'.[43] Most of the existing judges opted to join the pension scheme, based on a sliding scale depending upon length of service with the maximum reached after fifteen years. Three did stay on to an advanced age – Farrant (seventy-seven), Tobin (eighty), Cluer (eighty-two) – but there were no complaints about their faculties and Farrant, in particular, was valued for his services as a chairman of quarter sessions.[44]

Dealing with the judges was easy in comparison with satisfying registrars who spoke of resignation and clerks who threatened strikes. If Bridgeman had not been so wedded to the old way of

38 Schuster to Lord Stamfordham, 17 June 1920, PRO LCO 2/2539.

39 Public Accounts Committee, *PP* 1914 (249) X, q. 1278.

40 *Ibid.*, qq. 1011 ff., 1252–82; *PP* 1914–16 (125, 270) IV, qq. 714 ff.

41 *PP* 1914 [Cd 6761] XXX.

42 PRO LCO 2/436, 606. It is characteristic of LCO record-keeping before Schuster that one judge's undertaking had been lost.

43 County Court Judges (Retirement and Pensions) Act 1919 ss. 1–2.

44 PRO LCO 2/606, 12/39. Nineteen seem not to have joined the scheme.

doing things the government could have driven a hard bargain during the war, instead of which the Treasury put off the day of reckoning with hefty deficiency payments to compensate registrars for the loss of fee income. In aggregate the payments were not ungenerous but 'unfortunately owing to the manner in which the deficiency bonus was distributed and the capricious limits set by the Treasury upon those who were to receive it, the Registrars, though in fact they received payment as a class of a very large sum of public money to which they were not entitled, were left with a wholly justified sense of grievance, and thus the worst was made of all possible worlds'.[45]

Time was of the essence, not only because of the immediate threat of strikes and bankruptcies but because a revival in litigation would raise registrars' incomes and strengthen their bargaining position. Apart from the handful who were wholly salaried, the registrars all depended at least in part on fees, and it is ironical that the county courts, a characteristic product of Victorian reform, should have been almost unique among public offices in carrying into the twentieth century one of the most deplored features of Old Corruption – the vested interest of public officials in what was charged to the users. The irony had not amused the MacDonnell Commission nor, despite Bridgeman's assertion that it was an incentive to diligence, had they found it acceptable. Lowe pointed out that besides clerks in smaller courts 'touting for business', he was placed in an invidious position when, as under the Emergency Powers Act, he had discretion to remit payment of a fee.[46]

It was entirely predictable that the Swift Committee would recommend radical changes.[47] Ideally the registrar should be a full-time salaried civil servant, appointed by the Lord Chancellor and retiring at a fixed age on a pension.[48] The part-time registrar was undesirable, for although forbidden from practising in his

[45] Memo. of 28 Jan. 1924, PRO LCO 2/938. They were particularly annoyed by a 'disingenuous letter' from Baldwin defending the refusal of the bonus to registrars appointed soon after the war began: F. W. Brown's evidence to the Swift Committee: BL BS 24/30, pp. 83–4. See also *Hansard* 1919 5th s., vol. 118 (HC), cols. 40–1.

[46] *MacDonnell Evidence*, qq. 53,460–2.

[47] Besides Mr Justice Rigby Swift it comprised Schuster, Bridgeman, Judge W. H. Roberts, A. Copson Peake of the Home Office and A. L. Lowe.

[48] *Swift Report*, pp. 6–10.

own court, his dual capacity sometimes led to suspicions of bias which were hard to dispel.[49]

The ideal, however, was an extravagance. If men of the right sort were to be recruited (men qualified seven years rather than five, and given the power to hear rather bigger defended actions as proposed) the salary had to be attractive, and the £800 to £1,200 which was proposed would far exceed the fee yield from the smaller courts. Much could be done by grouping neighbouring courts under a single registrar but some part-timers would still be necessary and they should be given a salary based on the plaint figure for 1913; like full-timers they would retire at seventy, but they would not be pensionable.

The remaining high bailiffs, those whose office had not been absorbed, overplayed their hand badly before the Committee and not only failed to secure a recommendation for more favourable treatment than the Treasury had offered but instead convinced it that they should have no successors.[50]

The situation of clerks and under bailiffs was defensible only on grounds of economy. Because the registrar was personally responsible for seeing that the immense number of tiny payments collected by his employees did not go astray, 'the Superintendent took the view that it was immaterial to the Treasury whether the funds reached their proper destination'.[51] Audit could therefore be limited to a very economical and superficial examination and 'the result was an orgy of defalcation',[52] albeit mostly on a trivial scale. Paid whatever wage the registrar chose, the men were unpensioned and lacked the formal job security which their association made its primary goal; yet in practice dismissals were rare and men were often kept on far too long out of compassion, filling the courts with old men 'who cannot or will not retire as long as they can walk or be carried to the court'.[53] True, as Bridgeman argued, establishing them as civil servants would

49 See e.g. PRO LCO 2/610: complaint against W. H. Hazard arising from *Hazard v. Smith* (Harleston CC, 1922).

50 *Swift Evidence*, evidence of V. H. Thomas, W. Young Hucks; *Swift Report*, pp. 12–13; Schuster's memo, May 1924, PRO LCO 2/711.

51 Schuster's memo, May 1924, PRO LCO 2/711.

52 *Ibid.*

53 *Swift Report*, p. 15. According to the figures in app. VI of the *Swift Evidence*, 299 out of 1,690 clerks and bailiffs were over sixty. For cases of hardship among them see Keane's evidence and app. VII.

introduce the whole paraphernalia of industrial relations and raise costs, but there was really no alternative.[54]

Bridgeman 'had done everything in his power to obstruct the deliberations of the [Swift] Committee'[55] but he surpassed himself by producing at the very last minute a 'memorandum' for publication which was tantamount to a minority report, traversing most of the Committee's conclusions and defending the *status quo*. The chairman was furious and added a stinging rejoinder pointing out that Bridgeman had helped to draft the Report, which was quite explicitly a compromise.[56] This episode completed Bridgeman's isolation even within the Treasury, but he delayed the implementation of the Report and had the satisfaction of seeing the Treasury reject its urgings that war bonuses be extended to registrars appointed in 1914.[57] Treasury opposition to increased expense was buttressed by the retrenchments imposed in 1920 through the Geddes Committee and negotiations had to be conducted on the basis that any new scheme would be financially neutral.[58]

One side of the financial equation could be adjusted by reducing the number of courts and registrars.[59] Schuster had already put this in hand through a committee under Judge Radcliffe which spent three years of painstaking work on a thorough review. Nothing very radical was attempted and local authorities threatened with the loss of a court were invited to make representations; no fewer than thirty-nine sent deputations and in the end courts were abolished only if their business was inconsiderable (like Rhyader); if they were closely adjacent (like Haslingden, Bacup and Rawtenstall); or obsolete because of railway changes (like Southam). Some circuits proved intractable – the Marches and mid-Wales were always a problem and circuit 55 straggled

54 *Swift Report*, Memorandum, pp. 22–4.

55 Schuster to R. S. Meiklejohn, 19 Jan. 1921, PRO LCO 2/525.

56 *Swift Report*, pp. 25 ff.

57 *Ibid.*, p. 6; Napier's summary, 24 Dec. 1920, PRO LCO 2/525.

58 *Hansard* 1919 5th s., vol. 121 (HC), col. 467; *PP* 1922 [Cmd 1589] IX, pp. 22–4.

59 The McKenna Committee on Retrenchment, after a very superficial inquiry, had noted with seeming approval the frequent representations for reorganisation (*PP* 1916 [Cd 8200] XV, p. 13), while the Machinery of Government Committee felt that 'the time has long been ripe for a complete geographical redistribution' (p. 78).

unmanageably across Wessex – and only two were actually abolished, with one new one proposed.[60]

Though unfortunately timed in that, while acknowledging the likely impact of motor traffic, it had still to be based on the railway, the Radcliffe Report supplied a sound basis for a programme of progressive consolidation, assisted by statutory authority for registrars to be appointed to more than one court, to reside outside their district and to hold court when the judge was not sitting.[61] They could now be moved from court to court and rules were produced enabling 'branch courts' to be designated and giving the registrar greater flexibility to organise his district. As a result the number of registrars was more than halved by 1938 to 229, of whom about seventy were part-time.[62]

Economies were helpful but they were not enough. It was understood that there would have to be fee increases too, for in 1920 the gap between receipts and expenses was still £350,000.[63] Preliminary discussions on the proper principle for funding the courts enabled markers to be laid down for future reference but both sides acknowledged that the halcyon days of lucrative small debt undefendeds were gone for good.[64] Some fees must be raised and the overall structure simplified, since it was 'so complicated and obscure that even the experienced officers of the Courts have difficulty in finding their way through the bewildering mazes of the schedules and often ... are unable to say with any certainty what is the proper fee to be charged in a particular case'.[65]

This task was given to the last of the trio of committees on county court matters, under Mr Justice MacNaghten.[66] The Committee recommended that as a general rule fees in the smallest cases (not above £20) ought not to be raised significantly, while for the rest the county court should be only slightly cheaper than

60 *PP* 1919 [Cmd 431] XIIIa; see also pp. 214–15 below.
61 County Courts Act 1919 ss. 9, 15.
62 *Civil Judicial Statistics*, *PP* 1938–9 [Cmd 6135] XXV.
63 *MacNaghten Report*, pp. 4–5.
64 Schuster to R. S. Meiklejohn, 19 Jan. 1921, PRO LCO 2/525.
65 *MacNaghten Report*, para 10.
66 'The undistinguished son of a distinguished father' (Abel-Smith and Stevens, *Lawyers and the Courts*, p. 127 n. 3), best known for leading the judges' agitation against the cuts in their salaries in 1931. Committee papers are in PRO LCO 2/541–2.

the high court, most fees rising with the amount claimed.[67] Their proposals were calculated to yield about £110,000 and the most contentious of them was to end the automatic exemption of plaintiffs in workmen's compensation cases from the plaint fee, leaving the judge power to waive it in cases of hardship.[68]

Although the Law Society and creditors' organisations had naturally opposed any increases, the MacNaghten Report, published in March 1923, was generally well received, though it aroused far less interest than previous bouts of fee raising. Furthermore, by this time the pressure for big increases had eased, for a post-war litigation boom had seen Schedule A fees climb from £164,153 in 1919 to £393,406 in 1921, substantially reducing the deficit on the county court vote.[69]

The LCO had not waited for the outcome of the fees inquiry. Though Birkenhead had been unable to persuade the Treasury that existing legislation was wide enough to cover most of the Swift proposals for registrars, they had been embodied in the Economy (Miscellaneous Provisions) Bill 1922, and only when that measure was dropped was it decided to have a dedicated bill covering the whole range of staff reorganisation.[70]

Schuster negotiated deals with the staff association and with the registrars[71] but found the Treasury stubborn on several points, notably the fate of the 'old men' who would fall outside the new scheme and for whom he sought gratuities to ease them into retirement.[72] With agreement finally reached great care had to be taken to talk round interested MPs of all parties: 'what we want for the bill in its passage through Parliament is neither hostility nor too great a championing of the people we are trying to help, for if amendments were passed which overthrew the financial balance of the scheme the government would be obliged to drop it

67 *MacNaghten Report*, paras. 26–8, 37–9, 47.

68 The imposition of fees, though recommended in the (*Holman Gregory*) *Report on Workmen's Compensation* (*PP* 1920 [Cmd 816] XX), had been rejected by Parliament in 1920: Napier's summary of 1920 and sidenote of 1923, PRO LCO 2/525.

69 PRO LCO 2/541.

70 *MacNaghten Report*, pp. 1–5; Schuster's memo, 10 Jan. 1923; R. S. Meiklejohn to Lord Chancellor, 13 Apr. 1921 and correspondence between Birkenhead and Sir R. Horne, July 1921, all PRO LCO 2/525.

71 For details see PRO LCO 2/526 (registrars) and 2/527 (other staff) and pp. 286, 298–9 below.

72 For the Treasury viewpoint see: *Swift Evidence*, evidence of Meiklejohn.

and heaven knows whether an opportunity would ever occur again'.[73] Assuring the whips that the bill was uncontentious became even more crucial once Bonar Law's government fell and Labour had to be induced to find room for its orphans. Delay would also unravel the carefully constructed agreement because it was to be based on the fees income for 1922 and with litigation buoyant (the high court fees, recently raised, yielded so much that 'it was thought unsafe to disclose publicly the amount received'[74]) it was feared that the registrars would demand a renegotiation.

The County Courts Bill[75] did not follow the Swift Report to the letter; no salaries were specified; retirement for registrars was to be at seventy-two not seventy; and high bailiffs might still be appointed; it also contained elements from the MacNaghten Report and one or two miscellaneous clauses besides. There was some opposition to the Lord Chancellor appointing registrars. Dingle Foot felt that he 'already exercises power which is far too much for any frail mortal';[76] the Law Society claimed it might lead to jobbery and the judges awoke belatedly to the loss of their patronage, though as Schuster wrote, 'it is most vocal among those judges who have proved least competent to make satisfactory appointments'.[77] The only widespread feeling was against the imposition of a plaint fee in workmen's compensation, the failure to raise judges' salaries and the shabby treatment of the 'old men', 127 of whom were to receive gratuities averaging £300.[78]

Oddly enough, the only division was on a completely extraneous matter – Kingsley Wood's opportunist attempt to empower judges to grant injunctions *simpliciter* – and threatening only because it was ineptly handled by the novice Attorney-General, Sir Patrick Hastings.[79] To the great relief of the LCO the Bill squeezed

[73] To Burns, 23 Apr. 1923, PRO LCO 2/709. Financial calculations are in *PP* 1924 [Cmd 2140] XIX.

[74] Schuster's memo, 28 Jan. 1924, PRO LCO 2/938, p. 23.

[75] *PP* 1923 (211) I.

[76] *Hansard* 1924 5th s., vol. 175 (HC), col. 543. For attempts to talk Foot round see PRO LCO 2/710.

[77] Schuster's memo, 28 Jan. 1924, PRO LCO 2/938; Schuster to Attorney-General, 1 Nov. 1923, to E. R. Cook, 14 May 1924, PRO LCO 2/709. An amendment to restore the judges' patronage was defeated: *Hansard* 1924 5th s., vol. 175 (HC), cols. 1279–80.

[78] *Hansard* 1924 5th s., vol. 175 (HC), cols. 513–44, 1409–19; PRO LCO 8/57.

[79] *Hansard* 1924 5th s., vol. 175 (HC), cols. 1259–74. The clause was lost by 74 votes to 208.

through before Labour fell and with its implementation the reconstruction of the county courts was completed.[80]

There remained one item of unfinished business – the judges' salaries. The judges and their supporters made persistent representations but were met always with 'the doctrine of unripeness' – the constraints of the political and/or economic situation. The LCO was not prepared to advance their claims independently of other judicial officers, particularly the King's Bench masters, and it was 1937 before they finally received the £2,000 recommended as long ago as 1878.[81]

## NEW JURISDICTIONS

During the war all contentious legislation proposed by departments was put into abeyance unless directed to the war effort, but after the Armistice Schuster lost no time in resurrecting a County Courts Bill. Suggestions were invited from the Bar Council and the Law Society,[82] but the Society wanted to go well beyond the modest measure he had in mind and in the end they had to be given a blunt lesson in political realities:

> the proceedings of Parliament for the last few years are strewn with the wrecks of county court bills which have never reached harbour because they were overloaded. As long as those who are interested in the matter are content with nothing less than the indefinite enlargement of the jurisdiction and the grant of jurisdiction in divorce to the county court we can make no progress ... there is not the smallest chance at present of passing a contentious bill on the subject ... it seems very hard that this being so attempts to make minor alterations in the law should be impeded.[83]

Schuster backed up his argument with a blunt threat: 'I saw Cook on the subject ... and told him that if they proceeded in their endeavours to enlarge the scope of the bill we would drop the whole thing and cause it to be publicly known that we did so in

80 It was still a close-run thing. The whips wanted to abandon this bill to ensure others got through and Schuster wrote in alarm that it would be 'an appalling tragedy using the words in their literal sense': to A. F. Henning, 30 Jun. 1924, PRO LCO 2/711.

81 Stevens, *Independence of the Judiciary*, pp. 49–58.

82 *CCC* 47 (1919–20), 17, 30, 102; *LSG* 17 (1919–20), 64 ff.

83 Schuster to E. R. Cook, 13 May 1919, PRO LCO 2/434.

consequence of their obstruction; hence their hasty descent from the tree'.[84] Nevertheless, Cook was invited to assist with the drafting, a foretaste of the close and mutually beneficial relationship Schuster was cultivating with the Law Society.

The Bill was a ragbag of clauses, mostly extracted from the pre-war bills on the criterion of uncontentiousness. Some of the more important, however, originated from a committee of judges who had been asked to suggest ways of relieving congestion in the KBD;[85] by enlarging the scope for remitted actions in tort and raising the limit to £100, they expected to send down a lot of the speculative running down cases which were beginning to clog up the division.[86]

Though Halsbury was no longer on watch in the Lords, there were still eminent judges jealous for the high court, one of whom, Lord Phillimore, launched a rather wild attack, claiming that after this Bill, 'you might as well shut up the High Court of Justice altogether'.[87] Even coupled with a strengthening of the costs sanction, the modest expansion of remitted actions hardly warranted such hyperbole, but Phillimore was on stronger ground in criticising the absence of any appeal on fact from county court decisions, a notorious weakness but one not easily remedied.[88]

The wisdom of keeping the frail barque lightly laden was demonstrated when, after it had run out of time in the summer of 1919, it was rushed through in the autumn. The decline in parliamentary interest in the courts is clear; henceforth if the legal profession was squared, modest measures could be presented as essentially 'lawyers' law' and most laymen would be content to leave them to the lawyers.[89]

Apart from the remitted actions, the most important elements in the Act were those extending the role of registrars, who were enabled to hear defended cases up to £5 with the parties' consent

84 Schuster to Hon. H. Godley, 17 May 1919, PRO LCO 2/434.

85 *Hansard* 1919 5th s., vol. 37 (HL), cols. 301–3 (Birkenhead LC).

86 Schuster to Godley, 1 May 1919, PRO LCO 2/434; Schuster to W. Graham Harrison, 20 Nov. 1919, PRO LCO 2/435.

87 *Hansard* 1919 5th s., vol. 37 (HL), cols. 357–74.

88 Muir McKenzie, whose initial reaction to Phillimore's suggestion of a wider appeal was one of horror, was taken aback when he found that it had been in the bill of 1911: to Schuster, 21, 22 Nov. 1919, PRO LCO 2/435.

89 There were, however, some protests at the speed at which the Bill was pushed through the Commons: *Hansard* 1919 5th s., vol. 122 (HC), cols. 1088–94.

and given more extensive powers to make instalment orders and take references from the judge.[90] As Schuster made clear to the Law Society, it had been decided not to support proposals to send divorces to the county courts even though the divorce judges were overwhelmed and their brethren of the KBD reluctant to come to their aid.[91] However, the divorce question, as well as being controversial in its own right, was closely bound up with the problem of financing pauper litigation. The poor needed legal assistance if they were to be able to divorce at all and the Poor Persons' Procedure devised to assist them depended upon the goodwill of the legal profession in supplying services free of charge.[92] Both branches had to co-operate if it were to be extended to county courts, but barristers and solicitors were unable to agree over rights of audience and the Lawrence Committee, charged with trying to improve the scheme, divided along professional lines; the chairman's vote therefore became decisive and, as a former head of the Bar Council, he predictably cast it against county courts.[93] Curiously enough however, while county court judges were spared divorce work, some of their registrars were not: certain assize towns were chosen to relieve the divorce registry and those who doubled as district registrars of the high court found that they had to handle the preliminaries, work some found distasteful as well as novel.[94]

Reforms in the 1920s brought the county courts into play in

[90] Ss. 5, 7, 9.

[91] In 1918 Lord Buckmaster, a former Lord Chancellor, introduced a bill to reform both the substance and the procedure in divorce. It empowered a county court judge to deal with a divorce suit provided that, *inter alia*, the plaintiff established that he lacked the means to use the high court. Acknowledging that this was controversial, he substituted in the bill presented in the next session a provision enabling county court judges to sit as commissioners and handle divorce in that capacity: *Hansard* 1918 5th s., vol. 31 (HL), cols. 1191–2; 1920, vol. 39 (HL), col. 342. The bill failed but the initiative attracted so much support that the government was forced into making the courts more accessible for divorces.

[92] R. I. Morgan, The Introduction of Civil Legal Aid in England and Wales, 1914–1949, *Twentieth Century British History* 5 (1994), 38–76 largely supersedes older accounts such as F. C. G. Gurney-Champion, *Justice and the Poor in England* (London, 1926).

[93] *PP* 1919 [Cmd 430] XXVII; Schuster's memo in PRO LCO 2/938; PRO LCO 2/644.

[94] Introduced by RSC (Poor Persons) Order 1925, following the report of the second Lawrence Committee (*PP* 1924–5 [Cmd 2358] XV). *PP* 1929–30 [Cmd 3375] XVII at p. 265; evidence of registrars in PRO LCO 2/1057.

other branches of family law. This was not at the behest of the LCO – indeed jurisdiction under the Adoption Act 1926 was conferred by an amendment which was accepted against its wishes and the Legitimacy Act was also rather unexpected, necessitating a hasty bout of rule-making.[95] Neither Act produced very much work at first, but they were significant as incursions into a field normally regarded as the province of magistrates, marking a further stage in the march towards complete civil jurisdiction.[96]

For many judges the worst thing that Parliament inflicted on them was the Rent Acts. In his farewell address Parry excoriated them as 'a curse to the county courts of this country' and Crawford wrote that 'no more anxious, difficult and unpleasant work was ever imposed upon judges'.[97] Hopes of an early return to freedom of contract were quickly dashed as successive inquiries conceded that immediate decontrol was politically impossible. It was finally accepted in 1933 that some controls would be needed indefinitely and the National government switched tactics, adopting 'creeping decontrol', which would gradually free houses from the top end of the market downwards.[98]

The policy of rent control and security of tenure in peacetime was bitterly divisive but the quality of the legislation was generally condemned as enmeshing unfortunate judges (and far more unfortunate laymen) in a dreadful web of intricate definitions, yawning gaps and unnervingly wide discretions.[99] It added greatly to the judge's difficulties that in most cases, especially in the flood of possession summonses which followed the relaxations introduced in 1923, the tenant, and often the landlord too, was unrepresented, leaving him to construe the law as best he could, aided, in his smaller courts, only by a basic textbook.[100] The stakes made appeals worthwhile for landlords and because this

95 Napier to Judge Cann, 9 Jul. 1926, PRO LCO 2/112; PRO LCO 2/854, especially Napier to Cann, 20 Dec. 1926, 15 Jan. 1927.

96 In 1938, for instance, 498 petitions were presented under the Adoption Act and sixty-five under the Legitimacy Act. There were also twelve under the Guardianship Act 1925: *PP* 1938–9 [Cmd 6135] XXV.

97 *LN* 46 (1927), 163; *Reflections and Recollections* (London, 1936), p. 87.

98 Englander, *Landlord and Tenant*, pp. 305–16.

99 Crawford, *Reflections and Recollections*, pp. 107–12. The popular view of this tangled law is neatly exemplified by the *Daily Express* cartoon reproduced as a frontispiece to Rider's book.

100 Judge F. H. Bradley, Rent Restriction in the County Court *LQR* 39 (1923), 441–57; C. Mullins, *In Quest of Justice* (London, 1930), p. 37.

legislation (unlike workmen's compensation) did not curtail the 'double appeal', it happened more than once that the voices of authority pronounced contradictory verdicts.[101] Many judges were too closely acquainted with the misery caused by the chronic housing shortage to wish the Acts repealed *in toto*, but whereas they had little instinctive sympathy for retail traders and employers, their background and education did make many of them uncomfortable with such a drastic interference with the property rights of landlords, as emerges in Crawford's crepuscular account of his struggles with 'this Protean monster of the law'.[102]

The judges were very sensitive, however, to any suggestion that they were not impartial. The 1923 Act enabled a landlord to regain possession if it were reasonable and some judges were said to consider only what was reasonable for the landlord. When the Divisional Court, in *Shrimpton v. Rabbits*, seemed to echo this criticism the judges' society was provoked into a rare collective pronouncement denying that they had ever acted on that basis.[103] Dan Rider, who saw more than anyone of the courts at work in this field, was much less critical of judges than magistrates, lay or stipendiary, and it was said that landlords always preferred to try to get possession summonses heard in magistrates' courts.[104] It is no surprise to find Parry cutting through the technicalities of the statute by a crushing reference to the Ten Commandments, nor Cluer contemptuously dismissing a landlord's claim to be shocked by a tenant's foul language, but there are instances of other judges, less well known, showing sympathy for the tenants.[105] If landlords on their side felt unfairly treated they did not complain to authority and in the present (very imperfect) state of knowledge there is little with which to oppose the testimony gathered by a departmental committee in 1930 before which 'almost all witnesses, including advocates of Rent Courts, expressed complete satisfaction with, and appreciation of, the work of the County ... Courts'.[106]

101 Mullins, *In Quest of Justice*, pp. 34–40.

102 *Reflections and Recollections*; the quotation is from *LQR* 37 (1921), at 85.

103 *LJCCR* 13 (1924), 25.

104 *Landlords and Tenants*, pp. 278–9. But he felt that the newer judges tended to be less humane (p. 313).

105 *Ibid.*, pp. 251, 229.

106 *PP* 1930–1 [Cmd 3911] XVII, para. 99.

If the Rent Acts were the most radical interposition of the state between landlord and tenant they were not the first nor the only one. Well before 1914 the county courts had practically exclusive jurisdiction over disputes arising under the compensation provisions for tenants in the Agricultural Holdings Acts,[107] and in 1927 the Landlord and Tenant Act conferred wider rights on tenants of business premises to which goodwill had become attached; again, the county court was to be the main forum.[108] However, predictions of extensive business under this Act were not borne out, any more than the fears that the courts would be swamped by cases under the Housing Acts, which gave local authorities strong powers for slum clearance and the repair or demolition of substandard housing.[109] The right of appeal to the courts under these statutes was controversial, and when they did come into court they were strongly and professionally fought.

New statutes also intruded into the relationship between debtors and creditors, where the county court judges usually felt more at ease. One was an amendment to the Moneylenders Act 1900, which had empowered the courts to open 'harsh and unconscionable' bargains.[110] Following the report of a committee under Lord Darling,[111] the 1927 Act decreed that an interest rate exceeding 48 per cent p. a. was *prima facie* to be deemed extortionate, but though the ACCR President described it as 'about the most drastic Act he recollected to have been put on the statute book',[112] it was probably little more effective than its predecessor.

Another measure was much more important and badly overdue.

107 *LJ* 58 (1923), 607–9 (Judge B. Lailey).

108 *LT* 181 (1936), 420–1 (L. G. H. Horton-Smith).

109 *LT* 165 (1928), 310–11 (reporting the ACCR AGM); *SJ* 79 (1935), 278. In 1938 there were 342 applications under Housing Act 1936 s. 15; twenty-seven for compensation and fifty-four for new leases under the Landlord and Tenant Act 1927.

110 Following the *Report of the Select Committee on Moneylending*, *PP* 1897 (364) XI; 1898 (260) XI, to which several county court judges gave evidence. P. S. Atiyah, *The Rise and Fall of Freedom of Contract* (Oxford, 1979), pp. 709–13.

111 *PP* 1924–5 (153) VIII. Chalmers and Schuster gave evidence, the latter expressing concern at the idea of ousting the high court (q. 1142). Representatives of the Moneylenders Association also deprecated that notion, alleging that 'some of the [county court] judges have shown that they have distinctly an absolute prejudice against the trade of moneylending' (q. 3).

112 ACCR, minutes of AGM 1926. The Crowther Committee (*PP* 1970–1 [Cmnd 4596] IX at pp. 274–5 judged it ineffective. However, the experienced London registrar Gilbert Hicks said that this and the Bills of Sale legislation 'have

Judge Bacon had started on its way to the House of Lords the crucial case of *Helby v. Matthews*, which clothed the hire purchase transaction in its definitive legal shape. Already in widespread use for furniture, pianos and sewing machines, hire purchase facilitated a great expansion in the range of consumer durables, bringing motor cars, radios and gramophones within the range of the less affluent.[113] This accessibility was bought at a high price though. The 'snatchback' of goods on default in a single instalment, the lack of remedy for defective goods and the concealment of the terms of the bargain were abuses the reputable firms, through their trade organisation, had been regularly deploring since the nineteenth century.[114]

Scotland had legislated in 1932 but in England it was left to a private members' bill presented by Ellen Wilkinson and adroitly supported by the LCO and the parliamentary counsel to bring redress.[115] Several county court judges had drawn attention to the abuses attendant on hire purchase, Frankland in particular campaigning vigorously for action and supplying ammunition for the debates.[116] The 1938 Act gave judges wide powers in repossession actions to alter instalments and other terms. As usual, not all judges and registrars were pleased at the width of their discretion, but before any of them had much chance to operate it[117] war came and any scruples at interfering with contracts were subsumed within the all-embracing powers conferred by emergency legislation.

practically driven moneylenders out of business': to G. P. Coldstream, 15 Mar. 1946, PRO LCO 2/3295.

113 [1895] AC 471. Cornish and Clark, *Law and Society*, pp. 242–6.

114 PRO LCO 2/1511. The argument about venue (see below) was clearly influenced by abuses in hire purchase; see examples in PRO LCO 2/1288.

115 PRO LCO 2/1511–13; H. S. Kent, *In on the Act: Memoirs of a Lawmaker* (1979), pp. 101–2.

116 PRO LCO 2/1511 contains observations by several judges. Frankland was extensively quoted in the debates: *Hansard* 1938 5th s., vol. 330 (HC), cols. 729–63, 1194–1212.

117 In 1945 Hicks produced an appraisal of the Act to meet a request from Eire to the Board of Trade: PRO LCO 2/1513.

## BETWEEN THE WARS

### County courts at work

Common law business, as measured by plaints issued, did not reach pre-war levels until 1932 and at no point matched the 1910 peak of more than 1.3 million. However, in nominal terms there was a notable increase in the bigger actions; those between £20 and £50, never much above 13,000 before 1914, shot up to 38,000 in 1921 and remained in the 30,000s throughout; from a pre-war peak of 2,500, actions above £50 passed 9,000 in 1922 and, though falling back, generally remained above 7,000. Of course, inflation makes these figures misleading – there was a rise in larger actions but in real terms it was nowhere near so pronounced.

Common law business still predominated, in 1938 comprising 1,150,300 out of a grand total of 1,294,000 actions commenced. With equity and admiralty still numerically insignificant, the biggest sources of other business were statutory.[118] Tithe Act applications, for instance, surged from 5,000 in 1924 to nearly 49,000 in 1938, orders rising from 1,200 to 18,000. Most of this was purely formal, but in the 'tithe wars' of the 1930s it became a delicate and unruly business in parts of Kent and East Anglia.[119]

Landlord and tenant matters were also taking an increasing share of the courts' time. There were Rent Act cases in large numbers: 19,593 summonses in 1929, leading to 16,021 orders for possession; 20,472 in 1938, and 15,613 orders. There was also a roughly similar volume of possession and ejectment claims outside the Acts: 26,394 (17,001 orders) in 1929; 19,476 (12,476 orders) in 1938.[120]

Workmen's compensation continued to provide a steady flow of work. Applications for the judge to arbitrate ran at about 4–5,000 a year, though around half never reached a hearing. In addition, about 20,000 memoranda of agreement were presented annually for registration; this devolved upon registrars, who referred to the judge those which were felt to be unsatisfactory.[121] It was testing

118 *Civil Judicial Statistics*, *PP* 1938–9 (Cmd 6135) XXV. The failure of the equity jurisdiction is discussed by Judge Bradley in *LJ* 58 (1923), 537–8.

119 For the problems of enforcing tithe judgments see Polden, *Guide to Records of the LCD*, pp. 317–18.

120 *Civil Judicial Statistics*.

121 Bartrip, *Workmen's Compensation*, pp. 133–4.

work, for despite a consolidation Act in 1925 it was still 'a legal minefield'[122] in which incautious judges were regularly blown up in the appeal courts. The Holman Gregory Committee[123] was critical of judges' differing approaches, but it is unlikely that their suggestion for 'periodical convocations of the county court judges and of county court registrars ... at which the administration of the Act by the Courts should be discussed and an effort made to bring about uniformity as far as practicable'[124] would have been effective. Another suggestion, that registrars should dispense free advice to workmen and act as mediators if requested, was disapproved by their Assocation and by the legal press.[125]

What most judges and registrars wanted was to be able to exercise greater control over the settlement of admitted claims. In evidence to the Committee they stoutly defended the vetting of settlements, endorsing what Fossett Lock said: 'I do not look upon a free contract between unequal parties as such a fetish as Lord Bramwell did.'[126] They had no objection to lump sum settlements *per se*, provided that they were held in court and the judge given control over their release to prevent the beneficiaries from wasting their capital in ill-advised business ventures.[127] That, however, was a degree of paternalism that neither the Committee nor the Home Office would accept. Despite a preference for American-style 'District Commissions', the Committee concluded that 'the county court has given satisfaction as a tribunal'[128] and there is abundant evidence testifying to the anxious care that judges and registrars gave to this work.[129]

Though it is impossible to isolate different causes of common law action under the ordinary jurisdiction, there was certainly a decided increase in claims arising out of motor accidents. Running down cases were nothing new of course – only the instrument of mischief had changed – but the imposition of compulsory third-

122 *Ibid.*, p. 135.
123 *PP* 1920 [Cmd 816, report; 908, 909, evidence] XXVI.
124 Cmd 816, at pp. 91–2.
125 *Ibid.*, p. 92; *LJCCR* 9 (1920), 53.
126 Cmd 909, at q. 6578.
127 *Ibid.*, qq. 10,230 (Ruegg) and 15,031 (Bray, for most judges).
128 Cmd 816, p. 92.
129 See e.g. *Swift Evidence*; Parry, *The Gospel and the Law*, pp. 111–52; Crawford, *Reflections and Recollections*, pp. 189–212, and the records of the Rule Committee (PRO LCO 2).

party insurance in 1930 made a big difference,[130] ensuring that the culprit would be worth suing and that the insurers would defend if they felt they had a chance. By 1930 these cases were a substantial element in county court business and a major factor in the delays which bedevilled the KBD, whose highly conservative masters thwarted attempts to relieve the pressure by procedural reforms and were also reluctant to remit suitable cases to the county court.[131] Since Scrutton once found that of fifty-two cases waiting for him at Liverpool, forty-two were running down actions, they evidently also gave a fillip to the assizes.[132] One inquiry in the 1930s suggested that all such actions with a claim not above £500 might go to the county court, but Schuster saw to it that nothing came of that.[133]

Running down cases tended to be lengthy because witnesses were usually required. They were probably the first to bring middle-class men who were not traders into the county courts in any numbers and judges soon discovered that otherwise respectable citizens were tempted into outrageous perjury:

> The following is an instance of the regular course of evidence given before me, over and over again, in a cross-road running-down case. Driver A, doing a steady 17, slows up at the opening of the cross-road and hoots. He sees B cutting the corner, swerves to avoid an accident, and is at a standstill when B's car crashes into him.
>
> B is also doing a steady 17, and is half across the road when he sees A. He immediately stops dead, leaving A room to pass when A swerves and crashes into him.
>
> Assuming each witness to be a man of good character and sound memory, it was clear that two cars skilfully handled, travelling at 17 miles an hour, had met at cross-roads and each had been brought to a standstill. After that, the two cars had flung themselves at each other with such vicious force that they had destroyed their own machinery and maimed that of their owners.[134]

But for all the judges' grumbles they probably enjoyed motoring cases more than most business. It was familiar common

130 Cornish and Clark, *Law and Society*, pp. 538–9.

131 *LJ* 60 (1925), 1042–3; Schuster to Lord Hanworth MR, 17 Oct. 1933, PRO LCO 2/1759.

132 *LJ(CCR)* 68 (1929), 51.

133 The Danesfort Committee: *HLJ* 65, (1932–3), 11, 260ff., 334–5.

134 Parry, *My Own Way*, p. 214. Cf. Crawford, Reflections and Recollections, pp. 123–5.

law, usually turning on questions of fact and therefore immune from appeal, and the parties were frequently represented.

The wide range of their duties meant that judges were sometimes confronted with altogether more perplexing matters. Hill-Kelly at Northampton once had a liquidation followed by a probate, both rarities and perhaps a stimulating change; Judge Dumas, however, probably failed to derive much enjoyment from a fraught encounter with the intricacies of income tax; and a complex issue like that in *Schalit v. Joseph Nader & Co.* stretched a judge to the limit.[135] On the other hand they still had occasional absurd or grotesque disputes – a stuffed civet cat was the object in dispute before Tobin, while another stuffed feline, this time with two heads, was paraded before the judge at Bridlington. There was certainly no shortage of variety.[136]

More cases of a demanding nature were arriving, particularly once the high court became rather freer in remitting actions – so much so that in 1938 the Court of Appeal signalled its disapproval of the tendency to remit almost automatically whenever a tort plaintiff could not provide security for costs.[137] Between 1,500 and 2,000 cases were remitted each year, mostly to the London courts and to Westminster in particular, which in Woodfall's time had over 150 a year.[138]

Fluctuations in the level of business from year to year were often hard to explain. A fall in 1926 was plausibly put down partly to the General Strike, which even dented the upward trend in committals.[139] But Schuster was puzzled when business actually went up during the slump, contradicting the accumulated wisdom of the department: 'it is some change in the population that one cannot understand'.[140] The superintendent felt that MPs were better placed to chart social trends than his civil servants, who had no explanation for a sudden fall in hire purchase cases in the mid-1930s.[141]

135 *LJ(CCR)* 63 (1927), 1; *LJ* 87 (1939), 86; *SJ* 79 (1935), 374.

136 J. Tudor Rees, *Reserved Judgment* (London, 1956), pp. 177–8; 'Richard Roe' (Lord Bessborough), *Straws from my Wig* (London, 1954), p. 113.

137 *LT* 181 (1936), 187–8; *LN* 56 (1937), 88–91 (*Culver v. Beard*); *LT* 185 (1938), 313–14.

138 *Civil Judicial Statistics*; *County Courts (Plaints and Sittings)*, the annual series which ended in 1920.

139 *PP* 1928 (35, 99) V, at qq. 1870, 1894–5.

140 *PP* 1933–4 (36, 97, 98) V, q. 17.

141 *Ibid.*, q. 35; *PP* 1935–6 (45,144) V, q. 1724.

Obviously courts remained very different from each other, as Parry found when he forsook wideawake Manchester for sleepy west Kent. They took their character in part from the locality but in part too from their judge, though there seems to have been a slow reduction in the exuberant diversity once characteristic of the bench, probably due to the more responsible use the Lord Chancellor made of his patronage and to changes in the culture of the bar and the judiciary.[142]

In the early 1930s Ensor generalised that county court judgeships attracted the type of barrister who had worked up a practice of £2–4,000 a year and felt himself unlikely to get much further.[143] Most appointments were well received,[144] though inevitably not all turned out well; the choice of F. K. Archer, for instance, was applauded, but he won few admirers at the LCO.[145] Some, such as Snagge and Kennedy, would have adorned the high court[146] and it was never explained why Acton's promotion was not followed up. Many county court judges were considered good enough to go as commissioners on assize and the presence of some good men tended to attract others; thus Gerald Hurst was impressed at finding half a dozen Lincoln's Inn benchers among their number.[147] Though as a body they were not the equal of the high court, Lord Carnock's contemptuous reference to 'briefless barristers' was fifty years out of date.[148]

There were still pungent characters on the bench but they were growing fewer. Granger was 'the last of the old school'[149] and Parry and Cluer left no successors, though Crawford aspired to be

142 *My Own Way*, pp. 240–6; Gerald Hurst remarked on the passing of the 'heroic' type of county court judge: *Lincoln's Inn Essays* (London, 1949), p. 93.

143 *Courts and Judges in France, Germany and England* (Oxford, 1933), p. 7. See also, pp. 241–50 below.

144 The appointments of 1934, for example, were described as 'men of the highest calibre': *LJ* 78 (1934), 141.

145 Archer was 'a notable accession', *LJ* 83 (1937), 161. For unflattering views of him in the LCO see PRO LCO 2/3284.

146 As would E. W. Cave, of whom Schuster wrote, 'but for a stroke of ill-fortune, he would some years ago have been placed upon the Bench of the High Court': to Sir R. Scott, 12 Feb. 1937, PRO LCO 2/6654.

147 Polden, Judicial Independence, part two, *AALR* 25 (1996), 133–162, at 143; PRO LCO 2/6874; G. B. Hurst, *Closed Chapters* (Manchester, 1942), p. 316.

148 *Hansard* 1937–8 5th s., vol. 107 (HL), col. 982.

149 *LJ* 63 (1927), 65. Criticising a husband for failing to try the effect of physical chastisement on his drunken, quarrelsome wife was felt by the *Law Journal* to be rather out of date, *LJ* 54 (1919), 305.

a second Parry. Oddities there certainly were: Turner was 'a comic sort of judge' who nevertheless 'succeeded in dispensing a rough and ready justice, which, even if the manner thereof were unusual, was nevertheless in most cases correct';[150] Rowlands 'was inclined to disregard the sanctity of classical legal decisions by eminent judges of a bygone day';[151] Tobin was renowned for almost compelling the parties to settle to avoid his having to give judgment; and Farrant 'had the unsatisfactory inclination to divide the plaintiff's claim by two and give judgment to that amount'.[152] For all his sketchy law Farrant was 'universally beloved'[153] but there were a few 'holy terrors',[154] the worst of them Hill-Kelly, whose obituarist was restrained in referring to 'a none too gracious judicial manner'.[155] There was also one whose blatant favouritism led to a deputation from the local bar to the LCO.[156]

Most judges seem also to have been now less prone to extravagant *obiter dicta* on morals or public affairs, though Cluer found himself in hot water at least once and Sturges' views on sterilisation led to a question in Parliament.[157] More striking is the fact that in the wake of the debate started by the London Chamber of Commerce broadside, in which several judges had vigorously joined, their council passed a resolution deprecating such participation; why they felt this self-denying ordinance to be desirable is not clear.[158]

## *Rules and procedures*

The tendency towards homogenisation in the judicial style owed something to the Rule Committee. Strengthened in 1919, the

[150] H. Cecil (Judge H. C. Leon), *Just Within the Law* (London, 1975), p. 52; *The Times*, 14 Nov. 1932; *SJ* 76 (1932), 833.

[151] *LJ* 79 (1935), 67–8.

[152] Lord Hailsham, *A Sparrow's Flight* (London, 1990), pp. 154, 245.

[153] *Ibid.*, p. 154.

[154] Lord Hailsham's phrase, *The Door Wherein I Went* (London, 1975), p. 257.

[155] *The Times*, 22 Oct. 1949. Compare the harsher strictures of Cecil, *Just Within the Law*, p. 46 and N. Faulks, *No Mitigating Circumstances* (London, 1977), p. 52.

[156] S. Shetreet, *Judges on Trial* (Amsterdam, 1976), p. 256; Lord Shawcross, *Life Sentence* (London, 1996), pp. 36–37.

[157] *LJ* 60 (1925), 839; *SJ* 73 (1929), 237.

[158] Polden, *Judicial Independence*, part two, pp. 158–9.

Committee did not limit its activities to churning out new rules whenever a new Act imposed duties on the courts but actively sought out gaps and defects in the existing code.[159] Of course there were strict limits to what they could accomplish. Divergent practice was sometimes the outcome of legitimate exercises in judicial discretion and there were deep-seated differences, often of a regional nature, which could not be eradicated.[160] Simplifying procedure also proved frustratingly difficult as all too often an attempt to tackle an unsatisfactory rule came to grief on the discovery that it concealed awkward controversies or unsettled law.[161] Nevertheless the major revision carried out in 1936 was a valuable exercise, especially in recasting the rules in a shape similar to the *White Book*.[162]

The revision followed hard on a very necessary consolidation Act in 1934, this time encompassing the admiralty jurisdiction which had escaped in 1888 and originating in a labour of love by Judge R. A. McLeary.[163] Finding the 1888 Act 'a sort of museum of legal archaeology' which, by consolidating statutes of a pre-Judicature Acts vintage, perpetuated 'the most surprising anomalies, archaisms and discrepancies in drafting',[164] the parliamentary counsel quickly concluded that the undertaking would not be worthwhile without preceding it by an amending measure filling up *lacunae* and tidying up ambiguities and inconsistencies; the exercise therefore turned out to be more valuable than a pure consolidation.[165]

Another factor working towards harmonisation was the increasingly common presence of advocates, especially junior counsel. If not quite 'the Mecca of the young advocate',[166] the county courts had now become a regular training ground and a source of work not usually forsaken until a high court practice had really taken

[159] See pp. 220–1 below.

[160] PRO LCO 2/3300: evidence of W. R. Davies to the Austin Jones Committee, 1948. Similar regional differences bedevilled attempts to regularise the use of executions for part only of sums due: 2/3276.

[161] See e.g. PRO LCO 2/537 (1923), 2/833 (1925).

[162] County Court Rules 1936 (626/L 17), summarised in *SJ* 80 (1936).

[163] J. A. Stainton to Napier, 30 Jul. 1931, PRO LCO 2/1252. Oddly, however, McLeary was passed over for the Rule Committee: 2/5094.

[164] Stainton to Napier, 31 Mar. 1932: PRO LCO 2/1253.

[165] See SJ 78 (1934), 164, 375.

[166] So described in Sir Patrick Hastings' *Autobiography* (London, 1948), p. 127.

off.[167] It was not an unmixed blessing, for Schuster said that the indulgence of county court judges towards tiros learning the rudiments of their trade prolonged hearings,[168] but a judge served by advocates, even not very competent ones, was more likely to temper justice with law. Since the ban on solicitor-advocates was a dead letter in many courts, it was usually easy enough for anyone with means to find a decent representative and the judges quickly came to know who was trustworthy in their district; outside London and the big cities the great majority probably were.

It is always difficult to measure the level of public satisfaction with the courts, but the county courts do not seem to have been unpopular. That is not to say that they were always helpful or 'user friendly' however; they still refused to list their telephone numbers – in 1939 the LCO had to insist that they disclose them to regular users – and they were also slow to accept cheques.[169] In the 1920s many of the staff were elderly men who frequently displayed an addiction to entrenched routines which could be exasperating.[170]

In fairness, they often had to work in poorly designed or adapted buildings. The slow progress in replacing the worst county courts came to an abrupt end with the slump and opponents of wider jurisdiction had a legitimate point when they criticised the facilities for litigants and advisers in many county courts.[171] Another venerable complaint was the absence of fixed hearing times, which left people hanging around all day, sometimes only to find their case postponed to the next sitting day.[172] Sankey was briefed that adjournments were in fact unusual, and with registrars now taking most of the undefendeds and many of the small suits, judges could usually be more accommodating than formerly.[173] Almost all the justified complaints came from the

[167] See e.g. Lord Kilmuir, *Political Adventure* (London, 1964), p. 299.

[168] Minutes of Hanworth Committee, 4 Apr. 1933, PRO LCO 2/1604.

[169] *Hansard* 1937–8 5th s., vol. 330 (HC), col. 402; circular 6 of 1939, PRO LCO 8/6; circular 12 of 1927, PRO LCO 8/88.

[170] In 1924 three officers whose years of service totalled 153 retired from Westminster; three others from Lambeth totalled 128 years between them: *LJ* 59 (1924), 637. And see pp. 298–9 below.

[171] E.g. *SJ* 78 (1934), 428; C. Mullins, The Poor Man's Court of Justice, *The Nineteenth Century and After*, 113 (1933), 207–19; H. Hart, *The Way to Justice* (London, 1941), pp. 65–6.

[172] E.g. *LJ* 64 (1927), 45; *LJ* 66 (1928), 4–5.

[173] *Hansard* 1932–3 5th s., vol. 88 (HL), cols. 551–68.

London courts but that was especially unfortunate since, if more high court business were removed to the county courts, they would bear the brunt of it.[174]

The procedure of the county court had always been precariously poised between processing debt collection rapidly and cheaply and protecting the poor from oppression by their creditors. In 1918 the Bar Council suggested that it was awry on both counts; that while defendants could still delay judgment and create extra expense by putting in notional or hopeless defences, some registrars too freely granted leave to sue outside the defendant's home district. These two issues posed the Rule Committee its most difficult questions, for besides the direct impact upon litigants, they influenced a plaintiff's decision whether to use the high court or the county court.[175]

Venue became an urgent question when Judge Turner reversed the complacent practice of his predecessor in the show court of Westminster and began taking a strict line on allowing transfer of actions solely on a routine 'jurisdiction affidavit'.[176] Some metropolitan courts processed hundreds of these a day for big creditors and if one court proved punctilious they flocked to another, especially to Bow.[177] Though the registrars defended their practice against Turner's criticisms, the Rule Committee became convinced that safeguards were too weak, and after much painstaking work produced a new rule in the 1936 revision which tilted the balance slightly in the defendant's favour.[178] Strenuous lobbying from trade organisations ensued – the Hire Purchase Traders Association, for instance, maintaining that credit trading would never have got off the ground under these rules;[179] but the Committee stood firm, arguing that creditors would benefit from the streamlining of paperwork that accompanied the revised procedure. Crucial to the effect of the change, however, was the extent to which judges would allow agents and affidavit evidence to be used in the defendant's home court.

174 A point taken in the *Hanworth Report*, *PP* 1933–34 [Cmd 4471] XI, para. 75.

175 *LJCCR* 8 (1919), 1. For discussions in the Rule Committee see PRO LCO 2/529–34.

176 *LJ* 70 (1930), 45; PRO LCO 2/1288.

177 Bow Registrar to Martin, 13 Nov. 1931 and Martin's memo, 28 Jan. 1935, PRO LCO 2/1288.

178 PRO LCO 2/1288–9; County Court Rules 1936 o. 2, o. 16 r. 1(2).

179 Meeting with deputation of credit traders, 10 Jul. 1936, PRO LCO 2/1289.

The weakness of the procedure for judgment by default also exercised the Rule Committee. Tentative changes just after the war still seemed to give protection to the undeserving, with the result that many creditors continued to resort to the high court.[180] Judge Crawford, arguing with some justification that it was the more generous scale of costs as much as the superiority of the process that was the attraction, began campaigning to have all small debt claims forced into the county court.[181] As Schuster explained, the costs sanction worked poorly, partly because of interference by the former senior master in the KBD, the immensely influential Sir Thomas Chitty. Not only had Chitty persuaded everyone that the changes had unfairly deprived plaintiffs of their high court option and so had them modified by a little-noticed clause in the Administration of Justice Act 1925, but he also ensured that King's Bench practice was such that the sanction was scarcely ever imposed.[182]

Crawford made enough noise, and enough sense, for Mr Justice Talbot to be asked to head an inquiry, but Crawford lacked the energy and determination to follow up his bold pronouncements with hard evidence and Talbot, testily finding 'there was nothing to enquire into', abruptly called off his investigation.[183] Sankey was quite willing to give the county courts a counterpart to RSC order 14 as had so often been demanded, but the Rule Committee opted instead to fine tune their existing rules, still retaining safeguards for the defendant.[184]

Creditors also complained, and with reason, of the ineffective methods of enforcing judgments. Execution against goods continued to be the main resort, with more than 400,000 warrants issued every year in the 1930s, but as well as the problems posed by the spread of hire purchase, the convenient practice of 'walking possession', which made execution reasonably economical, rested on shaky legal foundations and the statutory amendment which

180 Administration of Justice Act 1920 s. 20; *LJ* 59 (1924), 29–30 (W. H. Whitelock).

181 PRO LCO 2/1063.

182 Schuster to Talbot, 25 June, 22 July 1929, PRO LCO 2/1063. Returns reluctantly supplied by Master Bonner showed that fixed costs on the high court scale were allowed without exception.

183 Memo of Nov. 1930, *ibid.*

184 Napier to Hill-Kelly, 6 Feb. 1935, PRO LCO 2/1279, and 2/1279–80, *passim*. Order 14 permitted judgment to be entered in default of appearance by the defendant.

regularised it[185] was shown in *Day v. Davies* to be largely inefficacious.[186]

In the absence of any reliable alternative, the judgment summons backed up by the threat of committal was bound to keep its hold. Emergency legislation and the absence of many debtors at the front had all but stopped the practice during the war – at least one judge declared that under no circumstances would he commit a soldier – leading humanitarians to predict its demise.[187] They were rudely disillusioned as the numbers rose again, passing 1,000 in 1922 and reaching 4,000 by 1932. But there was curiously little public concern. Parry continued to inveigh against it and one or two judges joined in[188] but there was no real pressure for reform, and when adverse publicity about the larger number gaoled by magistrates for non-payment of rates, fines and maintenance led the Home Office to mount an inquiry, the LCO had the county courts excluded from its scope.[189]

Indeed the LCO seems to have been content to let sleeping dogs lie and to take action only if stirred by others. When the Home Office drew attention to the inconvenience of Judge Campbell's three-day committal orders, he was asked to adopt a more orthodox approach,[190] and when the Chancery judges became critical about the widespread use of committal orders which were automatically invoked on any default, it was agreed that a practice direction should be issued; that it had to be circulated at regular intervals suggests that it was not very effective.[191] Though the judicial statistics no longer showed them, variations in practice were still widespread and imprisonment still

185 *Civil Judicial Statistics.* The amendment, by Administration of Justice Act 1928 s. 19, followed an investigation by a small committee under Mr Justice Rigby Swift, PRO LCO 2/844. *Hansard* 1928 5th s., vol. 219 (HC), cols. 785–845 and PRO LCO 2/807.

186 [1938] 2 KB 74. The subject was discussed by the Lilley Committee on Distress for Rent, whose deliberations were halted by the war (PRO LCO 2/1343–4).

187 *County Courts (Plaints and Sittings)*; *SJ* 62 (1917–18), 101; *LJ* 55 (1920), 21.

188 *SJ* 69 (1924–5), 357; *SJ* 73 (1929), 180; T. A. Jones, *Without My Wig* (Liverpool, 1944), pp. 110–21, reprinted from the *Quarterly Review* for 1938.

189 The Fischer-Williams Committee, *PP* 1935–6 [Cmd 4649] XI.

190 PRO LCO 2/1301.

191 *In re a Judgment Debtor* TLR 51 (1935), 524. For the background see PRO LCO 2/1146.

commonplace: what had changed was that few people now seemed interested.[192]

## *The cost of justice*

Though debt collecting would always be its bedrock, there was now scope for the county courts to attract litigation in which the man of modest means might be the plaintiff for a change. Road accidents, faulty consumer goods, marriage breakdown and the Rent Acts all created rights which a working man might wish to assert. Yet in 1922 the only form of legal aid available in the 'poor man's court', the *in forma pauperis* procedure, was ruled to be outside its powers.[193]

On purely practical grounds the Finlay Committee, which reviewed legal aid in 1928, was right not to recommend that the scheme run by the Law Society for the high court be extended,[194] and neither the judges nor the registrars who gave evidence showed much enthusiasm for free representation. Bray and Snagge told the Committee: 'it could rarely happen that a person with a genuine grievance and a legal claim was unable to obtain justice and assistance',[195] and even Lias, the only one among the judges Bray had consulted to take a different view, did not claim it was urgent; Lailey was probably more typical when he wrote sharply, 'I do not think that it is in the public interest that the county court should become more a dispensary or a soup kitchen than it is now.'[196]

The Committee may have been justified in taking the view that 'a large proportion of the cases in the county court are simple in character, and the Judge is well able to ascertain the facts, so that it is neither necessary nor advantageous that there should be any legal assistance at all'.[197] However, they were also imbued with a fear of encouraging litigation ('we believe that any scheme which might tend to make people more litigious should be depre-

192 One exception was 'Solicitor', who wrote *English Justice* (London, 1932); see pp. 195–209.
193 *Cook v. Imperial Tobacco Co. Ltd* [1922] 2 KB 158.
194 *Second Report of the Committee on Legal Aid for the Poor, PP* 1928 [Cmd 3016], XI.
195 Evidence, 38th day, PRO LCO 2/981.
196 PRO LCO 2/983.
197 *PP* 1928 [Cmd 3016] XI, p.13.

cated'[198]) and would not even adopt the Judges Council recommendation that the judge should be able to waive court fees.[199] Yet defamation was outside the county court's jurisdiction and nothing in the experience of those, such as the Bentham Committee, who did help the poor assert their rights suggested there would be a great influx of 'hopeless actions'.[200] But then, they were not invited to give evidence and it is difficult to disagree with Jackson's verdict that the Committee's attitude was 'a compound of ignorance and stupidity'.[201]

The Finlay Report undoubtedly reflected the prevailing view in the LCO, which was faced with a real dilemma. Fee income must be maintained or the Treasury would press for increases. If business boomed fees could be reduced, as they were in 1931; but if costs rose, or business slipped, fees had to go up again, as they did in 1936 over the protests of judges and registrars.[202]

In fact the LCO was boxed into a corner. The government would not pay for a public legal aid service; the voluntary scheme could not be extended to the county courts; more business could not be sent into the county courts because the effect would be to deprive the poor of the free representation they might have in the high court. The result was a paradox whereby poor persons were aided only in the most expensive, least suitable forum. It is impossible to guess how many potential actions were stifled by the combination of relatively big court fees, fear of liability for costs and the absence of legal aid, nor how many defendants might have fared better with access to representation, but the Finlay Committee's complacency about county court business was certainly misplaced; a substantial part of it, not least the Rent Acts, was far from simple.

The judicial system was about to face criticism from a more formidable quarter than the champions of the poor. In 1930 the London Chamber of Commerce (LCC) issued a well-researched and carefully argued paper condemning the courts from the

198 *Ibid.*
199 *Ibid.*, p. 14.
200 R. Egerton, Historical Aspects of Legal Aid, *LQR* 61 (1945), 87–94.
201 *Machinery of Justice*, p. 259. Morgan, Introduction of Civil Legal Aid, 50–1, is less severe.
202 PRO LCO 2/1248, 1249, especially Martin to Treasury Secretary, 18 May 1931, Napier to Martin, 28 Jul. 1936.

perspective of the business community as slow, costly and ineffective. Though Schuster was initially dismissive, the LCC initiative proved impossible to brush aside and he soon realised that it could be used to further policy goals of his own.[203] Neither the LCC nor Schuster saw an extension of county court powers as any part of the solution; the LCC, which admitted that its perspective was metropolitan, because it wanted only the best judges and found the London county courts already congested;[204] Schuster because it would revive the legal aid question and encourage further agitation to pay the judges more.

In contrast, Albert Napier, in day-to-day charge of county court business, took a different line, arguing for a modest extension: a £300 limit would, in his view, take 744 cases a year out of the KBD.[205] Most of those who gave evidence to the Hanworth Committee, which was charged with finding ways of improving the higher courts, also favoured some extension, but while the Bar Council trotted out its familiar platitudes with undiminished vigour, the Law Society was equivocal.[206] The Committee was dominated by superior court judges, many sharing Atkin's belief that the proper job of the county court judges was attending to small claims, 'and they should be proud to do it'.[207] Like Finlay's Committee, Hanworth's feared giving any encouragement to the poor to go to law, rejecting county court defamation since 'there is danger in providing too easy access to local courts for petty quarrels'.[208] As for deflecting litigation above £100 value into the county courts by means of the costs sanction, 'the question appears to give its own answer'.[209] All the Hanworth Committee

203 London Chamber of Commerce, *Memorandum on the Expense of Litigation* (London, 1930). On its impact see Abel-Smith and Stevens, *Lawyers and the Courts*, pp. 102–3. Schuster's plans are in 'The Administration of Justice in the Superior Courts of Law', Dec. 1931, PRO LCO 2/1596.

204 Schuster to Sankey, 29 May 1930 and note of meeting with deputation, 6 Nov. 1930, PRO LCO 2/1702.

205 Memo to Hanworth Committee, 18 Mar. 1933, PRO LCO 2/1606 and his evidence in 2/1604. Schuster, acknowledging their differences, suggested that the Committee hear Napier: minutes of meeting on 4 Apr. 1933, 2/1604.

206 Minutes, evidence and other papers are in PRO LCO 2/1597–1604, especially 1600, 1604. Whereas the Liverpool Law Society came out strongly for an extension, the Law Society did not and in its evidence to the Peel Commission (2/1611, paper 126) ignored county courts altogether.

207 Evidence to Peel Commission, qq. 3402–8, PRO LCO 2/1613.

208 *PP* 1933–4 (Cmd 4471) XI, para. 77.

209 *Ibid.*, para. 75.

offered the county courts was jurisdiction in common law matters up to £150, but with no costs sanction above £100; registrars should be able to take disputed cases up to £10 by leave of the judge and with the consent of the parties; and (what Sankey had failed to persuade the Council of Judges to accept) county court appeals to go direct to the Court of Appeal.[210]

No wonder those who sought a wider jurisdiction were downcast and tried vainly to pursue it through the County Courts Amendment Bill.[211] Schuster maintained that, 'except for details, the judicial system of England was as nearly perfect as it could be, and it was important that nothing was done to damage the system'.[212] The only trouble, in his view, was that Hewart LCJ was an incompetent manager of the KBD and was indifferent to litigants' interests. Chiefly to bring pressure to bear on Hewart, the Hanworth Committee was followed by a royal commission (the Peel Commission) on the business of the KBD, which was expected to confine its deliberations to 'reform on conservative and constitutional lines'.[213] As its lay chairman uncomfortably observed, it was packed with lawyers and advocates of wider changes got short shrift, especially as Schuster had the judicial statistics at his fingertips.[214]

The evidence to the Peel Commission is neatly summed up by Jackson: 'in brief it may be said that those connected with the county courts advocated extension of jurisdiction. High court judges and leading barristers opposed extension.'[215] Both investigations operated in a fog of ignorance about the state of the county courts which they did not seek to disperse by asking for detailed statistical returns. Schuster exploited the deficiencies of his own department's publications to expose the inadequacies of F. F. Smith, the registrars' representative, and Judge Snagge's

210 *Ibid.*, paras. 75–8; minutes of Council, 8 Jun. 1931, PRO LCO 2/1266(1). Atkin criticised even the direct appeal to the Court of Appeal for lumbering the latter with trivial matters: *Hansard* 1933–4 5th s., vol. 92 (HL), cols. 789–801.

211 Standing Committee on County Courts (Amendment) Bill, *PP* 1933–4 (65) V.

212 Minutes of Peel Commission meeting, 24 May 1935, PRO LCO 2/1614.

213 Schuster's draft letter to Lord Hanworth, Oct. 1934 and Lord Chancellor's memo to cabinet, CP226(34), PRO LCO 2/1610. The Commission's papers are in 2/1610–17.

214 Minutes of 18 Feb., 29 Mar. 1935, PRO LCO 2/1614.

215 *Machinery of Justice*, pp. 322–3.

ignorance about the speed of business on assize;[216] he did little to enlighten the Commission when they were faced both with complaints of overcrowded courts and the contrary assertion of their judges that the motor car gave them the flexibility to cope with more business.[217]

Despite Schuster's endeavours, the role of the county courts caused the only real uncertainty for most of the Commission, and they finally accepted Walter Monckton's compromise that the concurrent jurisdiction be raised to £300 with an absolute right for the defendant to remove any action above £100 to the high court with no costs sanction; the Hanworth proposal to raise registrars' jurisdiction to £10 was endorsed.[218] Since it was estimated that these changes would result in only 750 cases a year leaving the KBD,[219] it is a mark of the narrow perspective of some of the judges that Lord Roche condemned the proposal as 'an absolute revolution in county court jurisdiction'.[220] And it is a measure of the strength of the judiciary and the bar that, whereas Labour efforts in the Commons to delete the right of removal and to provide legal aid failed, a Lords amendment reducing the extension to £200 was accepted.[221] Allowing for inflation, this barely restored the real value of the concession Rollit had won with such difficulty in 1903, and it was correctly predicted that its effect would be nugatory.[222]

216 PRO LCO 2/1613: qq. 4678–82 (Smith) and 1715–852 (Snagge).

217 *Ibid.* Compare qq. 984 ff. (bar) with 1029–125 (judges).

218 PRO LCO 2/1611, paper 21 and 2/1614, minutes of 24 May, 15 Nov. 1935. The report is *PP* 1935–36 (Cmd 5065) VIII, with the county court recommendations at paras. 192–205; Clement Davies' dissenting note (paras. 42–58) offered a more radical view. The fact that the Bar Council was 'immensely impressed' by the Report (*Hansard* 1937–8 5th s., vol. 335 (HC), cols. 1347–9 (D. Maxwell Fyfe)) is a sure sign that it posed no threat to vested interests.

219 *Hansard* 1937–8 5th s., vol. 107 (HL), cols. 985–7. The proposals were in the Administration of Justice (Miscellaneous Provisions) Bill.

220 *Ibid.*, cols. 977–8. Since Roche had become a high court judge in 1917 it is unlikely that he had seen the inside of a county court since before the Great War.

221 *Hansard* 1937–8 5th s., vol. 338 (HC), cols. 2596–643; vol. 108 (HL), cols. 357–66, 559–67. A private member's bill to raise the jurisdiction to £200 in places where it would not impede the discharge of other business had been presented in 1936 but was dropped after failing to secure government support: PRO LCO 2/1292; *PP* 1935–6 (40) I; *Hansard* 5th s., vol. 308 (HC), col. 503.

222 *LT* 185 (1938), 161. A view borne out by events: *PP* 1948–9 (Cmd 7764) XIV, p. 20 (*Interim Report of the Committee on Supreme Court Practice and Procedure*).

It seemed that while the judges of the county courts could be trusted with statutory powers of appalling complexity, a running down case for a couple of hundred pounds' damages was still reckoned beyond them.[223] Many small debt cases were still taken to the high court for more generous costs, while slanders could not be heard in the only affordable forum. Meanwhile there was a growing tendency for the courts to be bypassed altogether in favour of administrative tribunals, a tendency now threatened to be extended to workmen's compensation.[224] And it was not only those of 'extreme left wing views' who found much to criticise in Schuster's 'nearly perfect' system.[225]

## THE SECOND WORLD WAR

However ill-prepared for war the country was in other respects, a great deal had been done to ensure that a legal framework for wartime conditions would be ready for immediate use.[226] As early as 1935 the Treasury had set discussions in motion, but their notion of giving the courts the extensive power to rewrite contracts which had been contained in Acts of 1917 and 1919 was too drastic for the Lord Chancellor to countenance.[227] In most respects, however, the Courts (Emergency Powers) Act 1939 was like its predecessors in more than name: in particular it had the key provision, in s. 1(4), whereby judgment was not to be enforced against a debtor who was 'unable to meet the debt immediately by reason of circumstances attributable directly or indirectly to the war'.[228]

Despite this close resemblance to previous legislation, the courts were not inclined to rely very much on decisions on the earlier Acts,[229] so the scope and meaning of the new Act had to be

[223] A point made by Judge Snagge: PRO LCO 2/1613 at q. 1715.

[224] Bartrip, *Workmen's Compensation*, pp. 168–71. This was proposed by the TUC to a royal commission set up in 1938, but its deliberations were suspended without a report in 1940.

[225] 'Barrister', *Justice in England* (1938), so described by R. M. Jackson *MLR* 2 (1938–9), p. 251.

[226] Kent, *In on the Act*, pp. 107–11.

[227] Schuster to Hopkins, 31 Mar. 1938, PRO LCO 2/1353.

[228] There is a good summary of the 1939 and 1940 Acts by P. H. Thorold Rogers in The Courts (Emergency Powers) Acts 1939 and 1940: a View in Retrospect, *Conv.* ns 5 (1940–1), 4–23.

[229] *Ibid.*, 4–5.

determined afresh. In *A v. B*[230] it was emphasised that the policy of the legislation was to protect debtors, not to encourage the distribution of their assets by a sort of quasi-bankruptcy, and that the protection was from execution not obligations. Notwithstanding this there were many feckless persons who felt that they had entered a 'debtors' paradise' where their liabilities would fall magically from their shoulders;[231] a feature of this sort of protection which the LCO disliked from the outset was that it encouraged debtors to wish away the day of reckoning.

Further decisions cascaded from the higher courts to inform the proceedings in the lower, where some registrars and a few judges could still remember applying the Great War Acts.[232] This war posed altogether more complex problems though, one of the most difficult being the service of summonses, for in addition to the familiar cases where servicemen were overseas, there was now the mass migration of civilians and the complete dislocation of whole areas by bombing.[233] Personal service, even where it was practicable at all, was costly and slow, while substituted or postal service might well fail to come to the defendant's attention. It was a situation open to exploitation by the unscrupulous, and Napier, on whom the making of rules devolved, was therefore wary of acceding too readily to the deluge of creditors' complaints, though many of them were plainly justified.[234]

Landlords were particularly aggrieved, and through the National Federation of Property Owners clamoured for concessions going beyond the rules of November 1939 which had put them, with mortgagees and hire purchase creditors, in a privileged position.[235] There were severe delays in some of the London courts and many tenants could not be traced to be served with possession summonses; East-enders had understandably decamped in large numbers, leaving their homes locked behind them. Many county court judges sympathised with the landlords'

230 [1940] 1 KB 217.

231 Rogers, The Courts (Emergency Powers) Acts 1939 and 1940, 7–9.

232 Master Mosse commented that 'the output of these decisions continues with unrivalled and undesirable prolixity': *LJ* 90 (1940), 4.

233 Predicted in *LJ* 87 (1939), 406–7. For the problem of servicemen see PRO LCO 2/1321 and 2858 (especially F. Axmann to Napier, 17 Feb. 1940).

234 Examples are in PRO LCO 2/1355.

235 County Courts (Emergency Powers) (no. 2) Rules 1939/1610 (L27), summarised in *SJ* 83 (1939).

plight and since government departments and the armed forces were implacably opposed to providing information for tracing debtors, the cabinet was warned that the Lord Chancellor might have to propose special legislation.[236] To compound the difficulties, hire purchase firms, for whom there was less sympathy, were equally anxious to be able to repossess the furniture locked away in empty houses.[237] Indecision in fact prevailed for so long that the problem solved itself as the tenants drifted back to their homes.[238]

Sheer pragmatism, as well as justice to creditors, dictated a more relaxed approach to the use of postal service, for court wages were too low to retain those able-bodied bailiffs who were not called up,[239] and when they lost their petrol ration in 1943 the service became so inefficient that a shift in emphasis was unavoidable. Registrars however remained commendably determined to protect defendants and a sharp circular had to be sent urging them to follow the approved line.[240]

While the Emergency Powers Acts offered protection for ordinary debts and the Rent Acts were easily adapted to assist tenants in wartime, there was now a much larger class of home-owners who were vulnerable because of the very strong legal powers of mortgagees. Masters and county court judges had long been aware that some mortgagees (building societies among them) were quick and ruthless in exercising their rights,[241] and if proof were needed that they could not be relied upon to be more compassionate in wartime, cases like *Temperance BS v. Nevitt*[242] soon provided it; consequently Acts and rules had several times to be amended in the mortgagor's favour.[243]

To these national problems were added local ones. When invasion threatened after Dunkirk great stretches of the south and east coasts were declared 'evacuation zones', from which civilians

236 PRO LCO 2/2680.

237 *Ibid.*, and 2/2681, especially Napier to R. C. L. Gregory, 23 Sep. 1943.

238 PRO LCO 2/1680.

239 Coldstream's note of 13 Mar. 1941, *ibid.*

240 Circular of 26 Sep. 1944, PRO LCO 2/3280.

241 The means whereby the courts 'tempered the winds to the shorn lamb' are summarised in the *Payne Report*.

242 [1940] 3 All ER 237.

243 Possession of Mortgaged Land (Emergency Powers) Act 1939; PRO LCO 2/1378; Courts (Emergency Powers) Act 1942 (see *LJ* 92 (1942), 354).

on non-essential work were cleared and a moratorium declared for all those who were thereby deprived of the beneficial use of their property.[244] The LCO deplored such undiscriminating approaches to debts and some of the judges were also unenthusiastic; in Sussex, Archer (who decried the whole evacuation programme and had to be told to desist from publicly criticising it[245]) did his best to wreck it by holding that merely storing furniture was a substantial benefit.[246] But at the insistence of the Home Office, both the evacuated areas policy and the moratorium were maintained long after the invasion threat had passed despite cogent LCO objections that the longer the day of reckoning was put off for debtors the greater would be the political difficulties when they had to meet their obligations at last.[247]

It was to this end that the LCO devised the imaginative and far-sighted scheme embodied in the Liabilities (War-time Adjustment) Acts. Loosely based on administration orders, this 'kind of preventive bankruptcy without stigma'[248] invited a person in money difficulties not to wait passively for the roof to fall in but to take his troubles to a Liabilities Adjustment Officer (LAO). The LAO would compile a schedule of debts and negotiate with creditors for their orderly liquidation or for a temporary suspension of payments until the debtor was in a position to start discharging them, the sanction behind the LAO being the coercive power of the county court to impose a settlement.

Some commentators were enthusiastic about the scheme but others, among them several very experienced registrars, were deeply sceptical, and the sceptics were proved right.[249] In the first six months only 940 applications were accepted,[250] and though narrow interpretations of the Act by the Court of Appeal and

244 Courts (Emergency Powers) (Evacuated Areas) Rules 1940/1421 (L21).

245 A. Johnston (Ministry of Home Affairs) to Napier, 10 Dec. 1940, PRO LCO 2/2726.

246 Coldstream to H. S. Kent (PCO), 24 Sep. 1941, *ibid*.

247 PRO LCO 2/2726.

248 Napier to T. Barnes, 10 Jan. 1941, PRO LCO 2/1400. The scheme was produced by the Wartime Liabilities sub-committee.

249 'Sired by eyewash out of least resistance': Gilbert Hicks to Napier, 19 Feb. 1941, PRO LCO 2/1400. M. Harnik jnr in M. Finer, The Liabilities (War-time Adjustment) Act 1941, *MLR* 5 (1941–2), 125–8 was especially enthusiastic; see also P. H. Thorold Rogers, The Liabilities (War-time Adjustment) Act 1941, *Conv*. ns 6 (1941–2), 31–49.

250 PRO LCO 2/2759.

some LAOs were partly responsible,[251] the real problem was more fundamental, mirroring the disappointments experienced with administration orders. If this was 'a prodigal's charter',[252] prodigals were singularly lacking in the wit to take advantage of it, notwithstanding efforts to publicise its virtues.[253]

More than anything, the attempt to sell the scheme to debtors probably foundered on the inability to bring debts owed to public bodies within its compass. The utilities continued to coerce through disconnections;[254] the Ministry of Health seemed minded to allow rates to be included, only to retreat at the last minute, leaving the civil servant who had committed them embarrassed and angry;[255] above all, the Inland Revenue were impregnable in refusing to abandon their priority.[256] In consequence, a painstakingly crafted amending Act, which it was hoped would also ease the transition from the moratorium, proved ineffective.[257]

As in the Great War, county court business tumbled, from 1,121,202 suits in 1939 to 236,625 in 1945,[258] but that at least made it easier to economise and to cope with the shortage of manpower and materials. Early closing became the rule,[259] some London courts were amalgamated and little-used provincial ones closed, along with High Wycombe, after an unseemly squabble ended with the judge finding himself locked out.[260] While the LCO struggled on from the House of Lords with whatever staff it could obtain (among them Judge Austin Jones from Westminster) the county courts branch took up safer quarters in Thame, issuing a stream of circulars imposing whatever economies could be

251 Judge Konstam to Napier, 27 Mar. 1942, *ibid.*

252 *LJ* 91 (1941), 125.

253 *SJ* 86 (1942), 369; *SJ* 87 (1943), 1.

254 Finer, The Liabilities (War-time Adjustment) Act 1941, 120–5. Disconnections had figured strongly in the debates on the Courts (Emergency Powers) Amendment Bill in 1940: *Hansard* 1939–40 5th s., vol. 362 (HC), cols. 935–70.

255 A. N. C. Shelley to Napier, 8 Jul. 1944, PRO LCO 2/3610.

256 Minutes of inter-departmental committee, 19, 26 May 1944, PRO LCO 2/3419.

257 *LJ* 94 (1944), 283–4. But Judge Gerald Hurst was one who thought it useful: *Closed Chapters*, p. 153.

258 No civil judicial statistics were issued as Parliamentary papers. Bald summaries can be found in the legal press.

259 County Court (no. 2) Rules 1939/1351 (L22).

260 County Court Districts (no. 2) Order 1943/1283 (L24); *SJ* 86 (1942), 261.

devised.[261] Happily, as the Law Society found, most judges and registrars were not disposed to insist on formalities where their absence did not prejudice litigants and co-operativeness seems to have been the rule.[262]

Some judges undertook other duties, which led rather curiously to the only casualty among them, Judge Edwin Burgis, shot and wounded by a would-be conscientious objector whose claim he had rejected.[263] Death from natural causes claimed the two judges who, in different ways, epitomised the best of the lower bench: Parry, author, playwright and passionate opponent of imprisonment for debt,[264] and Cluer, 'an intellectual giant' who bent his intellect to doing 'justice administered among the poor as it ought to be administered; with sympathy and insight, and without a shred of mercy towards those who sought to oppress them'.[265]

These two died in the dark days of the war but by 1944 the sunlit uplands were visible on the horizon and with attention turning to the reconstruction of British institutions it was inevitable that the legal system would again come under scrutiny. For the county courts it was likely to be an eventful centenary.[266]

261 PRO LCO 8/6.

262 *LSG* 37 (1940), 117.

263 Hurst, *Closed Chapters*, p. 28. Burgis recovered and remained a judge until his death in 1950.

264 *LT* 196 (1943), 220; *SJ* 87 (1943), 433; *LJ* 93 (1943), 394.

265 *SJ* 86 (1942), 23.

266 Among many articles see *LJ* 93 (1943), 34, 54; C. P. Harvey, Law Reform after the War, *MLR* 6 (1943), 39–46; *Solicitor* 11 (1944), 21–2, 146; *LJ* 95 (1945), 68.

# 5

# 'PATCHING UP THE COURTS'

## TINKERING WITH THE MACHINERY OF JUSTICE

Reform of the courts was in the air again at the end of the war, with a lively correspondence in *The Times* in 1944[1] and a continuing debate on legal aid,[2] but it was not a high priority for Attlee's government, which preferred for the most part to create tribunals to deal with new entitlements and disputes.[3]

Tribunals were a familiar feature of wartime emergency legislation and now even the courts' role in deciding purely private disputes was being questioned. The Uthwatt Committee on Tenure and Rents of Business Premises, for example, while reluctantly giving jurisdiction over its scheme to the county court, had wished to find a way of 'avoiding as far as possible the atmosphere of litigation associated with its normal procedure'.[4] Another committee was able to keep the fixing of 'fair rents' for controlled housing away from the courts, though most county court judges were happy to lose that, having quite enough to do with possession cases.[5] Still, the lack of confidence in their

1 *LSG* 41 (1944), 150; *Solicitor* 11 (1944), 21–2, 146. For other examples see Abel-Smith and Stevens, *Lawyers and the Courts*, p. 247 n. 1.

2 'It would be difficult to find another subject which has attracted a similar amount of attention in late years': E. J. Cohn, The Political Parties and Legal Aid, *MLR* 8 (1945), 97–117 at 97 n. 2, listing recent articles.

3 Abel-Smith and Stevens, *Lawyers and the Courts*, pp. 258–61, 285. A comparison between the first and second editions of W. A. Robson, *Justice and Administrative Law* (London, 1931, 1947) shows the growth of tribunals.

4 *PP* 1948–9 [Cmd 7706] XII, interim report, p. 95. The final report (*PP* 1950 [Cmd 7982] XII) proposed the county courts until it could be seen how the new Lands Tribunal was working.

5 The Ridley Report (*PP* 1944–5 [Cmd 6641] V) recommended tribunals and the Act creating them was vainly opposed by lawyers: *Hansard* 1945–6 5th s., vol. 415 (HC), cols. 1938–2011.

capacity was worrying, especially when it also deprived them of workmen's compensation,[6] felt by the *Solicitor* to be the harbinger of 'a process [which], if allowed to continue indefinitely, would eventually lead to the Courts becoming quiet backwaters, like Doctors' Commons at the beginning of the 19th century'.[7] It did not happen, but the anxiety was understandable.

At the same time the Lord Chancellor's Department (LCD) (as the Office was becoming more generally known) belatedly became aware that their policy of seeking to move civil actions out of the magistrates' courts and into the county courts was being undermined by local Acts obtained by councils and statutory undertakers allowing them to recover debts in courts of summary jurisdiction,[8] a facility more important, and more contentious, now that local authorities had extended their activities to the 'trading field', e.g. in the supply of central heating equipment.[9] A similar clause had been removed from the Crown Proceedings Bill in 1947[10] but the parliamentary counsel declined to take action on local bills, where there were precedents of long standing.[11]

While law reform was not a priority for Labour, it certainly did not intend to be inactive. In September 1945 a cabinet committee was set up with Jowitt, the Lord Chancellor, as chairman. It decided against a royal commission ranging across the whole field of civil justice with a remit extending to state-controlled legal services and fusion of the professions, opting instead for more limited inquiries, beginning with the most

[6] National Insurance (Industrial Injuries) Act 1946 (9 & 10 Geo. VI c. 62); Bartrip, *Workmen's Compensation*, pp. 212–13. The legislation was based on the Beveridge Report (*PP* 1942–3 [Cmd 6404, 6405] VI), para. 98, but neither the Report nor the critical account by Wilson and Levy (*Workmen's Compensation*) lends any support to the Labour MP quoted by Abel-Smith and Stevens, *Lawyers and the Courts*, p. 259 as claiming that county court judges were not always sympathetic to workmen.

[7] 11 (1944), 146. As the *Law Times* noted (203 (1947), 224), the growth of tribunals threatened the county courts more than the high court.

[8] Correspondence with Sir Cecil Carr, 1946, in PRO LCO 2/3151, and with the Home Office in 2/3047.

[9] A. Napier to G. Ram, 18 Mar. 1947, PRO LCO 2/3151.

[10] J. A. Stainton to Napier, 24 Mar. 1947, *ibid.*

[11] D. W. Dobson to Stainton, 17 Jan. 1949, *ibid.* For examples see PRO LCO 2/3147 (Manchester Corporation Bill 1944), 2/3150 (Long Eaton UDC Bill 1946) and 2/3179 (Salford Corporation Bill 1948).

clamorous demands, for a new divorce procedure and the review of legal aid.[12]

Divorce was the more urgent, as 'the avalanche of divorce suits now being brought is barely being held in check by the Divorce judges in London and the Provinces and by the King's Bench judges in the Provinces, and that only by the adoption of *ad hoc* expedients'.[13] The cabinet thereupon set up the Denning Committee, whose speed and clarity almost justify the hyberbole its chairman used in his reminiscences.[14]

At first sight it is curious that the Committee, like the recent Wedgwood Committee of 1943 on provincial divorce arrangements,[15] rejected the obvious solution of depositing undefendeds in the county courts.[16] Jowitt admitted that the most commonly urged objection, 'that [it] would endanger an essential feature of divorce – uniformity of decision and practice',[17] was greatly exaggerated and some of the cabinet, notably Bevan, strongly favoured it, but there was almost hysterical opposition from the President of the Probate, Divorce and Admiralty Division (PDA) and predictable protest from the divorce bar, fearful lest they lose exclusive audience. In the event Denning proposed a truly British compromise.[18] A whole host of 'Special Divorce Commissioners'[19] was to be appointed, among them the whole of the county court bench (excepting any who had conscientious scruples); they would sit in their own courtrooms, specially designated, would change

12 Stevens, *Independence of the Judiciary*, p. 114; Coldstream's draft memorandum of 20 Oct. 1945, PRO LCO 2/3927.

13 Coldstream's memo, PRO LCO 2/3927.

14 *The Due Process of Law* (London, 1980), pp. 191–3; Stevens, *Independence of the Judiciary*, pp. 114–16. The reports are *PP* 1945–6 [Cmd 6881, 6945] XIII and *PP* 1946–7 [Cmd 7024] XIII.

15 *PP* 1942–3 [Cmd 6480] V, para. 28. Judge Finnemore amended the draft, adding that it would dislocate county court business if they took defended divorces (PRO LCO 2/4172). Schuster was adamantly opposed and the Committee decided very early in its deliberations that it would not even be desirable to use county court judges to do divorce as commissioners of assize; they heard the views of supporters only as a matter of form: Wedgwood to Schuster, 18 Jan. 1943, PRO LCO 2/4172.

16 *PP* 1945–6 [Cmd 6945] XIII, p. 7.

17 Retreating from the position he had taken in an earlier paper: Stevens, *Independence of the Judiciary*, p. 114.

18 Stevens, *Independence of the Judiciary*, pp. 114–16; S. M. Cretney, 'Tell Me the Old, Old Story' – the Denning Report 50 Years On, *Child and Family Law Quarterly* 7 (1995), 163–79.

19 The phrase seems to have originated with Granville Ram: PRO LCO 2/4197.

their purple robes for black and be paid piecework rates for their labour.[20] Though this charade was criticised in Parliament and the press,[21] it served its immediate purpose and was perpetuated by the Morton Commission in the 1950s, which agreed that the sanctity of marriage was in some mysterious way reinforced by having its dissolution pronounced by a judge in black rather than one in purple.[22]

Divorce and legal aid were closely linked, though it was not yet appreciated quite how voraciously the appetite for divorce would gnaw away at the legal aid fund. The Rushcliffe Report on Legal Aid and Advice was waiting for Jowitt and embodied a pretty wide consensus that legal aid should be available for county court, as well as high court actions, though there was some unwillingness to extend it to judgment summonses and cases where only the mode of payment was in question. However, both the practical complications of preparing a workable scheme and the difficulty of finding space in the legislative programme led to a considerable delay in implementation which the beleaguered Treasury was almost alone in welcoming.[23]

Meanwhile the law reform programme had moved onto its next stage, yet another investigation into costs and delays in litigation. It was not to be comprehensive, for it omitted to deal with the civil business of the magistrates' courts,[24] and it would not have a 'free hand' because the Treasury made it clear at the outset that utopian projects involving public funds were off-limits.[25] Jowitt and his officials further limited its scope by creating separate committees to consider the high court and the county courts, chaired by Lord Evershed MR and Mr Justice Austin Jones respectively.[26] Unlike the inter-war inquiries, each contained a

[20] Correspondence with county court judges on the proposed arrangements is in PRO LCO 2/3952–6.

[21] Abel-Smith and Stevens, *Lawyers and the Courts*, p. 323.

[22] *PP* 1955–6 [Cmd 9678] XXIII. Paragraphs 748–51 deal perfunctorily with county court divorce, adopting the views of the Gorell Commission of 1912. For a critical account of the Commission see O. R. McGregor, *Divorce in England* (London, 1957).

[23] *PP* 1944–5 [Cmd 6641] V, especially paras. 162–5. For a rare dissenting voice see C. Mullins, Legal Aid ad infinitum, *LJ* 95 (1945), 215–16. The Conservative party's view was in *Looking Ahead*: see *Solicitor* 12 (1945), 50–1.

[24] Note by Coldstream and Napier, 13 May 1947, PRO LCO 2/3293.

[25] Correspondence in PRO LCO 2/3929.

[26] Stevens, *Independence of the Judiciary*, p. 116. Austin Jones had recently been

substantial minority of laymen, but it was always intended that the real work would be done by the lawyers,[27] and the more independently minded laymen on the Evershed Committee were reduced to impotence by restrictive directions from Jowitt, by the conservatism of the chairman and Coldstream's watchful eye.[28]

The decision to give the High Court Committee responsibility for considering how far the limits of county courts jurisdiction should be raised[29] made it predictable that any increase would be modest, especially since their interim report on this question was produced when the caseload of the high court was easily manageable.[30] This report, the product of a working party under Mr Justice Lynskey, found the bar (to no-one's surprise) opposed to any extension and the Law Society mostly concerned with securing more generous costs. Though the County Courts Committee had confirmed that a rise to £500 could be accommodated,[31] Lynskey's choice was only £350,[32] though he also proposed to end the absolute right to transfer any claim over £100 to the high court. The Committees also differed over the costs for plaintiffs securing judgment under RSC order 14, and here again the unwillingness of masters and judges to deny suitors the high court option prevailed.[33] The interim report did not appear until August 1949, shortly after the final report of the County Courts Committee, but the Evershed Committee ploughed doggedly on for another three years with diminishing returns, allowing the momentum of court reform to fade.

promoted from the county court, the first since 1920. He was 'domesticated', having been seconded to the LCO during the war, where he was in charge of the Liabilities (War-time Adjustment) Acts.

27 Jowitt to J. A. Pugh, 17 Mar. 1947, PRO LCO 2/3293, makes this clear. Minutes of the legal sub-committee are in 2/3296.

28 Stevens, *Independence of the Judiciary*, pp. 116–17. See the dissents appended to the final report: *PP* 1952–3 [Cmd 8746] XIV. Coldstream set himself to stop the committee 'pursuing hopeless hares' (PRO LCO 2/3929), and cf. 'scheme of work', 31 Jan. 1949, 2/3931.

29 Jones to Jowitt, 22 Apr. 1947 and Coldstream's reply, 22 Apr. 1947, PRO LCO 2/3293.

30 *PP* 1948–9 [Cmd 7764] XIV.

31 Calculations in PRO LCO 2/3295, sent to the Evershed Committee.

32 *PP* 1948–9 [Cmd 7764] XIV, pt II, paras. 27–8. Papers of sub-committee 'A' are in PRO LCO 2/3968, minutes in 2/4029.

33 *PP* 1948–9 [Cmd 7668] XIII, paras. 104–9; memo to Evershed Committee, PRO LCO 2/3293; minutes, 15 Jun. 1948, 2/3296; discussion on draft report, 2/3304. For the masters' attitudes see Evershed sub-committee 'B', 2/4001–4.

The Austin Jones Committee faced fewer problems, technical and 'political', but one reason why it needed less time was the unexpected level of indifference and apathy among those whom it consulted. The county courts superintendent found it 'the most surprising thing about county court work today, how indifferent people are'[34] and when the chairman, anxiously trying to get at the feelings of that habitually under-represented group, the debtors, questioned the National Council for Social Service he was surprised to find them claiming that there were 'few grumbles'.[35] Even the organisations representing regular plaintiffs were unusually moderate in their tone, so it is no wonder that Coldstream reported that 'Mr Justice Jones has got it firmly into his head that there is nothing whatever wrong with the county court system, and that the less interference there is, the better for all concerned.'[36]

In fact, although the primary object of the Committee was to seek ways of cheapening the county courts,[37] they found that most complaints were not about cost but delay, and in particular adjournments. This was considered serious and urgent, since although practically confined to the busier courts, in London in particular adjournments had reached an unacceptable level: 1,335 in 1947 out of 23,189 defended cases heard by a judge.[38] It was therefore decided to tackle them in an interim report.

Naturally, users tended to blame the courts for unrealistic and inflexible listing while the registrars and judges blamed solicitors for being ill-prepared.[39] The Committee had no dramatic solution to offer, but agreed with the ACCR that it was 'a matter for good teamwork'[40] and suggested that the key to the problem lay in the clerk of the court systematically reviewing the state of all cases in the list one week beforehand; large and small cases should be kept apart and nothing should normally be listed after 12.30 pm. In addition, the telephone should be regarded as a useful aid to be

34 Evidence of 27 Jan. 1948, PRO LCO 2/3299.
35 Evidence of 10 Feb. 1948, *ibid.*
36 To Napier, 17 Jan. 1948, PRO LCO 2/3295.
37 Jowitt to J. A. Pugh, 17 Mar. 1947, PRO LCO 2/3293.
38 *PP* 1947–8 [Cmd 7468] XI.
39 Compare e.g. Barristers' Clerks Association with Registrar D. Freeman Coutts, PRO LCO 2/3300.
40 Memorandum of evidence in PRO LCO 2/3295.

exploited, not a nuisance to be kept secret.[41] All this was innocuous enough, but at the end of the report was a recommendation that the LCD should seek quarterly returns to enable it to ensure that timely assistance was provided when a backlog developed.[42] This suggestion did not come from the Department, and when a circular was duly sent to those courts which seemed to be falling behind, it

> raised rather a storm and was generally taken objection to. The reason may have been the wording of the letter but I am inclined to think it was rather the essence of the scheme itself, which is bureaucratic in the extreme and is an attempt at central interference in the administration of the courts, which is primarily the concern of the judges and registrars.[43]

Returns continued to be sought but were not systematically acted upon.[44]

The main Report, appearing a year later, was equally undramatic,[45] almost every relatively radical suggestion (such as Martin's to combine default and ordinary summonses in a single form) failing to survive the sceptical scrutiny of the sub-committee which really ran the show.[46] To its own surprise the Committee found that there was no anxiety to make the courts' atmosphere and process more informal,[47] though many witnesses were contemptuous of the capacity of litigants to understand even the simplest thing; said Judge Gamon 'you cannot treat the ordinary county court person as a middle class person; that kind of person is absolutely feckless and hopeless'; his registrar Cohen, opposed to him on many things, added 'you cannot explain things to people. They drive you mad.'[48] To the Committee's relief, voluntary bodies testified that county court officials were in fact

[41] *PP* 1947–8 [Cmd 7468] XI, paras. 12–23. Coldstream still had some doubts about encouraging its use: evidence of B. Humfrey, 13 Jan. 1948, PRO LCO 2/3299.

[42] *PP* 1947–8 [Cmd 7468] XI, para. 23.

[43] Note by R. Rieu, 1949, PRO LCO 2/3307.

[44] PRO LCO 2/3307–10; Polden, Judicial Independence, part one, 14–15.

[45] *PP* 1948–9 [Cmd 7668] XIII. It was greeted with lukewarm approval, e.g. 'much to commend and little at which to cavil', *LT* 207 (1949), 291–3.

[46] Minutes of sub-committee, PRO LCO 2/3296. See 2/3294 for the 'beehive' of suggestions, with their fate annotated.

[47] They were impressed with the evidence of Cambridge House on this point (PRO LCO 2/3300); Coldstream to Jowitt, 5 Mar. 1948, 2/3293; *Austin Jones Report*, para. 53.

[48] Evidence of 9 Mar., 6 Apr. 1948, PRO LCO 2/3300.

helpful and patient, but the safeguards for debtors of the lower class could not, it seemed, be safely removed in order to streamline debt collection and reduce costs.[49] Even the recommendation that postal service should become the normal mode was strongly opposed by some registrars and by the county courts branch[50] after the retirement of Martin, who supported it and regarded the bailiffs as 'a little Victorian'.[51] Furthermore in some areas where the Committee might have wished to act it was not a free agent. It was prepared to relax the rules of evidence but had to adopt a more cautious line to accord with the Evershed Committee,[52] and might have investigated attachment of wages had not Coldstream warned them off, saying that it 'would arouse the most acute political controversy'.[53]

In the narrower world of the law even some of their modest recommendations were controversial. It was rousing a sleeping but surly dog to suggest the repeal of the prohibition on solicitor-advocates, even though the barristers on the Committee were strangely complaisant.[54] It was contentious to demand more effective powers to bring debtors into court for examination of means, since that was inextricably bound up with the question of committals which the Committee studiously ignored.[55] Even raising the registrar's jurisdiction to £20 with the judge's leave and absent any objection from the parties was opposed by the bar.[56] The Committee found its main object, to find ways of reducing the cost of litigation, very difficult.[57] Though it was

49 PRO LCO 2/3299, 3300; *Austin Jones Report*, paras. 20–1.

50 *Austin Jones Report*, paras. 30–9. Registrars Hicks and Marshall fought a rearguard action on the sub-committee (PRO LCO 2/3296, e.g. 1 June 1948). The views of the county courts branch are in 2/3317; Coldstream described some of their arguments as 'highly specious'.

51 PRO LCO 2/3299.

52 Minutes of 19 Oct. 1948, PRO LCO 2/3296. The cautious recommendations in the Report (paras. 54–61) were greatly praised in the legal press, e.g. *SJ* 93 (1949), 272; *LJ* 99 (1949), 241–3, 255–6.

53 Minutes of 20 Jan. 1948, PRO LCO 2/3296. See also 9 Mar., 23 Nov. 1948, showing the chairman as very apprehensive on this score.

54 *Austin Jones Report*, para. 50. At para. 52 it is proposed to allow managing clerks to appear in chambers, as they already could in the high court. In 1950 T. G. Lund, the Law Society's secretary, was told that the barristers on the Committee had opposed it, but there is no record of that in the minutes.

55 *Ibid.*, paras. 77–86. Para. 77 was a late insertion, based on a report by Judge Davies to the Committee: 21 Dec. 1948, PRO LCO 2/3296.

56 *Austin Jones Report*, para. 9; Bar Council's evidence, PRO LCO 2/3299.

57 Minutes of 20 Apr. 1948, PRO LCO 2/3296.

hoped that the freer acceptance of affidavit evidence and other procedural changes might have some economical effect, it came down largely to considering reductions in court fees and lawyers' costs. With mighty labour the Committee devised a new fees table, the main feature of which was the abolition of the hearing fee, the plaint fee being raised to compensate; overall however there could be no significant reduction without enlarging the state's subsidy, for, as Martin explained, 'the business of the county courts is of much higher class than formerly. The good business does not pay for itself and it never has done. It is the routine business ... that has always paid for the costs of administration.'[58]

Lawyers' costs proved equally intractable. The Law Society's slowness in getting its evidence together was a handicap,[59] especially as the Committee was not itself very well informed about practice, initially failing to appreciate that many solicitors acted under specific agreements with their clients, which made the taxation of costs irrelevant.[60] On the whole judges regarded lawyers benignly and wanted a wide discretion to depart from the scale where a case proved complex or demanding; their registrars for the most part opposed this, feeling that judges were too much inclined to generosity.[61] A new scale was rather unconvincingly put together but only Gilbert Hicks, notorious for his meanness towards solicitors, was fully persuaded of its merits.[62]

An official summed up the Committee's labours thus: 'The Committee have made 87 recommendations of which 19 would require legislation, 43 would necessitate amendments to the county court rules, 11 would be dealt with by administrative action and 5 would need other actions such as the prescribing of a new fees order. The remaining 9 recommendations do not involve

58 PRO LCO 2/3299; *Austin Jones Report*, paras. 121–8 and app. VI.

59 Not presented until 27 July 1948 and heavily criticised by registrars Hicks and Marshall: minutes of 13, 27 July 1948, PRO LCO 2/3296.

60 Evidence of H. B. Surridge and C. K. Duthie, PRO LCO 2/3300, and see 2/3318.

61 PRO LCO 2/3295 (Council of Judges); cf. G. Hicks (4 Nov. 1947, 2/3296) and the ACCR representatives' evidence in 2/3299.

62 Hicks remained 'quite impenitent about the rejection of a single scale and the provision of low charges for mere uncontested debt cases' (PRO LCO 2/3318). The latter were quite at variance with the views of the Rushcliffe Committee (*PP* 1944–5 [Cmd 6641] V, para. 98).

any changes in the present system.'[63] Most proposals were seen as uncontroversial, though some, on the law of evidence and an ending to wartime emergency legislation, had to await the determinations of the Evershed Committee. Contentious ones included the costs proposals, involving substantial reductions in undefended cases, and the power to bring judgment debtors forcibly to court for examination.[64] Many of the straightforward recommendations were rapidly implemented through the revived Rule Committee,[65] though its attempt to extend judges' powers over recalcitrant judgment debtors, despite Coldstream's warning that Jowitt was personally opposed to it, resulted in the first exercise of the Lord Chancellor's power to disallow a proposed rule.[66]

The times were unpropitious for any legal reform which threatened to increase calls on the Exchequer. Postal service of process had to be postponed,[67] and much more important, the legal aid scheme, though it was not axed, limped in maimed by the sacrifice of the county courts.[68] This had a paradoxical effect on the proposals for widening county court jurisdiction. If the county court became the prescribed forum parties would be denied legal aid and for that reason, where they did have a choice, it would seldom be the county court, with the result that the legal aid fund would be saddled with the bill for a costlier high court action. Though the Chancellor of the Exchequer disingenuously affected not to see the connection between the two proposals,[69] everyone else did, and Lord Chief Justice Goddard was adamant that any widening of county court jurisdiction must await the extension of legal aid.[70]

The legal aid scheme also added a new dimension to the sensitive question of lawyers' costs. The Law Society mounted a

63 File note, Apr. 1949, PRO LCO 2/3312. 64 *Ibid.*

65 PRO LCO 2/3315–16, 3321. Most were in the County Court (Amendment) Rules 1950 (SI 1231/L21), on which see GMB in *SJ* 94 (1950), 543–6. For the revival of the Rule Committee see pp. 221–2 below.

66 See p. 225 below.

67 J. I. C. Crombie to Napier, 15 Jan. 1949, R. Rieu to Judge Hancock, 21 Nov. 1949, PRO LCO 2/3321.

68 Announced to Parliament on 14 Nov. 1949: *Hansard* 1948–9 5th s., vol. 469 (HC), cols. 1658–61.

69 To Lord Chancellor Simonds, 20 Dec. 1951, PRO LCO 2/4980, rejecting the bid to extend legal aid, costed at £100,000 p. a.

70 Rieu to Napier, 8 Oct. 1951, and correspondence with Goddard and L. Heald, Nov. 1951, PRO LCO 2/4980.

formidable campaign against the Austin Jones costs proposals and a more searching investigation convinced him that his Committee had gone wrong.[71] Unfortunately the implication of that admission was that a more generous provision must be made, undermining any hopes of achieving the stated aim of the Committee to reduce the cost of going to law,[72] and in the end the Law Society had to be fended off with the promise of a full review as soon as legal aid was extended to the county courts.[73] Nor could court fees be reduced, or even held down, for the Treasury was demanding a renewed effort to close the gap between fee income and the cost of the courts, and since the Evershed Committee had not come out uncompromisingly against the view that the litigants should largely pay for the service,[74] the LCD could hardly stand out against increases to compensate for inflation. Since it had also to deal with insistent demands for a judges' pay rise,[75] it is hardly surprising that legislation to implement even the less contentious proposals was put off.

It was not until 1954 that the log-jam broke. First Churchill proved accommodating over judges' salaries, then the imminence of a general election opened the Treasury coffers for an expansion of the legal aid scheme.[76] By now the Evershed Committee had finished its deliberations and its final report covered two tricky and related matters. Embarrassing delays in the QBD as litigation boomed reconciled Evershed to sending more matters into the county courts and, since experience had shown that the existing costs sanctions were not effective, it was proposed to strengthen them by imposing a 'gateway' into the high court with the masters as gatekeepers, entry being allowed to actions within the county court limits only on showing special cause.[77] The *quid pro quo* was to be a wider appeal from the county courts.

[71] PRO LCO 2/3318. On 18 Apr. 1949 Coldstream noted 'obviously we are in for a battle', 2/3319.

[72] The dilemma is well explained in correspondence with Judge J. D. Hurst, PRO LCO 2/3318.

[73] PRO LCO 2/4975, leading to County Court Fees Order 1956 (501 L4); Rieu to Hicks, 12 Nov. 1953, 2/5035.

[74] Neither had the Austin Jones Committee, though the chairman had some inclinations that way: minutes of 8 Jun. 1948, PRO LCO 2/3296.

[75] Stevens, *Independence of the Judiciary*, pp. 119–25; PRO LCO 2/4979–82.

[76] Stevens, *Independence of the Judiciary*, p. 125; Abel-Smith and Stevens, *Lawyers and the Courts*, p. 333.

[77] *Final Report* (*PP* 1952–3 [Cmd 8746] XIV), section VI.

Appeals were a problem Evershed had found 'one of obstinate difficulty . . . which has given rise to a remarkable diversity of view amongst the witnesses whose opinions we sought'.[78] With county court judges strongly against appeals on questions of fact and the Lord Chief Justice and the bar equally forceful in favour, the Committee compromised by confining them to actions above £200, excluding landlord and tenant cases involving judgments on 'greater hardship' etc.[79]

In 1954 two bills were put in hand, one (which became the County Courts Act 1955) dealing with Austin Jones' Report, the other (the Administration of Justice Act 1956) with Evershed's. The issues which proved difficult were: the limit of jurisdiction; sanctions; appeals; the number of judges; the strengthening of judges' powers; and registrars' powers.[80]

Inflation had rendered the Evershed proposal for £350 out of date, but while Coldstream was prepared to go to £1,000, the Lord Chief Justice balked at even £500 and the law officers were still more unenthusiastic, the Solicitor-General even being reluctant to drop the absolute right of transfer, which was acknowledged to have sabotaged the 1938 increase.[81] The limit of their support was a rise to just £400, but with the valuable concession (opposed by Labour in Parliament) of a power to make a further rise to £500 by order in council.[82]

The attitude of the law officers in particular was inimical to any attempt to compel litigants into the county courts and the LCD had a hard time with them. Coldstream brought Lynskey in to try to strengthen his hand only to find that he was also conservative when it came to sanctions, and in the end the 'gateway' was given up,[83] probably not too unwillingly, since the likelihood of the masters operating it as intended must have been small. Under a

[78] *Ibid.*, p. 552.

[79] *Ibid.*, pp. 552–60. For deliberations following the working parties on appeals see PRO LCO 2/3994–5.

[80] PRO LCO 2/4984.

[81] Coldstream to Thesiger and Rieu, 11 Jan. 1954; memo of 26 May 1954 and note of meeting, 30 Jun. 1954, PRO LCO 2/4982.

[82] Kilmuir to Manningham Buller (Attorney-General), 25 Nov. 1954, PRO LCO 2/4984; *Hansard* 1955 5th s., vol. 543 (HC), cols. 1018–30.

[83] Coldstream to Lynskey, 8 July 1954, to Kilmuir, 19 July 1954, PRO LCO 2/4982.

revised costs sanction[84] it was estimated that 30 per cent of Queen's Bench actions would go into the county courts, but in exchange for even this much Kilmuir had to drop the Department's opposition to appeals on fact, broadly accepting the Evershed proposals.[85]

While the bills were in preparation prolonged negotiations with the Law Society were taking place over the new costs scale. The LCD was handicapped by inability to find among the registrars and masters anyone who had a realistic appreciation of the economics of solicitors' practices. There was much truth in the Law Society's complaints that registrars were generally grudging, but the Chief Taxing Master proved to be even worse, being one of those people with whom 'it is very difficult ... to get it into their heads that the £ has changed its value'.[86] Although the Society's threats not to recommend solicitors to do legal aid work in the county court were regarded as a bluff, Coldstream felt that they had got the better of the negotiations and feared that Parliament would see the scales as too generous.[87]

The Law Society and the Bar Council also exposed the weakness of the LCD's position over the costs sanction. Deputations followed the first reading of the County Courts Bill and, though the Law Society was mollified by being encouraged to introduce a clause into the Administration of Justice Bill empowering registrars to strike out hopeless defences,[88] it became clear that the lawyers mustered such a parliamentary presence that concessions would have to be made; costs on the county court scale would be awarded unless a master certified that the resort to the high court had been justified if less than £300 was awarded, not £400 as proposed.[89]

[84] *PP* 1954–5 (74) II, County Courts Bill cl. 1.

[85] Kilmuir to Manningham Buller, 25 Nov. 1954, PRO LCO 2/4984. According to Coldstream's note of 2 Dec., even Evershed was now opposed to appeals, but at a meeting the following day Kilmuir gave way.

[86] Meeting with Law Society, 25 Oct. 1954, PRO LCO 2/5038.

[87] Rieu's note, 4 Nov. 1955; Coldstream to Kilmuir, 16 Nov. 1955, PRO LCO 2/5040.

[88] The Law Society thought the LCD had agreed to give it support and were annoyed to find otherwise: H. Horsfall Turner to Dobson, 25 Apr. 1956. The LCD thereupon circularised registrars and, finding 'a striking cleavage of opinion', declined to back it: Dobson to Attorney-General, 27 May 1956, PRO LCO 2/5073.

[89] *Hansard* 1954–5 5th s., vol. 192 (HL), cols. 198–233; 1955–6 5th s., vol. 193 (HL),

Lawyers monopolised the debates on the Bill[90] and nothing exercised them nearly so much as this parochial question. Few voices were raised in favour of a wider extension and some were critical even of this modest one. Ominously, Lord Hailsham was among the latter, hoping 'that this is the last of the series of Acts enlarging the jurisdiction of the county courts which I shall see in my lifetime'.[91]

The passage of these Acts completed the laggardly implementation of the work of the two committees. For the county courts the effect was pretty limited, certainly compared with the significance of at last having legal aid available. There would be more judges and the quality of their business (as measured in money terms) would be somewhat improved; their armoury of remedies had been enlarged by charging orders and equitable execution; powers over truculent and recalcitrant defendants were increased and the ability of the LCD to respond to fluctuations in business by appointing temporary judges and deputies improved. Nevertheless it all amounted to tinkering with the civil justice structure rather than giving it the overhaul that might have been expected.

## COURTS UNDER PRESSURE

With the return of peace the high court experienced a boom in litigation, followed by a slump in the mid-1950s and a recovery in the 1960s.[92] In county courts the fluctuations, measured by the number of plaints in money claims, were rather less marked, a steady recovery from the all-time low of 212,483 in 1945 to 727,154 in 1955 being followed by three years of 'phenomenal increase', then a more gradual rise to 1,677,738 in 1961. Throughout the 1960s plaints stayed above 1,500,000 and began to rise sharply again when the money limit on jurisdiction was raised in 1969. In non-money claims the pattern is different: a peak of 73,751 in 1948 was not scaled again until 1969 and for

cols. 911–24; vol. 542 (HC), cols. 1649–1734; vol. 543 (HC), cols. 999–1016. PRO LCO 2/4985, especially Manningham Buller to Coldstream, 28 Jun. 1955.

90 *Hansard* 1955–6 5th s., vol. 542 (HC), col. 1682: 'a kind of lawyers' field day' (G. Finlay).

91 *Hansard* 1955–6 5th s., vol. 193 (HL), col. 916.

92 Abel-Smith and Stevens, *Lawyers and the Courts*, pp. 256–7.

most of the decade after 1956 the number hovered around 50,000. Since many of these were claims to the possession of land, fluctuations are probably due largely to the changes in statutory protection for tenants.[93]

Notwithstanding the continuing growth in tribunals, the range of county court business grew ever wider. In 1958 the *Annual Practice* listed more than 140 different statutory jurisdictions, and though some were arcane and seldom invoked, others brought in a lot of business.[94] Tithe actions, for instance, amounted to 20,000 a year (albeit most were purely formal) and though statutory changes reduced their number, were still over 2,000 in 1968.[95] The recovery of unpaid tax became much more prominent, with 11,000 actions in 1969, and the Married Women's Property Act 1882, scarcely significant before the war, assumed a much greater importance. Bankruptcy also featured more largely; from about 3,000 in the late 1940s, notices had passed 9,000 by the end of the 1960s,[96] and though equity remained sluggish, the high court continued to remit between 1,000 and 2,000 common law cases each year.

As a result, the numerical dominance of contractual debts diminished, though they still made up between 80 and 85 per cent of all plaints.[97] The limitations of official statistics[98] and the impact of inflation make meaningful comparisons with the inter-war years difficult, but figures produced for the Payne Committee suggest that very small claims continued to predominate: about 65 per cent were for under £20, compared with 80 per cent before the war; fewer than 15 per cent exceeded £30 and no more than 2 per

93 *Ibid.* at p. 257; *Civil Judicial Statistics*, various years.

94 For a selection of the more rarefied see *SJ* 104 (1960), 100–1.

95 *Civil Judicial Statistics*; *Halsbury's Laws of England*, 4th edn, vol. XIV (1975), paras. 1212 ff.

96 The Blagden Committee (*PP* 1956–7 [Cmnd 221] VIII) reviewed the county court bankruptcy jurisdiction and did not endorse the criticism made by Raeburn of the bankruptcy bar, that because they handled so few, county court judges and registrars 'lack a sense of proportion' and were inclined to be severe. The LCD, however, admitted there was some force in this: Dobson's note, 9 July 1956, PRO LCO 2/5827.

97 *Payne Report*, app. 7, table 1.

98 Publication resumed in 1948 and they were presented in slightly more enlightening form from 1969 following the report of the Adams Committee (*PP* 1967–8 [Cmnd 3684] XVIII). They remained, however, 'too blunt an instrument for research purposes': G. Drewry, How Vital Statistics?, *NLJ* 119 (1969), 771.

cent were for more than £200; these last, however, were naturally more significant by volume – £8 million in 1967 out of a total of £37 million at stake.[99] As ever, only a small proportion (2.5 per cent in 1969) of actions ever came to trial before a judge or registrar, who now heard cases in almost equal numbers. Many simply lapsed, while a proportion, declining slightly from well over one-third in 1950, were either withdrawn or struck out at a preliminary hearing.[100]

The national figures probably conceal interesting regional trends, reflected indirectly in the continuing process of re-arranging circuits and courts. Though small courts everywhere were always under threat and part-time registrars continued to be phased out as it became economic to do so, the major changes mirrored the drift of population and wealth to the south-east; thus Kingston (where plaints had doubled) was given a new court in 1961 and the south-eastern districts were reorganised and their 'judge power' increased.[101]

Pre-war trends in the conduct of business became more marked. Though judges sat as often as their predecessors and were seldom publicly accused of indolence,[102] they were unable to dispatch business at the old speed. This may have been due in part to their diversion to divorce and criminal work – the deputies who sat for them being understandably slower unless they were retired judges – but it also resulted from changes in the trials themselves.

Some actions, bankruptcy and housing possessions among them, were notoriously resistant to rapid disposal, but even in common law matters the county courts were coming increasingly to resemble the high court.[103] The Master of the Rolls urged judges to assist the Court of Appeal by being stricter with the

99 *Payne Report*, app. 7, table 1.

100 Not shown separately until 1969: *PP* 1970–1 [Cmnd 4416] XXVIII, p. 8. In that year the two together comprised 232,922 of the 435,644 listed as 'otherwise disposed of'.

101 *LT* 232 (1961), 26; *LT* 224 (1963), 528; *LT* 220 (1955), 28.

102 Though Leon's admission that he had been able to spend thirteen weeks a year writing was adversely commented upon: *SJ* 111 (1967), 745, 813. A registrar wrote that all his judges took far less holiday: *ibid.*, 884.

103 A very experienced registrar, D. Freeman Coutts, said that Landlord and Tenant Act 1954 cases were 'far more substantial than anything tried in the county courts before the war': to D. R. Wells, 18 May 1960, PRO LCO 2/7104. He also noted that there were far more interlocutory hearings.

rules of evidence,[104] and it is not surprising that, with proper pleadings becoming a more common feature,[105] one commentator noted that the poor man's court was no longer adapted to the litigant in person.[106]

This growing formality, which strengthened the case for legal aid, was intensified once it arrived, for legal aid led to more legal representation and counsel were attracted to courts where they could claim 100 per cent of their costs, not 90 per cent as in legally aided high court actions.[107] Barristers like St John Field (pupil master to Lord Chancellors Gardiner and Elwyn Jones), who appeared in a county court only once in his life, were becoming rarer,[108] and fewer solicitors' firms disdained the lower courts; if income from county court business was relatively unimportant to most solicitors, it was only because they had become unhealthily dependent upon conveyancing.

Though it could sometimes shorten trials, legal representation more often prolonged them for, with the profession suffering a severe manpower shortage, inexperienced and often sketchily briefed advocates were sent to court.[109] Moreover if, as 'a reflection of the malaise in the High Court',[110] bigger cases were brought by choice in county courts, busier counsel came with them and these birds of passage, juggling appointments and timetables, were prone to disrupt the lists and aggravate the problem of actions adjourned part-heard. 'Rough' pre-war judges like Cluer would have had short shrift with counsel of either description but there were fewer of his sort on the bench now and most were more patient with advocates, less ruthless in driving through the list.[111] They were also more burdened by the need to take notes in case of an appeal, for they still had no shorthand writer

104 Address to county court judges, 25 Oct. 1958.

105 I. H. Jacob, The Present Importance of Pleadings, *CLP* 13 (1960), 171–92 at 176, 182–3. See also *SJ* 108 (1964), 209.

106 *SJ* 110 (1966), 580 (JKH).

107 Abel-Smith and Stevens, *Lawyers and the Courts*, pp. 333–43.

108 M. Box, *Rebel Advocate* (London, 1983), pp. 46–8; Lord Elwyn Jones, *In My Time* (London, 1983), p. 42.

109 Judges sometimes complained of advocates' ignorance of the rules of evidence; in the past the boot had more often been on the other foot.

110 Abel-Smith and Stevens, *Lawyers and the Courts*, p. 257.

111 Lord Hailsham, *Door Wherein I Went*, p. 257.

nor recording equipment to save them the labour.[112] It is no wonder that everything slowed down.

Regular users complained. While the Hire Purchase Traders Association was vexed especially about delays in bringing matters to trial,[113] the Bar Council again took up adjournments, especially what the *Daily Telegraph* called 'trials in instalments'.[114] Richard Rieu and the county courts branch were inclined to be both sceptical and fatalistic, unpersuaded that there was a widespread problem and feeling that in any event it was one inherent in the system. The bar's favourite solution, the appointment of extra judges, held no appeal since it appeared that few were overworked and many regularly finished early because the list had broken down.[115]

There was, however, a general awareness that listing was becoming more difficult with the increasing complexity of the business, Rieu observing accurately but unhelpfully that 'it begins to emerge that the county court system as it is at present is not altogether suitable for handling a good deal of the work which has come as a result of the increase in jurisdiction'.[116] One shrewd registrar wrote that effective change would need 'something in the nature of a major surgical operation'[117] and Coldstream, though less complaisant than his juniors, would not countenance that; nevertheless the evidence produced by the Bar Council and replies to a circular to registrars were strong enough for him to create a working party under Judge Alan Pugh.[118]

Pugh did not enjoy the experience, not least because the Law Society saddled him with a solicitor named Gunn who proved purely obstructive and drove him to distraction.[119] The group had

112 An experiment with recording in Westminster county court in 1951 was said to have been unsuccessful: *Hansard* 1954–5 5th s., vol. 191 (HL), col. 232. The Committee on Mechanical Recording (*PP* 1966–7 [Cmd 3096] XXVI) urged further trials.

113 PRO LCO 2/7159.

114 Meeting of 27 Jun. 1958, PRO LCO 2/7146.

115 Rieu to F. Mayell, 24 Mar. 1959; Mayell to Rieu, 22 Apr. 1959, PRO LCO 8/85.

116 Rieu to Judge Carr, 8 July 1958, PRO LCO 2/7147. See also F. Axmann to Rieu, 23 Apr. 1959.

117 D. Fearn (Southwark), 11 Aug. 1958, *ibid.*

118 PRO LCO 2/7158. The members were Rieu, Judge Nicklin, registrars Welfare and Hankinson, D. Ackner, E. A. Williams and M. Gunn. H. F. Cobb, a senior clerk at Clerkenwell, acted as secretary.

119 'One of the most unpleasant experiences I have ever had ... I would not have

no difficulty in agreeing that the problem was real: while 'judge days' had risen from 8,807 in 1955 to 10,142 in 1958, trials had fallen from 18,306 to 17,110 and still there were delays.[120] They were not nationwide however, and there was no clear agreement on the causes, for while some judges and registrars were content to put the blame on the lawyers, others demanded fundamental changes in the system.[121] Anxious to avoid 'a roving examination of the working of the county court system', Pugh found it difficult to focus attention on less ambitious proposals.[122]

Even at this level the working party found that their freedom to make proposals was heavily circumscribed. They wanted an end to judges acting as divorce commissioners but that was beyond their remit.[123] United on the deplorable condition of many court buildings, they wanted to call for a crown building on every circuit but the Assistant Secretary to the Ministry of Works told them it was impracticable, also dismissing the old chestnut of a central county court for London as 'quite hopeless at present'.[124] Their own members blocked other proposals. Judge Nicklin objected that they had neither the expertise nor the evidence to justify suggestions for changes to staff recruitment and training,[125] while Desmond Ackner's astringent reference to judges' neglect to implement the Austin Jones Report's recommendations on listing was felt by others to smack too much of an encroachment on judicial independence and was replaced by a more anodyne paragraph.[126]

In the end the Pugh Report contained two connected proposals

thought it possible for a man to be so maliciously obstructive as this man has been from beginning to the end': to Coldstream, 16 July 1960, PRO LCO 2/7163.

120 Rieu's papers, no. 3, PRO LCO 2/7160.

121 K. M. Newman to W. Sproule Bolton, 11 Aug. 1958 and discussion of the 12th, PRO LCO 2/7146, plus the returns in 2/7147–8. Nicklin could not understand how Cumberland escaped the list of black spots, since it was a byword for delays and only practitioners' affection for the judge kept them quiet: 2/7158 (12 May 1959).

122 Cobb's circular, 16 Nov. 1959, PRO LCO 2/7161.

123 First meeting, 23 May 1959, PRO LCO 2/7160.

124 PRO LCO 2/7161: evidence of A. S. Lee, 3 Dec. 1959 and minutes of 12th meeting. See also pp. 320–1 below.

125 *Ibid.*: Nicklin to Pugh, 31 Mar. 1960 and Rieu's comments on the draft.

126 Rieu warned Pugh not to be stampeded by Desmond Ackner, the future Law Lord, PRO LCO 2/7159. Minutes of meetings, especially comments by Rieu and Hankinson on the first draft on 16 May 1960, 2/7160–1.

of substance.[127] There should be a 'New Special Procedure' available (but not compulsory) for cases likely to be defended and to last beyond two hours, with a preliminary hearing to ensure that they were listed on a day when they could be completed. To free judges for such trials registrars should hear the steadily increasing number of judgment summonses; the saving of judges' time would be considerable as Kewish was 'assured that the judges generally devote more of their time and attention to all their work and I should say this is particularly noticeable in relation to the hearing of judgment summonses'.[128]

The Report was circulated to the judges,[129] whose replies showed dismaying diversity on both proposals; the first fifty-nine replies were analysed as follows:[130]

> New Special Procedure: for 25; against 29; inconclusive 5
> Registrars' Judgment Summonses: for 36; against 17; inconclusive 6.

By and large, London judges tended to favour the new procedure while some others doubted the ability of their registrars to cope. It was drily noted that one who 'did not believe in any brave new world to be created by a New Special Procedure'[131] was Reid, whose Kingston court was among the most frequently criticised. As the breakdown shows, there was more support for the judgment summons proposal, but for every two judges who, with Pugh, believed 'we are now in the affluent society and the Victorian and Edwardian poor have disappeared except in the minds of some of my brethren',[132] there was a Cohen who was 'probably old-fashioned in thinking judges should be in the closest touch with the poorest of the poor in the Poor Man's Court'.[133]

Naturally judges and registrars, while admitting that the influx

[127] After an interim report in 1959 the final report was delivered in June 1960. Much of the delay arose from the Law Society's slowness in submitting their evidence (PRO LCO 2/7159).

[128] Memo of 16 May 1960, PRO LCO 2/7164.

[129] Gunn's note of dissent was merely summarised for circulation, PRO LCO 2/7166.

[130] Memo of 17 Feb. 1961, PRO LCO 2/7164.

[131] *Ibid.* Reid's response to the report, 13 Dec. 1960, PRO LCO 2/7166.

[132] Memo of 14 Mar. 1961. He was dismayed that three members of the Rule Committee (Hurst, McKee and Temple Morris) were among those hostile to the judgment summons proposal, PRO LCO 2/7164.

[133] Reply of 6 Jan. 1961, PRO LCO 2/7166.

of judgment summonses did create some problems, played down the extent of dissatisfaction among users and, like Reid, would not admit to any mismanagement on their own part, though Howard for one was prepared to be outspoken on the organisational ineptitude of some of his brethren.[134] Rieu, never enthusiastic about the inquiry, felt that these divisions doomed the proposals, especially since it would be politically impossible to downgrade committal hearings without conceding a right of appeal. Coldstream reluctantly concurred.[135]

Pugh was naturally disappointed with this outcome and, concluding that it was the freedom of the defendant to produce a defence only at the trial that was a fundamental cause of delays, he and Judge Hurst set about persuading the Rule Committee to insist on prior disclosure.[136] However, since the LCD regarded this freedom as 'an essential feature of the county court',[137] which it was prepared to relax only where the registrar had given a specific direction for disclosure, he had only limited success.[138]

Nevertheless, the Department was committed to devolving more high court work onto the county courts if the judges felt able to cope,[139] so Coldstream had to pin his faith in administrative action through the new head of the county courts branch, Douglas Kewish.[140] Kewish must have had some success, for the complaints died down for several years, but the most effective innovation was one suggested by Rieu: 'floating judges', known to the bar as 'call girls', nominally assigned to a district as the law required but sent to whichever district was falling into arrears.[141] The floaters, along with LCD insistence that judges seek help at

134 Howard to Rieu, 10 Nov. 1960, PRO LCO 2/7165.

135 PRO LCO 2/7146.

136 Pugh's memo, 14 Mar. 1961, *ibid.*

137 Rieu to Hurst, 10 May 1961, PRO LCO 2/7168.

138 *Ibid.* County Court (Amendment) Rules 1961 (SI 1526), reviewed in *LJ* 111 (1961), 541–2 and *SJ* 105 (1961), 796, 816: 'the main effect of the new provisions is likely to be that the actual hearing date of cases will be delayed and costs increased'.

139 When the judges were consulted on this point in 1962 Pugh, still sore about the fate of his report, expressed concern that the LCD seemed to be giving them some sort of veto over changes: 21 Feb. 1962, PRO LCO 2/7163.

140 See pp. 207–8 below.

141 Rieu's suggestions, 1 Jun. 1959, PRO LCO 2/7159. Elizabeth Lane was one: *Hear the Other Side* (London, 1985), pp. 123–4. It was understood that they would have a district of their own on the first suitable vacancy.

the first sign of difficulty, probably achieved more than any rule changes.[142]

## COURTS IN ACTION

The addition of the 'floaters' was part of a steady expansion in the number of county court judges, which had been more or less static between fifty-five and sixty during the first century. By 1955 there were eighty and by 1968, ninety-seven. Only in the mid-1960s did the Treasury start to offer more than token resistance to these additions (aided by Gardiner's indiscreet remark that some judges 'did a good deal less than would normally be accepted as a full working week')[143] and other interested parties were more likely to profess anxiety as to whether the proposed manpower could cope with an increased workload than to question the need for more judges.[144]

In the immediate post-war years Lord Chancellors sometimes claimed that recruiting the right calibre of man was difficult – Jowitt claimed (albeit in making the case for a pay rise) that he was forced to resort to 'burnt-out barristers'.[145] Obviously the attractions of the lower bench did fluctuate with the prospects and prosperity of the bar, but Henry Cecil, who was well placed to know, felt that the standard had risen and the LCD had some success in persuading suitable candidates to make themselves available at an earlier age.[146]

Oddly, however, one of the inducements continued to be withheld – the prospect of promotion. Jowitt raised four judges to the high court, one of whom, the county courts' 'star turn', Benjamin Ormerod, went on to the Court of Appeal and was, some thought, fit for the House of Lords.[147] But for all Kilmuir's professed

142 Rieu to Judge Howard, 26 Jun. 1961, PRO LCO 12/83.

143 P. Allen to Coldstream, 22 Nov. 1965, PRO LCO 12/46.

144 E.g. *NLJ* 118 (1969), 1012–13 (G. Borrie and J. Pyke); *NLJ* 119 (1969), 589–90. But the LCD viewed some judges' requests for deputies with scepticism: R. Gregory's memo, 28 Mar. 1962, PRO LCO 2/7182.

145 Stevens, *Independence of the Judiciary*, pp. 119–38.

146 *The English Judge* (London, 1970), pp. 160–1. For sidelights on the recruitment position in the 1960s see PRO LCO 2/7703.

147 Napier's memo, July 1947, PRO LCO 2/5094; Nield, *Farewell to the Assizes*, p. 244. The others were Austin Jones, D. L. Finnemore and C. A. Colling-

solicitude for the county courts, the 1950s saw just one promotion, leading to criticism in Parliament.[148] Promotions were then resumed, but they remained too infrequent to suggest any sort of career ladder.[149]

The promotions included Elizabeth Lane, the first woman judge, but if Gardiner was prepared to favour women, he did not extend his sympathies to solicitors. Both he and his equally dogmatic successor Hailsham were obdurate, and in Gardiner's case unpardonably scornful, against opening the judiciary to them;[150] the narrow breach made by the Courts Act represented a defeat rather than a concession.[151]

On the whole the bench was pretty homogeneous, containing many men with distinguished war records[152] and not a few with high academic honours,[153] as well as a sprinkling who had attained celebrity in sport[154] or other pastimes. There were still colourful characters: Lyall Wilkes whose 'sense of the ridiculous and his threshold of disgust were set too low to allow him to achieve the positions that might have been expected of him'; Wingate-Saul, the wit of the northern circuit who affected the dress of a bygone age; and Ingress Bell, 'variously soldier, sailor, boxer, MP and judge'. Some could still be styled 'a county court judge of the Old School' but others were clearly high court judges manqué.[155]

wood. In addition, D. Davies and G. Clark Williams became respectively First and Deputy Commissioner for National Insurance. The *Solicitor* 15 (1948), 123 thought it marked a real policy shift.

148 Cecil, *English Judge*, p. 161. Lord Kilmuir, *Political Adventure*, pp. 29–30. For criticisms see *Hansard* 1959–60 5th s., vol. 220 (HL), cols. 117, 119; 1960–1 5th s., vol. 226 (HL), cols. 973–5; 1961–2 5th s., vol. 235 (HL), cols. 860, 953–81.

149 Gardiner, who interested himself in the process of appointment to the county court bench, may have been influenced by unfavourable early impressions: Box, *Rebel Advocate*, pp. 47–8.

150 Even after Beeching had recommended it, Gardiner still dismissed it as 'of course, nonsense': Two Lawyers or One?, *Current Legal Problems*, 23 (1970), 1–22. For a particularly inflammatory interview see *SJ* 114 (1970), 795.

151 For pressure to open up the bench see Kirk, *Portrait of a Profession*, pp. 183–5.

152 Few so quixotic as C. T. Cohen, who had attacked a German tank with his walking stick: *The Times*, 28 Aug. 1971.

153 Blagden, for instance, an expert in bankruptcy. Unusually for a county court judge, he was chosen to head an inquiry on the subject.

154 Rowe Harding, for example, who won seventeen rugby caps for Wales and three for the British Lions.

155 The descriptions are all from obituaries in *The Times*. The judge of the old school was Daly Lewis, 'manqués' A. M. Lee and Barrington.

Nevertheless the impression is that there was greater circumspection on the bench. The more obvious pitfalls for the garrulous, opinionated or naïve judge came in divorce and crime[156] and it is perhaps significant that one who did get himself into a scrape, Judge Gamon, did so as a divorce commissioner.[157] On the whole they were discreet and seem actually to have welcomed the limits Kilmuir imposed upon their freedom of speech,[158] limits which one registrar believed even barred him from public comment on a matter so pertinent to the legal press as the holidays of the judges.[159] Not all were regarded as satisfactory – Done was horrendously slow, Archer worryingly erratic, Reid unduly prone to order arbitrations and Ingress Bell impertinent enough to urge divorcing couples to reconsider – but none was intolerable.[160]

Most judges regarded housing cases as the worst part of their job and, although the *Annual Practice* continued to exclude this branch of law from the main volume, it had become a permanent feature of county court life. The 'creeping decontrol' of the 1930s was abruptly reversed in wartime and controls were only half-heartedly pushed back by Conservative governments, while Labour greatly extended them both in the 1940s and the 1960s.[161] As a result of these political manoeuvres legislation which already had a bad reputation for complexity and opacity became a byword for both, even if Mackinnon was jocularly hyperbolical in alleging that it was 'hastening many of [the judges] to the grave'.[162] Each new Act dug fresh interpretative pitfalls for the unwary judge and Carr, for one, fell headlong when he read the 1957 Act as

156 The resurgence of criticism in the 1960s was directed principally at criminal trials: Abel-Smith and Stevens, *Lawyers and the Courts*, pp. 289–91, 299–310.

157 Stevens, *Independence of the Judiciary*, pp. 91–2.

158 *Ibid.*; Polden, Judicial Independence, part two, 160–1.

159 *SJ* 111 (1967), 813.

160 PRO LCO 2/3284 (Archer); 2/3309 (Done); 2/4999 (Reid). For Bell see *The Times*, 17 Aug. 1986.

161 They need to be seen in the context of the dramatic fall in the number of private rented homes from 6.2 million in 1951 to 2.9 million in 1969. Useful summaries of the legislation are in M. J. Barnett, *The Politics of Legislation* (London, 1969), pp. 19–27 and, from a different perspective, P. Beirne, *Fair Rent and Legal Fiction* (London, 1977), pp. 76–101, 111 ff.

162 R. E. Megarry, *The Rent Acts* (10th edn, London, 1967), vol. I, p. xxiii. The Rent Act 1965 runs to fifty pages and 'a number of important provisions are concealed in laconic paragraphs in the schedules': J. S. Colyer, The Rent Act 1965, *Conv.* ns 29 (1965), 429–63.

abolishing the greater hardship test:[163] no wonder Megarry dedicated his massive treatise 'to the draftsmen of the Acts with awe and affection and to the County Court Bench with a sympathy as profound as it is respectful'.[164]

The most difficult period for judges was just after the war, when demobilised servicemen came home to cities where bombing had created a desperate housing shortage. Laws could not create homes and their application of the 'greater hardship' test not surprisingly brought judges into conflict with the housing policies of harassed local authorities.

This brought about just the situation Conservatives had gloomily prophesied should Labour come into power: the Lord Chancellor pressed by party organisations, councils and a few MPs (Mrs Ridealgh the most persistent) to lean on judges to make decisions more in keeping with their notions of justice. Some judges were singled out for criticism – Gerald Hurst was one said to make possession orders too readily – and they angrily demanded protection from Jowitt. He bowed to political pressure so far as to send them a circular explaining the official view on local authorities' housing powers and duties, but held firmly to the line that he must not interfere with judges' decisions, though he did ask for explanations of the ones which aroused particular criticism.[165] There were renewed criticisms in 1947, but subsequent debates and official inquiries into the Rent Acts disclose no serious dissatisfaction with the judges,[166] while the Court of Appeal for its part showed no inclination to fetter their discretion by rigid guidelines.[167]

Business tenants also received more effective protection. Out of the Uthwatt–Jenkins Report came the Landlord and Tenant Act 1954 Part II, enabling them to obtain a renewal of their lease at market rent.[168] Happily, the balance struck by this Act proved

[163] *LJ* 107 (1957), 753; *SJ* 101 (1957), 907. The provision was Schedule VI para. 21.

[164] *Rent Acts.*

[165] Polden, Judicial Independence, part one, 35–7.

[166] *LT* 204 (1947), 296; *PP* 1965 [Cmnd 2605] XVII, the Milner Holland Report; *PP* 1970–1 [Cmnd 4609] XXXIII, the Francis Report.

[167] E.g. in *Coplans v. King* [1947] 2 All ER 393, Sir W. Greene MR expressly disapproved a dictum of Scott LJ in *Chandler v. Sharrett* (1946) 63 *TLR* 84 which tended to encourage appeals.

[168] *PP* 1948–9 [Cmd 7706] XII at p. 471; 1950 [Cmd 7982] XII at p. 703. The reports led first to the Leasehold Property (Temporary Provisions) Act 1951.

broadly acceptable to both main parties and it has remained unaltered in essentials;[169] it quickly became important too, with applications rising from 1,367 to 4,258 within a single year.

A jurisdiction which at least some judges found congenial was adoptions. Before the war the county courts' share of this business had never exceeded 10 per cent but they grew steadily more popular at the expense of magistrates' courts and finally overtook them in 1960; in the peak year for adoptions in England and Wales (1968) 16,499 out of 24,831 were handled by the county courts.[170] One reason for their expanding share was the growth in adoptions outside the child's own family, for with intra-family adoptions making up two-thirds of magistrates' court adoptions but only one-fifth in the county courts, a disproportionate growth in non-family adoptions favoured the latter.[171] Reasons for the different profile and for the magistrates' fall from favour are unclear; it was suggested to the Houghton Committee that some adopters feared that intimate information might more readily leak out from the magistrates' court,[172] but the decisive voices would more often be those of the professionals – local authorities, adoption agencies and solicitors.

There is also very little evidence on which to judge the performance of the county courts in this sensitive task. The two post-war committees do not mention any disquiet but there were suggestions of inconsistency in their approach.[173]

## COURTS UNDER SCRUTINY

By the mid-1960s divorce was eating up more than 60 per cent of the legal aid fund, forcing the government to seek economies.[174]

169 The workings of the Act are reviewed in *Law Commission Working Paper* 7 of 1969 and their *Report* no. 206 of 1992.

170 *PP* 1971–2 [Cmnd 5107] XXXVIII, app. B (the Houghton Report). In guardianship the magistrates court remained dominant (para. 260).

171 *Ibid.*, para. 264. M. Murch *et al.*, *The Overlapping Family Jurisdiction of the Magistrates' Courts and the County Courts* (Bristol, 1977).

172 *PP* 1971–72 [Cmnd 5107] XXXVIII, app. B, paras. 259–60.

173 *SJ* 113 (1969), 951–3 (S. M. Cretney). Gamon chaired a National Council for Social Services committee in 1947 (*LJ* 99 (9149), 608–9), Gerald Hurst an official one: *PP* 1953–4 [Cmd 9248] VIII.

174 *Hansard* 1966–7 5th s., vol. 74 (HC), Attorney-General at col. 66. It certainly upset the LCD's calculations most embarrassingly: *PP* 1963–4 (29) V: evidence

Gardiner let it be known that county court divorce was back on the agenda notwithstanding that it had been rejected by the Morton Commission less than a decade before, and with the Conservatives not voicing opposition, it was at last brought in by the Matrimonial Causes Act 1967.[175]

For those impatient for substantive divorce reform and for advocates of a 'Family Court' this was a wasted opportunity and few MPs outside the legal profession, for whom costs and audience were direct concerns, showed much interest in the debates. Some, using figures supplied by the divorce bar, suggested that county court judges were less adept and punctilious in sifting the shoals of undefended petitions for those which failed to meet the law's obsolescent requirements.[176] Others asserted that undefended petitions actually needed more expertise than the 'short defendeds' which were now to go to the high court.[177] But it was a rather apathetic debate; the bar was thriving and that took the edge off its fear of losing business,[178] while the Law Society's concerns centred on the level of costs, a matter for lobbying rather than confrontation. Most agreed with the Attorney-General that the bill 'reflected the reality of the situation'.[179]

Under the Act undefended divorces were to be taken in forty-nine 'divorce towns', the Principal Probate Registry in London acting as a sort of extra court. All the judges, floaters included, acquired jurisdiction and could at last pronounce the obsequies of a marriage in their own robes rather than the borrowed plumage of a commissioner; to ensure as much consistency as possible, however, rules for both the high and the county courts would be made by a new Matrimonial Causes Rule Committee.

Disquiet at the state of divorce law was matched by growing disillusion with the way the courts handled personal injury claims,

of Coldstream and H. Boggis-Rolfe to the Estimates Committee at pp. 15–21. Rising concern can be seen in successive reports of the Lord Chancellor's Advisory Committee on Legal Aid.

175 *SJ* 109 (1965), 615; *Hansard* 1966–7 5th s., vol. 744 (HC), cols. 58–119; vol. 749 (HC), cols. 74–80; vol. 280 (HL), cols. 168–204; vol. 281 (HL), cols. 547–50. Lords Denning and Pearce (both former judges in the PD & A) spoke against the Bill.

176 *Hansard* 1966–7 5th s., vol. 280 (HL), col. 198 (Lord Mansfield).

177 *Ibid.*, vol. 744 (HC), col. 81 (R. Body).

178 See however the bar's 'trade union' position expressed by A. Lyon in vol. 744 (HC) at col. 91.

179 *Ibid.* at col. 58.

and in 1967 there was an investigation headed by Lord Justice Winn. Posterity has been unkind to the Winn Report which, despite proclaiming its innovations in research, is regarded as disappointingly superficial.[180] The Committee seems to have resolved early on in favour of a substantial extension of county court jurisdiction over torts and was not to be dislodged from this position by strong submissions casting doubt on their suitability to handle more and larger actions. The TUC criticised county court judges as too mean with damages; Lloyds claimed they were still very difficult to appeal from; the Law Society and Bar Council submitted that arrangements for hearing dates were poor and adjournments common. All these concerns were dismissed rather than rebutted by the Committee.[181]

Winn's Committee clearly felt that some criticisms were motivated by self-interest. So long as county court work remained 'financially unattractive and inconvenient',[182] lawyers would continue to use the high court where possible, so a mixture of sticks and carrots would be required if the diversion was to be effective. They proposed raising the county court maximum to £1,000 or £1,500 but the bigger cases would be held only at designated courts with 'more and better accommodation'.[183] Judges should be freed for these duties by giving judgment summonses to registrars and lawyers' costs revised to make the forum attractive. As usual, the 'costs buffer' posed a major problem and a further adjustment was proposed.[184]

As the era of austerity gave way to the affluent society credit became a way of life for the middle classes as it had long been for the rich and the poor. Buying on the 'never-never' became socially acceptable and, as an ever-wider range of consumer goods was aggressively advertised (the television fuelling demand for the others), sales on hire purchase soared, only restrained by sporadic and clumsy credit controls.[185] While landlords, tradesmen and utilities still accounted for the bulk of county court plaints, hire

[180] *PP* 1967–8 [Cmnd 3691], XXX; J. C. Harper and P. Kimber, The Winn Committee, *MLR* 32 (1969), 67–75.

[181] *PP* 1967–8 [Cmnd 3691] XXX, paras. 416–84, esp. paras. 433–44.

[182] *Ibid.*, para. 432. [183] *Ibid.*, paras. 445–50. [184] *Ibid.*, paras. 473–6.

[185] R. Harris and A. Seldon (eds.), *Hire Purchase in a Free Society* (London, 1958), pp. 44, 53; but they note at p. 40 that hire purchase 'still played quite a modest role in the economy as a whole'.

purchase firms and their linked finance houses became increasingly prominent.

Though some judges still disliked this incentive to improvidence,[186] most implemented the statutory protections for hirers with vigour, some sharing a widespread view that they were insufficient both financially (though the limit was raised to £300 in 1954 to allow for inflation) and qualitatively.[187] The standard form of hire purchase contract included an 'option' designed to ensure that in the event of a default by the hirer he could (and in effect must) purchase the goods outright at a predetermined valuation. *Bridge v. Campbell Discount Co. Ltd*[188] showed that judicial opinion was divided on whether the courts were able to protect the hirer from the rigorous enforcement of such clauses, and the Molony Report on Consumer Protection,[189] noted in an aside that the existing rules on venue could also disadvantage the hirer. A major revision of hire purchase law followed in 1964, giving the courts considerably enlarged powers,[190] and HP actions in the county courts rose from 58,644 to 83,972 over the next two years.[191]

From the mid-1950s criticism from creditors of the way their claims were handled began to mount. In 1957, following a complaint from the Finance Houses Association (FHA) that hearing dates were fixed for distant periods, Coldstream circularised registrars that cases should normally be heard within four weeks.[192] He also knew that the FHA's other complaint, that some judges had 'idiosyncracies' and made derisory instalments, had some foundation.[193] Some judges were soft on debtors, but that

186 Hurst, *Closed Chapters*, p. 142.

187 R. W. Harding, The Hire Purchase Act 1964, *Journal of Business Law* (1965), 15–21. There is a summary of the legislation in A. G. Guest, *The Law of Hire Purchase* (London, 1966).

188 [1962] AC 600.

189 *PP* 1961–2 [Cmnd 1781] XII at para. 572. It took evidence from Judge Harold Brown and nine registrars.

190 The county court was given exclusive jurisdiction over any recovery action for 'protected goods' or where less than one-third of the price had been paid or tendered: Hire Purchase Act 1965 s. 49 (1); Guest, *Law of Hire Purchase*, paras. 1191–255. Such actions must be entered in the defendant's home district: County Court Rules o. 2 r. (9)(a).

191 *Civil Judicial Statistics*.

192 FHA to Coldstream, 18 Jun. 1957 and circular of 22 July 1957, PRO LCO 2/5091.

193 Some support for this can be found in the minutes of the County Court Rule

was nothing new; of the three judges who gave evidence together to the Austin Jones Committee, Dale was strongly pro-creditor, Langman equally strongly pro-debtor and Engelbach somewhere in the middle.[194] Where a judge was known to be 'brisk' with debtors his courts would attract judgment summonses and, since a court which was lax about proof of means would not allow the costs of a witness whose presence would be indispensable in a stricter court, it was essential to be familiar with the court's peculiarities.[195]

Registrars too were prone to 'grandmotherly nonsense' which the LCO did its best to discourage:[196] 'whenever I hear that a registrar is being difficult I write and refer him to the Rules, which some of them even ask us to amend in order to make things even more difficult for the hire purchase companies'.[197]

It was said that bailiffs, often with the indulgence or encouragement of their superiors, were lax both in serving judgment summonses and in enforcing executions.[198] Evidence to the Austin Jones Committee makes it clear that they often had enormous discretion – 'sometimes frightening', said Bruce Humfrey[199] – and an attempt to remove their 'seven day discretion' antagonised some judges, was never properly enforced and was reversed ten years later.[200] But even when the bailiffs had the will to be severe they often lacked the means, for to keep costs down the county courts branch was miserly with manpower and transport.[201] Moreover they faced the increasing complexity of the

Committee, 1956, PRO LCO 2/5082. The popular press, however, was more inclined to pick out manifestations of 'harshness': *SJ* 104 (1964), 670.

194 PRO LCO 2/3299, 28 Oct. 1947.

195 One agent said he kept an 'idiosyncrasy book': PRO LCO 2/5064. See also *LSG* 61 (1964), 663–4.

196 Rieu to Coldstream, 27 Jun. 1957, PRO, LCO 2/5064. See also correspondence in 2/5060, 5062 showing some registrars to be 'officious and obstructive' (Rieu to Judge Dale, 27 Sep. 1955 in 5062) and to act outside the powers conferred by the 1938 Act.

197 Rieu to Coldstream, 27 Jun. 1957, PRO LCO 2/5091.

198 See e.g. Law Society annual report for 1957 in *SJ* 101 (1957), 487 and correspondence at 514, 521, 536–7, 577, 587; also Leiderman and Leigh's letter in *LJ* 106 (1956), 78. There are many other complaints.

199 Evidence of 13 Jan. 1948, PRO LCO 2/3299. See also E. C. Martin (27 Jan.) and the bailiffs' evidence (2/3300, 23 Jan. 1948).

200 *Austin Jones Report*, para. 69; PRO LCO 2/3317.

201 Bailiffs' evidence, PRO LCO 2/3300; minutes of Wheatcroft Committee, 2/5063–4.

law when called upon to enforce possession orders and execution upon goods.[202]

The problems of enforcement were long-standing and intractable. Judges in those courts which did not rely on professional agents to provide evidence of debtors' means lacked the power to get debtors into court for questioning. Defaults on instalments were common, so it is no wonder that creditors resorted to cat and mouse games with part warrants, disliked by bailiffs whose time was wasted and by judges who felt they were a way of screwing bigger instalments out of the debtor than the court would have ordered.[203]

What could be done without legislation was done. Coldstream asked Master Wheatcroft 'to investigate the efficiency of the system of executing judgments in the county courts and to make recommendations within the framework of the existing system'[204] and gave the rather complacent county courts branch a good shaking up after Mayell's retirement.[205] Coldstream was pleased with Wheatcroft's report, which urged that bailiffs be freed from serving process in order to concentrate on executing judgments; that part warrants be limited to a minimum of £2 or one instalment; and that the registrar review progress of executions on warrants above £20 fortnightly.[206] More significantly, Wheatcroft called for 'a basic change in the attitude of court staff', evidence having confirmed that there was a reluctance to keep the creditor informed and that effective supervision of bailiffs was wanting.[207]

Meanwhile the deficiencies of county court recovery processes had begun to manifest themselves in the most undesirable shape,

202 Discussion on suggested amendments, 1951, PRO LCO 2/4996; *NLJ* 119 (1969), 393–4 (V. Powell-Smith).

203 There are frequent discussions of part warrants in the LCO papers from the Austin Jones Committee onwards, e.g. 2/5088 (Rule Committee, 1957). The Administration of Justice Act 1956 s. 28 conferred a power to restrict part warrants by rule.

204 Papers are in PRO LCO 2/5063–7. The report was published in Aug. 1956.

205 See pp. 206–7 below. Rieu noted that Mayell did not believe execution was defective: note of 26 Apr. 1956, PRO LCO 2/5063.

206 To Kilmuir, 6 Sep. 1956, PRO LCO 2/5064. The fate of larger warrants had been a particular grievance of the Law Society.

207 Despite circular 13 of 1949: 'it is necessary to tighten up very considerably the instructions on the supervision of bailiffs' work generally'; Law Society evidence and meeting of 1 May 1956, PRO LCO 2/5063. See also auditors' evidence in 2/5064 and Rieu to Judge Paton, 15 Apr. 1959, 2/6371.

for in 1960 the Inspector of Prisons drew attention to the steep rise in committals.[208] Though Coldstream was opposed in principle to the prison for debtors, the LCD did not trouble to make any detailed examination – they actually had less information about its use in the 1960s than in the 1900s – and most judges could see no alternative, insisting that it was needed as a sanction against the professional debtors who were 'well aware of the inefficiency of the law and disobey it with impunity'.[209]

Judges lacked faith in administration orders as an alternative (perhaps influenced by registrars and clerks to whom they were troublesome)[210] to such an extent that they had become almost obsolete until a skilful press campaign instigated by Lena Jager MP led in 1965 to a rise in their ceiling from £100 to £300.[211] After that they returned to favour to some extent while committals fell away again, judges perhaps realising that too ready resort to the threat of gaol might strengthen the case for abolition.[212]

It is greatly to Gardiner's credit that he grasped the nettle by setting up an inquiry into the whole matter of remedies for personal indebtedness, bankruptcy apart. The methods of the Committee, under a promoted county court judge, Sir Withers Payne, did not meet the exacting standard demanded by the new breed of socio-legal commentators, but it was more ambitious and intelligent than any previous review of a notoriously uninviting subject.

Composed chiefly of judges and lawyers, the Committee's experience was deep rather than broad, and while it acknowledged that information on debtors was meagre, it did not commission any research, possibly because of pressure of time.[213] Allowing for

[208] *Solicitor*, 27 (1960), 281–2. Mr Justice Danckwerts also launched a strong attack, Henry Cecil's book *Not Such an Ass* (London, 1961) included a chapter on the subject and the Treasury expressed concern at the cost: PRO LCO 8/81.

[209] Judge Andrew (Bow), telephone call to LCD, 2 Apr. 1952, PRO LCO 2/5007. Cf. Coldstream to Judge Neal, 1955, 2/5061.

[210] The strongest dislike was manifested by the County Court Officers' Association in evidence to the Austin Jones Committee: PRO LCO 2/3299.

[211] *LSG* 61 (1965), 134. Administration of Justice Act 1965 s. 20; *Hansard* 1964–5 5th s., vol. 261 (HL), cols. 506–22; vol. 705 (HC), cols. 203–56. Numbers rose from two in 1963 to 2,264 in 1967.

[212] Gardiner pointed out that they had fallen from 7,913 in 1962 to 2,789 in 1968: *Hansard* 1968–9 5th s., vol. 306 (HL), col. 202.

[213] However Professor McGregor 'grafted onto a very much wider scheme of research' a study of attachment orders in matrimonial proceedings.

its inevitable reliance on county court officers for data, it undertook a thorough examination[214] and produced 'a coherently argued interconnecting set of proposals',[215] albeit with a number of dissents and reservations which lessened their authority. Unfortunately it was eclipsed by the long awaited Beeching Report which weighed in at a mere 118 pages of crisp, clear explanation and dealt with the structures of justice while Payne offered the reader 370 pages, some mired in technicalities, on a subject many found sordid.[216]

The Payne Committee made up its mind suspiciously quickly on the only question of broad public interest, the future of imprisonment for wilful failure to meet a judgment order.[217] A rather perfunctory discussion concludes with an approving endorsement of the Walpole Report of 1873, the most partisan and superficial of the several reports available.[218] The Report conceded that the Committee's unanimity in condemning committals was fortuitous,[219] some being swayed by humanitarian arguments, others by economic; they were at one, however, in doubting whether there was adequate investigation of circumstances before the committal order with the result that 'the vast majority of debtors who are actually received in prison ... are inadequate, unfortunate, feckless or irresponsible persons; they are, for the most part, not dishonest and do not therefore require punishment'.[220]

Some of the Committee insisted that even if no effective alternative could be devised, imprisonment was still an unacceptable sanction, but others, probably a majority, felt that it was incumbent upon them to come up with a plausible alternative.

214 It received memoranda from seventy-three organisations and fifty-two individuals. Four judges gave oral evidence and a further six gave theirs in writing; most answered a questionnaire. The ACCR and Officers' Association both gave oral evidence, as did Kewish. Among the memoranda are submissions from Birmingham registrars collectively, five others individually and the chief clerk of the Westminster court.

215 C. Glasser, The Administration of Justice Act 1970, *MLR* 34 (1971), 61–70 at 61.

216 See Lord Chorley's praise of Beeching, The Report of the Royal Commission on Assizes and Quarter Sessions, *MLR* 33 (1970), 184–90.

217 *Payne Report*, para. 952. The Attorney-General announced its conclusion to the Commons on 22 June 1966.

218 *Ibid.*, paras. 952–1007. On the *Walpole Report* see pp. 85–6 above.

219 *Ibid.*, para. 954.

220 *Ibid.*, para. 982.

Interestingly, despite making severe criticisms of the judgment summons procedure,[221] the Report conceded that 'the threat of committal has been an effective means of enforcing a money judgment against a man who could afford to pay his debts, albeit by instalments'.[222]

The obvious replacement for this sanction was the attachment of earnings order which for working men had been effectively prohibited by the Truck Acts and the Wages Attachment Abolition Act 1870.[223] Since trade unions and employers' organisations had steadfastly opposed its revival, it was crucial that the TUC was at last willing to countenance this further breach in the 'integrity of the wage packet'.[224] Experience with maintenance orders had been rather discouraging, but it was suggested that the normal run of civil debtors would be more co-operative.[225] Though the difficulties in devising a system which, while informed by sufficient knowledge about the debtor, would not be too burdensome on employers or too costly to administer, were formidable, they were not felt to be insurmountable. Of course, the self-employed and unemployed would be freed of the threat of prison without being subjected to attachment and it was admitted that this hole could not be fully plugged.[226] Something might be done by improving existing remedies – garnishing bank accounts, appointing receivers by way of equitable execution and putting charging orders on land[227] – but in most instances execution against goods would still be the main recourse. The main proposal in relation to execution was to remove the option of resorting to *fi-fa* and the high court procedure, since that 'operates more harshly and more severely than it does in the county courts and above all is more costly';[228] this would, of course, threaten the livelihood of the under sheriffs and their men.[229]

The whole relationship between the courts greatly exercised the Committee. Unlike previous committees, this one was not domi-

[221] *Ibid.*, paras. 997, 983–90. [222] *Ibid.*, para. 995. [223] *Ibid.*, para. 585.

[224] *Ibid.*, paras. 586, 590. The only union to oppose its application to its members was the merchant seamen's, and they were duly excluded as a special case: Administration of Justice Act 1970 s. 26 (2) (e).

[225] *Ibid.*, para. 602 and app. 2.

[226] *Ibid.* Para. 588 promises a further discussion which fails to materialise.

[227] *Ibid.*, paras. 711–36, 855–99.

[228] *Ibid.*, para. 630, part of a discussion at paras. 630–57.

[229] *Ibid.*, paras. 658–67.

nated by high court judges, masters and London solicitors, which perhaps explains the lack of force behind the arguments the Report recounts for retaining the overlapping jurisdiction in liquidated claims. Payne met the preference for the greater speed and effectiveness of the high court in executing judgments by proposing a common regime for all judgments and gave the other objections to the county court little weight when set against its conviction that 'the aim should be to avoid overlapping, to achieve simplicity and to reduce expense to all parties'.[230]

The Committee became convinced that 'the costs sanction has largely failed'[231] and, rather than emphasising the rights of the suitor (in practice, his solicitor) to choose his forum, they frowned upon a system which 'gives a choice of courts as though litigation were a game in which players manoeuvre for better or worse chances'.[232] Prepared to urge a considerable tightening of the costs sanction if that were all that was acceptable, the Committee urged the consignment of all liquidated actions for less than £500 to the lower court, accepting that this was 'a far-reaching proposal which will alter substantially the pattern of litigation for the recovery of debts'.[233] Moreover, over the opposition of most of the public bodies which habitually resorted to the magistrates' courts on the grounds of cheapness, speed, informality and a more pro-creditor outlook,[234] Payne recommended that they lose jurisdiction over practically all civil liabilities, including rates, taxes and utilities charges.[235]

Under the Payne proposals the county court would become, with only minor exceptions, *the* court for small debts. To its 1.35 million plaints for debt would be added 75,000 high court judgments under Order XIV and an unknown number from the magistrates' courts,[236] while, in addition, it would be given an important power to postpone repossessions of homes by mortgagees;[237] it is an indication of the rising status of registrars that they were to be allowed to deal with these cases in chambers.

230 *Ibid.*, para. 89. 231 *Ibid.*, para. 101. 232 *Ibid.*, para. 119.

233 *Ibid.*, para. 120. 234 Gas Boards were an exception: *ibid.*, paras. 207–9.

235 *Ibid.*, para. 286. Excluded were London taxi fares and national insurance contributions.

236 The Report provides no figures and the absence of statistical information about magistrates' courts was a matter of growing complaint.

237 *Payne Report*, paras. 1345–433, especially para. 1399.

Beyond the hopeful assertion that the end of the judgment summons procedure should free a good deal of staff time no attempt was made to assess the manpower requirements and financial implications of this extra work.[238]

Although the substitution of attachment for committals and the ending of the overlapping jurisdictions were major reforms, the core of the Payne Report lay in its approach to enforcement generally rather than the remedies or the forum. Evershed, reviewing the high court alone, had 'adopted the principle that machinery of execution which is unplanned and untidy on paper ought not to be scrapped if it works satisfactorily in practice',[239] but while on the Payne Committee, 'there is no member ... who does not accept this principle ... the close examination of the law and practice of enforcement that we have been obliged to undertake has shown us that the machinery is not only unplanned and untidy on paper but does not work satisfactorily in practice'. They did not mince words: 'dissatisfaction and disillusion with the present system are widespread and there is evidence before us of creditors who will not pursue their remedies in the courts because of the feeling that it is a waste of time and of others who have recourse to private and sometimes ugly methods of enforcement'.[240]

The remedy was nothing if not ambitious. There should be

an integrated system for the enforcement of judgment debts of all courts which would

be capable of reaching out to all the income, assets and property of the debtor subject to specified exceptions
be capable of being employed concurrently or consecutively in one continuous process
be based on full information about the debtor's circumstances which he should be obliged to disclose
distribute the recovered monies fairly among the creditors
provide for the fair treatment of the debtor
provide for methods of controlling his access to credit and
be operated by machinery which should be efficient, effective, expeditious and fair.[241]

Although having the status of a court of record, presided over

238 *Ibid.*, para. 29, citing a work measurement survey of 1965 showing 5 per cent of clerks' time in county courts spent on judgment summonses.

239 *Ibid.*, para. 312.

240 *Ibid.*, para. 311.

241 *Ibid.*, para. 314.

by a county court registrar and coinciding with a county court district, the body charged with this daunting duty would not be a 'Debtors Court' as proposed by the Law Society, but an 'Enforcement Office'.[242] In order to be fully effective the Enforcement Office needed to encompass the debtor's non-judgment debts too and in fact to take complete command of his obligations and see to their ultimate discharge. This was to be accomplished through the medium of a modified and strengthened administration order.[243]

The Committee was enthusiastic about the potential of these cinderellas of the enforcement system, though noting that their present use was patchy, that they were sometimes abused by debtors and that, among other drawbacks, they could as yet be made only on the debtor's application.[244] They were seen as the basic tool of the Enforcement Office in most cases of multiple debts, but especially where the debtor was in business in a small way.

Imbued with the prevailing climate of opinion that the individual who reneged upon his obligations to society was in need of help,[245] the Committee succumbed to the urgings of welfare organisations and recommended that a 'Social Service Office for Debtors' be attached to each court, staffed by social workers who ought to be able 'to gain the confidence and co-operation of the debtor and his family' and recommend the most suitable order.[246]

What was proposed was a complete transformation of debtors from delinquents liable to imprisonment for the quasi-criminal offence of not paying debts when judged to have the means into 'inadequate personalities 'who 'succumb to the temptations of purchasing goods on credit beyond their means' or 'fall into debt from improvidence, misfortune or ill-health or accident ... Such debtors can no longer cope with life let alone with their financial affairs and may become resigned to their lot. Such debtors create problems which are primarily social and which require social rather than legal machinery for their solution.'[247] Accordingly the county court must be transformed into a quasi-welfare agency assisting (sometimes compelling) the inadequate personality to manage his life and money in the complex world of late capitalism.

242 *Ibid.*, paras. 330–42.
243 *Ibid.*, paras. 762–5, but note the reservations at pp. 377, 388–96.
244 *Ibid.*, para. 761. 245 *Ibid.*, paras. 1209–12. 246 *Ibid.*, para. 1214.
247 *Ibid.*, para. 1210.

Truly, Payne is in many ways a more remarkable document than Beeching.

Whether or not it is true that Sir Richard Beeching and his Commission 'in some ways got away from the LCD',[248] they certainly brought an iconoclastic approach to hallowed legal institutions which sets them apart from the long line of judge-led inquiries. The ruthlessly unsentimental approach which doomed the assizes extended also to such quaint survivals as the local courts in Liverpool, Bristol, Manchester and Norwich which the LCD had long wished, but never dared to abolish. Even now the City was powerful enough to preserve its Mayor's and City Court in name, but it became a county court in all essentials.[249]

The county courts themselves found more favour in the Commission's eyes. However tempting the prospect of rationalising the whole civil justice structure, Beeching acknowledged that his terms of reference were too narrow, and the composition of his Commission too restricted, to attempt it.[250] There would still be a high court and county courts but, as the Winn Report had proposed, the latter's jurisdiction should be raised to £1,000 and the registrars' to £100.[251] In fact the registrars should become judges proper, with the title of masters, and, as most of them wished, should finally shed the last vestiges of their original functions as administrators; the transformation begun in 1850 would thus be completed.[252] Perhaps surprisingly in view of its radicalism on most issues, Beeching did not discard the 'cushion', although it was proposed to make interchange between the courts easier.[253]

The Report praised the county court judges ('they do not always enjoy the status and reputation which they deserve'),[254] though reprobating the notion of a 'local' judge which some of them espoused. Now their role was to be widened to include criminal jurisdiction, for they, along with other junior judges, were to become circuit judges. Most of the county court judges

248 Stevens, *Independence of the Judiciary*, p. 117. Coldstream sat on the Commission, and oral evidence was given by judges Gage, Mais and Paton for the Society of County Court Judges. Written evidence was taken from the Council, the ACCR, the Officers' Association and judges Block, Harding and Bulger.

249 *PP* 1968–9 [Cmnd 4153] XXVIII. On county courts see paras. 368–73.

250 *Ibid.*, para. 205.

251 *Ibid.*, para. 175.

252 *Ibid.*, para. 176.

253 *Ibid.*, paras. 208–9, 216.

254 *Ibid.*, para. 108.

were already doing criminal work at quarter sessions but at least one entered a *nolle prosequi* and was allowed to confine himself to county court business.[255] It was acknowledged in the Report that the different backgrounds and expertises of the circuit judges would make a degree of functional specialisation sensible.[256]

The most dramatic outcome of implementing Beeching would be the end of the assizes, a sharp rupture in the continuity of English institutions. Equally important however, though much less remarked upon, was the alteration in the relations between the LCD and the judiciary. The Department was now to take responsibility for the staffing and operation of a 'unified court service' overseen at local level by 'Circuit Administrators'.[257] Hewart would have found all his worst fears realised but in a country which had found it convenient to allow the constitutional boundary between executive and judiciary to remain blurred it would rouse little public interest; nor, perhaps surprisingly, was there much murmuring from the judges.

## COURTS UNDER RECONSTRUCTION

With one major accession of business, undefended divorces, barely absorbed, there were now three important reports – Winn, Payne and Beeching – all recommending further substantial additions. Each inquiry had brushed aside objections that the county courts, if not inherently unsuited to what was proposed, were incapable of dispatching more and heavier business expeditiously and effectively. Nevertheless the legal profession was loud in its complaints, most of them familiar. Buildings, and not just the old ones, were badly designed and ill-equipped; the Lord Chancellor admitted that design briefs from the Home Office were skimpy and some of the recent courthouses appalling.[258] A high turnover among staff meant that they were often poorly trained and overstretched,[259] and though the number of judges kept on rising, the system was only kept going by an excessive use of deputies, who sat for more than a thousand days in

255 Judge Sumner: *The Times*, 18 May 1990. 256 *Beeching Report*, para. 250.
257 *Beeching Report*, para. 181. 258 See p. 321 below.
259 *SJ* 111 (1967), 10 (G. Williams); *SJ* 114 (1970), 575; *Law Guardian* 31 (1967), 29–30. See also pp. 301–4 below.

1968;[260] diverting judges to quarter sessions was robbing Peter to pay Paul, civil justice as usual being the victim of the robbery.[261]

A decade of inflation had also made a revision of the costs scales imperative, especially with the changes in divorce jurisdiction, but it was no longer a straightforward matter of little interest outside the profession and the Treasury. The extension of legal aid to the county courts meant that a part of any increase in lawyers' costs would be passed onto the taxpayer. Unfortunately, the issue also became entangled with a political argument over conveyancing charges.

The Labour government referred the matter of solicitors' incomes as a whole to its creature, the Prices and Incomes Board (PIB).[262] Appearing in February 1968, just ahead of a meeting of the Matrimonial Causes Rule Committee which was to fix a new costs scale, the PIB report[263] contained some interesting data on the economics of county court work. Barely one in seven of the solicitors' firms in its sample group derived more than 5 per cent of their income from that source and for most of those which did, it was currently uneconomic. An increase of 27 per cent in the costs scale would bring most of these 'specialists' back into profit but no less than 108 per cent would be needed to do the same for the larger group whose county court work accounted for 2 to 5 per cent of their income. The 35 per cent of firms in the sample whose county court engagements were negligible could not be expected to be taken into consideration.[264]

But the PIB did not intend to recommend any such increases. With unfounded confidence in its judgment and qualifications for such a task and an entire disregard for the impact of its proposals on the service the courts were supposed to provide, it set out to achieve a wholesale and rapid restructuring of the profession through the manipulation of scale charges for both contentious and non-contentious business. A rise of 55 per cent in county

260 *Hansard* 1967–8 5th s., vol. 288 (HL), cols. 602–10; G. Borrie and J. Pyke, The Administration of Justice Act, 1969, *NLJ* 119 (1969), 1012–13.

261 *NLJ* 119 (1969), 589–90.

262 For accounts of these events see Kirk, *Portrait of a Profession*, pp. 149–52 and Jackson, *Machinery of Justice* (6th edn.), pp. 427–9. The professional journals, especially the *LSG*, give blow-by-blow accounts.

263 *PP* 1967–8 [Cmnd 3529] XXVII. There is a useful summary in *NLJ* 118 (1968), 123–6, 149–52.

264 Table C.

court costs was to be balanced by reductions in conveyancing charges which would leave the total collective remuneration of the profession unchanged.[265] This would, it was supposed, make county court work profitable only to those firms willing to specialise in it; others could not complain if it was not profitable. The arrogance of the Board did not stop there, for it sought a standing reference and proposed in effect to reduce the rule committees to rubber stamps.[266]

To the disgust of solicitors, the rule committees meekly submitted. The Matrimonial Causes Rule Committee produced a costs scale ten years out of date[267] and the chairman of the county courts committee, Judge Temple Morris, obsequiously cancelled its meeting on the indefensible ground that the Lord Chancellor would not sign any rules increasing costs until the Law Society accepted the 'linkage' with conveyancing which the PIB insisted upon.[268]

Ministers' own performances in the debates on the matrimonial rules were scarcely more creditable[269] and the impasse persisted until the PIB's second report (1969) weakened the linkage and offered a slightly more generous county court scale.[270] Even then, solicitors were accepting a scale which would keep county court work unremunerative for most of them, so it is scarcely surprising that they were unenthusiastic about the LCD's cost-driven policy of forcing more litigation into that forum.[271] Either side of the general election of 1970 the three reports – Winn, Payne and Beeching – were implemented. In matters pertaining to civil justice there was little to distinguish Labour from Conservative: Hailsham, like Gardiner, was a fierce defender of the bar's privileged position on audience and judicial appointments and the

[265] *PP* 1967–8 [Cmnd 3529] XXVII, para. 65, and see the patronising criticisms of courts and solicitors at para. 63.

[266] *Ibid.*, paras. 70–7. There is a sympathetic appraisal by B. Easton in *NLJ* 118 (1968), 161–2.

[267] Lengthy negotiations over the scale had broken down in 1967: *LSG* 64 (1967), 233, 461, 467, 471. The solicitor members refused to sign the Matrimonial Causes Rules (SI 219 of 1968) which imposed the new scale.

[268] Scathingly criticised in the legal press: *NLJ* 118 (1968), 361–3; *NLJ* 119 (1969), 167; *LSG* 66 (1969), 73–4.

[269] *Hansard* 1967–8 5th s., vol. 291 (HL), cols. 1424–58.

[270] *PP* 1969–70 [Cmnd 4217] XXV, paras. 29–41.

[271] *SJ* 113 (1969), 373; *NLJ* 119 (1969), 451. The June supplement of the *LSG* has a full account, with correspondence.

two men ensured that law reforms would proceed without factious opposition in a way that recalled Selborne and Cairns a hundred years before.[272] More radical reformers decried the tendency to legislate piecemeal changes but the practice of frequent Administration of Justice Acts filled with assorted reforms was by now firmly established.[273]

The Act of 1969 went some way to implement the Winn Report by raising the county court limit and the 'cushion' in proportion. The increase was only to £750 however, for as Gardiner admitted, there was not the money to spend on improving facilities and recording judgments which Winn had said would be necessary;[274] the Lord Chancellor was however empowered to raise the limit to any extent by order in council.[275] Registrars were given jurisdiction in contested actions up to £75 unless one of the parties made an objection, and at last the obsolescent ban on 'attorney-advocates' was repealed: 'the barristers – I am not blaming them – hung onto it as long as they could', said Gardiner condescendingly.[276]

Though Dilhorne and Denning regretted the change in the character of the county court,[277] the Lords offered little criticism, but the Bill had a rougher passage in the Commons, where the unsuitability of the county courts for personal injury claims was strongly pressed and the large increase in equity jurisdiction from a level where it was seldom used to one with the potential to affect the Chancery division quite seriously also came under fire.[278] The heaviest fire, however, was directed at the costs sanction. The Bill not only followed Winn in uprating the cushion to 80 per cent of the sum claimed but anticipated Payne by repealing the

272 See their mutual congratulations in *Hansard* 1969–70 5th s., vol. 310 (HL), cols. 1039–40. Gardiner's contribution is evaluated by R. F. V. Heuston, *Lives of the Lord Chancellors, 1940–70* (Oxford, 1987), pp. 225–39, Hailsham's by G. Lewis, *Lord Hailsham, a Life* (London, 1997).

273 S. M. Cretney, The Administration of Justice Act 1969, *SJ* 113 (1969), 951–3; G. Borrie and J. Pyke, The Administration of Justice Act 1969, *NLJ* 119 (1969), 1012–13.

274 *Hansard*, 1968–9 5th s., vol. 297 (HL), cols. 433–5; J. C.Harper, Personal Injuries Litigation, *MLR* 34 (1971), 70–4.

275 Administration of Justice Act 1969 s. 10.

276 *Hansard* 1968–9 5th s., vol. 297 (HL), col. 437. Criticism from the PIB (*PP* 1967–8 [Cmnd 3529] XXVII, paras. 61–2) may have emboldened the government finally to confront this old anomaly. As late as 1958 Judge Southall had tried to enforce it: *Davis & Co. v. Dye*, *LJ* 108 (1958), 113.

277 *Hansard* 1968–9, 5th s., vol. 297 (HL), cols. 458–70.

278 *Ibid.*, vol. 777 (HC), cols. 408–78.

intricate provisions of s. 47 (4) County Courts Act 1959, which had made the high court an attractive option for unopposed debt collection.[279]

It did not assist those who had to defend the change (which would not bind the Crown) that the Department of Health and Social Security had recently removed all its debt actions into the high court,[280] nor that the Payne Report, which appeared before the Bill reached the Commons, linked its suggestion for repeal with proposals to improve county court executions. In standing committee the government was resoundingly defeated by 'a remarkable non-party coalition'[281] on an amendment thickening the cushion by £100, and another, to lower from £150 to £75 the minimum sum required to be recovered before costs might be awarded, was lost only on the chairman's casting vote.[282] By the time the Bill had reached the report stage, the Under-Sheriffs' Association had shown convincingly that they would be so hard hit by the undefended costs proposal that their other, indispensable functions for the high court would be put in jeopardy and accordingly Gardiner conceded a reduction to £100.[283]

The next year it was the turn of the Payne Report, or rather, parts of it. Beyond enacting the proposal that the courts should be able to postpone mortgage repossessions in certain circumstances (outside London and Lancashire this power was given exclusively to county courts),[284] the Bill did little more than abolish imprisonment for breach of money judgment orders (retaining it for maintenance orders) and introduce attachment of earnings; only at the committee stage in the Commons was the court given the power to impose an administration order on its own initiative.[285]

279 *PP* 1967–8 [Cmnd 3684] XXX, paras. 473–6; *Payne Report*, para. 119; *PP* 1968–9 (HC 60) I, Administration of Justice Bill cl. 4.

280 Noticed by Sir Ian Percival at the report stage (*Hansard* 1968–9 5th s., vol. 788 (HC), cols. 789–90, and by commentators, e.g. S. M. Cretney, The Administration of Justice Act 1970, *SJ* 114 (1970), 596–9.

281 Cretney's phrase, The Administration of Justice Act 1969, *SJ* 113 (1969), 953. *PP* 1968–9 V: standing committees, HC, cl. 4.

282 *Hansard* 1968–9 5th s., vol. 788 (HC), cols. 790–4. At the report stage Percival's amendment was lost by 121 to 146 in a vote along party lines.

283 *Ibid.*, vol. 304 (HL), cols. 1614–17. This was estimated to reduce the transfer of undefended debt actions from 47 per cent to 30 per cent.

284 Administration of Justice Act 1970 s. 37. For doubts about the competence of the county courts see E. L. G. Tyler, *NLJ* 120 (1970), 808.

285 *NLJ* 120 (1970), 564–6.

Gardiner defended the 'staging' of the Payne proposals as being in line with the Committee's own suggestion, but what was being done was really more along the lines of the 'Reservation' entered by Wheatcroft and Shufflebotham, who cautiously favoured taking things one at a time and seeing how each turned out before proceeding further.[286] Outline provision for the most ambitious, and contentious, element, the Enforcement Office, had been in the original Bill but was dropped before it was presented in the Lords. Though the LCD was sceptical of its merits the decisive voice was probably the Treasury's, for it was estimated that the introduction of attachment orders alone would cost £70,000, the Enforcement Office far more.[287]

Selwyn Lloyd and Donaldson were particularly critical of the omission of 'the kernel' of the Payne Report[288] but most speakers' main concern was the working of attachment orders.[289] Some lawyers, and doubtless many judges, were sorry to be deprived of the weapon of committals but not one peer or MP was prepared to stand up in Parliament and speak for its retention: it was one grand old institution they were glad to see the end of.[290]

Finally Dobson and his team, to whom Gardiner paid gracious tribute,[291] were able to present the Courts Bill, embodying most of the recommendations of the Beeching Commission. It fell to Hailsham to introduce it and he acknowledged that he would have liked to integrate the civil side of the courts as completely as the criminal side was now proposed to be, but the resources could not yet be found.[292]

Although the position of their judges underwent drastic changes, the county courts themselves were not very greatly affected by the biggest upheaval in the courts since the Judicature

286 *Payne Report*, paras. 33–5 and pp. 400–3; Glasser, Administration of Justice Act 1970, at 67–8.

287 *Hansard* 1969–70 5th s., vol. 306 (HL), col. 222.

288 *Hansard* 1968–9 5th s., vol. 306 (HL), cols. 218–25, 229.

289 *Ibid.*, vol. 306 (HL), cols. 874, 924; vol. 307 (HL), cols. 13–66; standing committee, vol. 801 (HC), cols. 1603–22.

290 For appraisals of the Act see Glasser, Administration of Justice Act 1970, Cretney, Administration of Justice Act 1970, and G. Borrie and J. Pyke, Administration of Justice Act 1970, *NLJ* 120 (1970), 540–2, 564–6.

291 *Hansard*, 1970–1 5th s., vol. 312 (HL), cols. 1254 ff. Denis Dobson succeeded Coldstream as Permanent Secretary in 1968. It appears that he was not wholly pleased with the Beeching Report: *The Times*, 16 Dec. 1995.

292 *Hansard*, 1970–1 5th s., vol. 312 (HL), col. 1307.

Acts. There was no further increase in their jurisdiction and Beeching's idea of styling registrars masters was dropped. But though the integrated civil court remained a pipedream the Courts Act did mark the end of an era; the county courts branch of the LCD was subsumed within the new courts' service and the county court judges were now to be circuit judges with a much wider range of duties.[293]

Just as the Judicature Acts were not intended to mark the limits of reform and reconstruction, neither was the Courts Act. However satisfactory the county courts seemed to Beeching, evidence was mounting which showed that, as they increasingly took on work which had belonged to the high court, so they reopened the very gap they had been created to fill. In the same session as the Courts Bill, Michael Meacher's Small Claims Courts Bill made its first appearance, testimony to the view put forward in an influential report from the Consumer Council that many would-be suitors still found only 'Justice out of Reach'.[294]

[293] Courts Act 1971 s. 43.
[294] Published in 1970.

6

# CENTRAL ORGANISATION AND FINANCES

## THE LORD CHANCELLOR'S DEPARTMENT

Although three departments initially shared the duties involved in running the new courts, the Home Office had the lion's share, handling accommodation and sittings, prison facilities for debtors, complaints by and about judges and, in conjunction with the Treasury, fees and salaries. Most initiatives came from outside, however, and the Home Secretaries of the period do not seem to have been very enthusiastic about their new charge.[1]

The Home Office of the 1840s was a small unit organised along old-fashioned lines with particular clerks holding expertise in the several branches of its work within their own heads.[2] New areas of responsibility were invariably treated by the clerks as inferior and, although one of them was given an extra allowance for the correspondence generated by the County Courts Act, it is unlikely that anyone took much interest in it. The Home Secretary's need to offer economies in the clerical organisation and the fact that no patronage went with his responsibilities probably explain why he willingly surrendered them to the Lord Chancellor, a curiously timed change, with major inquiries into the organisation of legal services imminent.[3]

In June 1868 three bags of Home Office papers arrived, unaccompanied by any clerks. The Chancellor would have the

[1] There were six Home Secretaries between 1847 and 1866, of whom Sir George Grey (1846–52, 1855–8 and 1861–6) was in post for more than half of that time.

[2] J. Pellew, Law and Order: Expertise and the Victorian Home Office, in R. McLeod (ed.), *Government and Expertise* (Cambridge, 1988), pp. 59–72.

[3] J. Pellew, *The Home Office, 1848–1914* (London, 1982), ch. 2; PRO HO 86/1–3; A. P. Donagrodski, New Roles for Old: the Northcote-Trevelyan Report and the Clerks of the Home Office, 1832–48, in G. Sutherland (ed.), *Studies in the Growth of Nineteenth Century Government*, (London, 1972), pp. 82–110.

assistance of his private secretary and Henry Nicol, who already acted as a sort of county courts secretary and in the absence until the 1880s of any recognisably 'modern' departmental structure with an accessible record system, Nicol was indispensable and very influential; his own attempt to play down his role before the Childers Committee was utterly unconvincing.[4]

After Nicol's retirement in 1894 his role in the LCO devolved upon the Permanent Secretary, always a barrister and usually imbued, like most Lord Chancellors, with a conviction of the overriding importance of upholding the pre-eminence of the high court and the position of the bar.[5] It was departmental policy until after the Second World War that while county court jurisdiction might be judiciously enlarged, it should not be allowed to make any serious inroads into the position of the high court. This did not change with the capture of the county courts department from the Treasury in 1922; the administration of the county and high courts was in no way integrated and movement of personnel between them, from the judges down to the clerks, was minimal and certainly not systematic.

The Treasury still had a part to play, being necessarily involved in setting fees, scrutinising judges' allowances and controlling building expenditure, but its hand was generally light. Even in the 1860s, when parliamentary opinion most strongly endorsed parsimony in public expenditure, Treasury supervision of the everyday activities of government departments was relatively ineffective, and it scarcely existed at all where the courts were concerned:[6] at most, as Sir Thomas Farrar observed, 'we can cheat them in big things; they may bully us in small things'.[7] Events in the 1870s showed that the Treasury could not enforce major economies in the provision of county courts and judges even when that provision seemed extravagant and judges underworked. It could be

4 PRO HO 86/3, f. 447; *Childers Report*, qq. 1906 ff.

5 Polden, *Guide to the Records of the LCD*, pp. 13–33. Muir McKenzie did claim that he had always favoured an extension of the jurisdiction: *Hansard*, 1919 5th s., vol. 37 (HL), cols. 351–4.

6 H. Roseveare, *The Treasury* (London, 1969), ch. 7; Wright, *Treasury Control of the Civil Service*; M. Wright, Treasury Control, 1854–1914, in Sutherland (ed.), *Studies*, pp. 195–227. None of these studies does more than glance at the problems of expenditure on the legal system.

7 Quoted in Wright, Treasury Control, 1854–1914, p. 199. Farrar was formerly under-secretary at the Board of Trade.

cheeseparing with judges' expenses but could not make them work harder.[8]

Generally speaking, 'if there was no demand for increased expenditure there was "virtually no Treasury control"'[9] and it was not until the advent of legal aid in 1949 that the LCD began making substantial extra demands on the public purse. Even then, worthwhile savings could only be secured if the Treasury was prepared to engage in a dispute with the judiciary for which it had no stomach. However, by then it had become LCD policy to divert more business to the county court rather than expand the number of high court judges and trial facilities. Some Chancellors were reluctant, particularly Hailsham, but as legal aid costs rose the relative cheapness of the county courts made it practically unavoidable.[10] Treasury demands were focused more on getting extra money out of litigants than on improving the efficiency of the courts and, though it dictated terms in pay negotiations for court staff,[11] what is striking – as borne out by the relative ease with which they secured more judges – is rather the freedom than the constraints.

Within the LCD work expanded generally and in county court matters increasing reliance came to be placed upon Roy Gregory. Entering the Department in 1948, he achieved a unique status as 'the Lord Chancellor's expert adviser on practice and procedure in all civil courts'. Working directly to the Permanent Secretary, he was secretary to the County Court Rule Committee from 1961, chiefly responsible for the *County Court Practice* and the official *Handbook*, and for county court fees and records.[12] Gregory's biggest achievements with the small claims procedure in 1973 and the rules revision of 1981, were still to come, but by 1970 he was already as indispensable as Nicol or Selfe in their day.[13]

[8] See pp. 253–4 below.
[9] Wright, Treasury Control, 1854–1914, p. 197; the internal quotation is from R. E. Welby's evidence to the Ridley Commission (1887).
[10] See ch. 5 above.
[11] See e.g. PRO LCO 8/54.
[12] Sir G. P. Coldstream, The Lord Chancellor's Office, *Graya* 55 (1962), 13–21; Report of Treasury inspector on Gregory's post, 20 May 1966, PRO LCO 4/348.
[13] *The Times*, 25 Jul. 1997.

## THE COUNTY COURTS BRANCH

Henry Nicol, a second-class clerk in the Treasury since 1850, was in charge of the treasurers' accounts and other financial aspects of county courts, and this became a distinct 'county courts department' in 1861.[14] For the next thirty years Nicol and his assistant Quentin Twiss[15] formed the core of a unit which gradually assumed its enduring shape as the treasurers were phased out and replaced by peripatetic 'Examiners of Accounts' (initially their own clerks);[16] these men, twenty-odd in number, and a handful of office clerks were scattered around three floors of the Treasury building.

Their superintendent had only a modest place in the Treasury hierarchy but considerable independence.[17] B. J. Bridgeman, Nicol's successor,[18] described the functions of his department thus: '[i]ts duties are primarily financial. It considers the financial effect of draft rules; it issues, under the general supervision of the Treasury, instructions to officers of County Courts as to accounts, book-keeping, fees, &c., and authorities for making payments, and acts generally as a department entrusted with the "accountant" duties of the County Courts.'[19] He added that 'certain duties not strictly financial' also fell within its remit because although 'the administration of the County Courts properly appertains to the Lord Chancellor's department ... the Lord Chancellor has no itinerant staff through whom he could promptly and effectively obtain independent information needed in dealing with 500

[14] *Select Committee, 1878*, qq. 4969 ff. He was formerly in the department of the law clerk (PRO T 10/1, f. 178).

[15] Twiss 'entered the Treasury in 1856 and set some sort of record by remaining there for thirty-five years without promotion ... He was quite a celebrated comic actor, whose "duties as a Treasury clerk", recorded his *Times* obituary, left him a good deal of time to devote to his favourite occupation': Roseveare, *The Treasury*, p. 172.

[16] For treasurers see p. 63 above.

[17] *MacDonnell Evidence*, Bridgeman at q. 51,783. For the structure of the Treasury see Roseveare, *The Treasury*, pp. 210–11.

[18] Nicol retired with a CB and a pension of £700: *PP* 1896 (322) XL. Alfred Pike was briefly superintendent (1894–8); he had been a civil list clerk in the accounts branch. Bridgeman came from the treasury solicitor's department where he was clerk in charge of accounts.

[19] *MacDonnell Evidence*, q. 51,630.

County Court offices, in which the majority of the judges scarcely ever set foot'.[20]

Rules and instructions were transmitted to the courts by the department and if it became aware of misconduct, not necessarily of a financial sort, it would report to the LCO.[21] Its reach went further, however, for 'the department also observes how the office work is done, and acts if there is any inefficiency'; registrars would be instructed to take appropriate steps, and only in the last resort would the authority of the Lord Chancellor be invoked.[22]

The department also organised the supply of stationery and office equipment and assessed judges' claims for ushers, books and travelling expenses.[23] Moreover, whilst insisting that the court staff were not civil servants, it nevertheless took upon itself to judge whether an illness justified the registrar in employing a substitute and whether an injury should be compensated out of public funds.[24] If an officer was threatened with a law suit for malfeasance, neglect or (most commonly) for exceeding his powers, the law officers' opinion would usually be sought to determine whether to defend him at public expense,[25] but other complaints were usually dealt with without reference to higher authority.[26] In theory all proposals involving public expenditure had to be approved by the principal in the Treasury's legal division, but Bridgeman implied that except where substantial sums were involved (usually for new or extended buildings) this was a formality.[27]

Few matters, then, went beyond the superintendent. But whereas Nicol had been universally respected, Bridgeman made himself extremely unpopular. He took no pains to conceal his opinion that many judges were underworked, that registrars needed the incentive of payment by results to provide a decent service and that clerks were men well below civil service calibre doing straightforward, undemanding jobs.[28] There was a good

20 *Ibid.*, q. 51,633.
21 *Ibid.*, qq. 51,634–6.
22 *Ibid.*, qq. 51,637–8. For an example, see p. 204 below.
23 *Ibid.*, qq. 51,639–45.
24 *Ibid.*, q. 51,646.
25 Examples are in PRO T 10.
26 *MacDonnell Evidence*, qq. 51,647–9.
27 *Ibid.*, qq. 51,650–2.
28 *Ibid.*, qq. 51,857, 51,715, 51,666.

deal of truth in these propositions. Nicol had been under few illusions about the courts, telling a select committee that a registrar 'may decrease [business] amazingly by simply not giving facilities', and implying that they would always give priority to their private practice; he had 'frequently heard that some judges do not sit as often as they might' and knew that suitors' fears of biased judges were sometimes justified.[29] All in all, 'it is astonishing what people put up with'.[30]

Bridgeman, however, appeared to registrars autocratic and ungenerous, more concerned with economy than the administration of justice. His decisions were effectively unappealable and, during the Great War, when circumstances put them at his mercy, they found him wanting in sympathy. The registrar on the Swift Committee, Arthur Jennings, was insistent that there must be some appeal on questions such as the interpretation of a fee order and from his decisions on, for example, the proper allowance for clerk hire: 'it is no good writing to the Secretary to the Treasury, because the superintendent is his adviser'.[31] Letters from registrars amply confirmed the 'widespread feeling that registrars are up against a particular official'.[32]

Bridgeman's departure, and the transfer of the department to the LCO in 1922, were therefore welcomed. His successor, H. P. Boland, had a new responsibility, for as courts became 'established' their staff became civil servants, and in conjunction with other departments the county courts branch had to arrange for recruitment, promotion and retirement, in due course becoming responsible for the careers of several thousand men and women.

The system of accounting and audit was also overhauled, since registrars would no longer be liable without fault for losses to the suitors or the public. The 1888 Act had given the Treasury a free hand in the choice of auditors and they were invariably chosen by the superintendent from a waiting list of county court clerks.[33] The examiners conducted a quarterly audit at each court, the

29 *Select Committee, 1878*, qq. 5115, 5187, 5173–5.

30 *Lisgar Evidence*, q. 7429.

31 *Swift Evidence*, 4B–H.

32 *Ibid.*, 4G. None of the witnesses or respondents had anything complimentary to say about the superintendent.

33 County Courts Act 1888 s. 38; *MacDonnell Evidence*, qq. 51,776–82. They were usually about thirty-five years old when appointed.

largest taking several days. They concentrated on seeing that the books balanced and that fees had been duly collected and accounted for, making only test audits in the ledgers recording the innumerable ins and outs of small sums.[34] A full audit was thought impracticable and superfluous, for if it was necessary to trace a default to a particular clerk the registrar, being liable for the loss, had every incentive to do it himself.

As Bridgeman said, the examiners were also on the look-out for other infractions: one, for example, discovered that a new registrar had been issuing judgment summonses without the prescribed affidavit.[35] The visit of the examiner, resplendent in his frock coat and silk hat, was therefore a momentous event, especially in the smaller courts; as a young clerk, Barker was deputed to take him his glass of egg and milk, receiving a few coppers and a religious tract as his reward.[36] It was a great thing for a clerk to become an examiner, for they were paid £200 to £450 a year, had the coveted civil service pension and might even end up as a clerk in the department.[37]

Boland's brief tenure was dominated by the negotiations over staff establishment and the work of a small committee on accounts, whose report, recommending a major overhaul in bookkeeping in the courts, was his parting gift.[38] This was what Schuster wanted, for serious irregularities had come to light in one court, the defaulter killing himself when exposed; the fraud had been going on for years and Schuster felt that the elderly examiner ought to have found it out much sooner.[39]

Since the new system required more elaborate quarterly returns and fuller bookkeeping by bailiffs, it was more burdensome to staff and naturally caused grumbling;[40] nor was it foolproof, but Schuster defended it as the best that could be done without

34 *MacDonnell Evidence*, qq. 51,893–5, 52,135–42. Bridgeman guessed there were 8 or 9 million postings from cashbooks to ledgers.

35 *Swift Evidence*, 61 L–M (W. E. Jones).

36 *CCO* 26 (1947–9), 155. Barker does not reveal that he later became an auditor himself.

37 Examples are H. S. Grazebrook and H. Baber in the 1890s.

38 PRO LCO 8/44. The report was not published.

39 *PP* 1926 (26, 155) V, qq. 1328 ff., with an implied censure on the county courts department at q. 1341.

40 Circulars in PRO LCO 8/88, especially 15/1924, 21/1924, 3/1925, 3A/1925, 2/1927. See also p. 299 below.

unacceptable expense.[41] The examiners were retitled auditors to emphasise their extended role,[42] but the LCO denied the claim made by their union (the Society of Civil Servants) that they were a 'travelling inspectorate' with responsibilities beyond the audit;[43] however it was certainly believed that they were used to recommend clerks for promotion.[44]

With the move the branch acquired a new role, compiling the annual civil justice statistics, hitherto prepared in the Home Office with material provided by the LCO. As an economy measure the elaborate and informative productions pioneered by Sir John MacDonnell were reduced to a bare set of tables and the separate sets of county court returns ceased publication; since the last of these had sold just seven copies, there was no outcry.[45]

In 1924 Boland was succeeded by Ernest Martin, a Treasury principal with no experience of the courts.[46] Martin proved a good choice and made useful innovations. His main helpers were the establishment officer, A. J. Hill, and the assistant superintendent, A. E.Tilley, each succeeded in turn by S. J. H. Dunn who, starting out as a clerk in the Bridport county court in 1895, became successively an examiner, a clerk, establishment officer and finally, in 1939, assistant superintendent.[47]

As accounting officer Schuster was careful to keep in touch with matters of importance, but day-to-day responsibility was delegated to the Assistant Secretary Albert Napier. Napier had charge of the Rule Committee and interviewed prospective registrars, though during the war, with the LCO stretched to its limits, Martin, having earned Napier's confidence, was given more responsibilities and a special allowance. Generally however, the superintendent enjoyed less independence under the LCO even though the branch was physically detached, the LCO clinging tenaciously to its coveted rooms in the House of Lords while the branch was moved first to Millbank (1935) and

41 *PP* 1930–1 (48, 114) V, q. 706.

42 *PP* 1926 (26, 155) V, q. 1351.

43 *CCO* 28 (1951), 45.

44 E. Slack, *CCO* 38 (1963–4), 10.

45 *Chitty Committee Report*, PRO LCO 29/11, p. 29. Boland and Napier both sat on the Committee.

46 Boland, a principal in the Establishments Office, was appointed on 1 Sep. 1922 and took a post in his native Ireland in July 1924.

47 *CCO* 24 (1945–7), 66. Dunn retired in 1945.

later, after an evacuation to Thame (1939–45), to Dean's Yard, Westminster.[48]

When Martin retired in 1949 his branch consisted of twelve clerks, forty typists, twenty-three auditors and two inspectors under the three senior men, and was responsible for 2,041 court staff.[49] Martin's successor was Frank Mayell, who had begun at Scotland Yard, transferring to the LCO in 1940.[50] The assistant superintendent since 1945 was A. J. Cole, who had come into the department in 1912 as a boy clerk, and the establishment officer was F. G. Axmann, first a county court clerk in Fakenham, Norfolk (1920), then an auditor (1939).[51]

The branch was essentially concerned with administration rather than policy and under Mayell's less forceful and imaginative leadership it became highly conservative. Even when the hand of the Treasury was at its lightest, the branch was always alert to prevent waste and extravagance and as the visible face of official resistance to claims for better pay and conditions it could not expect to be popular; but though the unpopularity was sometimes undeserved, as when there were delays in wage increases, it also stemmed from a generally negative outlook. The branch seemed indifferent to innovations promising no immediate saving, therefore rejecting both staff training and an O & M committee out of hand[52] and disparaging several proposals in the Austin Jones Report, even postal service extensions which soon came to be generally accepted.[53]

Coldstream had seen this resistance with some impatience and had become dissatisfied with the leadership of the branch. In 1956 Master Wheatcroft, heading a committee on execution of judgments, was unfavourably impressed with Mayell's denial, in the face of widespread criticism, that the system was defective, and by Cole's negative attitude to suggested changes.[54] At Coldstream's suggestion, he sent a personal letter to the Lord Chancellor in

[48] Martin to Napier, 12 Aug. 1946, PRO LCO 4/22. From 1936, Martin was paid at Assistant Secretary rates, and in 1946 his salary was raised to £1,800.

[49] PRO LCO 4/22.

[50] PRO LCO 4/221; *CCO* 36 (1959–60), 138.

[51] *CCO* 36 (1959–60), 260; Kewish to Coldstream, 8 Mar. 1960, PRO LCO 4/118; *CCO* 24 (1945–7), 66.

[52] *CCO* 30 (1953), 168–74; *CCO* 36 (1959–60), 42–3.

[53] PRO LCO 2/3299 (evidence); 2/3317 (discussions on the Report).

[54] Rieu's note, 26 Apr. 1955, PRO LCO 2/5063; 19th meeting, 2/5064. For this report see p. 183 above.

which he claimed that the branch was unable to arrange prompt inspections of courts alleged to be failing and needed a chief with higher rank, supported by a younger registrar as his deputy and roving 'troubleshooter'.[55] Since Mayell was pressing for the upgrading of his lieutenants and for the appointment of a welfare officer (a staff-side suggestion[56]), he could not well demur at Coldstream's invitation to the Treasury to send in a staff inspector, ostensibly to report on the claims of Cole and Axmann, but with a wider remit too, albeit he was urged to take 'a broad view of a somewhat peculiar organisation'.[57]

Coldstream was keen to enhance the role of the auditors, sharing Rieu's view that 'at the present time the auditors have little opportunity of carrying out inspections which are probably essential if there is to be any central control. The absence of such control seems to be at the root of the widespread criticism on the subject of the efficiency of the system.'[58] The inspector reported unfavourably on the claims of the incumbents, recommending that both the head and his deputy should be legally qualified, the former at assistant secretary level; on Mayell's retirement in 1960 a lawyer came to head the branch, the first since Nicol.[59]

Coldstream wanted an outsider, a similar appointment to the Supreme Court Taxing Office having 'pulled the whole place together in a remarkable manner',[60] and his choice was Douglas Kewish, a highly regarded Liverpool registrar with a good army record.[61] Kewish evidently made some difference because a Treasury O & M man engaged in a study of the handling of suitors' funds wrote that 'our discussions ... with officers of the branch have been rather protracted but with the departure of some of them from the scene recently, it has been possible to make some progress with their successors'.[62] Kewish had his difficulties – lack

55 10 Aug. 1956, PRO LCO 4/118.

56 *Ibid.*, note of April 1957 and H. Boggis-Rolfe to Coldstream, 16 Oct. 1958.

57 Coldstream to J. W. Winnifrith, 16 Oct. 1958, *ibid.*

58 R. Rieu to Judge Paton, 15 Apr. 1959, PRO LCO 2/6371. At the suggestion of C. J. Hayes, in charge of the review, several judges were written to for opinions.

59 PRO LCO 4/118.

60 Coldstream to Sir L. Holmes [July, 1957], *ibid.*

61 Holmes to Coldstream, 2 Aug. 1957, *ibid.* Registrars Pownall and Fraser confirmed the favourable view of Kewish.

62 H. E. N. Cullingford to R. E. K. Thesiger, 31 July 1961, PRO LCO 4/119. Cole retired in October 1960, Axmann in 1962.

of a civil service background perhaps contributed to his mistakes in the conduct of wage negotiations[63] – but overdue progress was made on training and structural reforms; union resistance to clerical assistants was overcome and at the end of the 1960s a new system of audit and inspection was introduced.[64]

As well as staff discontents beyond its power to address, the branch had to undertake the heavy task of readying the courts for the influx of divorce business after the 1967 Act[65] and not long afterwards was itself involved in a bigger upheaval, the Courts Act 1971 bringing its separate existence to an end and leading to the overdue creation of a unified courts service.

### *The Whitley Councils*

In response to an alarming upsurge in industrial unrest during the Great War, an official sub-committee 'recommended the introduction into industry of machinery to regularize relations between employers and employed, and the joint co-operation of employers and employed in the functions of management and control'.[66] Ironically, almost the only place where this hopeful vision was permanently translated into a practical reality, and then with more modest aspirations, was the public service and when county courts staffs became 'established', they also came within the scope of the national Whitley Council for the civil service.

'Whitleyism', however, was also intended to operate at departmental and branch level, and in 1919 the County Court Officers Association (CCOA) approached Schuster, flourishing the Ministry of Labour's blueprint for setting up departmental councils.[67] Uneasy at this novel prospect, especially in view of the Association's links with a big civil service union and the militancy staff had been recently displaying, Schuster consulted Sir Michael Ramsay, head of the Treasury's newly created establishments division,[68] and they decided upon a policy of prevarication, first

63 See PRO LCO 8/54. 64 See pp. 300–4 below.

65 J. Garnham and D. Templeman, Operation Divorce, *CCO* 40 (1967–8), 274.

66 H. Parris, *Staff Relations in the Civil Service* (London, 1973), p. 25.

67 9 Sep. 1919, PRO LCO 2/670.

68 *Ibid.*, note to A. Napier, 6 Nov., Schuster to Ramsay, 7 Nov. 1919. Ramsay became the first chairman of the National Whitley Council: Parris, *Staff Relations*, pp. 28–31.

using the pending Swift Report as an excuse and then relying on the Association's preoccupation with the negotiations about establishment.[69]

These evasions succeeded until 1926, when the union's conference pressed for the renewal of talks,[70] and what emerged was typical of the peculiar slants to which standard administrative practices were prone when they came into contact with the courts. A departmental council was established, set up in appropriate terms and having similar functions to a Whitley Council, but not actually comprising one. It was unusual in that the 'staff side' represented just one union, the CCOA, other unions with members in the courts never seeking representation.[71]

The council was to meet at the request of either side and after its inaugural meeting in February 1927 to discuss a bailiffs' pay claim it met irregularly, with a two-and-a-half-year gap after 1929, probably because the staff side, having experienced little success, was pinning its hopes on the Tomlin Commission.[72] Besides pay, the issues of most concern were regrading, holidays and relief staff.[73] Meetings actually became more frequent in the early part of the Second World War, but this came to an abrupt halt when, failing to win concessions on bailiffs' travel, the union called in Len White, general secretary of the Civil Service Clerical Association (CSCA), to lend his experience of national Whitleyism to their efforts. White's less deferential style shocked and offended the official side, his view being that 'even a cursory survey of the history of this Department over the years leads inevitably to the conclusion that its affairs have not been conducted with due regard to the obligation imposed upon the Official Side by the Government's acceptance of the Whitley system'.[74] Schuster himself, on the eve of retirement, made a wrathful intervention and it was believed that at least one of

69 PRO LCO 2/670. Schuster sat on the national council and was one of the few non-Treasury members to impress his personality on the staff side: Parris, *Staff Relations*, p. 41.

70 Incited by the future cabinet minister Douglas Houghton, then a youthful General Secretary of the Tax Officers Association.

71 N. Walsh, 'Whitleyism in the County Courts, *CCO* 41 (1969–70), 156–9, 185–90, 249–56. This account is drawn from the *County Court Officer* as no background papers to meetings survive in the PRO.

72 Short History, CCO 28 (1951–2), 27–8.

73 Walsh, Whitleyism, 157–8.

74 *Ibid.*, 158.

the staff side, Reg Bennett, was victimised by being denied promotion.[75]

There were no more meetings until 1947 but thenceforth annual meetings soon became the rule, with extra ones when the official side had urgent business, such as the cuts of 1952 or the introduction of clerical assistants in 1964.[76] Most items came from the staff side, with unit scales, bailiffs' allowances, training, promotions and the transfer of registrars' duties to clerks all making frequent appearances on the agenda. The union found the official side generally negative,[77] while Axmann for his part told them on his retirement that 'some of the tripe that was talked in those days made his blood boil'.[78]

Gradually the atmosphere improved and meetings became more constructive except in the stand-offs over pay, a mark of this being the creation of standing sub-committees for training, promotions and efficiency.[79] Even so, in this department as in others, the Whitley Council seldom lived up to the ideal of securing 'the greatest measure of co-operation in matters affecting the staffs, with a view to increased efficiency in the department, combined with the well-being of those employed'.[80]

The 'spirit of Whitleyism' also encompassed the creation of local committees in large workplaces but these were delayed by caution on both sides. The union executive had to be impelled into action by its conference on behalf of the Liverpool court, while the officials had to refer it to the Lord Chancellor himself. Liverpool eventually got its committee in 1962, followed by Birmingham, Manchester, Sheffield and Bristol.[81]

## COUNTY COURT DISTRICT ORGANISATION

The 1846 Act set no limit on the number of courts or judges but Cottenham's instructions to Bethune contemplated fifty-nine districts (Bethune said they should be called circuits) and he wanted

[75] *CCO* 23 (1943–5), 109, 147–9; 37 (1961–2), 95.
[76] *CCO* 29 (1952), 43; 38 (1963–4), 248.
[77] *CCO* 29 (1952), 130 is a good example.
[78] *CCO* 37 (1961–2), 189.
[79] Walsh, Whitleyism, 249.
[80] *Ibid.* [81] *Ibid.*

places with courts of requests to be included where practicable.[82] Bethune made a net addition of one to the number of districts – despite the appellation county courts, there was no serious attempt to make districts coterminous with counties – and expected less controversy about the districts than the choice of court towns.[83] For those he took as his starting point the 619 places which were districts for the purposes of the Registration Acts and reduced them to 454; metropolitan courts were settled on a more *ad hoc* basis. Cottenham had desired that everyone should be within seven miles of a court and Bethune's scheme came impressively close, though the districts ranged quite widely in population, from 312,000 in Hampshire down to 202,000 in mid-Wales. Provision was very generous; with a population of 304,000, Northumberland had ten courts; Leicestershire's 244,000 had thirteen, the 469,000 in districts 47 and 48 (Kent), seventeen.[84] Except where towns were closely clustered, few places of any consequence were denied a court and some which Bethune regarded as 'inconsiderable'[85] were included. An instruction which caused him difficulty was that each district must have a named chief court; in Anglesey, for instance, he had to elevate the unimportant Llangefni above Beaumaris, Amlwch and Holyhead because of its central location.[86]

Though Bethune's scheme was already informed by consultations with local leaders,[87] it was only to be expected that it would be modified by strenuous lobbying after publication. Strong political pressure reinstated Gateshead for instance, even though it was just eight minutes' walk from the court at Newcastle;[88] Folkestone, which had been displaced by Hythe, was restored to the number, and the small Cornish town of Camelford crept back

82 Bethune to Cottenham, 19 Dec. 1846, PRO LCO 8/1; he calls them circuits throughout. Drinkwater Bethune was counsel to the Home Office 1833–47. He subsequently went to India as legislative member of the Supreme Council and died at Calcutta in 1851: *Boase*, vol. I, p. 264.

83 Cottenham to Bethune, 16 Sep. 1846, PRO LCO 8/1; *LR* 5 (1846–7), 194–213.

84 PRO LCO 8/1. See also *LM* 6 (1847), 120–9. Bethune was aided by Captain Dawson, an assistant tithe commissioner, and Nicol.

85 PRO LCO 8/1, describing Bellingham in Northumberland.

86 *Ibid.*

87 *Ibid.*: circular to clerks of the peace, urging them to consult widely with the gentlemen of the county; *LT* 8 (1846–7), 298, 326.

88 PRO LCO 8/1; Order in Council, 6 Feb. 1847; *Judicature Commission Evidence*, *PP* 1872 (C 631–I) II, qq. 268–91 (H. Nicol).

in. In the final order made on 10 March 1847, the number of courts rose to 491.

Bethune had paid more attention to settling the boundaries of the districts than to the area of each court, sensibly reckoning that the latter would have to be altered in the light of experience in any case. Such alterations were fairly common, and there were additions too, though the early ones were not predominantly new industrial townships as might have been expected: an order of December 1848, for example, gave courts to Woolwich, Henley, Fishguard, Axbridge and Sandwich.[89] A few courts, beginning with Boston (Yorks.) and Clutton, were even abolished. Since the courts were supposed to pay their way and an early investigation showed that more than 300 were failing to do so, a much more drastic cull was mooted, 'but nothing was ever done upon it, because the opposition was so very great. It was Gateshead over again, and so it has been ever since.'[90]

Changes on this scale – Nicol envisaged about sixty courts closing[91] – implied that districts should also be reduced, but there were doubts whether the Act permitted that and when it became imperative to send a second judge to Liverpool a statute was passed which also restricted the number of judges to sixty.[92] A little-used South Midlands circuit (36) was abolished and the following ones confusingly renumbered.[93]

External pressure for more concentration of resources soon began to be felt. The Judicature Commission wanted each district to have a central court and satellites, with the smallest being closed,[94] and though Lord Chancellors did not adopt this model, they were pressed hard to economise now that the principle of self-sufficiency had been abandoned.[95] With the judges' sitting days falling the case was a persuasive one, but unfortunately, although two further districts were abolished in 1872,[96] the

[89] PRO LCO 8/1 contains the alterations down to the end of 1854. See also PRO HO 86/1–3 for correspondence with the Treasury.

[90] *Judicature Commission Evidence*: Nicol at q. 2718.

[91] *Lisgar Evidence*: Nicol at q. 7402.

[92] County Courts Act 1858 s. 3; *Childers Report*: Nicol's evidence at qq. 1851–5.

[93] The practice of renumbering districts was not repeated.

[94] *Second Report*, pp. 17–18.

[95] See pp. 226–7 below.

[96] District 34, covering the Fens and the Wash, was absorbed on 28 August 1872, Judge Ellis-McTaggart being transferred to Marylebone. Bridgewater (Somerset), district 56 (formerly 57) was abolished on 8 Apr. 1872, on the death of Judge Saunders.

abolition of district 10 in Lancashire disclosed a major obstacle in retrenchment strategies, for the neighbouring Manchester judge to whom one of its courts (Salford) was transferred promptly rebalanced his workload by sitting fewer days in both Salford and Manchester; when the nearby district 5 fell vacant soon afterwards, Nicol advised against its dismemberment for fear of the same outcome.[97]

If judges were one obstacle, local sentiment was another, which foiled the attempted abolition of the Sussex district in 1877.[98] In fact with business rising again the case for closures became less compelling and the number of courts, 499 in 1878, remained practically unchanged until 1914, the few closures offset by the opening of new ones.[99]

There were a few more significant initiatives. In 1893 Herschell instructed a small committee to review the arrangements for London and duly abolished district 46 (Southwark and Wandsworth); their other proposal, for a central county court in London to handle remitted actions, did not find favour.[100] London was most likely to need regular alteration and judges' complaints of overwork were partly met in 1908 by the abolition of a rural district (23, in Hereford and Worcestershire) to provide another metropolitan judge.[101] More ambitious changes, removing many of the fifty-one courts with fewer than 200 plaints annually, were also mooted, but were probably frustrated by political pressures;[102]

[97] See p. 255 below. Nicol was quizzed on this episode with uncomfortable pertinacity by the Childers Committee (*Childers Report*, qq. 1822–43, 1906–80, 2001–18).

[98] CCC 26 (1877), 203.

[99] In Essex, for instance, Clacton, Grays and Ilford were opened, Rochford closed; in Sussex, Haywards Heath opened, Cuckfield closed; in Durham, Consett opened, Shotley Bridge closed.

[100] *SJ* 37 (1892–3), 538, 678, 793; *LJ* 28 (1893), 322, 514. The report is in PRO LCO 2/830 and contains an appendix with every judge's views on redistribution possibilities for his circuit. The committee comprised D. Brynmor Jones, Judges Holroyd and Selfe, T. T. Woodhouse (solicitor), Nicol and Muir McKenzie; they considered a report by the metropolitan judges which Herschell had requested (9 May 1893) and Holl's supplemental report – he differed on the remit of the proposed central court.

[101] *SJ* 52 (1907–8), 271; *CCC* 41 (1908), 355.

[102] Selfe's proposals, 1899, PRO LCO 2/111; *MacDonnell Evidence*: Muir McKenzie at q. 55,472. Loreburn, who was keen on a redistribution (PRO LCO 2/204), was in conflict with the Liberal party over his refusal to 'job' the magistracy.

even when a committee examining complaints in Lancashire suggested closing Garstang and Haslingden they had to be reprieved.[103]

Against this background it is not surprising that when a committee was set up under Judge Radcliffe with broad terms, there was scepticism about the fate of its recommendations and the Committee openly acknowledged that 'so many interests . . . have grown up around the county courts' that it was realistic to limit changes to those which offered a substantial advantage in economy or convenience.[104] Schuster knew the limits of what could be achieved and was looking for a redistribution rather than a contraction, while the Committee was further impelled to moderation when proposed closures suggested in an interim report were implemented very selectively: in East Kent, for instance, they had wanted to axe Hythe, Sandwich, Sheerness, Romney, Tenterden and Cranbrook but only Romney was closed; in the final report Sandwich alone was listed for closure.[105] A similar sense of realism informed their final proposals for other districts, notably the Welsh district 29, where the number of courts was unjustifiably generous but only Llangollen was marked down for closure.[106] The Committee did not propose any net reduction in districts, but many of the remaining small courts would have reduced facilities once registrars were allowed to hold court in the absence of the judge.[107]

The Radcliffe Committee toiled for nearly three years[108] and its report was treated not as a blueprint but a foundation, implemented with considerable variations over the next decade.[109] In

[103] PRO LCO 2/295; *LJ* 49 (1914), 444.

[104] *Radcliffe Report*, p. 1; *LT* 142 (1916–17), 124; *PP* 1918 [Cd 9230] XII, p. 78.

[105] *Radcliffe Report*, p. 28. I have not seen the interim report, nor the evidence the main report says was preserved.

[106] *Ibid.*, pp. 44–9. For the criteria the Committee adopted for closure see pp. 120–1 above. It also proposed 'a considerable number of circuits which involve little travelling and are therefore suitable for more elderly or delicate judges' (p. 29).

[107] *Ibid.* This became feasible by the 1919 County Courts Act (c. 73) s. 9.

[108] 11 Dec. 1916 to 29 Oct. 1919. Members were Radcliffe, Bridgeman, A. H. Coley, J. H. Cunliffe, A. O. Jennings; Alfred Seneschall, chairman of the Commercial Travellers Benevolent Association, was later added in a rare concession to court users.

[109] Some changes had been made in advance of the final report (e.g. *LJ* 54 (1919), 149); others quickly followed – see *SJ* 63 and 64 (1918–19); *LJ* 55 (1920), 7, 66, 184. Individual orders are in PRO LCO 12.

1928 there were fifty-five districts and 444 courts, plus sixty-three 'branch courts'; in 1938 there were still fifty-five districts, with 432 courts and fifty-two branch courts – not so very different from the original plan when allowance is made for the great advances in communications.[110] The creation of the branch courts, smaller courts 'grouped' under a common registrar, was the major change and this, rather than large-scale closures, was the LCO's preferred strategy, though relegation to branch court status sometimes marked out a court for future closure.[111]

Wartime brought further closures, some permanent, and the dismemberment of district 53. Afterwards it became more common for a judge to be given auxiliary duties in a district other than his own; thus in 1947 H. M. Pratt was appointed to district 34 with additional duties on 58, H. J. C. Whitmee to 38 with duties on 39, J. A. Pugh to 37 and additionally at Bow (40).[112] The steady expansion in the number of judges from the mid-1950s onwards was not matched by a rise in the number of courts or districts, though there was some necessary adjustment to reflect changes in population distribution. The most substantial were in the south. In 1963 district 53 (Hampshire and Wiltshire) had to be re-created and by 1968 there were sixty-five districts, including single centre districts for Bromley, Ilford and Croydon and two-centre ones for Cardiff with Barry and Kingston with Reigate; the practice of linking a London court with a town in the home counties, which had been in vogue, was abandoned; within inner London Bloomsbury was amalgamated with Marylebone.

In the 1960s the Department made short-term plans for closures on seven circuits, but there was some danger that closures simply led to underemployed judges who could not easily be moved.[113] There was also a much more radical scheme involving the redrawing of circuit boundaries to enable judges to sit for several days at a time at selected centres, leaving registrars to hold court in the smaller towns; this made the staff union decidedly anxious about the future, especially as they were denied consultation on closures.[114] In fact, however, nothing drastic could be attempted

110 *PP* 1938–9 [Cmd 6135] XXV.

111 Napier's note, 7 Jul. 1926, PRO LCO 12/58.

112 *LJ* 97 (1947), 7.

113 Notes of meeting with judges on 14 Oct. 1966, PRO LCO 12/90.

114 Dobson's note to Lord Chancellor, 11 Oct. 1966, *ibid.*

until the LCD had more control of court accommodation[115] and the plans were overtaken by the Beeching Report, which introduced entirely new considerations into the distribution of local courts.

## THE RULE COMMITTEE

The founding Act made provision for rules to flesh out the statutory bones. Previous bills had envisaged this being done by a group of judges of the new courts, but with none yet appointed the duty was given to five superior court judges chosen by the Lord Chancellor.[116] The Act of 1850 substituted a committee of five county court judges, their labours subject to the scrutiny of three superior court judges and both groups chosen by the Lord Chancellor. The new Rule Committee was soon at work elaborating on the rather sketchy code of 1847 and in 1850 it expanded it from 52 rules to 210, the first in a series of revisions necessitated partly by inevitable defects and omissions but also by the rapid accumulation of new jurisdictions.[117]

With the addition of, *inter alia*, the Bankruptcy Acts of 1861 and 1863 (78 rules), the equitable jurisdiction (113) and admiralty (77) and an overhaul of the the main body of rules after the 1867 Act the total was carried beyond 500.[118] Following the Judicature Acts they were assimilated to the freshly issued rules of the new Supreme Court both in wording and layout; the familiar division into orders and rules dates from a revision of 1876.[119]

The original Rule Committee consisted of A. S. Dowling, R. Brandt, J. Espinasse C. J. Gale and W. Furner[120] but the personnel was changed several times before the 1856 Act removed the Chancellor's power to alter its composition except upon a vacancy. This meant that judges might now accumulate long

115 Dobson to R. Puttam (Treasury), 14 Feb. 1967, PRO LCO 12/46.

116 County Courts Act 1846 s. 78.

117 County Courts Act 1850 s. 12. The 1847 code is in (*inter alia*) *LT* 8 (1845–7), 498, that of 1850 in *LT* 17 (1851), 134, reviewed in *LM* 15 (1851), 141–6.

118 S. Rosenbaum, Rule Making in the County Courts, *LQR* 31 (1915), 304–13 at 308.

119 *Ibid.*, 308–9.

120 Curiously, none was a judge in London, nor to my knowledge had an established reputation as a draftsman.

service, but all were outlasted by Nicol, who was their secretary from the beginning.[121]

In the early years all the judges were occasionally circularised for suggestions when a new Act was passed but that was soon abandoned.[122] Informed critics were not always complimentary to the rules[123] and from time to time a rule was claimed (sometimes correctly) to be *ultra vires*,[124] hardly surprisingly since the terms of the rule-making power were wide and vague.[125] Nor were the rules always popular. Costs and committals were particularly sensitive subjects. The Committee was given the duty of framing costs in 1852[126] and promptly ran into difficulties. Their overseers regarded their scale as too generous – much to the disgust of attorneys, who alleged that the superior court judges had adopted the highly interested views of their taxing masters.[127]

Committals were an even more touchy subject. In 1859 the Committee was, for the only time, used as an investigating body following strong public criticism and in line with the judges' views, recommended only that the power to commit for non-appearance to a judgment summons be abolished and that credit for the purchase of beer be restricted.[128]

The Rule Committee would have been abolished under Cairns' ill-fated bill of 1878–9 and its functions performed by the Supreme Court Rule Committee (SCRC),[129] but in the event the latter was merely required to scrutinise the draft rules, which proved far less valuable than the unofficial comments of law societies and the registrars' association.[130] There were plenty of

121 County Courts Act 1856 s. 32; *Select Committee, 1878*, q. 4969.

122 PRO LCO 8/2, f. 193; 8/3, circular of 27 Feb. 1856. Judge Owen told a select committee in 1897, 'we are never consulted', *PP* 1897 (364) XI, q. 4442.

123 E.g. *LM* 15 (1851), 141–6; *SJ* 9 (1864–5), 1010.

124 E.g. *LJ* 5 (1870), 267; *Select Committee, 1878*, q. 1572 (Sir R. Harington); Rosenbaum, Rule Making in the County Courts, 312.

125 County Courts Act 1850, s. 12.

126 County Courts Act 1852 s. 1, following animated debates: *Hansard* 1851–2 3rd s., vol. 119, cols. 754–62.

127 *LO* 44 (1852), 343; 45 (1852–3), 103; 46 (1853), 85; *LR* 19 (1854), 257–71.

128 *Hansard* 1858–9 3rd s., vol. 154, cols. 773–5. The report and replies were not published until 1867, *PP* 1867 (209) LVII.

129 *LT* 66 (1878–9), 310–11, 328.

130 Rosenbaum, Rule Making in the County Courts, 306–7. Between 1856 and 1884 only the concurrence of the Lord Chancellor was required. The change, by Supreme Court of Judicature Act 1884 s. 24, was not debated in Parliament.

rules to scrutinise, for after a quiet interlude the Committee sprang into vigorous life under the influence of the young Birmingham judge McKenzie Chalmers and his associate G. W. Heywood, who effected a revision in 1886.[131]

With Nicol retiring in 1892 and Chalmers leaving the bench soon after, the Committee came under the sway of two men who would mould its proceedings for the next twenty years, its secretary Muir McKenzie and chairman Sir Lucius Selfe.[132] Though other judges clocked up long service[133] and more than pulled their weight, Selfe was the draftsman, Muir McKenzie the setter of agendas and without their backing nothing could be done. From 1894 rules flowed unceasingly, one set every year and often more.[134] New legislation continued to make demands – the Workmen's Compensation Acts generated 100 rules and 80 forms, the Tithe Act 58 rules and 35 forms – but the Committee also produced a steady stream of amendments to existing rules. Some were in response to decisions in the higher courts,[135] rather more from suggestions received from practitioners, registrars and judges, while some of the members had favourite topics of their own, like Smyly's administration orders.[136] Where the complaint was of varied interpretations from court to court the Committee usually felt there was little it could do,[137] and sometimes a rule was found to be such a minefield that they decided not to try to improve it.[138] Even so, following a fresh consolidation by the indefatigable Selfe in 1903, the code totalled well over 1,000 rules by the outbreak of war.[139]

131 *Ibid.*, 309. Summarised in *SJ* 30 (1885–6), 334–5, 351–2, 367–8, 497–9.

132 Selfe (1845–1924) was the son of a police magistrate and attended Rugby, Corpus Christi, Oxford and the Inner Temple (called 1870). He was briefly Principal Secretary to the Lord Chancellor in 1880 and was a county court judge from 1882 to 1920.

133 Notably A. Martineau, W. C. Smyly, H. J. Stonor, Sir R. Harington and R. Woodfall.

134 The Rule Committee papers in PRO LCO 2 are substantially complete from 1895. Earlier survivals are fragmentary.

135 E.g. *Millar v. Solomon* [1906] 2 KB 91; *Willis v. Lovick* [1901] 2 KB 195; *Kinnell and Co. v. Harding, Wace and Co.* [1918] 1 KB 155, 405.

136 PRO LCO 2/114.

137 E.g. PRO LCO 2/220, on letter from Dod, Longstaff and Son and Frederick.

138 E.g. Selfe to Muir McKenzie, 28 Jan. 1907: 'the difficulties raised by s. 156 [on interpleader] are simply frightful' (PRO LCO 2/117), and 2/162 (1903, on o. 7 r. 10).

139 Rosenbaum, Rule Making in the County Courts, 312.

Selfe's Committee burned its fingers rather badly on one notoriously contentious issue, that of venue. Feeling that recent decisions, especially *Northey, Stone & Co. v. Gidney*,[140] had given plaintiffs too much latitude under s. 74, which allowed defendants to be sued in a distant court 'in the district within which the cause of action or claim wholly or in part arose', and learning that 10 per cent of actions were being pursued in this way (which was of course highly convenient for bulk plaintiffs), the Rule Committee went to the very verge of its powers with a highly restrictive rule which raised a storm among solicitors and the powerful and well-represented wholesale traders' lobby.[141] Selfe had acknowledged that the rule in question (o. 5 r. 9) was 'a vexed question'[142] but underestimated the strength of the reaction; the rule was first suspended for reconsideration then, chasteningly, withdrawn.[143] It was forty years before the Committee did anything as controversial again.

Though rules under the wartime emergency legislation were made by the Lord Chancellor (in practice by Selfe),[144] the Rule Committee continued to work but in a rather desultory way and without much inclination to pursue controversial points.[145] It was an ageing body until several long-serving members successively retired: Smyly in 1915, Tindal Atkinson in 1918, Woodfall in 1919 and Selfe in 1920. On Muir McKenzie's departure in 1915 they declined the offer of 'a secretary of their own' and Schuster took his place.[146]

The Birmingham registrar A. L. Lowe (president of the ACCR from 1907) had come to be regularly consulted and impressed Schuster enough to want him on the Committee.[147] The idea of a broader membership was not new[148] and the Law Society had long been pressing its claims for a representative, which would

140 [1894] 1 QB 99.

141 *SJ* 41 (1896–7), 266, 324–6.

142 To Muir McKenzie, 17 Jan. 1895, PRO LCO 2/113.

143 *SJ* 41 (1896–7), 399; *Hansard* 1898 4th s., vol. 47, col. 680; *CCC* 36 (1897–8), 89–92, 151. With unfortunate timing, Selfe's knighthood followed shortly after.

144 E.g. Schuster to Selfe, 2 Jun. 1916, PRO LCO 2/372 and 5 Mar. 1917, 2/378.

145 PRO LCO 2/356–66.

146 PRO LCO 2/308 includes a memo on the Committee's procedure for Schuster.

147 Lowe to Muir McKenzie, 14 June 1910, PRO LCO 2/229; Schuster to Buckmaster, 22 Jan. 1916, PRO LCO 2/357.

148 See e.g. T. W. Wheeler *LJ* 23 (1888), 289–90.

inevitably mean having a barrister as well. Pre-war government bills adopted the Gorell Committee's preference for one solicitor, a barrister, a registrar and a Treasury representative rather than Rollit's more expansive ideas[149] but the 1919 bill dropped the Treasury man as a concession to the Law Society, fobbing the Treasury off with a promise to show them the draft rules before they went to the SCRC, which was already the practice anyway.[150]

Fittingly, Selfe's long reign ended along with the old Committee. None of his successors as chairman could match Selfe's encyclopaedic grasp of the arcana of county court practice and none exerted such a powerful influence.[151] The presence of a registrar proved invaluable and, after the death of Lowe in 1928, Arthur Jennings was permitted to take his place without relinquishing the presidency of the ACCR, which enabled him to speak with authority on their concerns.[152] Jennings was a hard man to replace; two well-qualified candidates, F. G. Glanfield and H. P. Stanes, were each put aside as 'not a gent' and a younger man, the 47-year-old Gilbert Hicks, registrar of Northampton and later of Shoreditch, son of a canon and educated at a minor public school, was chosen.[153] Hicks quickly made his mark, sharing with Judge Procter the main responsibility for the 1936 rules revision.

The first solicitor representative, A. H. Coley of Birmingham, also pulled his weight,[154] but the barristers were less useful, though H. Bensley Wells, E. Hancock and J. A. Pugh all became county court judges, and the last two chairmen of the Committee.[155] Now that they retired at seventy-two, judges came and went at shorter intervals. A balance was sought between London

149 *PP* 1909 (71) LXXII, at p. 34; PRO LCO 2/207–9; *PP* 1902 (26) I, cl. 16.

150 Schuster to W. Godley, 21 Apr. 1919; G. B. Barstow to Schuster, 1 Dec. 1919, PRO LCO 2/434.

151 Chairmen after Selfe were Sir W. Howland Roberts, Sir E. Bray (1922), Sir W. Cann (1925) and Sir A. Hill-Kelly (1931). Selfe claimed that the tradition was that the longest-serving judge on the Committee became chairman, but Granger declined. In 1922 Cann was passed over for Bray because he did not live in London.

152 PRO LCO 2/5094.

153 *Ibid.*, Napier's memo, 12 Mar. 1934.

154 *Ibid.*, suggested by Selfe (to Roberts, 18 Mar. 1920). Coley retired in 1933 and died almost immediately.

155 *Ibid.* H. M. Giveen (1920–9) attended only one meeting.

and provincial judges and seniority counted for something unless, like Max Konstam, a judge had 'not a very good manner in argument' or, like Gerald Hargreaves, 'showed no businesslike qualities'.[156]

Napier, who acted as secretary from about 1920, seems seldom to have tried to impose a departmental view on the Committee, though he did seek to dissuade it from tangling unnecessarily with notoriously difficult matters.[157] There was always ample business without looking for more, often enough to require more than one meeting a year. Though internal differences were occasionally pressed to a vote, the Committee managed to avoid controversy until, in the course of a consolidation in 1934, it made another attempt to curb the liberal use of s. 74 to assist plaintiffs. Their efforts roused a predictable outcry and led to some vigorous lobbying of the members, but this time they were able to defend their handiwork, making only minor concessions.[158] However, they had to yield to the Law Society over their attempt to squeeze commercial process servers out.[159]

In 1939, unlike 1914, the Rule Committee was put into abeyance and the Lord Chancellor left to make rules.[160] Napier was usually content to consult Hicks, who was close to hand, knowledgeable and self-confident to the point of impatience with opposing viewpoints; but a wider range of opinions might sometimes have been useful, as when 'a storm of protest' followed an amendment to the rules on warrants of delivery which inadvertently jeopardised a widespread and convenient practice and had to be hurriedly withdrawn.[161]

Though the vacant places were filled in 1947,[162] the LCD was in no hurry to convene a meeting, Napier being content to

156 Napier's note, 6 Mar. 1940, PRO LCO 2/5094.

157 E.g. PRO LCO 2/537, on ejectment actions. A rare instance in which Napier asked the Lord Chancellor whether he should try to influence deliberations is in 2/854(1), on the question of rules under the Legitimacy Act.

158 See p. 139 above and PRO LCO 2/1280, 1288–90.

159 PRO LCO 2/1296; *SJ* 81 (1937), 119, 162–3. The concessions were in County Court Amendment Rules 1936/1312 (L35).

160 PRO LCO 2/1721. Administration of Justice (Emergency Provisions) Act 1939 s. 2.

161 PRO LCO 2/3274.

162 Some had been filled earlier because the Committee was still responsible for workmen's compensation rules: H. H. Churchill to R. Gregory, 31 Oct. 1962, PRO LCO 2/6985.

circulate draft rules.[163] It took a timid intimation from the Austin Jones Committee[164] to restore it to life in December 1949, a full decade after its last meeting. Judge Hancock took the chair but retired before the next meeting, and his successor, a reluctant Donald Hurst,[165] found plenty of work.

The Austin Jones Report contained forty-three recommendations requiring rule changes[166] and there was an unending succession of statutes and an accelerating trend for the draftsman to leave ever more of the detail to be filled up by rule.[167] In due course the Wheatcroft and Pugh Reports also had to be implemented.[168]

Suggestions for rule changes came from a wider range of sources too. Some judges (such as Gamon), registrars (D. R. White) and even chief clerks (Burden) were more fertile in ideas than was really welcome,[169] and now there was the staff suggestions committee[170] as well as the ACCR and the professional bodies. Even with two meetings a year agendas lengthened, to thirty-one items in 1959;[171] and though some were trivial,[172] leading to complaints that the Committee was endlessly and fussily tinkering, to the exasperation of harassed practitioners,[173] apparently minor matters could have serious implications.[174] Strangely, however, there was a lull in the mid-1960s and in 1966, for the first time in many years, it was felt that no meeting need be held, the small amount of business being dealt with by correspondence.

The growth of business brought about some changes in procedure, with items distributed beforehand to individuals for investi-

163 County Courts (Crown Proceedings) Rules 1947/2576 (L36); PRO LCO 2/3327.

164 Minutes of 4 Jan. 1949, PRO LCO 2/3296.

165 PRO LCO 2/3252, 4496.

166 Note to Lord Chancellor, Apr. 1949, PRO LCO 2/3312.

167 *SJ* 99 (1955), 825–6.

168 County Court Amendment (No. 2) Rules 1957/1136 (L8) and Amendment Rules 1961/1526.

169 For Gamon see e.g. PRO LCO 2/4775; for some of White's suggestions see PRO LCO 2/5052, 5044, 5086, 5093. On Burden see Gregory's note, 26 Aug. 1950, 2/4496.

170 E.g. PRO LCO 2/5150, 5000–1.

171 PRO LCO 2/7170.

172 E.g. PRO LCO 2/5044: discussions on whether full names or initials should appear in the praecipe, 1953.

173 *SJ* 105 (1961), 796.

174 E.g. PRO LCO 2/5047 (judgment summonses from the high court).

gation and report and preliminary drafting,[175] textual amendments at the meeting being heavily discouraged.[176] More was settled in advance of meetings, though they were no formality,[177] and a more active LCD management style seems to have evolved. Coldstream, the secretary from 1954, only attended for really important business,[178] leaving the Committee to more junior officials, and in 1961 Roy Gregory was made secretary, perhaps the greatest expert on the rules since Selfe.

In 1956 the Committee was enlarged by the addition of a second, provincial registrar, and a second solicitor and barrister, bringing the members to eleven.[179] As before, the solicitors tended to be more useful, especially Ralph Davies;[180] by contrast the longest-serving barrister, Monier Williams had 'never been much use'.[181] The Committee was also emancipated at last from the scrutiny of the SCRC and the President of the Board of Trade lost his role in relation to rules on administration orders.[182] Around 1960 its make-up changed quite markedly, enough to make Judge Andrew retire now that his friends were all gone.[183] Rather oddly, it was only in 1962 that the officials suggested that future appointments to the Committee should be limited to three years, though they were readily renewed if the incumbents proved satisfactory.[184] Another change was that on Hurst's retirement Judge Pugh was formally appointed chairman by the Lord Chancellor rather than simply being chosen by the Committee, a decision probably made with a view to the next vacancy, Owen Temple Morris being favoured ahead of the longer-serving Donald McKee.[185] It is unlikely that they guessed how important it would be to have an acquiescent chairman.

175 E.g. PRO LCO 2/7170, 5088.
176 PRO LCO 2/5055 (1957).
177 E.g. Rieu to Hurst, 30 Sep. 1952, PRO LCO 2/4997.
178 PRO LCO 2/5012.
179 Administration of Justice Act 1956 s. 32 (2). The CCOA unsuccessfully sought a representative: *CCO* 37 (1961–2), 32.
180 Private communication from R. Gregory.
181 Coldstream to Kilmuir, 5 Nov. 1959, PRO LCO 2/6985.
182 Administration of Justice Act 1956 s. 32 (1, 3). The President's role was described as 'an anomalous relic' in the briefing paper for the debates: PRO LCO 2/6312.
183 Andrew to Rieu, 12, 19 Jun. 1961, PRO LCO 2/6985.
184 PRO LCO 2/6985, *passim.*
185 *Ibid.*

The other important position was the London registrar, which fell vacant with D. Freeman Coutts' death in 1966. Officials stressed the special position he occupied: 'it is the practice to show him draft items from the agenda ... at the meetings it is to the London registrar that the committee will obviously turn first for information and advice in matters of procedure and office routine'.[186] Indeed Gregory found that 'the easiest way to get a proposed rule passed was to try to persuade the senior registrar member to sponsor it'.[187] They chose G. A. Everett, a protégé of Hicks, as Freeman Coutts' successor.[188]

The Committee frequently found itself in a dilemma. Some members were keen to tighten up the rules to promote more uniform practice and interpretations, and many outside suggestions stemmed from encounters with diversity;[189] but attempts to tamper with some of the rules and forms in question revealed irreconcileable differences among judges and registrars. Even redesigning forms to make them more 'user-friendly', which Jowitt had personally urged them to do, created unforeseen difficulties.[190]

On the whole the Committee's work was well received, though not everyone approved of their insistence on retaining non-suit, a relic of the days before the Judicature Acts which had come to light like the coelacanth.[191] One of its most frustrating endeavours was to bestow flexibility upon judges in cases where a payment into court had been made. The Court of Appeal repeatedly thwarted this intention, leading one commentator to explain that they 'have been indulging in a sort of duel, the former making proposals designed to help solicitors to recover more costs in some cases where an action is concluded by paying them into court, and the Court of Appeal busily preventing them from doing so'.[192] In

186 Gregory's note, 28 Feb. 1966, *ibid.*

187 Private communication, *ibid.*

188 *Ibid.*

189 E.g. PRO LCO 2/5061 (1955), on o. 25 r. 2.

190 E.g. PRO LCO 2/5004 and 2/5017 (warrants of delivery, 1952).

191 *Clack v. Arthur's Engineering Ltd* (*The Times*, 15 May 1959). The Court of Appeal urged the abolition of non-suit ([1959] 2 QB 511), but the Rule Committee thought it still useful: PRO LCO 2/7171, 7179–80. County Court (Amendment) Rules 1960 1275 (L14); M.J. Prichard, *CLJ* 18 (1960), 88–96. For its history see P. Polden, The Strange Death of County Court Nonsuit, *Cambrian Law Review* 1999 (forthcoming).

192 *SJ* 108 (1964), 307–8.

the end the Committee had to abandon the search for flexibility in favour of a more generally liberal rule.[193]

Inevitably, they were drawn repeatedly into two inescapably contentious areas, judgment summonses and scales of costs, and serious conflicts arose from each. The Austin Jones Committee had wanted judges to be given more effective powers to compel the appearance of debtors as a counter to the accusation that their instalment orders, and sometimes subsequent committal orders, were based upon insufficient investigation.[194] Hurst was strongly in favour of action but found the LCD unwilling to tackle the subject by any means,[195] partly because of doubts about the *vires* of a rule, but mostly because any attempt to strengthen the power to imprison debtors was 'political dynamite'.[196] Though Coldstream attended the meeting at which the proposed rule was discussed he had told Hurst that 'it is no business of mine, as secretary to the Rule Committee, to argue points before the Rule Committee'.[197] Hurst and Pugh carried the Committee with them in determining to make the rule even in the knowledge that the Lord Chancellor would disallow it, and in fact the whole batch was jettisoned rather than put forth a feeble collection shorn of the centrepiece.[198]

At the same time the Committee was struggling to produce a new costs order to replace the one made, without its involvement, in 1949.[199] With the coming of legal aid to the county court a new costs scale would, via the legal aid fund, have a direct impact upon public spending as well as feeding the spiral of rising wages and prices which governments were struggling to tame. The Rule

193 County Court (Amendment) Rules 1963/403 (L1). The cases were *Hopkins v. Manners* and *Herbert v. Rhondda Transport* [1963] 1 All ER 33. *Hansard* 1962–3 5th s., vol. 669 (HC), cols. 482–96; *LSG* 60 (1963), 165; *LJ* 113 (1963), 177.

194 *Austin Jones Report*, section 5, paras. 77–86.

195 PRO LCO 2/5007. The Lord Chancellor was personally unfavourable: note of meeting, 16 Apr. 1953 in 2/5012.

196 Minutes of 30 Jul. 1953, PRO LCO 2/4977; note of meeting with Law Officers, 2 Apr. 1953, 2/5012.

197 11 Jun. 1952, PRO LCO 2/5007.

198 PRO LCO 2/5012.

199 PRO LCO 2/5036–40 show that only Hicks was closely involved in 1949 and that the Committee was presented with a scale which it adopted. County Court (Amendment) Rules 1955/1799 (L14); *LSG* 52 (1955), 519–21.

Committee might find itself in a delicate position in trying to carry out its statutory duties in isolation from the wider world.

By the time that came about the chairman was Temple Morris, once unflatteringly described by Coldstream as 'the champion self-advertiser on the bench ... always asking for preferment of one sort or another'.[200] He refused to call the Committee together while the Prices and Incomes Board was preparing a report on solicitors' incomes and, when the report was issued, he led it in supinely rubber-stamping the LCD's proposed scale based upon the report.[201] Not surprisingly, the Committee's evident lack of independence led to demands for changes in its composition. Temple Morris retired soon after, clutching his knighthood,[202] and almost the first act of his successor McKee was symbolic of a new era – a rule imposing a decimal coinage on the courts.[203]

## COUNTY COURT FINANCES

### *Fees*

Local courts were financed by suitors' fees, local taxes or a combination of both. The Common Law Commissioners airily declared that 'very moderate fees, to be paid in each cause, would supply a fund sufficient to defray every expense attendant on the establishment of Local Courts',[204] and that was the course adopted for the new county courts, although at least one of the earlier bills had envisaged that fees might have to be supplemented out of the consolidated fund.[205]

Fees were initially set at quite a high level and any surplus beyond the ceilings set for the officers' earnings supplemented a 'General Fund' to pay for courthouses and offices, principally resourced by a levy of 6d on moderate-sized suits (20s to 40s) and 5 per cent on larger ones.[206] This 'tax on suitors' came in for bitter

200 PRO LCO 2/4987.
201 See pp. 192–3 above. The row can be followed in the *Law Society's Gazette*.
202 Temple Morris' *Times* obituary (24 Apr. 1985) does not mention this episode.
203 County Court (Amendment) Rules 1970/1201.
204 *Fifth Report*, p. 21.
205 *HLSP* 1841 vol. I (Bill 43, cl. 18).
206 County Courts Act 1846 ss. 77, 50–4 and Schedules.

criticism and there was a widespread conviction that the fees were generally much too high.[207] Although some reductions were made in 1850, it was commented that for the biggest actions county courts actually charged more than the superior courts,[208] and continuing pressure in Parliament on this topic[209] was the chief reason for setting up the Romilly Commission, enjoined to see 'whether the fees can be made reduced, or levied in a less burdensome manner'.[210]

With the fee yield comfortably exceeding what would be needed to meet the salaries of judges and registrars and the very modest building programme,[211] a body dominated by the legal profession would find that question easy to answer. The Commission's examination was superficial, drawing on a report by the judges responsible for the 1850 revision, and members evidently shared Judge Uvedale Corbet's view that 'you must not legislate too much for economy'.[212]

The most important proposition in the Report was the rebuttal of the basis of the 1846 Act. Courts should not be self-supporting; suitors should pay only for the services of the officers, judges and buildings being provided at the expense of the general taxpayer. On this basis a fee table was drawn up embodying substantial reductions and with the sanguine note that 'experience renders deficit improbable'.[213]

Brougham ensured that the campaign for lower fees did not flag[214] and in 1856 the government accepted the Romilly principle. The new fees table which shortly followed was estimated to have a margin of £30,000 over the budget for judges' salaries, and with the building programme dwindling that seemed ample.[215] However, around 1870 the extravagance of the county courts came under fire, first from the Judicature Commission, which expected

207 E.g. *CCC* 2 (1849), 273; *LO* 41 (1850–1), 109; *LR* 7 (1847–8), 217; *LT* 10 (1847–8), 7, 194, 470; 11 (1848), 31; *Hansard* 1847–8 3rd s., vol. 99, col. 429.

208 E.g. *LT* 16 (1850–1), 73; *Westminster Review*, 54 (1850), 104–17.

209 E.g. *Hansard* 1852–3 3rd s., vol. 128, cols. 253 ff.; 1853–4 3rd s., vol. 132, col. 831; vol. 138, col. 2135.

210 *Romilly Report*, p. 1.

211 For 1854 the gross fees were £230,604: *PP* 1854–5 (350) XLII.

212 *Romilly Report*, q. 1677.

213 *Ibid.*, pp. 38–44.

214 *Hansard* 1856 3rd s., vol. 140, col. 147; vol. 141, col. 122; vol. 143, cols. 684–92.

215 *PP* 1856 (340) L.

by abolishing the 'banking system' and other changes to bring down the fees from a level 'stated to be oppressive',[216] and then from a select committee more concerned at the burden on the taxpayer. Despite an increase in fees in 1864, the net charge stood at £195,000 in 1871–2. However, the Committee directed its criticisms at the inadequate mechanisms for controlling expenditure rather than the underlying principle,[217] and the ensuing Lisgar Commission did not take Nicol up on his assertion that if they abolished the banking function there would be no saving to the public because 'if you do not render the services for which the fees are collected, you must not collect the fees'.[218]

The actual operation of the system was obscured by the peculiar form in which it was presented in the public finances.[219] The Public Accounts Committee (PAC) occasionally voiced impatience at the imprecision of income estimates, but Nicol and Bridgeman always countered that all their experience did not enable them to forecast the trend in volumes of litigation.[220] The PAC also criticised the way the strict letter of the law was not observed. Plaints were averaged over four years for the purpose of assessing the registrars' allowance for staff and, even where the average showed a fall as against the previous four years, no reduction in allowance was made until there was a staff vacancy. This was defended on grounds of convenience and common humanity but it was some years before it had any statutory sanction.[221]

Spasmodic criticism of the level of fees in the legal press and in Parliament[222] intensified in the mid-1890s, perhaps fuelled by the exposure in the civil judicial statistics of the proportion of fees to sums recovered.[223] In 1897 the Law Society's committee on county courts advocated the halving of the *ad valorem* fee of one shilling in the pound on ordinary plaints and similar reductions on

216 *Second Report*, p. 20.
217 *Childers Report*, q. 1734 and 'Recommendations', p. ix.
218 *Lisgar Evidence*, q. 7419.
219 *MacDonnell Evidence*, q. 51,537 (Bridgeman).
220 *PP* 1909 (18, 58, 126, 158, 284) VI, qq. 1361–5; *MacDonnell Evidence*, qq. 51,528–36.
221 *PP* 1883 (77, 187, 233) XI, qq. 210–34; *PP* 1884 (98, 237) VIII, qq. 216–47; The position was partly regularised by County Courts (Expenses) Act 1887, (50 & 51 Vict. c. 3).
222 E.g. *Select Committee, 1878*, qq. 1631, 5538; *LT* 66 (1878–9), 409; 73 (1882), 162–3; 80 (1885–6), 62; *SJ* 32 (1887–8), 468.
223 Beginning with *PP* 1896 [C 8263] XCIV.

others, especially those chargeable on smaller actions, a package the Treasury estimated would cost £178,000 in lost fees on the (questionable) assumption that there would be no offset from more cases being brought.[224] It was powerfully pressed in the Commons by Sir Charles Dilke[225] and even the Rule Committee recommended an official inquiry, which was ultimately conceded.[226]

Revisions based on the inquiry's deliberations fell well short of the Law Society's demands, as they must if, as a Treasury official later asserted, the inquiry shared the 'generally accepted ... constitutional doctrine that the courts and the judges should be supplied gratis to the suitor by the state',[227] but that suitors collectively should meet the other costs of the civil justice system. This formula was in fact a significant shift of ground, for there had hitherto been a no-man's land in county court finances covering the costs of stationery, office equipment and incidental expenses which were in the aggregate quite substantial. Defenders of the proposition were fond of pointing out that the high court did, on this formula, cover its costs, but they usually omitted to explain that this was only because of the 'unearned income' from uncontested probate fees.[228] If county court registrars had been entrusted with this essentially administrative chore, the financial positions of the courts would rapidly have been reversed.

There remained, therefore, what *The Times* styled 'deep dissatisfaction, not wholly unreasonable, at the excessive rate of county court fees'[229] and critics were not impressed by the standard official defence, that the suitor was given more assistance for his money.[230] It was true enough, but some suitors did not want the assistance and others found it ineffective; the man who paid out £1 3s 6d on a £5 claim, then a further £1 11s 6d to the

224 *SJ* 39 (1894–5), 442; *LJ* 37 (1902), 455; *LSG* 11 (1913–14), 150–1.

225 *Hansard* 1898 4th s., vol. 55, col. 183; 1899 4th s., vol. 68, col. 16; vol. 74, col. 193.

226 PRO LCO 2/114; they were shown the report in confidence in May 1900 but no copy is among the LCO papers.

227 *LSG* 11 (1913–14), 150–1.

228 This was still the case in 1946, when probates yielded £648,834 out of a total of £1,050,353: Evershed Committee, *Second Interim Report*, *PP* 1950–1 [Cmd 8176], XVI, para. 145.

229 Quoted in *SJ* 49 (1904–5), 756.

230 E.g. *PP* 1909 (71) LXXII, p. 31.

bailiffs for a dilatory execution hardly felt he had received value for money.[231]

The LCO gave little support to the critics, perhaps because they felt the *status quo* was preferable to reopening the wider arguments of the 1870s; a subsidy of well over £100,000 a year was not lightly to be brought into question. Without strong official or parliamentary support the Law Society's renewed campaign in 1913 was never likely to be very successful and they were offered only the chance to rearrange the incidence of fees without making any reduction in the overall yield.[232]

In fact the Treasury was doing rather well out of the county courts, for applying their own principle they showed a 'profit' for most of the decade ending in 1914. Then, of course, the fee yield collapsed, to £145,383 in 1918, less than a third of the pre-war peak. When Schuster presented the post-war Treasury with the Swift Report and sought acceptance of proposals for judges' pensions and the incorporation of court staff into the civil service, he knew that the price would be a hefty fees increase to offset the extra burden on general taxation.

In the initial skirmishing the Treasury sought to gain acceptance of the 'principle' (as a long-term goal) that suitors should pay all court expenses save the cost of judges and buildings, but this was merely mandarins at play;[233] both sides knew that the county courts could not be run on that basis and equally both knew that there would have to be higher fees. The MacNaghten Committee noted the Treasury position perfunctorily and passed quickly onto the more messy reality.[234]

In fact, contrary to pessimistic forecasts, fee revenue recovered so rapidly, passing the £500,000 mark in 1922, that the pressure for a really big increase slackened. Workmen's compensation fees apart, the 1924 order proved relatively uncontroversial and certainly tidied up the mess considerably.[235] Even with moderate increases, fee yields rose so much that complaints again became audible, and though in 1928 Schuster told the PAC 'if we once

231 *LJ* 43 (1908), 586.
232 *LSG* 11 (1913–14), 150–1.
233 PRO LCO 2/525.
234 *MacNaghten Report*, p. 6.
235 *Hansard* 1924 5th s., vols. 173, 175 (HC). Comment in *LJ* 59 (1924), 574; *LT* 158 (1924), 189–90.

dropped the fees we could never go back again',[236] three years later some modest reductions were made, notably in possession fees and plaint fees on bigger claims, in order, the Treasury was told, to forestall pressure for bigger, more general ones.[237]

These reductions did not meet the main complaint of registrars, that the plaint fee on the smallest claims was too high,[238] and within a few years falling receipts, partly the result of procedural changes, required some fees to be increased.[239] On the whole, however, this was a period notable for harmony between the Treasury and the LCO on the finances of the courts and one in which public discontents seldom reached an embarrassing level.

The fees rules, consolidated in 1943,[240] were nevertheless criticised as too lengthy and complex by the Austin Jones Committee.[241] The chairman was disappointed at their inability to make a serious attack on the fees themselves, but few of the Committee had the stomach for an out and out fight on principle.[242] Instead they confined their recommendations to shifting the burden from the much criticised hearing fee to the plaint fee, limiting adjournment fees and doing some useful tidying up.[243]

Unfortunately, while the LCD wished to encourage suitors to use the county court, it was unable to control the expense of providing the service, and inexorable pressure on wages and prices began to widen the gap between fee income and the total cost to the point where the Treasury was bound to intervene. After some stalling the LCD had to put together a package in 1956 estimated to bring in another £150,000, but relief was only temporary.[244] The next year Rieu warned the Lord Chancellor that 'the Financial Secretary is agitating for a complete review of county court finances. He thinks the county court should be self-supporting, as it was before the war, and that the current deficit – this year the

236 *PP* 1928 (35, 99) V, q. 1880.

237 SI 1931/487 (L12); Martin to Treasury, 18 May 1931, PRO LCO 2/1248. The LCO was particularly concerned about criticism from the former judge, Sir Edward Parry.

238 PRO LCO 2/1249.

239 *Ibid.*; SI 1936/160 (L27).

240 SI 1359 (L28).

241 *Austin Jones Report*, para. 122.

242 Sub-committee meeting of 8 June 1948, PRO LCO 2/3296. Judges and registrars wanted fees reduced: see evidence in 2/3293.

243 *Austin Jones Report*, section X.

244 PRO LCO 2/4975; SI 1956/501 (L4).

estimate is £600,000 – should be met by increasing the fees all round.'[245]

While the LCD found the suggestion of a 40 per cent rise unthinkable (it would in some cases bring county court fees above high court equivalents which could hardly be raised while probate revenues kept it solvent[246]), they were disconcerted by the vigour with which the Treasury pressed the case for the adoption of the alleged principle that only judges and buildings came free to suitors.[247] The Lord Chancellor had told the Evershed Committee that it was merely a 'rough and ready rule to be borne in mind'[248] and they stated it in vague terms as 'a principle ... accepted by Parliament and the country for many generations, viz., that suitors in the courts should bear some proportion of the costs of the machinery of justice'.[249]

Though unable to move the Treasury from its position, the LCD eventually escaped with another series of rises, much bigger this time,[250] and had to concede further ground in 1961;[251] in all these three fee orders in just five years were estimated to increase the yield by more than £750,000, yet the estimates spiralled upwards, to just short of £1 million for 1961–2.[252] The greater the cost of the county courts the less feasible it became to make the suitors meet the bulk of that cost, and with legal aid now in the county court some of the fees simply represented a recycling of public funds. Though spared annual reviews[253] the Department now experienced stronger and more persistent Treasury pressure than ever before. Further rises in the 1960s led to complaints that suitors were paying more for a service which, in terms of its capacity to deliver effective judgments, was very unsatisfactory; the suitors, however, were still meeting only a part of the cost.[254]

245 3 June 1957, PRO LCO 2/7137.
246 Memo. by H. Boggis-Rolfe, 2 June 1958, *ibid.*
247 *Ibid.*, and Hayes to Boggis-Rolfe, 15 Sep. 1958, D. Heathcote-Amory to Kilmuir, 5 Dec. 1958.
248 *PP* 1950–1 [Cmd 8176] XVI, part V, para. 145.
249 *Ibid.*, para. 141.
250 SI 2154 (L16) (December 1958).
251 SI 1961/355. This time the Treasury did not press the 'principle': D. M. B. Butt to R. K. Thesiger, 1 Mar. 1960, PRO LCO 2/7198.
252 *Ibid.*, Rieu to Coldstream, 9 Jan. 1961. The LCD was given a hard time on their estimates in the 1960s: see e.g. *PP* 1963–4 (29) V, pp. 15–21.
253 PRO LCO 8/81.
254 E.g. W. T. West, *SJ* 110 (1966), 450.

### The registry of county court judgments

One part of the county court system which did pay its way was the registry of judgments. Created by the Treasury at the end of 1852,[255] it had various locations until it settled in Treasury chambers in 1890 from where it followed the county courts branch to its successive homes.[256] But though its origins are clear, and likewise its purpose 'to enable parties to ascertain the credit of tradesmen and others whom they might be inclined to trust, by searching to see if there were any judgments registered against the person in question',[257] it remains a mystery why the Treasury should have benignly established such a facility at public expense.

That a public subsidy was involved was clear by the early 1870s, for the office, employing a superintendent, two clerks and a writer, and charging only 6d for a search, cost more than £2,500 a year to run while its income was less than £100.[258] All common law judgments of £10 and upwards which remained unsatisfied after fourteen days were entered, along with all equity decrees and (the few) admiralty orders made in county courts. Over time the register also acquired other entries, such as deserted wives' petitions for protection against process, but none of these was of lasting importance.[259]

Any debtor might have the registration cancelled on proof that he had satisfied the judgment,[260] but since very few did so the registers swelled steadily; 25,156 entries were made in 1874 and in

255 Circular of 10 Nov. 1852, PRO LCO 8/2, f. 139; County Courts Act 1852 s. 18. The width of the power given to the Treasury was criticised in *LO* 44 (1852), 369.

256 Starting out at 1 Parliament Street, it was at 2 New Street, Spring Gardens by 1858 and moved to Treasury chambers when the post of superintendent was abolished: PRO LCO 8/4, f. 73.

257 M. D. Ross to Sir R. W.Payne, 7 Dec. 1967, PRO LCO 31/3; *Lisgar Commission*, p. 99.

258 *Lisgar Evidence*: T. C. Hamilton at q. 7620, and *Lisgar Commission*, pp. 99–100. For earlier figures see *PP* 1865 (160) XXX and *PP* 1856 (119) L. As recommended by the Commission the post of superintendent was abolished on the next vacancy; a senior Treasury official performed the role until the county courts branch was transferred to the LCO, when it was assumed by the head of the branch.

259 *Lisgar Evidence*, qq. 7583–606.

260 *Ibid.*, q. 7573.

1965 no fewer than 450,000, often 2–3,000 a day.[261] But long before then the finances of the registry had been transformed.

In 1930, in response to a 'machine-made' agitation by trade protection societies for a similar facility for high court judgments, Napier explained what had happened, though not when and how.[262] While one copy of the daily returns was given to the registry, another was sent to the Mercantile Press Association (MPA) for insertion, in convenient form, in *Stubbs' Gazette*. The MPA paid nearly £2,000 p. a. for this, and contracts with other trade organisations for judgments of interest to their members yielded a further £500.[263] No wonder personal inspections yielded only £6 a year. Although this arrangement kept the Treasury and the traders happy it is not surprising that Napier marked his memorandum 'highly confidential' and that the LCO gave no encouragement to expansion of registration either then or when it was considered by Evershed in the 1950s.[264]

The only people registration did not suit (debtors, presumably, excepted) were the staff on whom the burden of preparing and processing these daily returns fell. It is not therefore surprising that the ACCR and CCOA were among those who told the Austin Jones Committee that it should be abolished.[265] The MPA and other commercial interests were equally vehement for its retention[266] and, though the Committee was divided, Martin made the telling point that the best evidence of the worth of the register was that users evidently valued the service enough to pay for it.[267] The Committee rather grudgingly yielded.[268]

By contrast the Payne Committee, so far from considering its abolition, envisaged a more extended register covering the judgments of all civil courts and possibly extending to judgments of

261 *Lisgar Commission*, p. 99; *Payne Report*, para. 1184. Since records were kept for twenty years the space problem had become acute: J. P. Lowry, Register of County Court Judgments, *CCO* 40 (1967–8), 113.

262 Memo of 11 Dec. 1930 and Schuster to Attorney-General, 5 Nov. 1930, PRO LCO 2/1069.

263 *Ibid*.: Napier's memo.

264 *Ibid*. Registration of Unsatisfied Judgments Bill *PP* 1930 (50) I; *PP* 1952–3 [Cmd 8878], CI, paras. 464–70.

265 PRO LCO 2/3295.

266 PRO LCO 2/3302.

267 PRO LCO 2/3299 and sub-committee discussions in 2/3296 (23 Nov. 1948).

268 *Austin Jones Report*, para. 66.

£5.[269] Unlike the earlier report, Payne was quite open in describing the role of the commercial press in disseminating judgments and evinced none of the disapproval evident in Austin Jones and Evershed. Its approval ensured that the registry would survive.

## *Funds in court*

Although large quantities of suitors' money passed through the 'banking system' of the county courts, it was not until they acquired an equity jurisdiction in 1865 that they became custodians of capital sums or property pending the happening of a specified contingency, usually the person entitled reaching a prescribed age.[270] These deposits were later augmented by sums from two other sources: lump sums awarded as compensation to the widow and/or children of a deceased workman under the Workmen's Compensation Acts and, following the Branson Report of 1923,[271] damages awarded in the KBD to infants and lunatics, and also damages under the Fatal Accidents Acts awarded to widows, hitherto expensively administered by the Public Trustee.[272] By 1930 between £4 and 5 million was in court, mostly invested in some 35,000 individual Post Office Savings accounts opened by the registrar of the court in question.[273]

In 1931 the government contemplated a raid upon 'dormant funds' (defined as funds on which no dealing had taken place for at least fifteen years[274]) to alleviate the plight of the Exchequer. Schuster hoped to seize the opportunity to rescue his ravaged county court building programme by persuading the Treasury to introduce a limitation period for claims on dormant funds and to earmark the unclaimed county court ones for courthouses, but the Treasury would not agree and the investigating committee would not accept that the policy of a limitation period was within its

269 *Payne Report*, paras. 1172–208.

270 County Courts (Equitable Jurisdiction) Act 1865 (28 & 29 Vict. c. 99).

271 *PP* 1923 [Cmd 1870] XII(2).

272 Administration of Justice Act 1925 s. 21, later County Courts Act 1934 s. 164; P. Polden, The Public Trustee in England, 1906–1986: the Failure of an Experiment?, *JLH* 10 (1989), 228–55, at 239–40.

273 *Report of the Committee on Dormant Funds*, *PP* 1931–2 (Cmd 4132) VII, paras. 46–54.

274 Supreme Court Funds Rules 1927/1184 (L27). In the county courts funds unclaimed after six years were transferred to the Exchequer, but with no bar on recovery.

terms of reference. £148,000 of dormant funds remained tantalisingly out of reach.[275]

What did emerge from the Tomlin Committee's deliberations was a simplified procedure for investment.[276] To the registrars' indignation, they were now required to remit all capital sums to the Accountant-General.[277] Each was kept for a month in a local deposit account earning 2.5 per cent interest and if there then remained £50 or more, it was transferred to an 'investment account' at 3 per cent. Behind the scenes the money was invested by the National Debt Commissioners, almost invariably in government securities.[278] This system had some advantages to the suitors in that their capital and the prescribed income were guaranteed even though it became impossible actually to produce that return from authorised investments. In wartime, as Martin wrote, 'we cannot possibly earn this rate ... our fund has been seriously bankrupt and will undoubtedly be so for a long time'.[279]

The drawbacks for suitors, however, quickly became apparent:

> The County Court system has had unfortunate results for the beneficiaries, in that the funds have earned interest at a less[er] rate than could have been obtained from other investments, and most of the beneficiaries have on the basis of present market values suffered a serious capital depreciation, in the sense of a diminution of the number of pounds, as well as the decline in the real value (purchasing power) of each pound.[280]

The LCD and the judiciary were rather complacent in not seeking to improve the handling of funds in court and this was not the only part of their practice that came in for criticism.[281]

Under the workmen's compensation legislation, county court

275 Schuster to Rae, 28 Sep. 1931, to G. H. S. Pinsent, 30 Nov. 1931; Pinsent to Schuster, 2 Dec. 1931, PRO LCO 2/1645. *PP* 1931–2 [Cmd 4132] VII, paras. 42, 46–54.

276 For the negotiations see PRO LCO 2/1257.

277 ACCR AGM, reported in *LJ* 79 (1935), 350–1.

278 County Courts Act 1934 ss. 158–66; County Court Funds Rules 1934/1315 (L28). An annual report was made to Parliament from 1937 onwards: see *PP* 1936–7 (85) XXI.

279 Martin to Napier, Jan. 1942, PRO LCO 2/4242. Before agreeing to the 3 per cent return, the Treasury had required an undertaking that the LCO would accept an immediate reduction if the National Debt Commissioners reported that they could not generate that return: LCO 2/1323.

280 *PP* 1958–9 [Cmnd 818] XIII, para. 50. The performance of investments in war loans was so embarrassing that there were fears that the beneficiaries might sue: PRO LCO 2/6028.

281 In fairness, the LCD did tackle the high court masters about this, but found

judges and registrars had been accustomed to exercising control over lump sums for the benefit of widows and children. With no experience of handling substantial sums, many widows were easy prey to blandishments to buy hopeless businesses – like the men, they seemed to have a quite desperate inclination for fried fish shops.[282] The courts had no compunction about protecting these people from themselves. Notwithstanding the doubtful *vires* of the rule under which they acted[283] and a decision which seemed to narrow their discretion,[284] money payable to children was routinely detained in court after they had become adults and, despite repeated complaints, the practice was only relinquished when the Court of Appeal ruled against it.[285]

By then workmen's compensation cases were almost at an end, but the widows who had been smuggled into the same protective regime in 1925 continued to be the objects of unabashed paternalism. Complaints arose not only at the way their capital was eroded under the courts' management but also at their being treated as incompetent to manage their own affairs.[286] Some judges added insult to injury by insisting on hearing applications for payment of money in open court[287] and the county courts adhered to their tradition of making periodical payments monthly to women whose budgeting was a weekly affair.[288] These criticisms, along with judgments questioning the *vires* of the rule

them very evasive and unhelpful: Dobson to Boggis-Rolfe, 8 Dec. 1957, PRO LCO 2/6028.

282 This topic is barely mentioned in Wilson and Levy, *Workmen's Compensation* or Bartrip, *Workmen's Compensation*, though both deal extensively with the controversial practice of making lump sum agreements with the injured workman: see especially Wilson and Levy, vol. II, pp. 151–63. It was a recurrent concern of the Rule Committee.

283 This rule (19) was discussed in 1924 (PRO LCO 2/1077–8) and amended in 1930 (2/866, 869, 1081–2).

284 *Johnston v. Henry Liston and Co.* [1920] 1 KB 99; Bartrip, *Workmen's Compensation*, pp. 162–3; PRO LCO 2/1943.

285 *Re Embleton* [1946] 2 All ER 542. Judge Procter was particularly criticised: PRO LCO 2/6225.

286 See the evidence of T. K. P. Barrett for the *News of the World* in PRO LCO 2/6031. Some judges were also rather mean: R. Gregory to Coldstream, 25 Mar. 1957, PRO LCO 2/6225.

287 *PP* 1959 [Cmnd 818] XIII, para. 63(e), inserted on the initiative of the secretary, N. H. Turner: PRO LCO 2/6033, 12th meeting of the Pearson Committee.

288 19th meeting, PRO LCO 2/6032. Only Judge Pugh and the registrar H. Reeve-Allerton supported monthly payments. The report (para. 25 (2)) emphasised

in question,[289] induced the LCD to set up the Pearson Committee.[290]

The most surprising feature of the Committee's deliberations is that opposition to paternalism was so muted. The best-documented case against continuing the controls was presented by the *News of the World*, which had been championing the widows' cause, and though the bar took the same side, the Law Society echoed the unanimous opposition of masters and registrars.[291] So did Coldstream, who wrote, 'to abandon [the present practice] ... simply on grounds of logic ... or because it is thought to be inconsistent with the implications of the welfare state, seems to be to encourage all that is worst in modern society'.[292] The Committee not only came out in favour of continuing controls on widows, whether or not with dependent children, but even wanted them extended to damages awarded under the Carriage by Air Act 1932 and to settlements of claims.[293]

It was, however, acknowledged that the handling of investments by all courts needed radical change. The Pearson proposals were influenced by those of the Nathan Report, which had examined similar grievances about charitable funds.[294] Rejecting the bar's preference for individual trusts on grounds of cost and practicality, it opted for pooling in a central fund comprising two trusts, one for short-term, the other for longer-term holdings. Investment would be the function of a 'Central Fund Corporation' run along the lines of a unit trust, but decisions on payments to beneficiaries and transfers between the short- and long-term trusts would still be made by the court.[295] Most Queen's Bench awards

that the criterion should be the beneficiary's interests, not the court's convenience.

289 *McCann v. Belfast Corporation* [1952] (LR) NI 49. Upjohn J changed the usual practice by giving the widow her money out and out: *Smith v. Boulton and Paul* (*The Times*, 24 Oct. 1957) and *Lawrence v. Greenholm Plant Hire* ((1957) Ch. D.), leading to queries from county court registrars: PRO LCO 2/6028. The Committee was split on the *vires* of the Supreme Court rule.

290 PRO LCO 2/6028.

291 Evidence is in PRO LCO 2/6030–3. The LCD representative, Thesiger, felt obliged to put the case for decontrol himself: 1st meeting, 2/6030.

292 Coldstream's note, 18 Nov. 1957, PRO LCO 2/6028.

293 *PP* 1958–9 [Cmnd 818] XIII, para. 22B.

294 *PP* 1952 [Cmd 8710] VIII.

295 *PP* 1958–9 [Cmnd 818] XIII, paras. 54–62. The range of investments would be considerably widened. It was felt that the National Debt Commissioners would not use any wider powers of selection: 12th meeting, 2/6033.

would continue to be administered by a county court, whose judge might delegate to his registrar.[296] Hearings should no longer be held in open court, weekly payments should be made in appropriate cases and 'in the exercise of the discretionary power to control widows' damages, an application for the payment of the whole of the money to the widow should be regarded in a comparatively cautious attitude at the stage of the initial directions as to disposal but with a somewhat greater readiness to accede to such an application when made some years later'.[297]

Although the report appeared in July 1959, it was not implemented until 1965 and then restricted to widows with dependent children.[298] Moreover, the scheme was altered in some important respects. The new investment account was to be under the Public Trustee, short-term deposits remaining under the existing county court arrangements, now made available to the high court too.[299] In an age of inflation the return on these investments could no longer be allowed to remain static and by several stages it had risen to 7 per cent by 1970.[300]

296 *PP* 1958–9 [Cmnd 818] XIII, para. 63. Chancery and admiralty funds were not to be subject to this recommendation.

297 *Ibid.*, para. 32.

298 *Hansard* 1964–5 5th s., vol. 261 (HL), cols. 506–23, 535–46, 1238–72. Dilhorne (then Sir R. Manningham-Buller) had been critical of 'grandmotherly legislation': to Coldstream, 27 Jan. 1959, PRO LCO 2/6029.

299 Administration of Justice Act 1965 ss. 9, 19.

300 County Court Funds (Amendment) Rules 1970/228 (L9).

7

# JUDGES

## THE POWER OF APPOINTMENT

After the passage of the 1846 Act sixty judges were soon appointed,[1] it being affirmed in *R v. Parham*[2] that the Act did indeed envisage one judge per district, not one for each court. In the 1870s, following the Judicature Commissioners' recommendation for a drastic reduction in courts,[3] the Lord Chancellor came under strong pressure to cut the number of judges substantially,[4] but the reductions were modest and in 1914 there were still fifty-five judges. Little changed between the wars, judges being increased by two, but afterwards the statutory maximum was progressively raised, to sixty-five in 1949, thereafter by stages to ninety-seven in 1968 and in 1970, in preparation for the Beeching reforms, to 125.[5] This doubling in twenty years of numbers which had been more or less static for a century was driven by necessity, for the LCD continued to oppose 'dilution' of the judiciary at all levels.[6] Thus the 1955 expansion was directly linked to the coming of legal aid and a wider jurisdiction and that of 1968 to the acquisition of divorce and the increasing general workload.[7] For the most part, a single judge continued to cover a district, though from 1959 he might call upon a 'floater' to cope with congestion.

1 The County Courts Act 1846 authorised 'as many fit persons as are needed'.
2 (1849) 13 QB 858.
3 *Second Report*, at p. 14.
4 See the proceedings in the *Childers Report* and the *Lisgar Commission*.
5 High Court and County Court Judges Act 1949 s. 2; County Courts Act 1955 s. 9; Administration of Justice Acts 1964 s. 5(2) and 1968 s. 1.
6 See e.g. their submission to the Franks Tribunal (Abel-Smith and Stevens, *Lawyers and the Courts*, p. 263) and PRO LCO 2/7182.
7 Coldstream to G. Grey, 24 Nov. 1954, PRO LCO 2/4984; Dobson's note, 8 July 1963, 12/106; *Hansard* 1967–8 5th s., vol. 288 (HL), cols. 602–10.

However, by 1963 there were nineteen districts, including all the London ones, with two judges and one, Marylebone, with three, and this trend continued through the decade.

Patronage had been one of the thorniest obstacles to the creation of the new courts but Cottenham, less concerned than the Conservatives with preserving the rights of the local gentry from government encroachment, gave full powers to the Lord Chancellor. He made three exceptions, two temporary, the other permanent. Existing judges in Bristol, Bath, Liverpool and Manchester, the County Clerk of Middlesex and the Steward of the Manor of Sheffield were permitted to become judges of their county courts and the lords of eight manors were allowed to appoint to the next vacancy in the county court superseding their manorial court; because of this Sheffield was manned by a nominee of the Duke of Norfolk until Thomas Ellison died in 1896.[8] The permanent exception was for districts exclusively within the Duchy of Lancaster, in which the Chancellor of the Duchy had both the right to appoint and the power to dismiss.[9] One of the Chancellor's early choices, William Ramshay in Liverpool, turned out disastrously[10] and there was some criticism of later Duchy appointments,[11] but while the Duchy did tend to favour local candidates its choices do not seem to have been worse than the Lord Chancellor's.

## CHOOSING THE JUDGES

### *Eligibility*

The qualification for a county court judgeship was at least seven years' standing at the bar, or seven years' practising partly as a barrister and partly as a special pleader.[12] Despite vigorous

8 County Courts Act 1846, ss. 10–12; *LJ* 31 (1896), 246. The other manors were Birmingham, Cirencester, St Albans, Stourbridge, Kidderminster, Stockport and Ashton-under-Lyne. The Conservative bill had given most of the patronage to the *Custos Rotulorum* of each county: *LM* ns 5 (1846), 217 at 221.

9 County Courts Act 1846 s. 16.

10 Polden, Judicial Selkirks, 255–6; *Ex p. Ramshay* (1852) 18 QB 174.

11 *LJ* 48 (1913), 222.

12 Delaying the call to the bar in order to gain experience as a special pleader was common in the early part of the nineteenth century: Duman, *English and*

lobbying, attorneys were excluded, although attorneys who were judges of existing local courts, or those acting as county clerks were eligible.[13] Two were chosen, and though William Furner subsequently went to the bar, James Stansfeld did not. Stansfeld died in 1871,[14] and it was a full century before solicitors again became eligible to sit on the county court bench.[15]

## *Information*

The convention established in the last century that high court judgeships are not openly sought[16] has never applied to junior judgeships, though applications were not, until recently, publicly invited.[17] There has never been an absolute shortage of candidates. The *Law Times* claimed to have heard that more than 750, including all but four of the serjeants, had put themselves forward for the initial batch of appointments.[18] This was probably an exaggeration, but until Schuster introduced systematic records of applications it is impossible to have any accurate picture of numbers or the selection process.

From about 1920, if not earlier, candidates had to provide the names of referees and a standard body of information. Those thought to merit serious consideration were interviewed by senior civil servants and when a vacancy occurred the Lord Chancellor would usually be furnished with an annotated short list.[19] At no time did the Chancellor feel obliged to confine his choice to those who put themselves forward. Several Victorian judges boasted that they had received their places unsolicited[20] but in the

*Colonial Bars*, p. 83. The less stringent qualification – the Common Law Commissioners had proposed ten years – was welcomed as enlarging the field of choice; *LM* ns 5 (1846), 220–1.

13 County Courts Act 1846 s. 9. *Hansard* 1845–6 3rd s., vol. 88, cols. 919 ff.

14 *Boase*, vol. I, p. 1113; vol. III, p. 712; *Walford's County Families of the United Kingdom* (London, 1865 edn).

15 See p. 175 above and Cecil, *English Judge*, pp. 12–17.

16 As Schuster explained to a barrister who perpetrated this solecism: PRO LCO 2/2226.

17 See now the LCD's publication *Judicial Appointments*.

18 *LT* 8 (1846–7), 380. For numbers between the wars see Polden, 'Oiling the Machinery': the Lord Chancellor's Office and the County Court Bench, 1927–1944, *JLH* 19 (1998), 224–44. The annual average in the 1950s was about fifteen: Rieu's minute, 8 May 1959, PRO LCO 2/7703.

19 Polden, 'Oiling the Machinery'.

20 E.g. *DNB*, vol. I, p. 142; *Select Committee, 1878*, q. 1956. Hatherley offered a

twentieth century the diminishing opportunities for Chancellors to gain personal knowledge of the bar has made it unusual for them to go outside the officials' list, though there were certainly instances between the wars of choices which the officials disapproved of.[21]

## *Applicants' motives*

The county court bench never carried anything like the same prestige as the superior courts – it was not so much a lower division as a lesser league. The poor quality of many nineteenth-century appointments ensured that its status remained low for a long time, that 'friends' would express surprise when a barrister of eminence joined its ranks; in the contemptuous phrase of an outspoken KC it was 'that respectable shelf'.[22] Slowly the quality improved and with it the prestige, until Gerald Hurst could be impressed by finding that several fellow benchers of Lincoln's Inn were among the judges.[23] Even so, what impelled candidates to come forward does need explanation, though it can only be tentative.

First there were successful men who had worn themselves out and wanted a quiet life: Manning and G. L. Russell openly admitted as much and it clearly applies to Willis too.[24] Others had felt themselves to be in line for the high court but found the prize had somehow slipped from their grasp. They might, like Meadows White, have fallen victim to one of Halsbury's dubious 'jobs'[25] or, like Archer and Thompson, they may have been unfortunate in finding themselves among a very talented cohort at the Chancery bar,[26] where the number of judgeships was very small. A few, like Dumas perhaps, gave up hope a little too soon.[27]

Men such as Prentice, Galbraith and W. H. G. Bagshawe, fell into that embarrassing category of successful juniors who gambled

judgeship to S. T. Thring when the bankruptcy commissioners became redundant: *Childers Report*, q. 4964.

21 Polden, 'Oiling the Machinery'.

22 J. H. Balfour Browne, *Forty Years at the Bar* (London, 1916), p. 166.

23 *Closed Chapters*, p. 136.

24 *LM & R* ns 22 (1867), 174; *Select Committee, 1878*, q. 915; *DNB*, 2nd supp., vol. III, p. 683.

25 *Law Gazette* 6 (1892–3), 449; *CCC* 34 (1893–4), 187.

26 *The Times*, 18 Jan. 1958; 25 June 1962.

27 *Ibid.*, 19 Jan. 1952, 5 Nov. 1940; PRO LCO 2/6654.

on silk and lost;[28] they have usually been the recipients of outdoor relief in some form. Others accepted that they had reached the limits of a solid junior practice or, as silks, were never going to make the top flight. They are the men, earning £2,000 to £4,000, whom Ensor (writing in 1933) regarded as typical county court judges[29] and they overlap with a group who, while demonstrating many of the qualities needed for success, were held back by the absence of others: Bray lacked the 'push' which his more eminent brother had in abundance; Moore was too nervous, Scully too 'otherworldly', Graham too prone to 'asperity'.[30] The lower bench also had its fair share of scholarly men, ill-suited to the Darwinian world of the bar.[31]

In a different category are men who put personal considerations ahead of their profession. Both Lee and Wingate were among the select band who had turned down the high court: Lee was in poor health and would not leave his beloved Hampshire; Wingate had married late and would not leave his family to go on circuit.[32] Into this category also fall Allchin, desolated by bereavement,[33] and Cecil Beresford and Roope Reeve, who found the life of a country gentleman mingled with some light judging more agreeable than London.[34] The most unusual case is that of Hildyard, a Master in Lunacy who inherited a country estate and took a county court judgeship to be able to live on it.[35]

Finally, there are men who had forsaken practice for politics or official life, or who had gone to war and subsequently found themselves unable or unwilling to resume their profession. Aside from MPs,[36] they include colonial judges like Kershaw, Braund, Blagden and Chapman,[37] secretaries to Lord Chancellors (Scott,

28 *Law Gazette* 7 (1893–4), 449–50; *The Times*, 30 Jan. 1945; *LJ* 36 (1901), 566.
29 *Courts and Judges*, p. 7.
30 *The Times*, 21 June 1926, 19 June 1934, 6 Feb. 1929, 8 Aug. 1930.
31 E.g. Sir G. S. Baker, *The Times*, 16 Mar. 1923.
32 *The Times*, 17 Jan. 1983, 6 Aug. 1990.
33 Hailsham, *Sparrow's Flight*, p. 107.
34 *The Times*, 15 Feb. 1912, 19 Feb. 1952.
35 *Ibid.*, 22 Apr. 1956.
36 See p. 260 below.
37 Kershaw was a judge of the mixed court in Egypt who fell 'victim of a notorious judicial scandal', resigned on principle and returned to England without a pension. Made a judge in 1927, he died soon afterwards: *The Times*, 17 June 1927. Braund and Blagden were judges in India and Burma respectively (*WWW* 1961–70, pp. 102, 129), Chapman in Ireland: *The Times*, 22 July 1933.

Bradshaw)[38] and Bacon, who had been secretary to his father the Vice-Chancellor.[39] Some, like Higgins, had been to war and found that their injuries precluded them from rebuilding a practice or, like Donald Hurst, made them anxious to give up early.[40]

## *Factors in the selection of judges*

### *Political influences*

Labelling judicial appointments 'political' can be misleading.[41] The choice of men who were, or had been, active in political life was almost unavoidable given the remarkable number of barristers who entered the House of Commons – 309 between 1832 and 1886 – and the many others who had stood for election, actively campaigned for a party or written party propaganda.[42]

It is not surprising therefore that thirty-eight judges were or had recently been MPs when appointed, and none was so controversial as the first of them, Edmond Beales in 1870, whose selection sparked off a considerable political row.[43] Lord Chancellors of all parties made MPs into judges and in the 1950s Kilmuir quite openly espoused a policy of trying to increase their number at all levels of the judiciary, though he was thwarted by the shortage of suitable men;[44] not everyone thought it desirable but no-one regarded it as illegitimate. Indeed some of the twentieth-century MP-judges were outstanding – Kennedy and Gerald Hurst were very near to high court standard[45] – and if one or two were rather undistinguished, only Stavely-Hill turned out really badly.[46] Among the earlier appointments Tom Hughes and

38 *Boase*, vol. III, p. 461; *Foster*, p. 51.

39 *The Times*, 12 June 1911; *CCC* 43 (1911–12), 156.

40 PRO LCO 33/40. Cecil, *English Judge*, p. 26 states that 90 of the 117 judges he examined had served in the armed forces.

41 A. Paterson, Judges, A Political Elite?, *British Journal of Law and Society*, 1 (1974), 118–35.

42 Duman, *English and Colonial Bars*, p. 170, table 6.1.

43 D. Duman, *The Judicial Bench in England, 1727–1875* (London, 1982), pp. 95–6. Hatherley had feared trouble: M. R. D. Foot and H. C. G. Matthew (eds.), *The Gladstone Diaries*, VII, p. 356.

44 Rieu's minute, PRO LCO 2/7703.

45 *CCO*, 18 (1937–8), pt 6; *LT* 195 (1943), 67.

46 Stavely-Hill was reputed to come to court armed with *Everyman's Guide to the Law* and *Ruff's Guide to the Turf*: *Hansard* 1966–7 5th s., vol. 749 (HC), col. 1765.

Morgan Howard were singled out for criticism[47] but Halsbury earned plaudits for following Herschell in choosing political opponents[48] and, though unimpressed with the generality of Loreburn's choices, the *Solicitors' Journal* admitted that 'in the main they were middle aged men with a good circuit, local or commercial court practice, and not mere party hacks'.[49]

Victorian politicians however did view minor judicial posts in a different light from their successors and most Chancellors came under pressure from their party, though the patronage secretary at the Treasury never succeeded in bringing the Chancellor's appointments within his grasp.[50] Loreburn and Haldane put a stop to the use of high court judgeships as a political reward and refused to 'job' the lay magistracy.[51] The former and present Liberal MPs who were made county court judges all had sound credentials: then and afterwards, political services helped, but were not sufficient.

Earlier Chancellors undoubtedly made some judges to assist the Prime Minister – as Halsbury did with Marten – or to oblige a cabinet colleague, as Cairns did with Horatio Lloyd.[52] The legal profession found these men acceptable, but others were not; for instance, Roebuck got a judgeship for T. F. Falconer, a man with a negligible practice and who had volunteered himself for a colonial secretaryship.[53] Similar circumstances may explain other appointments contemporaries found baffling.

Some critics objected to political considerations having any influence, arguing for instance that Vernon Lushington, though well qualified, should not have been appointed merely to save on a pension.[54] But indignation was greatest about the use of the bench

47 For Hughes see *CCC* 28 (1882), 369 and for Howard *SJ* 32 (1887–8), 37, though according to the *Law Journal* (22 (1887), 609), 'his claims to a higher seat were of a kind which have often been found irresistible'.

48 *LJ* 29 (1894), 169; 32 (1897), 113.

49 *SJ* 56 (1911–12), 590.

50 Duman, *Judicial Bench*, p. 119; H. J. Hanham, Political Patronage at the Treasury, 1870–1912, *Historical Journal* 3 (1960), 75–84.

51 Heuston, *Lord Chancellors, 1885–1940*, pp. 153–8. The party took it out on the Lord Chancellor's private secretaries by refusing them a pay rise: E. David (ed.), *Inside Asquith's Cabinet* (London, 1977), p. 82.

52 Heuston, *Lord Chancellors, 1885–1940*, p. 49; Hanham, *Political Patronage*, 78–9.

53 *LM* ns 16 (1851), 129. He was Roebuck's brother-in-law.

54 *LJ* 12 (1877), 593; cf., on Bacon, *LJ* 13 (1878), 741.

to reward men who had no other claim beyond services to ministers or judges, men like Scott and Bradshaw. As well as being unfair to other contenders, it devalued the whole county court bench at a time when it needed boosting.

*Nepotism*

Nineteenth-century Chancellors used their patronage to assist their own families, giving rise in Halsbury's case to a widely circulated, if perhaps unfair joke.[55] He provides the only obvious example in the county courts. His brother was made a judge by Cairns in 1875, but Halsbury himself chose Melville ('whom we hear of for the first time'[56]), a relation of Lady Halsbury, and Robert Woodfall, his brother-in-law.[57]

*Age*

In 1878 Henry Nicol suggested that county court judges should be appointed at no older than forty-five, or fifty at the outside,[58] and this view, that their duties placed a greater premium on the vigour of youth than the seasoned wisdom of comparative old age, was later endorsed by Haldane[59] and was received wisdom in the 1950s, when candidates for junior judgeships were 'in the danger zone' at fifty-eight.[60] The goal would have been easy enough to achieve at the outset but when Nicol expressed it the bar was at its most ruthlessly competitive; overcrowding made it harder to reach eminence quickly, and bigger earnings made barristers in their prime more reluctant to quit.[61] Consequently, the choice often lay between an able, but inexperienced younger man and a well-known but considerably older one. The age at which judges in all

[55] Heuston, *Lord Chancellors, 1885–1940*, pp. 36–7.

[56] *CCC* 32 (1889), 215.

[57] Duman, *English and Colonial Bars*, pp. 101–2, quotes Muir McKenzie's letter recommending him but without mentioning this additional claim. Unlike Melville, he was an excellent judge, though 'his success as an advocate was not commensurate with his ability': *The Times*, 17 Feb. 1920. Halsbury did choose his brother J. W. Giffard for the first vacancy on the Rule Committee.

[58] *Select Committee, 1878*, q. 5040.

[59] *Royal Commission on Delays in the KBD, Second Report, PP* 1914 [Cd 7177], XXXVII, q. 4727.

[60] P. Polden, Safety First: the Appointment of Metropolitan Stipendiary Magistrates, 1950–61, *Cambrian Law Review* 27 (1996), 57–74 at 65.

[61] Duman, *English and Colonial Bars*, pp. 143–7.

courts were appointed rose,[62] and in county courts there was only a short period around 1900 when over- and under-50s were chosen in almost equal numbers; oddly, over-60s also had their best chance in the Halsbury era, but since the early 1920s, when one journal called the county courts 'the preserve of elderly KCs who have given up hopes of preferment',[63] they have been comparatively uncommon.

There has in fact been a marked reduction in appointments at either extreme. Among the original judges were Wing (thirty-four), Heath (thirty-six) and Harden (thirty-eight) and until around 1890 men in their thirties were not infrequently chosen; Cairns made an offer to Gathorne Hardy when he was only thirty-two,[64] Pollock accepted at thirty-three and others include two of the most illustrious, Chalmers and Parry, the latter, at thirty-one, probably the youngest of all.[65] In the twentieth century such precociousness has been unknown. Barely half a dozen have been under forty-five and the most youthful post-war judge was B. D. Bush at forty-four. Likewise the really elderly appointments have ceased, perhaps made more difficult by the requirement for a health check. At seventy-one Paterson and Christopher Temple, were probably the oldest of all,[66] while McIntyre, Powell, Nichols and Teed were all sixty-eight. Since 1918 the only three over sixty-five were Cave and Dumas, both unlucky in the high court stakes,[67] and Gurdon.

### *Sex*

The Sex Disqualification (Removal) Act 1919 made women eligible for the bench but although there was at least one candidate on the LCD's list in the 1940s,[68] and in 1946 Edith Hesling

62 Duman, *Judicial Bench*, pp. 72–3.

63 *SJ* 69 (1924–5), 118.

64 N. E. Johnson (ed.), *The Diary of Gathorne Hardy, later Lord Cranbrook* (Oxford, 1981), p. 358.

65 Doubts were expressed about the wisdom of sending Chalmers straight to Birmingham, one of the busiest courts: *SJ* 28 (1883–4), 793. Parry was surprised to be chosen: *My Own Way*, pp. 192–6.

66 I have seen no comment on Paterson's age. Temple (1784–1871) was appointed in 1855 and described as 'a very tottering old man' when transferred to an industrial district in Lancashire in 1858: *Select Committee, 1878*, q. 5436 (S. Wall).

67 *The Times*, 5 Nov. 1940; PRO LCO 2/6655.

68 PRO LCO 2/4596–7.

became the first woman to sit on the county court bench, as a deputy judge,[69] it was 1962 before Elizabeth Lane broke down the barrier, followed in 1968 by Dorothy Waddy.[70]

### *Health*

It emerged after Judge Napier's resignation that no evidence of good health was required of a new judge. The Treasury disclaimed any desire to query appointments on this score and Muir McKenzie was appalled at the prospect.[71] It was inevitable, however, that some form of test would be required in the Judicial Pensions Act and after much toing and froing a suitably vague provision was included.[72] Some judges before Napier's time had died after a few months[73] and one or two others, like William Barber, were never really well enough to do the job.[74] The fitness requirement could not prevent unexpected early deaths[75] but probably ensured that most judges were physically fit for their duties.

### *War service*

In 1927 the *Law Journal*[76] praised the Lord Chancellor for choosing men who had served in the front line, and the short lists to his successors always mentioned the candidates' war records: 'a good war' seems to have distinctly enhanced a candidate's chances for any judicial post and certainly offset the fact that he had less experience, or a smaller practice, than those who had been able to stay at home.[77]

### *Judicial experience*

Many candidates had served as deputies in the county court and a good report improved their chances, but as a rule Chancellors

69 *LSG* 43 (1946), 41.
70 Shetreet, *Judges on Trial*, p. 59.
71 *PP* 1914 (249) IV, qq. 1011–46, 1252–82.
72 S. 2. The negotiations are in PRO LCO 2/436.
73 Examples are David Leahy (1847), D. R. Blaine (1871) and Aeneas McIntyre (1889).
74 *SJ* 36 (1891–2), 400.
75 E.g. P. M. Wright (1959). J. M. Kennan (1960), G. H. Rountree (1962) and W. A. B. Goss (1963).
76 *LJCCR* 62 (1926), 69.
77 Polden, Safety First, 66, and 'Oiling the Machinery'; Stevens, *Independence of the Judiciary*, p. 42.

refused to appoint a judge's regular deputy to succeed him, even if petitions were presented in his support.[78] More junior posts were sometimes raided for judges; the Chancellor of the Duchy took men from the Salford Hundred Court and the Liverpool Court of Passage,[79] and stipendiaries were sometimes promoted.[80] In Cluer's case this caused a few raised eyebrows,[81] but the bar reserved its indignation for ex-colonial judges, who became significant competitors in the 1950s when several were left stranded by the retreat from empire.[82]

*Record at the bar*

The Victorian law journals reserved their sharpest condemnations for the selection of men 'unknown to the profession', either through having been in retirement, like Temple,[83] or more commonly never having really got started, like Ellicott.[84] It was said that of Halsbury's first twenty-one judges only six 'ever enjoyed anything like a large practice at the Bar'; three or four were experienced deputies, the rest practically unknown.[85] The bar, of course, regarded a good practice or, failing that, an established reputation for legal scholarship, as the *sine qua non* for a judgeship, but Victorian Chancellors did not accept the prescription, though how they persuaded themselves that some of their selections were suitable is a mystery. In the twentieth century, they have been less adventurous, or perhaps less casual. The more systematic, (though still rather amateur) method of appointment, involving the collection of views from judges and senior barristers, necessarily gives the bar's evaluation a greater weight.

78 G. Harris, *The Autobiography of George Harris* (London, 1888), p. 297. Derby solicitors vainly petitioned on behalf of J. W. Lowe in 1892: *Law Gazette* 4, (1891–2), p. 116.

79 E.g. R. Segar and T. W. Wheeler from Salford and H. Brown from Liverpool.

80 A. S. Hogg (Salford, 1913), T. Bishop (Pontypool, 1886), Sir R. Harington (London, 1872).

81 *SJ* 54 (1910–11), 662.

82 Note of meeting with the Bar Council, 7 Mar. 1955, PRO LCO 2/4985.

83 *LM* ns 23 (1855), 208.

84 Sir F. A. Bosanquet, *The Oxford Circuit* (London, 1951), p. 77.

85 *LJ* 27 (1892), 491.

## CONDITIONS OF SERVICE

### *Salaries*

Since there was a power to go up to £1,200 p.a., the government's decision to pay only £1,000, well below what fees were bringing in, caused much dissatisfaction,[86] greatly increased in 1852 when, on the back of the extended jurisdiction the Treasury determined to create differential salaries. The Treasury's scheme was ineptly constructed, requiring immediate and embarrassing alterations; in the end eighteen judges were paid either £1,500 or £1,350 and the rest £1,200.[87] When the equity jurisdiction offered a suitable justification for putting the judges up to £1,500, the scheme was scrapped.[88]

The judges were to remain on £1,500 for the next seventy years, despite a select committee in 1878 recommending that they receive £2,000[89] and regular representations from their own Council. Rollit's Act strengthened their claim, but although the LCO toyed briefly with a return to differential salaries[90] they denied that the judges were overworked and contended that the salary was good enough to attract men of the right sort, something the judges could hardly gainsay without seeming to slight recent recruits.[91] A war bonus to compensate for increases in the cost of living did in fact carry their earnings above the magic figure of £2,000 in the early 1920s,[92] but though they received fair words from Lord Chancellors, the LCO did not press their claim with any great vigour and time after time they were put off with the incantation that the time was not ripe.[93] The ripening process was so lengthy

86 County Courts Act 1846 s. 40; *HLSP* 1851 (176) XI.

87 County Courts Further Extension Act 1852 s. 14 raised the maximum to £1,500. Correspondence is in *HLSP* 1854–5 (38) I. Two made good their claims after the Act, necessitating an amending Act, the County Court (Salaries) Act 1857.

88 County Courts Act 1867 ss. 1, 3, 14.

89 *Select Committee, 1878*, pp. iii–iv.

90 Memo of Apr. 1903, PRO LCO 2/153; memorial of 2 Aug. 1911, 2/210.

91 Muir McKenzie to Judge W. H. Roberts, 26 Feb. 1906, PRO LCO 2/153; evidence of Loreburn and Haldane to the Royal Commission on Delays in the KBD, *PP* 1914 [Cd 7177], XXXVII.

92 Stevens, *Independence of the Judiciary*, p. 46.

93 *Ibid.*, pp. 45–50; PRO LCO 12/40.

that it was not completed until 1937 when (partly because the bonus had recently been ended) they were finally awarded their £2,000, by then worth far less than when it was first recommended.

Despite what they earned for working as divorce commissioners,[94] judges grew worse off in the 1940s because of higher taxation and were aggrieved not only by the absolute decline in their living standards, but also by the fear that they were losing ground relative to other professions, particularly civil servants.[95] This time their claim was acknowledged to be a strong one[96] but it became inextricably linked to those of other judges, enmeshing all of them in a web of pay relativities as arcane as any shipyard.[97] The LCD, however, rejected a Treasury suggestion to 'step' salaries according to experience or workload.[98] When the long-delayed increase, to £2,800, came in 1952,[99] it was not especially generous because in exchange the judges gave up their divorce earnings,[100] so it was not long before, like everyone else, judges pressed for further rises to compensate for endemic inflation. The first, to £3,750, eased the way for future increases by allowing them to be made by order in council rather than statute, and orders were regularly made, taking salaries to £6,550 in 1969. Salary rises were informally linked to the civil service,[101] which had the effect of narrowing the gap between county court and high court earnings: from 30 per cent, the county court judges closed to more than 60 per cent at one point but thereafter the gap was deliberately widened again.[102]

94 In 1950 this ranged from £1,000 plus to less than £50. *Hansard* 5th s., vol. 494 (HC), col. 2149.

95 Stevens, *Independence of the Judiciary*, pp. 119–22. In 1945 it was claimed that those with children received only £1,173 15s after tax: Judge Davies to Napier, 17 Dec. 1945, PRO LCO 12/54.

96 Jowitt called it 'overwhelming' and the position 'nothing short of a scandal', to Napier, 28 Apr. 1949, PRO LCO 12/54.

97 Stevens, *Independence of the Judiciary*, pp. 121–5.

98 PRO LCO 2/4610, 4614.

99 Judicial Officers (Salaries) Act 1952.

100 PRO LCO 2/4979.

101 Stevens, *Independence of the Judiciary*, p. 125; Abel-Smith and Stevens, *Lawyers and the Courts*, pp. 292–3.

102 Stevens, *Independence of the Judiciary*, p. 13.

## *Pensions*

Until 1920 no judge had any entitlement to a pension,[103] but he might be given a gratuity of up to £1,000 p.a. if it was agreed that he should resign on the grounds of ill-health. It became the invariable practice to award the full amount but, ironically, it was the generosity in giving Napier £500 p.a. for the single day's work he felt able to perform which brought the arrangements into disrepute.[104] Under the terms of the 1919 Act, which was accepted by most of the serving judges, a judge completing fifteen years' service received two-thirds of his final salary plus a lump sum equal to twice the pension.[105] Pensions were subsequently uprated in line with other public servants and widows' pensions were introduced in 1949 to placate the judges for deferring their pay rise.[106] Even this modest enhancement to their conditions, to which all signed up bar Judge Fenwick, needed to be fought hard in cabinet.[107]

## *Residence and expenses*

The original Act imposed no conditions on where the judges should reside and a number quite legitimately chose to base themselves outside their district.[108] Despite occasional complaints of non-residence, some Lord Chancellors thought local residence inadvisable and others preferred to enforce it by means of a personal undertaking.[109] The Treasury, however, was to determine what 'reasonable travelling expenses' a judge might claim[110] and in 1872 attempted to reduce them by calculating expenses on

103 A clause in the Further Extension Bill of 1852 was taken out: *Hansard* 1851–2 3rd s., vol. 122, col. 374. The Select Committee of 1878 recommended a pension of two-thirds final salary after twenty years.

104 *PP* 1914 (249) V, q. 1252; Judge Smyly to Muir McKenzie, 4 May 1905, PRO LCO 2/160.

105 See p. 117 above. Nineteen judges opted out, PRO LCO 2/606.

106 PRO LCO 2/4608, Administration of Justice (Pensions) Act 1950.

107 PRO LCO 2/4609, 4610.

108 *LM & LR* ns 5 (1858), 307–14; *Debrett's House of Commons and Judicial Bench* (1868 edn).

109 *Hansard* 1871–2 3rd s., vol. 213, col. 47. An example, for W. Elmsley, is in PRO LCO 8/10.

110 S. 40.

the footing of residence in the central town in their district.[111] Unwisely and insensitively they tried to apply this to existing judges, only to be forced into ignominious retreat by their furious and well-supported protests.[112] Some judges did a great deal of travelling – Falconer for instance claimed to have travelled 3,635 miles in one eleven-month period[113] – and the calculation of expenses continued to give rise to occasional friction. In fact the allowances became distinctly generous and something of a 'quasi-vested interest' that the LCD was very wary of tackling[114] and such were judicial sensibilities that the Permanent Secretary was often involved in individual cases.[115]

## *Transfers*

Every judge was liable to be transferred to another district, and there were advocates of regular rotation.[116] That was never attempted, but the LCO did attempt to get the best judges for the most demanding courts and to move the frailer ones to districts with little travelling.[117] Plenty of judges were transferred at their own request – Parry from his beloved Manchester and Grainger from Cornwall, both when family circumstances changed – and in 1955 two Welsh judges were allowed to exchange.[118] Some were promised certain circuits when a vacancy occurred, but whereas officials were prepared to be helpful to judges held in high regard they were markedly less so to others.[119]

Some judges moved several times and there is no doubt that some were moved against their wishes. Thus, in 1893 Cecil Beresford, who had succeeded to his father's Welsh circuit, was moved to a Devon one when the Liberals took office because Herschell considered the party pledged to have only Welsh

[111] Minute of 22 June 1872, with Nicol's comment, PRO LCO 1/40.
[112] *Hansard* 1871–2 3rd s., vol. 213, cols. 47–9. Judges lobbied MPs and the Lord Chancellor, and one (Daniel) wrote a pamphlet to air the grievance. Expenses in 1870–1 totalled £14,545, Ingham claiming £450, Gurdon and Dinsdale over £400: *PP* 1872 (246) L.
[113] *LT* 44 (1867–8), 109.
[114] Napier's phrase, to P. G. Inch, 23 Nov. 1936, PRO LCO 12/110.
[115] E.g. PRO LCO 12/42 (East Yorkshire).
[116] E.g. *Jur.* 7 (1853), 437; 'Country Practitioner', in *LJ* 43 (1908), 698.
[117] *SJ* 54 (1910–11), 662; *PP* 1914–16 (249) V: Muir McKenzie at q. 1282.
[118] Polden, Judicial Independence, part one, 7–11.
[119] Polden, 'Oiling the Machinery'.

speakers on certain circuits. Beresford added to the controversy by permitting a group of Aberystwyth solicitors to petition for his retention.[120]

In other cases a move was the result of a judge's local unpopularity, though he may have welcomed the change. Homersham Cox was moved to Kent after denouncing the endemic perjury in his Welsh courts, while W. H. Cooke, thoroughly obnoxious in Norfolk, had interests in Oxford which made him happy to continue his unpleasant ways there.[121] But even in the 1870s it was acknowledged that a judge long settled in his district should not normally be uprooted in the interests of more efficiently arranged circuits[122] and the expectation developed that enforced removals would not be normal practice.

In fact where a judge could muster popular support in his favour they might not be easy to accomplish. In 1872, as part of a reorganisation of the South Lancashire circuits, it was planned to remove J. A. Russell from Manchester to Liverpool. Russell objected, a deputation came down from Manchester and the judge stayed put.[123] Manchester proved equally independent in 1912 when it was proposed to move Sturges away.[124] These episodes suggest inept management, perhaps through divided responsibility between the LCO and the Duchy, for in other cases judges were offered the chance to move before any public announcement; Jordan, for instance, was offered Manchester and Birmingham in succession and declined both.[125]

By the 1920s the Department was preparing elaborate games of musical chairs in anticipation of vacancies and had a comprehensive list of judges' requests. It also accepted that a judge might reasonably expect not to have to remain for too long on one of the circuits regarded as less desirable.[126]

## *The trappings of office*

County court judges gradually acquired an official dignity. From 1884 they could style themselves judge and be addressed as 'Your

[120] Polden, Judicial Independence, part one, 9–10.
[121] *SJ* 38 (1893–4), 821.
[122] Polden, Judicial Independence, part one, 10.
[123] *Ibid.* [124] *Ibid.* [125] *Ibid.*
[126] Polden, 'Oiling the Machinery'.

Honour'. Selborne also obtained for them, with some difficulty, a definite place in the order of precedence.[127] After initial hesitation, most began to wear robes of some sort,[128] but they did not design their robe of purple and black until the Great War and even then it remained unofficial and could not be worn at court functions.[129]

In the 1950s, to distract them from their pay grievance, they were gratified by being appointed by the Crown instead of the Lord Chancellor,[130] though told that their other request, automatic knighthoods after fifteen years' service, was out of the question.[131] A. G. Marten was probably the only judge to be knighted on being raised to the bench, as compensation for missing the high court,[132] and before the Great War only Lucius Selfe was knighted for purely county court services, though Kettle (for industrial arbitrations) and T. W. Snagge (services in connection with the attempt to stamp out the white slave traffic[133]) were also honoured. Then a clutch of the best known – Howland Roberts, C. L. Shand, T. S. Granger and Ernest Bray[134] – were all knighted and thereafter most chairmen of the Rule Committee and a handful of others – Parry, T. M. Snagge, Tobin, Greenwell, Burgis and Dale among them – followed down the years. Even so, it remained a rarity and it was not difficult for Coldstream to promise more liberality in recognising 'services rendered outside the strict confines of their duties'.[135]

127 *SJ* 39 (1884–5), 793; *LT* 77 (1884), 287. D. W. R. Bahlman (ed.), *The Diary of Sir Edward Walter Hamilton* (Oxford, 1972), vol. II, p. 641. In 1919, at the behest of a former judge, J. B. Edge, they were allowed to keep their style but not their precedence in retirement, PRO LCO 12/128.

128 *CCC* 1847–55, *passim*, especially 5 (1852), 59, 77–8.

129 *LJCCR* 5 (1916), 50; 8 (1919), 45; J. Derriman, *The Pageantry of the Law* (London, 1955), p. 179; R. W. Bankes to Judge Chapman, 5 Jan. 1925, PRO LCO 12/43.

130 Administration of Justice Act 1956 s. 21.

131 Note of 21 Dec. 1953, PRO LCO 2/4982.

132 Heuston, *Lord Chancellors, 1885–1940*, p. 49.

133 *Debrett's House of Commons and Judicial Bench* (1890 edn); *The Times*, 6 Feb. 1914.

134 There is nothing in the LCO papers to explain this sudden generosity.

135 Note of 21 Dec. 1953, PRO LCO 2/4982.

## *Collateral activities*

It was not long before an absolute ban on bar practice was introduced[136] but for a while the judges remained free to make money from doing arbitrations, and when Cairns, probably acting in response to strong criticism from Mr Justice Quain, issued a circular to stop it, he was defied by Quain's immediate target, the combative Thomas Terrell.[137] In 1888 a statutory prohibition on paid arbitrations was introduced and later strictly enforced by the Bar Council.[138]

Municipal recorderships were both legally and practically compatible with a judgeship – Nathaniel Clarke accumulated no fewer than four – but as competition at the bar grew keener, newly appointed judges were criticised for clinging onto them.[139] Herschell seems to have initiated the practice of requiring a judge to relinquish recorderships and though Halsbury did not immediately follow suit, it soon became settled LCO policy, adopted also by the Duchy.[140] The Home Office was even more disposed to keeping the posts in separate hands and they made it impossible for the LCO to be flexible when it wished. In 1941 the united intransigence of the Home Office and the Attorney-General, as head of the bar, cost them a judge, E. W. Sandlands refusing to accept without the added income of his recordership.[141]

In contrast to recorderships, both the LCO and the Home Office positively encouraged judges to play a part at quarter sessions. There had always been instances where they had been chairmen or deputy chairmen,[142] but after 1938, when additional powers were conferred only upon quarter sessions which had a

136 County Courts Further Extension Act 1852 s. 16. The original provision, County Courts Act 1846 s. 17, was unclear and Judge Wildman sought clarification on whether he might practise at the neighbouring assize: PRO HO 86/1.

137 *LT* 54 (1872–73), 413; *LM & R* ns 2 (1873), 479; the case was *Herbert v. Cooper. Select Committee, 1878*, q. 126.

138 Abel-Smith and Stevens, *Lawyers and Courts*, p. 93; County Courts Act 1888 s. 14.

139 Duman, *English and Colonial Bars*, 97–8; *Boase*, vol. I, p. 635; *LT* 27 (1856), 173.

140 PRO LCO 12/45.

141 *Ibid.*

142 Examples are C. F. A. Caillard (Wilts.), J. Johnes (Carmarthen), R. A. Kettle (Staffs.).

legally qualified chairman, the number naturally increased,[143] and with the reorganisation of London's criminal courts in 1963 following the Streatfeild Report the capital's county court judges also gained more criminal work.[144] Even excluding Manchester and Liverpool, whose Commissioners, created in 1956, were all county court judges, the Beeching Commission found thirty-eight of them acting as chairmen of quarter sessions and many others as deputy chairmen.[145]

The King's Bench judges who went on circuit often had to be supplemented by commissioners drawn from the top rank of the common law bar. The first county court judge to be used for this purpose was McKenzie Chalmers, Herschell intending it as a prelude to his promotion,[146] and thereafter the most highly regarded, such as F. R. Y. Radcliffe, were occasionally chosen until in the 1930s it became much more common.[147] It had been suggested that the county court judges might all be made commissioners,[148] but when this was revived by the Lord Chief Justice in 1960 it was again rejected, an LCD official pointing out that some of those who enjoyed the criminal side, not among the most suitable, would abuse the opportunity.[149]

Judges were also employed on a variety of temporary duties. Occasionally this took them abroad: Chalmers acted as temporary Chief Justice in Gibraltar, Pugh chaired an inquiry into the Bahamas police, Youds went to assist the High Court in Uganda.[150] In wartime some were seconded to *ad hoc* tribunals[151] and Austin Jones took charge of the Liabilities (War-time Adjustment) Acts for the LCD. More commonly, they sat on committees and commissions inquiring into aspects of county courts business

143 By 1947 fifty-eight out of sixty-four chairmen were legally qualified: PRO LCO 2/3444.

144 Dobson's note, 1963, PRO LCO 12/106; *Hansard* 1967–8 5th s., vol. 288 (HL), cols. 602–10.

145 *Beeching Report*, app. 9. This excludes London.

146 *DNB*, 1922–30, pp. 166–8.

147 *LJ* 58 (1923), 31; PRO LCO 2/6514.

148 *LT* 54 (1892–3), 53, 161–2. A bill to this effect drawn by Judge Sir Richard Harington for Selborne was, he claimed, blocked because it allowed the judges extra remuneration.

149 Lord Chief Justice Parker to Coldstream, 11 Dec. 1961 and Thesiger's note, 13 Dec., PRO LCO 2/7182.

150 *DNB*, 1922–30, pp. 166–8; *SJ* 113 (1969), 192; *The Times*, 15 Nov. 1971.

151 PRO LCO 2/4299.

or organisation and, as their reputation improved, they were entrusted with chairing some of the less momentous inquiries: Lilley was given distress for rent, Gerald Hurst adoptions, Hancock the interaction of industrial injuries and war pension awards, Dale industrial diseases.[152] It was meant as a real compliment to the lower bench when Blagden chaired the Bankruptcy Law Committee in 1955.[153]

## LEAVING OFFICE

### *Promotion*

Few county court judges were ever promoted. Pitt Taylor and Chalmers probably would have been, but the Chancellors who favoured them never had the opportunity to translate expectations into reality.[154] H. T. J. MacNamara was, though not to the high court but to that oddity the Railways and Canals Commission and his case remained unique (and almost forgotten) for nearly fifty years.[155] Schuster acknowledged that there had been men of high enough calibre – Howland Roberts was almost certainly one of those he had in mind – but somehow they were always too old when their name came up for a suitable vacancy,[156] and when at last a promotion was made the fortunate man was not an obvious choice. Edward Acton was competent enough and young enough, having been on the bench only two years – but it was Birkenhead's preference for men from his old college and town that lifted him over the heads of more obviously qualified judges.[157] The failure to follow up his promotion surprised and disappointed county court judges[158] but under Jowitt all that changed. Four men were promoted and one, Ormerod, was later elevated to the Court of

152 PRO LCO 2/3055.

153 Newman to Coldstream, 28 June 1955, PRO LCO 2/5827.

154 *Select Committee, 1878*, q. 517; *DNB*, 1922–30, pp. 166–8.

155 *LJ* 12 (1877), 75. It was said that he would have gone to the high court if his health had been better.

156 PRO LCO 2/2539.

157 J. Campbell, *F. E. Smith* (London, 1983), pp. 48, 479; C. Schuster, Lord Birkenhead, in W. R. Inge (ed.), *The Post-Victorians* (London, 1933), p. 91.

158 Cecil, *Just Within the Law*, p. 56, questionably states that Acton's failure blighted the chances of more able men such as Mordaunt Snagge.

Appeal. Since Finnemore was very well regarded as a trial judge and neither Austin Jones nor Collingwood fell below the general level of puisnes,[159] the reluctance of Conservative Chancellors of the 1950s to continue the practice was puzzling; Wrangham was the only promotion and Kilmuir was sharply criticised in the press and Parliament.[160] Thereafter promotions were more frequent: R. W. Payne (1962), Elizabeth Lane (1965), H. G. Talbot (1968) and – at the very end of the separate county court judiciary – R. H. Mais and B. K. Hollings.[161] A total of eleven promotions to the high court in 125 years is unimpressive and not a true reflection of the quality of the county court bench.

## *Resignation*

Four judges entered Parliament, all in the nineteenth century. The first, George Clive, became parliamentary under-secretary at the Home Office (1859–62)[162] and the last, David Brynmor Jones, one of the youngest ever judges and still only forty when returned as a Liberal for Stroud in 1892, returned to the judicial ranks in 1914 as a Master in Lunacy.[163] The others were Sir John Eardley Wilmot, unflatteringly dismissed as 'an ass and bore of the first magnitude and as a party man useless',[164] and Sir George Russell, who retired on health grounds in 1885 but was fit enough to become Conservative MP for Wokingham in the same year.[165]

Two of the most gifted late-Victorian judges successively became permanent under-secretary at the Home Office, a post so intimately linked with the administration of justice that the advantages of judicial experience were seen to outweigh the constitutional objections to such moves. Kenelm Digby made the change in 1894, directly from the bench, and in 1906 was

159 Early views of their performance, with a view to transfer to the KBD, are in PRO LCO 6/2683, 2686, 2689, 2694. On Finnemore see J. Parris, *Under My Wig* (London, 1961), p. 61 and Faulks, *No Mitigating Circumstances* (London, 1975), p. 150.

160 *Hansard* 1961–2 5th s., vol. 235 (HL), cols. 860, 953–81.

161 Shetreet, *Judges on Trial*, p. 81.

162 *Boase*, vol. I, p. 652.

163 *The Dictionary of Welsh Biography* (Oxford, 1959), p. 453.

164 Johnson, *Gathorne Hardy Diary*, p. 217. *DNB*, vol. XXI, p. 541. For his role on the Select Committee of 1878 see pp. 78–9 above.

165 *LT* 104 (1897–8), 443.

succeeded by McKenzie Chalmers, who had gone first to India to revise the criminal code and then into the office of the parliamentary counsel.[166] A more drastic move was undertaken in 1928 by Harry Newell, seven years on the bench, who resigned to take up a business career in his native Derbyshire.[167] This aroused no comment at the time and presumably was not felt to pose any threat to the status or integrity of the judges.

It was only in the 1960s that the Bar Council issued a clear ruling that a county court judge might not return to practise at the bar.[168] Two eminent Victorian QCs had briefly tasted the life of a county court judge and found it so little to their liking that they resigned almost immediately and straightaway resumed their practices. Charles Chapman Barber, worn out by his labours at the Chancery bar (including the Tichborne trial), took a judgeship in the East Riding in 1874 only to come straight back to London,[169] and the same thing happened in 1885 when Halsbury's first (and 'unexceptionable') judge, G. B. Hughes, also realised his mistake very quickly.[170]

## *Dismissal*

A judge might be dismissed for 'inability or misbehaviour', terms scarcely elucidated by the scanty case law which attempts to invoke them have generated.[171] The only case of a judge being formally dismissed is that of William Ramshay in 1851,[172] but other judges resigned, sometimes with official encouragement and occasionally insistence, where their state of health or conduct had brought them within the statutory provisions. The tradition of discretion makes the frequency of these occurrences hard to estimate but the evidence suggests that Victorian Chancellors were not disposed towards intervention to remove ailing judges, though it may have happened with Abdy and Bayley in the 1890s after outspoken press criticism.[173]

166 *WWW 1916–28*; *The Times*, 24 Apr. 1916; *DNB* 1922–30, pp. 166–8; Pellew, *Home Office, 1848–1914*.

167 *The Times*, 6 Nov. 1937.

168 Shetreet, *Judges on Trial*, p. 374.

169 *SJ* 26 (1881–2), 224, 233.

170 *SJ* 39 (1884–5), 773, 793; *LJ* 20 (1885), 591, 657.

171 *R v. Owen* (1850) 15 QB 476; *Ex p. Ramshay* (1852) 18 QB 174.

172 Polden, Judicial Selkirks, 255–6.

173 *Law Gazette* 6 (1892–3), 161, 177.

There is one clear case of a judge disabled by the onset of mental illness, B.T. Williams in 1885, but he saved any difficulties by instantly resigning.[174] It is also possible that the extraordinary antics of Ramshay and Vaughan Williams were in fact manifestations of incipient or actual insanity. Judges at all levels have had a wide latitude in their conduct on the bench and county court judges like W. S. Owen, A. S. Hill-Kelly and W. H. Cooke were fully the equal, in their humbler sphere, of the Hawkinses, Granthams, Darlings and Hewarts who disgraced the superior courts.[175] The conclusion from cases of formal complaint is that only a continuing course of outrageous misconduct or a gross despotic abuse of power sufficed to secure their removal.[176] An example of the former is T. E. P. Lefroy, who finally goaded lawyers, newspaper proprietors and local MPs into making up a formidable deputation to the Lord Chancellor.[177] The latter are represented by Ramshay, who unwisely persecuted a local editor, and Vaughan Williams, who victimised an unfortunate cabman who had disputed right of way with him in the street.[178]

Financial problems caused the resignation of Stavely-Hill in 1928 when he went bankrupt[179] but P. M. Leonard's case was worse, for he engaged in such dubious dealings that he was forced to resign.[180] G. H. Higgins was threatened with prosecution by the Inland Revenue for failing to fill in tax returns and was lucky to escape a similar fate, but his case shows how cautious the LCO felt obliged to be in the light of the *Owen* decision.[181]

More recently the difficult decisions have often arisen out of judges' motoring misdemeanours. At least three county court judges committed driving offences of a fairly serious nature and one, Eifion Evans, who aggravated the original offence by aggres-

[174] *CCC* 30 (1885–6), 53; *Dictionary of Welsh Biography*, p. 1026.

[175] Sir F. A. Bosanquet, *The Oxford Circuit* (London, 1951), p. 77; Cecil, *Just Within the Law*, p. 46; Polden, Judicial Selkirks, 256–7.

[176] E.g. *R v. Marshall* (1855) 4 El & Bl 475; *LT* 83 (1887), 380; *CCC* 31 (1888), 294.

[177] Polden, Judicial Selkirks, 257–9.

[178] *Ibid.*, 255–6.

[179] *SJ* 72 (1928), 748.

[180] *Hansard* 1893 4th s., vol. 11, cols. 1626–7; vol. 16, cols. 1884–5; *CCC* 34 (1893–4), 60. Leonard had the effrontery to ask for a pension: Muir McKenzie to Halsbury, 7 Apr. 1898, BL Add. MSS. 56370, f. 158.

[181] PRO LCO 33/40 and 12/88.

sive behaviour towards the other driver, resigned after it had been made clear to him that he faced dismissal.[182]

### *Retirement*

Compulsory retirement at seventy-two was introduced in 1920 for future appointments,[183] so Gwynne James, Tobin and Cluer, who went on into their eighties, were the last of their kind. The Lord Chancellor had power on grounds of the 'public interest' to retain a judge's services up to the age of seventy-five and, although the permanent officials usually got their way in individual cases, Chancellors did vary decidedly in their interpretation of this phrase. Simonds took the view that anyone still fully physically and mentally fit had a *prima facie* claim but most others saw the power as a means of keeping those who were outstandingly good, were needed for other purposes (Cann on the Rule Committee, Farrant at quarter sessions) or whose retirement would create an inconvenient vacancy.[184] Altogether, of fifty-eight judges on the extensions file down to 1961, thirty-five were given some extension, but only eighteen for more than one year, and that includes seven in wartime, when a more liberal approach was followed.[185]

### *Death in office*

'Resignation is undreamt of ... quite as a phenomenal event, it should be recorded that Judge Holl resigned.'[186] This *Law Times* sarcasm exaggerates the position but in the days before compulsory retirement around half the judges died in office, the first of them, David Leahy, within a few months of the opening of the courts.[187] In a few cases the job was said to have contributed to their death: Adolphus for instance is said to have died of overwork, Cadman to have fallen victim to a notoriously unhealthy courthouse and Willes, with too delicate a constitution, was

182 Polden, Judicial Independence, part two, 151 and see now PRO LCO 12/38. Evans was appointed to the Foreign Compensation Commission in 1963.

183 PRO LCO 2/606.

184 Polden, Judicial Independence, part one, 18–19.

185 PRO LCO 12/39.

186 *LT* 100 (1895–6), 209.

187 *LT* 9 (1847), 284.

transferred too late from the climatic rigours of a bleak northern circuit.[188] Three died abroad, Lowndes perished by accidental drowning[189] and G. H. Head threw himself under an underground train at Victoria in a fit of depression following a bout of influenza.[190] Three (E. A. Parry, W. H. G. Bagshawe and E. C. Burgis) were subjected to murderous assaults in the course of their duties but fortunately survived and resumed their duties.[191]

## THE JUDGES' CHARACTERISTICS

### *Age*

The public usually thinks of judges as old men and the image is pertinacious although the reality, in the county courts as elsewhere, has for some time been that judges are more likely to be middle-aged than elderly.[192] The age structure however has undergone some interesting variations over time.

The first judges were appointed young – the majority were under fifty[193] – and because many of them stayed in office for a long time and their replacements were often rather older men, a quite striking ageing of the bench occurred over the next thirty years. By 1900 deaths and retirements had redressed the balance to some extent but Halsbury made several elderly judges, so quite a high proportion of the bench could be classed as 'old'; indeed, given that some sought the post because they felt worn out, they probably appeared even older than they really were. There was therefore a strong likelihood that the casual visitor would find a county court presided over by a veteran, and the image was

188 *CCC* 23 (1872), 236; *LT* 120 (1905–6), 397; *CCC* 16 (1863), 49.

189 *Boase*, vol. I, p. 1097; vol. II, p. 1138; vol. III, p. 1391 LM 12 ns (1850), 223.

190 G. Alexander, *After Court Hours* (London, 1950), p. 202.

191 Parry's assailant was a bailiff whom he was depriving of his certificate; Bagshawe's a German dentist; Burgis' (not in the county court) an unsuccessful would-be conscientious objector.

192 Cecil, *English Judge*, pp. 4–5, 11–12.

193 An analysis of the judges in 1848 showed that two had been called less than ten years; ten between ten and fifteen years; thirteen between fifteen and twenty years; eleven between twenty and twenty-five years; eight between twenty-five and thirty years; eight between thirty and thirty-five years; six between thirty-five and forty years and one more than forty years. The two solicitor-judges were excluded: *LT* 11 (1847–8), 460.

reinforced by the presence of the octogenarian Bayley in the most 'visible' court, Westminster.[194]

The retiring age gradually eliminated the really elderly judge but with the average age at appointment remaining in the fifties, there was actually an upward drift in the age profile of the judges between the wars. Some younger appointments, and the expansion of numbers, later brought about a reduction, but in 1960 it had only just become possible to say that the 'average' judge would be a man in his fifties rather than his sixties, and there was still a significant number in their seventies. More remarkably, there were then no judges under fifty.

## *Social background*

One of the expected changes in the parentage of judges over time has been the decline of the landed interest,[195] the clergy and the armed forces. In the nineteenth century more than one-fifth of the bench had a landed background,[196] while the clergy and in smaller numbers the armed forces between them provided around a quarter. Their successors came sometimes from commercial and (less commonly) manufacturing backgrounds, and increasingly from the newer professions – accountancy, schoolmastering, medicine, etc. The profiles of these judges however offer no support whatever to the bar's claim to be a career open to talents, if that is meant to include men from really humble backgrounds. Of more than 400 judges whose fathers' occupations are known, no more than two could be considered lower or working class and neither was English: Artemus Jones was the son of a Welsh stonemason, Henry Ruttle of a sergeant in the RUC.[197]

As would be expected, there are also plenty of names familiar to lawyers. Though the most famous and extensive of all the legal dynasties, the Pollocks, is not represented among county court

194 S. Mayer, *Reminiscences of a KC, Theatrical and Legal* (London, 1924), p. 141; *Law Gazette* 3 (1891–2), 7.

195 Part of a more general decline: D. Cannadine, *The Decline of the British Aristocracy* (rev. edn, London, 1996); M. Beard, *English Landed Society in the Twentieth Century* (London, 1989).

196 On the origins of barristers see Duman, *English and Colonial Bars*, pp. 16–21 and R. Abel, *The Legal Profession in England and Wales* (Oxford, 1988), table 1.21.

197 *The Times*, 18 Oct. 1943, 22 Sep. 1995.

judges,[198] the Russells, Stephens and Mellors are.[199] Moreover the county court produced dynasties of its own. Two families, the Haringtons and the Beresfords, have had three judges,[200] several others – Bagshawe, Tindal Atkinson, Snagge, Terrell, Leigh, Wheeler and Eardley Wilmot – two. Judges have also been the sons[201] or brothers[202] of higher judges and, beyond the period covered by this book, the Sumners, father and son, achieved the unusual feat of being circuit judges at the same time.[203]

## *Schooling*

Most judges have been to public schools. Even allowing for the fact that the quite numerous judges whose schooling is not known exaggerates the proportion of public school men, they form a clear majority throughout, with the highest proportion around 1930, that is among men mostly at school in the 1880s and 1890s.[204] The widening range of public schools available has meant that in the twentieth century few schools stand out as having produced more than a handful of judges. Eton, predictably, comes out first, followed at a distance by Charterhouse, Harrow, Shrewsbury, Rugby and Winchester.[205]

[198] Joseph Pollock, judge in Liverpool 1851–7, does not seem to have been a member of this remarkable family.

[199] Hon. Arthur Russell (judge 1900–7) was the son of the Lord Chief Justice. James Stephen (1871–94) was the only son of Serjeant Stephen and a cousin of Fitzjames. Francis Mellor (1911–25) was the tenth son of Sir John, judge in the Queen's Bench.

[200] Sir Richard Harington, Bt, judge 1872–1905; Richard, his third son, judge 1891–1912; John Charles Dundas, Sir Richard's twelfth son, judge 1958–73. William Beresford, judge 1878–91; Cecil Hugh Wriothesley, his second son, judge 1891–1912; Eric George Harold, William's grandson, judge 1959–76.

[201] Francis Henry Bacon, judge 1878–1911, Vernon Lushington, judge 1877–1900, Walter B. Lindley, judge 1909–34, Herbert W. Lush-Wilson, judge 1901–22, Alfred R. Kennedy, judge 1929–43, Francis Bayley, judge 1849–93, Edmond Turner, judge 1868–93.

[202] Edward Bray, judge 1905–26, W. H. Willes, judge 1859–63, John F. Collier, judge 1873–1907, Arthur L. B. Thesiger, judge 1931–47.

[203] *The Times*, 18 May 1990.

[204] There is no generally agreed list of public schools, but the lists compiled by J. R. de S. Honey, *Tom Brown's Universe* (London, 1977), are a good guide. In the 1950s the judges argued that their salaries needed to provide a public school education for their sons.

[205] Eton thirty-four, Rugby twenty-three, Winchester nineteen, Charterhouse eighteen, Shrewsbury sixteen, Harrow twelve.

### *Universities*

There has been a notable increase in the number of university-educated judges, though by no means all have read law. Among the county court judges they were always a majority, but whereas in the mid-nineteenth century it was around five-eighths, by 1900 it had risen to three-quarters; in 1960 only eight of the seventy-two had not been to university and only five appointed in the 1960s were not graduates. University has usually meant Oxford or Cambridge, and this remained so even among 1960s appointments, although there were, when they left school, several well-established civic universities offering law courses. Even the colleges of London University seem to have had few attractions except for a short period around the end of the last century and then probably for men with modest backgrounds; they were certainly never fashionable.

### *Life experience*

The judges' education was increasingly homogeneous. From their school, usually a boarding school, they went up to Oxford or Cambridge, then straight to an Inn and into pupillage. The bar did of course bring them into contact with all sorts and conditions of men, but their life experience was often a comparatively narrow one. However, two world wars gave most barristers an inescapable opportunity to broaden their knowledge of mankind. Most judges after 1920 were drawn from generations who had served in a world war, though not all were in the armed forces and some were able to make use of their professional skills in the judge advocate-general's department.[206] Many had very distinguished war records, several were taken prisoner-of-war (at least one would not otherwise have become a lawyer),[207] others carried wartime injuries for the rest of their lives.[208] It is impossible to gauge the effect the war had on their outlook, but it is a circumstance which should not be overlooked.

206 Examples are C. Cunliffe, H. Buttle, E. Steel, G. F. Leslie and F. Honig.

207 E.g. W. M. Andrew in the Great War, C. T. Cohen, D. Ranking and F. D. McIntyre (in Changi) in the Second World War. John Garrard was the man who turned to law in camp.

208 R. C. Essenhigh lost a leg in the Great War, T. Elder Jones an arm in the Second.

A small minority had not followed the conventional path outlined above. Aside from those who engaged in politics, there were some who had started out as solicitors and transferred to the bar.[209] Others came to the law from other trades or professions, mostly rather prosaic: Morgan Howard started out in Henry Peek's tea warehouse in Eastcheap, Tindal Atkinson as a Liverpool tradesman.[210] Some came from other professions: Preedy from medicine, Tebbs accountancy; Lias had been a headmaster, Raikes in the navy, Dewar an analytical chemist, Thesiger fourteen years in insurance.[211] A very few had done something more exotic: Jellinek had been art critic for a newspaper, Graham had spent two years in the Caucasus laying telephone cables.[212] Not all judges knew nothing but law.

## *Celebrity*

County court judges have seldom ever had more than a local celebrity; Cluer and Parry are exceptions (as is Commissioner Kerr in the Mayor's Court) but there have been very few others. Naturally things were different in the narrower world of the law. Some judges were remembered for their part in famous trials: Chapman Barber in the Tichborne case, Tobin in the trial of Dr Crippen. Others had begun textbooks which became established authorities: *Gale on Easements*, *Ruegg on Workmen's Compensation*.[213] A good many, in fact, were better known for legal authorship than as judges: it was their writings which earned Francillon, Petersdorff, J. W. Smith and Shiress Will a place in the *DNB*. Some had held professorships and lectureships: Amos and Starkie among the original judges;[214] Abdy, Lias, J. A. Russell and

209 T. Wheeler, D. R. Blaine, J. B. Edge, G. C. Rees, T. Hunter, J. Perrett and two promoted judges, Benjamin Ormerod and Reginald Withers Payne, are among them.

210 Sir E. Clarke, *The Story of My Life* (London, 1918), p. 79; *SJ* 15 (1870–1), 118.

211 *WWW 1941–50*, pp. 255, 684; *WWW 1929–40*, p. 1331; *WW 1994*, p. 511; *Al. Cant.*, vol. V, 233; *WWW 1961–70*, p. 1110.

212 *WWW 1971–80*; *The Times*, 10 Aug. 1929. The Master of the Rolls described Jellinek as 'a rough diamond', to Coldstream, 1 Feb. 1952, PRO LCO 12/38.

213 Gale wrote the editions of 1839 and 1849, Ruegg all editions down to 1922.

214 Andrew Amos (1791–1860), member of the first Criminal Law Commission, Downing Professor of the Laws of England at Cambridge, 1848–60. Thomas Starkie (1782–1849), his predecessor as Downing Professor, 1823–48 and lecturer to the Inner Temple.

Stephen among their successors.[215] Not all reputations came from erudition however; Digby Seymour and Willis were celebrated as advocates of the florid school.[216] Once on the bench it was easy enough to gain publicity by outrageous or controversial behaviour: men like J. W. Smith, Owen, Willis, R. W. Turner and Archer all managed to do that.[217] It was also possible to win general respect and affection by doing the job efficiently and humanely.[218] A few had sufficient opportunity to make or enhance a reputation in a particular field of work, as Daniel did in bankruptcy, but by and large the county court bench was not the place to win fame.

Judges might however be famous for other achievements unrelated to their profession, in sport for instance. Millis Coventry was 'the father of the boat race' and L. Bensley Wells had rowed in the 1912 Olympics;[219] Rowe Harding played rugby for Wales and the Lions; Nance was a good enough chess player to draw with Botwinnik; Farrant rode in the Grand National, Garrard in the Isle of Man TT; Roope Reeve held a world fishing record.[220]

Others followed more literary pursuits. Adolphus was the young man who had identified Walter Scott as the author of *Waverley*[221] and Tom Hughes would always be first and foremost the author of *Tom Brown's Schooldays*. Several others wrote novels or verse, but only H. C. Leon (as Henry Cecil) and Gordon Clark (as Cyril Hare) were really successful.[222] Robert Lambert had a play performed but one of Parry's was put on the West End, and Parry was the most prolific and successful author among them, with plays, books on various subjects and one of the few

215 J. T. Abdy (1822–99), Professor of Civil Law at Cambridge; W. J. Lias (1868–1941), Professor of International Law at Sheffield; John A. Russell (1816–99), Professor of English Law at University College, London; James Stephen (1820–94), Professor of Laws at King's College, London.

216 *DNB*, vol. LI, p. 3635 and *2nd supp.*, vol. III, pp. 682–3.

217 Polden, Judicial Selkirks, 248–53; Bosanquet, *Oxford Circuit*, p. 77; *DNB 2nd supp.*, vol. III, pp. 682–3; *The Times*, 14 Nov. 1932, 25 June 1962.

218 E.g. *The Times* 12 Mar. 1943, 9 Sep. 1986 (Kennedy and N. H. Curtis Raleigh).

219 *Al. Cant.*, vol. II, p. 154; *WWW 1961–70*, p. 1186.

220 *The Times*, 16 Feb. 1991, 5 June 1996, 20 Apr. 1946, 23 July 1990; *WWW 1951–60*, p. 915.

221 *DNB*, vol. I, p. 142.

222 Cecil is best known for the comic novels commencing with *Brothers-in-Law* (1955). He also wrote for radio and produced several books on the legal profession. Cyril Hare wrote several well-regarded crime novels, notably *Tragedy at Law* (1942).

autobiographies.[223] Judge Drabble, however, can claim literary celebrity by proxy, through his daughters.[224]

## THE LIFE OF A COUNTY COURT JUDGE

### *Workload*

The judges' workloads, as measured by the number of days they sat, were not equal, and could not be made so without an extension of bureaucratic control unacceptable to the judges and difficult to reconcile with the principle of permanent local circuits. It was acknowledged almost from the beginning that some judges were overworked, as was demonstrated by the breakdown of James Pollock.[225] London judges, and a few in other big cities, were usually excepted from complaints about lazy judges and on occasion rather disloyally joined in the criticism of their country cousins.[226]

It is not surprising that some judges tried to give themselves an easy life – that, after all, is why they had left the bar – and in some districts they could do so without seriously inconveniencing court users. But the annual returns showed that they were doing so. Thus in 1864, while three judges sat for 166, 168 and 174 days, three others managed with 109, 105 and 74, and in 1873 the average of 135 compared unfavourably with the 200 days of the superior judges' year.[227]

Inevitably, hard questions were asked. In answer to criticism it was said that country judges spent good a deal of time travelling and often had to waste their time at a court with little or no business. As Selfe put it: 'no-one who has not had practical experience of the county courts in country towns can adequately realise the waste of judicial time and public money'.[228] Even so Nicol was embarrassed by figures showing that some judges were managing to reduce their sitting days still further, and had

223 *WWW, 1941–50*, p. 887; *WWW 1971–80*, p. 450.
224 A. S. Byatt and Margaret Drabble, *The Times*, 5 Jan. 1982.
225 *LT* 31 (1858), 146.
226 E.g. *Select Committee, 1878*, qq. 570, 1044–6.
227 *PP* 1864 (536) XLVIII; *Lisgar Commission*, pp. 97–100.
228 Memo of Apr. 1899, PRO LCO 2/111.

to acknowledge that 'some higher authority' ought to regulate them.[229]

Some localities regarded themselves as ill-served: Nottingham compared their judge's diligence unfavourably with his neighbour in Derbyshire, while one of the many complaints from Bolton was that Crompton Hutton sat as few as eighty-five days.[230] With Henry Fowler persistently drawing attention to the statistics,[231] it is not surprising that the impression got about that country districts were something of a sinecure.[232] The judges could not be expected to agree, but Bridgeman and the LCO did, without feeling able to do much about it.[233] So Emden, Bacon and the other London judges battled grimly through their lists while Beresford enjoyed the life of a country gentleman; even in Manchester an investigation attributed arrears largely to Mellor's laziness.[234]

After the Great War both the complaints and the statistics disappeared. Plaints were slow to regain pre-war levels, registrars had wider jurisdiction, and the more systematic redistribution of business helped to ensure it was dealt with quickly. Not all judges were noted for celerity: men like Done and Tucker were famously slow[235] and at the end of the Second World War the problem of delays and adjournments became serious.[236] Judges were enabled to call upon 'congestion deputies' and given encouragement to seek help when they got behind, but before long Coldstream felt that some had become too willing, especially as they were not always prepared to provide an explanation for their need.[237] In the mid-1950s, when the average annual figure for sittings was 151 days, the Department felt that 168 was 'on the light side for an active judge' and that in a one-judge district in the provinces 180

229 *Childers Report*, q. 2078. See also qq. 1849–71, 1903–4.

230 *LT* 61 (1876), 202; *LJ* 22 (1887), 534.

231 E.g. *Hansard* 1893–4 4th s., vol. 17, col. 1383; 1899 4th s., vol. 75, col. 887. An earlier question produced the most detailed return on how judges spent their time: *PP* 1890–1 (362) LXIV, discussed in *LT* 93 (1892), 171–3.

232 E.g. *Strand Magazine* 1 (1891), 534.

233 Evidence to Royal Commission on KBD Delays, *PP* 1914 [Cd 7177], XXXVII and *MacDonnell Evidence*.

234 PRO LCO 2/3311 (q. 984); D. S. Smith to Muir McKenzie, 25 May 1914, PRO LCO 2/294.

235 PRO LCO 2/3311; note of meeting, 25 Nov. 1954, PRO LCO 2/4984.

236 See pp. 158–9 above.

237 Dobson's memos, 14 May, 10 July 1962, PRO LCO 2/7182.

was reasonable.[238] Variations were still enormous though: while two Welsh judges sat only 85 and 94 days, Fraser Harrison was clocking up 200 and Coldstream agreed that Barrington had reached 'saturation point'.[239]

This might suggest that little had changed in a hundred years, but there were no longer widely reported accusations of laziness and the Chancellor could obtain extra judges without strong objections from the Treasury or Parliament.[240] The variations were now accepted as arising from the structure of the county court system.

## *'Lifestyle'*

In 1903 Judge Parry described the work of a county court judge as a 'dull, grey life'.[241] In busy courts it involved the endless, rapid processing of debt cases, a form of judicial drudgery even less elevating than the work of a London police magistrate. Judges had to seek stimulation in the rich variety of human stories they encountered rather than the intellectual challenge of knotty points of law, and their satisfaction in protecting the poor from oppression rather than elucidating the law. Over time, they did slough off more of the small cases onto their registrars and more demanding matters came their way, though some of these, especially the Rent Acts, were unpalatable enough. By the 1950s a judge like Eric Beresford, who claimed to be fascinated by points of law,[242] had more chance of indulging his tastes and the diet of a county court judge was not so dissimilar from that of a QBD judge.[243]

But compared to such a judge, the county court judge's life was still, as it had always been, a rather lonely one. One woebegone

238 Statistics, 1954 in PRO LCO 2/4985; D. R. Wells to Dobson, 28 Nov. 1963, 12/106. In 1913 the view was that 170 days, or 200 on a non-travelling circuit, was reasonable: note of 24 Dec. 1913, 2/294.

239 PRO LCO 2/4985; Barrington to Coldstream, 20 Jan. 1959, and reply, 21 Jan., 2/4988.

240 Though see p. 174 above and PRO LCO 12/46 for Treasury resistance in 1965.

241 In *Fortnightly Review*, os 69 (1898), 797–804, he criticised newspaper presentations of the courts as full of droll judges and amusing incidents.

242 To Rieu, 5 Mar. 1961, PRO LCO 2/7190.

243 County court judges did not, of course, preside over criminal trials, but many were chairmen of quarter sessions.

judge in the 1890s lamented his lot in almost comical fashion,[244] but Gerald Hurst in the 1940s and Coldstream in the 1950s fully confirmed its essential truth.[245] Except in the handful of two-judge courts, he was isolated from his peers, meetings of the Council were poorly attended, and most were too distant to engage in the society of the Inns, which some found congenial.[246] Even where there was a local bar, the judge needed to be wary of too enthusiastic a fraternisation, for such links were quickly noticed and disapproved of by solicitors.[247]

Yet since there was seldom a shortage of good applicants, the life must have had its attractions. One was the degree of independence both in arranging the circuit and sittings and in deciding cases. Another was the opportunity to live in a favoured location and to become thoroughly involved in local society. The objection to permanently localised judges was based precisely on judges doing this, and rendering themselves vulnerable to conflicts of interests and suspicions of bias;[248] the Beeching Commission commented 'that some county court judges displayed in their evidence a proprietorial attitude towards those courts, and placed emphasis on the value of the expertise which results from specialization and local knowledge in a way which we found somewhat disturbing'.[249]

Some judges made a point of remaining aloof from local society but many did not, and lived in a manner which suggested that they did not expect to be asked to move. Two early judges in Suffolk were in this mould: William Gurdon delighted in the country house he had had built by P. C. Hardwick, and John Worlledge made 'for nearly twenty years our county courts . . . the most popular and best appreciated places of public entertainment in Suffolk'.[250] Horatio Lloyd was so well regarded in Cheshire that the Duke of Westminster presented him with a service of plate and 1,000 guineas for his services to the county.[251] Few were

244 *CCC* 34 (1893–4), 29.

245 Hurst, *Closed Chapters*, p. 149; Coldstream to Judge Neal, 26 Mar. 1953, PRO LCO 2/5019.

246 London judges could do so. Ifor Lloyd, notwithstanding his marriage, still lived in the Temple: *The Times*, 3 Aug. 1988.

247 H. Cecil, *Tipping the Scales* (London, 1964), pp. 231–5.

248 The 'conflicts of interest' file (PRO LCO 12/94) is very tame.

249 *Beeching Report*, p. 150.

250 *LJ* 7 (1872), 680; *Public Men of Ipswich and East Suffolk*, pp. 237–43.

251 E. Gaskell, *Cheshire Leaders, Social and Political* (Exter, 1896).

as fortunate as that, but Cecil Beresford was not the only one to be in the 'county' set; in the 1960s Donald Sumner's lifestyle in Kent was not dissimilar.[252]

There were other judges deeply attached to a city, usually their native place, who stayed there most of their lives and while on the bench played an active role in its civic life. In Liverpool, for instance, Dowdall's family had been prominent in the city for four generations and he was chairman of its Council for Social Service, Lord Mayor and Chancellor of the Diocese, marrying a daughter of Lord Borthwick, one of the leading citizens.[253] Another such judge was F. J. Greenwell, who spent his whole life in the north-east and was a judge in Durham for thirty-five years, marrying the daughter of another county court judge; he was recorder, chairman of quarter sessions, JP etc. 'His interests ... were bound up in his family house and in the welfare of the mining and agricultural people of Durham and Northumberland, among whom he had lived his life, and for whom he had an unbounded admiration and sympathy.'[254]

With so many judges, over so long a time, the keynote is bound to be diversity. The bar boasted of its 'characters' and celebrated the uninhibited individuality of judges, tolerating a wide range of behaviour – and misbehaviour. But from about 1900 commentators began to find a general improvement in quality and conduct. The best had always been excellent, so it was rather that the worst were becoming less bad. There were no longer Melvilles coming into court with their minders,[255] and though 'little book learning is required', 'Ruff's Guide to the Turf' would no longer be the judge's preferred reading.[256] No longer would a Wildman be able to go through a judicial career without condescending to give reasons for his judgments,[257] nor a Willis be 'so easily led away by his feelings, which inclined towards the servant as against the mistress, the employee as against the employer. He was at constant

[252] *The Times*, 18 May 1990.

[253] *WWW 1951–60*, p. 316.

[254] C. A. Manning, *Durham Lives* (London, 1897); C. Muir, *Justice in a Depressed Area* (London, 1936), p. 106.

[255] *LT* 92 (1891–2), 35.

[256] Hurst, *Closed Chapters*, p. 144. For the reference to Stavely-Hill's reading see n. 46 above.

[257] R. Mellors, *Men of Nottingham and Nottinghamshire* (Nottingham, 1924), p. 191.

war with counsel, and the "scenes" which were chronicled in the press left a poor impression of his sense of official decorum.'[258]

Some of the colour and idiosyncrasy was probably lost along the way, but if there were none quite like Pitt Taylor, Bacon and Tom Hughes, it should not be thought that there were no longer any 'characters': Lyall Wilkes, Claud Duveen and Basil Wingate Saul were fully the equal of their predecessors for pungency and flamboyance,[259] and the LCD's best attempts to appoint men like Whitmee, who possessed 'the quintessence of commonsense',[260] were not proof against ending up with the wilful independence of spirit of that 'most unjudicial judge' F. K. Archer[261] or J. R. Reid who 'seems to find it so difficult to cultivate a "county court mind"'.[262] Whatever the 'county court mind' was, it embraced patience and courtesy towards litigants in person, a pragmatic approach to the application of the law where the subject-matter was small and the parties poor, and the ability to dispatch business speedily.

Most county court judges would, one suspects, have been content with the verdicts accorded to two of them. Parry quoted against himself the judgment of two railway clerks on one of his cases:

1st clerk: 'How the — did he get to £5?'
2nd clerk: 'I don't know.'
1st clerk: 'I think he's a — fool.'
2nd clerk: 'I think he's a — fool' (a long pause, then as an after-thought), 'but I think he did his best.'[263]

Ruegg was no longer alive to hear the tribute of an MP: 'Heaven help any counsel who appeared before him and who thought that he might be clever at the expense of an ill-dressed, impoverished woman who came before the court. His courtesy and kindness to those who needed help was something which I shall never forget and which has always been an inspiration to me.'[264]

258 *DNB 2nd supp.*, vol. III, pp. 682–3. On one occasion this entangled him with the young F. E. Smith: Campbell, *F. E. Smith*, pp. 112–13.
259 *LJ* 23 (1888), 410; *SJ* 55 (1910–11), 584; E. A. Parry, *What the Judge Saw* (London, 1912), pp. 140–2; *The Times*, 5 Apr. 1991, 17 Sep. 1976, 8, 9 Oct. 1975.
260 *LT* 48 (1954), 185.
261 Napier's note, 13 Aug. 1946, PRO LCO 2/3284.
262 Rieu to Coldstream, 7 Apr. 1952, PRO LCO 2/5008.
263 *My Own Way*, p. 220.
264 *Hansard* 1951–2 5th s., vol. 494 (HC), col. 2402 (B. Stross).

## THE JUDICIAL ROLE OF REGISTRARS

By degrees the clerk, essentially an administrative officer, was transformed into a junior judge.[265] In 1850 he was given power to enter as a judgment an agreement by which the parties terminated a suit before the hearing, and in 1852 he acquired responsibility for taxing costs; though this was curtailed in 1856, the same Act added a number of 'quasi-judicial' powers.[266] Much more important were powers in insolvency. The Bankruptcy Act 1847 gave clerks in provincial county courts the functions of registrars and, momentously, the 1861 Bankruptcy Act gave them the extensive authority wielded by their erstwhile counterparts in the district bankruptcy courts. Although only a few county courts had bankruptcy jurisdiction, their registrars, 'undertaking critically important work in complex questions involving large sums of money',[267] were an elite both in the powers they exercised and the rewards they obtained.

Almost every time the county courts were entrusted with a new jurisdiction, the registrars had a judicial part in it. In 1865 the equity jurisdiction carried gave them all the authority of a Chancery master, potentially work of great intricacy and responsibility.[268] In 1869 a few of them acquired admiralty work[269] and from 1867 registrars in undefended debt actions were enabled to enter judgment and direct payment by instalments by the judge's leave, and most judges were happy to delegate this part of their work.[270]

The Judicature Commissioners' proposals would have given registrars (fewer and salaried) power to try contested debt cases up to £5[271] and some reformers had even more ambitious plans for 'judicial registrars' in principal courts with jurisdiction up to £20.[272] However, the barrister majority on the Select Committee of 1878 not only rejected much more modest extensions but urged

265 Bartrip, Registrars, pp. 349–79.
266 *Ibid.*, pp. 355–8.
267 *Ibid.*, p. 360.
268 *Ibid.*, pp. 361–2.
269 *Ibid.*, p. 362.
270 *Ibid.*, p. 363. Pitt Taylor was criticised for his refusal to do this.
271 *Ibid.*, pp. 365–6.
272 *LT* 62 (1876–7), 275, 313; *PP* 1877 (71) I cl. 10.

the withdrawal of all judicial functions from those still at liberty to practise as solicitors.[273]

Ten years later, however, the government's consolidation bill gave registrars trial of defended suits up to £2,[274] and pressure soon built up for the ceiling to be raised to £5.[275] Though Rollit had to jettison this to get his bill through[276] it soon found a place in the LCO's own bills,[277] which also tackled an anomalous (and widely evaded) restriction which prevented a registrar from holding 'his' court on the same day as his judge.[278] Both clauses became part of the 1919 Act.[279]

By that time the registrars had acquired one further important role and were on the verge of acquiring another. In workmen's compensation they were responsible for appraising the adequacy of settlements brought before the court for approval, and for looking after the fund if it was lodged in court.[280] They took great pains on the workmen's behalf, and though the Stewart Committee was not satisfied that all registrars carried their inquiries as far as they should, finding a worrying lack of uniformity,[281] for many registrars this work was among the most satisfying parts of their job and they relinquished it with real regret.

The other area was divorce. Though opposed to county court divorce, post-war governments could not fend off demands for some measure of devolution and twenty-three district registries,

273 *Select Committee, 1878*, especially p. 10 and report at iii–iv. Norwood had argued that registrars had too much power: *Hansard* 1877 3rd s., vol. 234, col. 590, and the Attorney-General (col. 597) had also opposed their right to try cases.

274 County Courts Act 1888 s. 92.

275 Charles Cautherley, a registrar who frequently wrote on county court topics, advocated £10: *LQR* 7 (1891), 346–53.

276 *PP* 1903 (122) I; Standing Committee proceedings, *PP* 1903 (97) V; *Hansard* 1903 4th s., vol. 118, cols. 1470–2. It was in the chambers of commerce bills, beginning with *PP* 1897 [bill 42] I.

277 PRO LCO 2/204–10, 285. In the debates on the 1911 bill Halsbury spoke contemptuously of registrars – 'they may have no legal training at all' – and Loreburn sharply retorted that Halsbury's own bills had proposed to enlarge their jurisdiction: *Hansard* 1911 5th s., vol. 9 (HL), cols. 402, 407–8.

278 For evasion of the rule see notes on draft bill of July 1904, PRO LCO 2/157. The rule had been criticised by the Judicature Commissioners (Bartrip, Registrars, p. 365).

279 Ss. 5, 9.

280 Bartrip, *Workmen's Compensation* and Wilson and Levy, *Workmen's Compensation* both ignore this aspect.

281 *PP* 1937–8 [Cmd 5657] XV, at p. 92.

soon augmented by a further fifteen, were chosen to handle the preliminary and interlocutory work. Most were manned by county court registrars, and the Schuster Committee, acknowledging that some of them found it distasteful (they had to be given financial recompense), reported that they were highly competent.[282]

A further extension of the registrars' common law jurisdiction came about in 1934, implementing a suggestion of the Hanworth Committee,[283] but it took much longer to implement the proposal in the Austin Jones Report for the ceiling of £20 (with the leave of the judge and neither party objecting) to be raised.[284] When a somewhat modified proposal was finally put forward it aroused none of the hostility Kilmuir had feared;[285] indeed, the Lord Chancellor was empowered to raise it to £30 by order.[286]

The most sensitive area of jurisdiction was judgment summonses, opposed by a minority of judges[287] on various grounds. The LCD felt it would be politically impossible to pass such a proposal without providing for an appeal to the judge, and that would deprive it of many of its attractions.[288] Hence even when proposed by the Winn Committee as a means of 'freeing-up' judges for bigger personal injury cases, it was still omitted when the registrars' jurisdiction was raised (again in line with the county court limit) to £75.[289] By this time it was generally accepted that, as the ACCR submitted to Beeching, registrars should have responsibility for all of the minor judicial work in these courts,[290]

282 *PP* 1929–30 [Cmd 3375] XVII and *Report of the Wedgwood Committee, PP* 1942–3 [Cmd 6480] V.

283 Hanworth Committee, group II minutes, PRO LCO 2/1604; *PP* 1933–4 [Cmd 4471] XI, para. 78; *Hansard* 1933–4 5th s., vol. 90, cols. 729–36; County Courts Act 1934 s. 87.

284 *Austin Jones Report*, paras. 6–9. For discussions about this recommendation see PRO LCO 2/3296.

285 Rieu's note, 6 Dec. 1954, Dobson to Fiennes (PCO), 5 Jan. 1955, PRO LCO 2/4984.

286 Administration of Justice Act 1956 s. 30.

287 PRO LCO 2/7166. Examples are judges Howard and Elder-Jones. 2/7163, pt 4.

288 PRO LCO 2/7169.

289 *PP* 1967–8 (Cmnd 3691) XXX, para. 447; Administration of Justice Act 1968 s. 9. It had already become a standing joke at the ACCR AGM: see e.g. Report of 1961.

290 *Beeching Report*, para. 176g.

though they had not been attracted to Payne's suggestion that they should be the men to run the Enforcement Offices.[291]

Since registrars are far more elusive, numerous and probably more diverse than judges, they are even less susceptible to any general conclusions about how, and how well, they performed their duties. The men who testified before inquiries, who served on the Rule Committee, were consulted by the LCO, wrote in the legal press, men like Thomas Marshall and F. F. Clarke at the end of the nineteenth century,[292] Lowe and Jennings between the wars,[293] Hicks and Freeman Coutts after the Second World War,[294] were men of undoubted ability and shrewd common sense. Many part-timers must have been a good deal less able, given the limited choice and moderate standards in the profession. No doubt the overall level improved as part-timers became fewer and competition for whole-time posts keener. Already in 1898 Yate Lee felt that they were better than judges at dealing with the small everyday disputes,[295] and Cecil's 1970 verdict, albeit rather patronising, may be reasonably accurate: 'most registrars in the county court try their cases sensibly, fairly, and compassionately. Few of them have any pretensions to being great lawyers, but most cases which they try involve questions of fact rather than questions of law.'[296]

However, for many years, their performance of their judicial role was tainted by suspicions arising from the system of payment by results and part-time registrars. Two suspicions were generated, neatly summed up by Judge Cann:

> It is . . . a very unfortunate state of affairs which puts a man into a position whereby he may one day act as Judge to someone who on another day is a client . . . The fact that a Registrar has his own clients before him causes attacks to be made on him, and suggestions are made that in giving leave to issue process out of the jurisdiction he is influenced by the fact that his remuneration will thereby be affected.[297]

291 *Payne Report*, paras. 350 ff.: reservation by registrar Bryson and others.

292 For Marshall see *SJ* 53 (1909–10), 266; F. F. Clarke of Walsall was chosen to give evidence to several inquiries and was also consulted on rules, e.g. in 1899: PRO LCO 2/110.

293 Successive presidents of the ACCR after Marshall and members of the rule committee (see pp. 219–20 above).

294 See pp. 220–4 above. Gregory did not regard Freeman Coutts so highly as Hicks (private communication).

295 *LM* 5th s., 24 (1897–8) 257–71.

296 *English Judge*, pp. 24–5.

297 *Swift Evidence*, 55AB.

While registrar Pybus could not see the objection in the first case ('I do not think that there is any reason for a Defendant to object to a Registrar hearing a case in which the Plaintiff is, or was, his client. He is not, and cannot be, his client in that case'[298]), Judge McCarthy pointed out that laymen might not share the registrar's confidence in his ability to keep his two roles quite distinct.[299] The Swift Committee, while anxious to disclaim any suggestion that there had been bias, agreed.[300]

Payment by results not only generated the suspicion explained by Cann, which was probably well grounded, but another besides. Since a registrar's income depended on plaints, he stood to gain by encouraging his clerks to drum up business, especially near the year's end. Though defended by Bridgeman as encouraging the courts to be 'user friendly',[301] it undoubtedly did lead to abuses: as Barker recalled, 'it was a case of "Go out into the highways and by-ways and bring them in", and some ingenious methods of swelling the total were used'.[302] Chalmers had rightly concluded that 'from a Treasury point of view there is a good deal to be said for the system of payment by results, but as a question of public morality the system is abominable'.[303] Its gradual abandonment made it politically feasible to extend the registrars' judicial role and improved their reputation with the public, leading to the much greater responsibilities they have come to be entrusted with in recent years.

298 *Ibid.*, 401. 299 *Ibid.*, 57E.
300 *Swift Report*, p. 8.
301 *MacDonnell Evidence*, qq. 51, 710–35.
302 *CCO* 26 (1947–9), 514.
303 *LQR* 5 (1889), 7.

# 8

# STAFF AND BUILDINGS

## REGISTRARS

### *Appointment*

The 1846 Act required each court to have its clerk, but it empowered the Lord Chancellor to sanction a joint appointment where business was unusually heavy and allowed a judge to appoint the same man to several of his courts, with assistant clerks to look after the less important ones.[1] Many judges found this convenient. Pluralism became widespread and could also be lucrative; Burrows was clerk both to Brompton and Brentford and to Marylebone, and apparently continued to run a flourishing private practice as well.[2] But it quickly fell out of favour with officialdom, perhaps because of doubts whether the registrar's supervision could really be effective where, as in West Wales, he controlled ten courts, nine of which he visited only on court days from his base at Carmarthen.[3] The County Courts Further Extension Act 1852 restricted it to exceptional cases authorised by the Lord Chancellor, and gradually the pluralists died out.[4]

The rule of one court, one registrar led to a rapid growth in numbers. There were 498 in 1874, and this remained practically unchanged until the Great War.[5] However, the principle had been

[1] Ss. 24, 27, 58. There is no full history of registrars but there is a helpful unpublished Ll B dissertation (County Court Registrars) by S. Fradley (Brunel University, 1975). For the first thirty years see Bartrip, Registrars.

[2] *LT* 16 (1850–1), 445.

[3] *LT* 27 (1856), 151.

[4] Bartrip, Registrars, p. 357; County Courts Act 1852 ss. 1, 14, 17. The County Courts Act 1856 s. 9 enabled the Treasury to end pluralism in any court and they acted against Morris, the Carmarthen registrar, under this provision.

[5] This figure was given both to the Lisgar Commission in 1874 and to the MacDonnell Commission in 1914.

adopted without full consideration of its implications. The small courts could not yield enough to induce a respectable solicitor to abandon his practice, so part-time registrars were common, yet the desire to make the registrar into a judicial officer sat uncomfortably with his being a local practitioner. It also perpetuated a system of payment by results which seemed increasingly anachronistic[6] and in 1888 the government had a hard job to defeat a proposal to make all registrars whole-timers, even though twenty earned barely more than the statutory minimum of £100.[7]

The obvious solution was to close courts that did not justify a whole-timer,[8] but since that was politically impossible, the LCO had to resort instead to a cautious process of 'grouping' small courts under one registrar.[9] This was given a more explicit sanction in 1919 and under rules made in 1921 a swift and purposeful programme was put into effect.[10] The combined impact of grouping and closures was striking. The number of registrars had fallen from 450 to 229 by 1938, including eight courts with two registrars each and 116 men who were covering more than one court.[11] Though Martin thought that the limits of grouping had almost been reached,[12] the widespread use of the motor car and the telephone enabled it to progress further: numbers fell to 123 in 1956 (some serving six or seven courts) and 108 in 1968, with just twenty part-timers.[13] One consequence was a reversal in the balance between the number of judges and registrars: for a hundred years judges had been greatly outnumbered, by as many as eight to one at one time, yet by the time the Courts Act 1971 was passed the number of judges had drawn ahead.

Apart from clerks in certain of the defunct courts of requests, all county court clerks were required to be attorneys.[14] In line with

[6] The *Romilly Report*, p. 44, which recommended salaries based on plaint numbers.

[7] *MacDonnell Evidence*: Muir McKenzie at q. 54,565; report of standing committee, *PP* 1888 (172) X; return of registrars' remuneration, *PP* 1888 (148) LXXXIII.

[8] Judicature Commission, *Second Report*, pp. 14–15.

[9] *MacDonnell Evidence*: Muir McKenzie at q. 55,467.

[10] County Courts Act 1919 s. 15.

[11] *CCO* 26 (1947–9), 145; *PP* 1938–9 [Cmd 6135], XXV.

[12] Evidence of 27 Jan. 1948, PRO LCO 2/3299.

[13] *Civil Judicial Statistics*.

[14] County Courts Act 1846 s. 24. When the Croydon registrar transferred to the bar a bill was introduced to try to prevent further instances: *LT* 92 (1891–2), 462; *LJ* 25 (1890), 429; *PP* 1890 (523) I.

their acquisition of increasing judicial responsibilities, the qualification was raised, to five years' experience in 1888 and seven in 1924,[15] it being 'eminently desirable that the office should be one sought after by men successful in their profession, and not be regarded merely as a refuge for those who have not attained success in practice'.[16] Though women were eligible from 1919, even in 1960 they were 'most unlikely [to] be appointed direct to a . . . registrarship'.[17]

Although patronage lay with the judges, their choices had to be approved by the Lord Chancellor and despite Muir McKenzie's assertion that the testimonials were carefully considered Schuster said that there had been 'disgraceful instances of nepotism'.[18] There were generalised allegations of corruption,[19] but particular appointments were criticised only on grounds of inexperience or because they were not local men. Judge Pitt Taylor was frowned upon for putting his son in charge of a substantial court when only six months qualified[20] and local practitioners, having come to regard these posts as their prize, were annoyed when a judge in Kent twice brought in an outsider and when Woodfall took F. B. McFea down from London to Plymouth, a practice which may have become more common when salaried 'whole-timers' were introduced in 1888.[21] Nepotism was common enough,[22] but it was a foolish judge who put an incompetent relation in charge of a court, and some were far from incompetent; registrar Thomas Marshall, for instance, was more highly regarded in Leeds than his father the judge.

The LCO disclaimed any wish to appoint all registrars, but where a town was made a district registry of the high court it was usual to avoid a wasteful proliferation of officials by making the

15 County Courts Act 1888 s. 25; County Courts Act 1924 s. 1 (2).

16 *Swift Report*, p. 8.

17 R. K. Thesiger to Coldstream, 28 Mar. 1961, PRO LCO 4/129.

18 *MacDonnell Evidence*, q. 55,462; Schuster to Attorney-General, 1 Nov. 1923, PRO LCO 2/709.

19 *Hansard* 1856 3rd s., vol. 141, cols. 279–88.

20 *SJ* 17 (1871–2), 122; cf. *CCC* 23 (1871–2), 27.

21 *LT* 110 (1900–1), 64; *CCC* 39 (1903), 123. F. W. Cooke, for instance, was a London solicitor asked by the judge, at the suggestion of the Lord Chancellor, to go to Norwich as a whole-time registrar: *Swift Evidence*, 7FG.

22 In the 1888 return are a Hulton, a Yates, an Atkinson, a Stephen, a Woodforde, a Pitt Taylor, a Clarke and a Francillon, all on circuits where there was or had been a judge of the same name.

local county court registrar the district registrar too.[23] The LCO view, endorsed by the MacDonnell Commission, was that in such centres the registrar should thenceforth be appointed by the Chancellor.[24]

In practice, it is unlikely that it made much difference whether the judge or the Chancellor had made the appointments, at least in small towns: 'it is really rather a blue ribbon in the small places, and everywhere except the largest places. You get on the whole, I think, the best solicitor in a place to take the ... Registrarship, because he just adds it to his business; he puts up "County Court Registrar" over his door.'[25] So in Sittingbourne, T. B. Bishop accepted the appointment because 'it was formerly held by one of the partners of the firm which I joined, and the appointment formed part of the business', and often, as Judge McCarthy remarked, there was really little choice.[26] It is not surprising to find them passing from father to son, like the Tassells in Faversham, or brother to brother, like the Lovells in Bath.[27]

The judges lost their patronage because it was considered incompatible with the registrars' new civil service status, but a judge's recommendation was still very influential. The LCO preferred men of forty to fifty with a good local practice, and had few problems getting them[28] until the 1960s, when they wanted a higher calibre of solicitor to undertake the increased responsibilities, and Kewish wrote to The *Law Society's Gazette* to encourage suitable candidates, suggesting that the ideal person was now younger, forty to forty-five.[29] It was the usual practice however for the local law society to nominate a man who had agreed to be put forward.[30]

### *Conditions of service*

The 1846 Act provided for payment out of fees unless and until an order in council substituted salaries.[31] Though some clerks did

23 *MacDonnell Evidence*, qq. 44,215–16, 55,459–61.

24 *MacDonnell Report*, pp. 44–5. The LCO's County Courts Bills from 1910 onwards all contained clauses to this effect.

25 *MacDonnell Evidence*, q. 44,225 (Muir McKenzie).

26 *Swift Evidence*, 45B, 56B.

27 *Ibid.*, 43J; *LT* 30 (1857–8), 77.

28 Martin's evidence to the Tomlin Commission, PRO LCO 4/121.

29 *LSG* 61 (1964), 669–70.

30 Fradley, County Court Registrars, p. 74.

31 The maximum salary was initially set at £500, raised to £600 in 1850 and £700 in 1852.

extraordinarily well out of the fees, surpassing the earnings of their judges, the majority did not, three-quarters earning less than £100.[32] Despite strenuous lobbying, just fifteen clerks were salaried by 1853.[33]

The Romilly Commission's proposals were the foundation for a three-tier structure which lasted for sixty years: a minimum salary for the smallest courts; for the rest, a rising scale based on plaint numbers up to a maximum of 6,000 plaints; and above that in the Treasury's discretion. But their proposed salaries were unrealistic and what emerged was a minimum of £120, a maximum of £1,200 gross for a court issuing up to 6,000 plaints and a maximum of £700 net for the bigger courts, with an allowance for clerk hire.[34]

This basic structure was later refined and complicated in several ways, notably by Schedule 'B' fees, additional remuneration for duties under various special statutory jurisdictions. In 1887 for instance, the Newcastle registrar added to his basic £662 10s, £581 1s 4d in bankruptcy fees and £510 as district registrar, though a Treasury minute restricted total earnings to £1,400 to prevent them exceeding those of the judges. Schedule 'B' fees widened the gap between big and small: on the same circuit other incomes ranged from Gateshead's £340 down to Rothby, Wooler and Alnwick, each £100; their gleanings under Schedule 'B' were from £18 9s (Gateshead) down to 2s 6d at Wooler.[35]

But the most significant changes came in two overlapping provisions in the 1888 Act. One, s. 25, enabled the Lord Chancellor to bar from private practice the next registrar appointed to a court with more than 8,000 plaints; by the other, s. 45, he might salary him up to £1,400 and exclude him from practice where the volume of business or the addition of a high court registry made it desirable.

Section 25 was a dead letter and under s. 45 only twenty-two registrars became salaried civil servants. However a further forty-five were required to give up, or restrict, their practice as a

32 Bartrip, Registrars, p. 357.

33 Under order in council of 30 July 1849, *PP* 1854–5 (350) XLIII. For the lobbying see *Hansard* 1849–50, 3rd s., vol. 109, cols. 816–17; vol. 110, cols. 131–52; *LT* 22 (1853–4), 132.

34 *Romilly Report*, pp. 44–5; *Hansard* 1856 3rd s., vol. 143, cols. 708 ff.; County Courts Act 1856 s. 82.

35 *PP* 1888 (148) LXXXIII. Judge Harington had claimed that some registrars earned much more than judges: *Select Committee, 1878*, q. 1575.

condition of appointment.[36] As a result the three classes of registrar by mode of payment – gross fees, fees plus staff allowance and fixed salary – were not congruent with the division according to status – part-time, whole-time and civil servant.

The devastating effects of the war on registrars' incomes, particularly those governed by the undertaking, were fatal to this anachronistic system,[37] but it took four years of hard bargaining and parliamentary manoeuvring to make the change recommended in the Swift Report.[38] Salaries under the scheme – £100 to £1,200 – were not very generous and the ACCR was disappointed at its failure to incorporate routine reviews; 'sombre acceptance' was their recommendation.[39] There was no general pay increase until 1938, when whole-timers were given 10 per cent,[40] but as civil servants the whole-timers received regular increases after the Second World War, and by 1964 there were three separate scales: £2,702 to £3,235; £3,113 to £3,700 and £3,445 to £3,975.[41] Part-timers had to negotiate their pay individually and their association could only help them by providing information on existing payments.[42] The 1924 Act also brought most registrars into the civil service pension scheme for which until then only a handful had been eligible, modified to take account of their unusual career pattern and, like the judges' scheme, providing for a pension after a minimum of fifteen years' service.[43]

When pluralism was barred, a residence requirement was introduced.[44] In 1888 a relaxation sought by Rollit was resisted[45] but there may have been a certain slackness, for in 1890 a general reminder was issued and in 1896 the Maldon registrar was being chased up for having left the district and put in charge a non-

36 *PP* 1888 (172) X; *SJ* 32 (1887–8), 416, 432, 468; *Swift Report*, pp. 4–5.

37 *Swift Report*, pp. 6–7, 23–6 and app. A and C; *Swift Evidence*, pp. 65 ff.

38 *Swift Report*, p. 8; PRO LCO 2/525–6, 709–11, 8/52, and pp. 117–24 above.

39 Jennings to Boland, 8 July 1923, PRO LCO 8/52 and circular to registrars, Feb. 1924. Thirty registrars were singled out for 'conversations' before the scheme was finalised in March 1925.

40 *LT* 184 (1938), 401. The claim had been for 15 per cent.

41 *LSG* 61 (1964), 669. In 1950 it was said that two of them earned more than their judges: *Hansard* 1950 5th s., vol. 482 (HC), cols. 112 ff.

42 ACCR AGM 1959.

43 *Swift Report*, p. 16; County Courts Act 1924 s. 2.

44 County Courts Act 1852 s. 17.

45 *Hansard* 1888 3rd s., vol. 330, cols. 359 ff.

resident deputy.[46] To facilitate grouping the rule was relaxed in 1920, the Lord Chancellor acquiring a dispensing power.[47]

Registrars were forbidden to practise in their own court either in person or through their partners,[48] and there are instances of registrars prosecuted for a breach of the rule; thus Glubb of Liskeard was fined the maximum of £50 in 1891 for acting through his son.[49] They were not barred, nor even discouraged, from filling other legal posts in the neighbourhood, such as clerk to the justices however.

### *Perquisites of office*

A registrar had little to look forward to. He was not eligible to become a judge[50] and there was no systematic promotion to bigger courts. The most that could be hoped for was an invitation to join the Rule Committee or to serve on a departmental committee. Kewish, uniquely, was invited to become head of the county courts branch.

Originally they did not even wear robes to dignify their office, but later, in a move not universally popular, they began to wear a plain black gown and bob wig. In the 1960s there were moves to make their dress more imposing but the LCD was unenthusiastic and they came to nothing, as did suggestions that they should be styled 'solicitor judges' to emphasise their main function.[51]

### *Assistant and deputy registrars*

Originally an *assistant* clerk was a man appointed to cover the less important courts of a pluralist clerk, while a *deputy* was chosen to fulfil the clerk's own functions in cases of illness or unavoidable absence; both were usually attorneys, though there was no statutory requirement that they be qualified.[52] Some deputies were employed very regularly and Robert Pybus was probably not the

46 Circular of 22 May, PRO LCO 8/4, f. 76; *Hansard* 1896 4th s., vol. 44, col. 110.

47 County Courts Act 1919 s. 15.

48 County Courts Act 1846 s. 61.

49 *CCC* 33 (1891–2), 155, 161.

50 Despite the Judicature Commissioners' recommendation: Bartrip, Registrars, p. 366.

51 ACCR AGM 1966, 1967.

52 County Courts Act 1846 ss. 24, 26.

only one to become registrar in turn.[53] 'Assistant registrars', who needed the same qualifications as registrars and were established civil servants appointed by the Lord Chancellor to serve busy courts, were reintroduced in the 1924 Act but remained rare until the 1950s.[54]

### *Leaving office*

As with judges, there was no statutory provision for registrars to retire, so they also tended to hang onto their office as long as they could; one arthritic veteran's occasional visits to the office involved such grotesque contortions that they were a spectacle for the local inhabitants.[55] They clocked up lengths of service surpassing anything the judges could show; Henry Dawes, Nuneaton's first registrar, was there for sixty years, George Wilkinson was at Holt for fifty-seven.[56]

Octogenarians were still to be found between the wars among those who had not joined the pension scheme (retirement at seventy-two was only for those appointed after the 1924 Act). Though some were sprightly and alert, like Pybus, who stayed on till he was eighty-seven, others became an embarrassment, whose inefficiency and reluctance to update their law and practice brought them at least to the verge of statutory 'inability'. In 1926 a concerted attempt was made to persuade six of these (and three high bailiffs) whom Napier had singled out to resign.[57] In response to ACCR protests he pointed out that one of them, Parker of Wellingborough, was still clinging onto his job although he had resigned through old age as town clerk.[58] Even in 1961 there were still two registrars, J. N. St G. Curwen in Workington and G. H. Twist in Nuneaton, who were over eighty and two others, H. H. Foster in Worcester and S. E. Wilkins of Aylesbury, who had been appointed before the Great War. There were no complaints about their performance but it was by now felt at

53 *Swift Evidence*, 12D.
54 County Courts Act 1924 s. 3 (they had been omitted from the 1888 Act); PRO LCO 2/5073.
55 G. F. Bamford, I Remember, *CCO* 33 (1956), 17.
56 *CCC* 41 (1907), 191; *County Courts Gazette* 1 (1913–14), 39.
57 Martin to Napier, 13 Dec. 1926, PRO LCO 12/117.
58 *Ibid.*: Napier and Jennings correspondence, Nov. 1926.

headquarters that it was undesirable to have junior judicial officers of such advanced age.[59]

Registrars, like judges, were liable to dismissal for inability or misbehaviour, but the power of dismissal lay with the judge[60] and its width was soon put to the test. W. Owen, who ran several North Wales courts under Judge A. J. Johnes, got himself into financial trouble and Johnes, sympathetic at first, became increasingly concerned as the extent of Owen's debts became apparent. When the registrar had to leave his home, his furniture seized by creditors, Johnes' patience gave way and he gave him notice. But the judges of the Queen's Bench, their authority invoked by a writ of *quo warranto*, ruled that since his person had not been seized, nor had he been made bankrupt, Owen was not prevented from carrying out his duties and financial embarrassment *per se* was not to be construed as misbehaviour. Owen was therefore restored to his place.[61]

The Owen case showed how invidious it was for a judge to have this responsibility and in 1850 it was transferred to the Lord Chancellor, the registrar also being deprived of his security of tenure.[62] The greater number of registrars and their access to suitors' money probably explains the fact that more use had to be made of the power of removal than in the case of judges. At all events, William Edge was removed from Cheadle in 1856, and Harman from High Wycombe and William Statham from Liverpool in 1861.[63] Statham's case is interesting because he was one of nine who had given up freehold offices in courts of requests to become county court registrars and a last-minute amendment to the Act had protected them from dismissal for anything short of 'gross misconduct'. Statham, however, had made off with £1,734 of public money, and even an 'irremovable' could not expect to keep his place after that.[64]

These were all dismissals for misbehaviour. The first for

59 PRO LCO 4/541.

60 County Courts Act 1846 s. 24. Dismissal was subject to the Lord Chancellor's approval.

61 *R v. Owen* (1850) 15 QB Ad & Ellis 476. The judge's own account is in *LR* 19 (1854), 257–71.

62 County Courts Act 1850 s. 4; *Hansard* 1849–50 3rd s., vol. 111, cols. 162–3; vol. 112, col. 1443.

63 PRO LCO 8/10.

64 PRO LCO 12/88; *Hansard* 1849–50 3rd s., vol. 113, cols. 77–80.

inability was John Bishop of Greenwich and Woolwich in 1872.[65] In the absence of pensions the Lord Chancellor would hesitate both from prudence and from humanity before acting in other than the clearest of cases (such as the insanity of the registrar of Ross-on-Wye in 1905).[66] Elderly registrars were therefore able to prolong their own tenure by making sons or nephews 'joint registrars'.[67] As with judges, public criticism became much rarer after the Great War, and the only known instance of serious misconduct was seemingly attributable to mental disorder.[68]

## *The Association of County Court Registrars*

Clerks on some circuits soon met to discuss matters of common concern and seem rapidly to have progressed to action on a wider scale. In 1849 their 'Society' was actively campaigning for legislation,[69] and though there is no further trace of this organisation,[70] the ACCR sprang from a successful agitation for a higher minimum salary and a change of name in the 1856 Bill and held its first general meeting in May 1857.[71] By the mid-1870s it had 250 members and it grew in influence under the presidency of Thomas Marshall, regarded as the real founder and leading actor in the association, an altogether more forceful figure than his predecessor Thomas Collins of Bury St Edmunds.[72] Soon after 1900, for instance, the Rule Committee began sending it draft rules for comment.[73]

Changes which took place after Marshall's death in 1910 however suggest that younger men felt that it needed a good shake-up. The hand of the new president, A. L. Lowe of Birmingham, may perhaps be seen in the innovation of practice notes begun in 1907 and distributed annually thereafter, and was

[65] *SJ* 17 (1872–3), 122. Bishop died, at seventy-three, soon afterwards: *LM* ns 2 (1873), 1144.
[66] PRO LCO 2/163.
[67] *LT* 98 (1894–5), 527; similarly with high bailiffs: *MacDonnell Evidence*, qq. 55,498–501.
[68] PRO LCO 2/7143.
[69] *LT* 9 (1847), 501; 13 (1849), 348.
[70] But in 1878 the ACCR president claimed to have been in office for twenty-five years: *Select Committee, 1878*, at q. 3142.
[71] *CCC* 10 (1857), 1.
[72] Report of AGM, 1874, PRO LCO 8/5. The records held by the Association do not extend back beyond the Great War. For Marshall see *SJ* 53 (1909–10), 266.
[73] *SJ* 47 (1902–3), 550.

certainly behind the first ever revision of its rules and the regular reports of the AGM in the law press.[74] A vigorous membership drive raised it to an impressive 341 in 1913, strengthening its position as a trade union in arguments with the Treasury and other departments. There were successes over national insurance, duties carried out for the Ministry of Pensions and, to some extent, over the war bonus.[75]

A further victory was the placing of Lowe on the Rule Committee. This left Arthur Jennings of Brighton to bear the main brunt of the arduous negotiations for establishment which dominated the ACCR's proceedings in the early 1920s. Ironically, by facilitating the grouping of courts, the attainment of this great goal was the direct cause of the association's steep decline in membership: from 377 members in 1919 to 192 in 1938 and just 110 in 1968.[76]

Though some were able men, none of Jennings' successors was so influential. The association continued to scrutinise new rules in draft and sometimes made proposals of its own; in 1933 for example, on the initiative of H. P. Stanes, it sought restrictions on the use of summonses out of the district.[77] It also sought to reverse changes it did not like; thus in 1938 Hicks was asked to bring forward its strong desire to recover discretion over solicitors' costs.[78]

The ACCR had direct negotiations with the professional bodies on matters such as robing and the listing of cases and with the Inland Revenue over unstamped documents.[79] Naturally, it often had to press the claims of its members on the LCO. It had little success in pressing salary claims, perhaps because it could not decide whether it wished to be linked with judges or civil servants,[80] but had more success in less momentous matters, taking up the cudgels against overbearing auditors and impertinent debt collectors,[81] and in the 1960s, when some registrars felt

74 AGMs for every year from 1911 to 1940 are reported in the *Law Journal* and the *Solicitors' Journal*.

75 *LJ* 48 (1913), 230; *LJCCR* 6 (1917), 30; 9 (1920), 21.

76 For the ACCR's concern about grouping see *LJCCR* 16 (1927), 21.

77 ACCR committee minutes, 28 Apr. 1933.

78 *LT* 185 (1938), 401–2.

79 ACCR committee minutes, 31 July 1931, 29 Jan. 1932.

80 See e.g. discussions at the 1967 AGM.

81 ACCR committee minutes, 31 Jan. 1930; AGM reports 1955, 1969.

themselves badly overworked, it made representations on that score.[82]

## CLERICAL STAFF

### *Before the Swift Report*

Registrars and high bailiffs employed clerical staff but Nicol did not even know how many there were, though in the bigger courts the Treasury confirmed their appointments and included them in the annual estimates.[83] In 1850 Brompton and Marylebone each had six but in the provinces they were generally fewer; Jones had two office clerks and an office boy in Huddersfield, while in Canterbury Furley had one full-time and one part-time clerk.[84] Part-timers were quite common in the smaller courts and most provincial clerks were probably drawn from the registrar's own solicitor's office, especially where his premises also accommodated the court office.

The clerks issued plaints and process, executions and warrants of all kinds, entering everything in the great ledgers which also recorded the fees they took in and the innumerable tiny instalments paid in by debtors. Clerks were not mere automata however. While the plaint book might be neglected for weeks at a stretch, some clerks kept their own books as well as the statutory ones for greater convenience.[85] Occasionally their initiatives were less innocent; the Wolverhampton registrar lost over £900 by a clerk's embezzlement and his colleague at Barnet was also a victim, partly due to his own negligent supervision.[86]

Members of a black-coated army of clerks a million strong by 1911,[87] the Victorian county court clerks are shadowy figures.[88] Even the most basic facts, such as their earnings, are scarce. In the 1850s one group ranged from as low as £30 to only £140 with

82 AGM report 1961.
83 *Second Report*, qq. 2654–65; *LT* 82 (1886), 124: petition of county court clerks.
84 *PP* 1850 (287) XLVI.
85 *Romilly Report*, qq. 1550–9.
86 *Select Committee, 1878*, q. 2940; PRO T 15/18, f. 111.
87 G. Anderson, *Victorian Clerks* (Manchester, 1976), p. 2.
88 A few returns besides that of 1850 (n. 84 above) provide a little information: see e.g. *PP* 1851 (654) XLVII and *PP* 1861 (398), LI.

most below £100 and in the 1870s most clerks outside London probably earned less than £150.[89] Working hours are more straightforward because the court office was open from ten o'clock till four o'clock on Saturdays, though it was sometimes necessary to stay late, especially when an audit was in prospect. Working conditions were no doubt as variable as in other offices.

The clerks' great aspiration was to be civil servants, for the modernisation of the civil service which began in the 1850s brought to its clerks (including those in the superior courts) the benefits of secure tenure followed by retirement on a pension, an immense boon to those who had to provide for old age by saving what they could from meagre salaries.[90] This was the chief goal of the Metropolitan County Court Clerks Association, which traces a more or less continuous succession from the body pioneered by the Shoreditch clerks around 1870.

Combinations in the civil service began in the 1850s and soon became more widespread and sometimes militant, but unionisation among private-sector clerks developed more slowly for reasons applying also to county courts. Clerks worked in very small units in close personal contact with an employer who had the power to dismiss them at will, and as their terms of employment and working conditions varied widely, so did their grievances. Furthermore county court clerks were apt to regard themselves as members of the legal profession and shared its abhorrence of working-class trade unionism.[91]

Even so, the performance of the early associations was strikingly feeble, exasperating more militant recruits. For years they 'had a dinner but no rules'[92] and apathy was interrupted only by fitful exertion. An attempt to exploit the government's difficulties in the Commons over the County Courts Bill 1888 was foiled by an adroitly ambiguous assurance from the Attorney-General; MPs

89 *PP* 1857–8 (245) XLVII; *SJ* 15 (1871), 263. Nicol said 'we do not know what they pay their clerks' (*Second Report*, q. 2542) but W. F. A. Dehane, treasurer to the metropolitan courts, said they were 'certainly paid at a higher rate than mercantile clerks': *Romilly Report*, q. 1586.

90 B. V. Humphreys, *Clerical Unions in the Civil Service* (Oxford, 1958), pp. 8 ff., 14.

91 *Ibid.*, pp. 28–40; Anderson, *Victorian Clerks*, pp. 108–28.

92 W. S. Hardman, The Evolution of the County Courts Officers Association, *CCO* 3 (1922–3), pts 7, 8; *County Courts Gazette* 2 (1914–16), 83–4.

were decorously lobbied; the committee once tremulously bearded Nicol, but all to no effect.[93]

At the turn of the century a new association, the County Court Officers' Association, was formed with a national embrace under the presidency of Grimsdale of Bow. Grimsdale pinned his hopes on a small committee set up by the LCO under Brynmor Jones, but its report (never seen by the association) was a sad disappointment. Though the chairman wrote that 'it would be expedient to place all the clerks and officers presently employed as wholetimers in county courts upon a pensionable basis', the report itself said that 'the object of the legislature was to create local courts, the actual working of which should be as far as possible independent of central control and therefore distinct from the usual organisation of the civil service'.[94]

Though the association began to spread and to establish provincial branches it was only when they finally jettisoned the president, Bradley of Wandsworth, for F. W. Cross that they made real progress. With the new secretary, John Keane, a colleague of Cross at Cardiff, he infused a vigour and purpose that had long been wanting.[95] The membership grew to over 600 and, riding on the back of a great upsurge in trade union activity,[96] more systematic lobbying was instituted. The long-standing policy of confining membership to the '6,000 plus courts' however led to the formation in 1913 of a rival body for the smaller courts, but after initial petulance, the association recognised that disunity would be disastrous and an amalgamation took place in 1914, just before the royal commission turned its attention to the legal departments.[97]

At last the Treasury was forced to find out how many clerks there were: including part-timers, they numbered 1,417 (plus eleven women), an average of only four or five per court; the biggest was Birmingham, with fifty-six clerks and ushers.[98] Most

[93] *Hansard* 1892 4th s., vol. 5, col. 555; Hardman, Evolution of the CCOA; *County Courts Gazette* 2 (1914–16), 66 (C. J. R. Tijou), 83–4 ('Only a Clerk').

[94] *MacDonnell Evidence*, qq. 51,998, 51,882–3, 51,905–7.

[95] Hardman, Evolution of the CCOA; *County Courts Gazette*, 2 (1914–16), 66, 83–4.

[96] Humphreys, *Clerical Unions*, pp. 59–71.

[97] *County Courts Gazette* 1 (1912–14), 74, 97, 129–30, 185; *MacDonnell Evidence*, qq. 51,911–21.

[98] *MacDonnell Evidence*, qq. 51,659, 51,866, 51,922, 52,072, 53,580.

came in straight from school at about fourteen. In Birmingham they were 'the sons of superior clerks, or clerks in solicitors' offices, and commercial gentlemen who are managers of departments – the ordinary clerk class'.[99] Less scrupulous registrars advertised for 'apprentices' whom they paid a pittance and discharged as soon as they became entitled to better pay, and some boy clerks in the smaller offices were very young indeed – the Faversham registrar took one at twelve. Some adults were recruited but the experience with two middle-aged men at Bristol was said to have been unfavourable. Older juniors might be unpopular with the incumbents as they could not so readily be subjected to the practical jokes and petty tyrannies which relieved the monotony of office life.[100]

Differing views were advanced on how much practical security of tenure the clerks had. Unwarranted dismissals were uncommon but Bamford was given a week's notice for declining to submit in silence to gross mistreatment and registrars and clerks alike, from opposite viewpoints, laid great stress on the absence of job security.[101] Clerks were vulnerable as most had limited marketability because of their narrow work experience. Bamford had to submit to injustice for months until a court vacancy came up and there was no official assistance with transfers, though in 1914 the association's journal opened a register.[102]

It is difficult to know how common career moves were. Certainly Coombs' small court regularly acted as a feeder to bigger ones and William Norman went from Northampton to Newport via Reading in search of better things, but the overall impression is that most stayed put unless they were badly treated or unusually ambitious.[103] Transferees in search of advancement

99 *Ibid.*, q. 53,397 (A. L. Lowe).

100 Bamford, I Remember, 17; A. C. Barker, Now When I Was a Young Man, *CCO* 26 (1947–9), 154–5; *Swift Evidence*, 43C (G. Tassell); *MacDonnell Evidence*, qq. 51,999–52,000.

101 *MacDonnell Evidence*, qq. 51,767, 52,056–68; Bamford, I Remember, 100.

102 *MacDonnell Evidence*, qq. 53,402, 54,096–7; *Swift Evidence*, 32C; *County Courts Gazette* 1 (1912–14), 175; 3 (1916–17), 114; Bamford, I Remember, 100.

103 *MacDonnell Evidence*, q. 54,126; *Swift Evidence*, 47J. The Birmingham registrar told the royal commission that in three years seven men left out of forty-two – two were sacked for dishonesty, one left for ill-health, one to be private secretary to a nobleman, two to set up in the motor trade, one to go to a commercial office (q. 53,407).

were not likely to be popular with their new colleagues, for promotion was a rarity in most courts. Even in Birmingham, an exception in promoting on merit rather than seniority, leapfrogging seldom took place and elsewhere it was usually a case of filling dead men's shoes, often quite literally given the absence of retirement provisions. Even then a promotion was not guaranteed if business had fallen away.[104]

It even tended to be difficult to acquire the whole range of skills necessary for a more responsible post: 'woebetide anybody who poked his nose into the mysteries of another man's job. If a clerk had the temerity to go near the desk of one of the senior men he would observe the latter discreetly cover the secrets of his craft with his blotting paper.'[105] This presumably was the clerks' way of ensuring they were indispensable.

Earnings still varied enormously. Young men were miserably paid: in Birmingham they began on 5s a week, rising to about 25s when the 'boy' was twenty-one. At Bow annual pay ranged from £80 to £400, at Lambeth from £80 to £300 and those are probably representative of London rates. In the provinces the range was much wider; in Faversham a clerk of forty-five years was getting only £155, Wade, the only clerk at Trowbridge, £140.[106] Moreover registrars exercised an unfettered discretion in determining the clerks' share of schedule B fees.[107]

Whether clerks as a body were underpaid depends of course on the appropriate comparison. Bridgeman and registrars naturally said no – their comparators being solicitors' clerks.[108] Clerks argued that they undertook complex and responsible work.[109] Certainly in the courts with a district registry attached, county court clerks did that work too and undoubtedly some matters were more than mere form filling, workmen's compensation being an example. On the whole though, it was work of 'a very specialised routine character', not requiring much learning or initiative.[110]

A chief clerk's role was often more demanding, either because

[104] *MacDonnell Evidence*, qq. 53,420–31, 51,932–9; Barker, Now When I Was a Young Man.

[105] Barker, Now When I Was a Young Man.

[106] *MacDonnell Evidence*, qq. 51,683, 52,028, 52,173, 53,370–5; *Swift Evidence*, 43D.

[107] *Swift Evidence*, 33D (W. S. Hardman).

[108] *MacDonnell Evidence*, q. 51,663. *Cf.* qq. 53,474 (Lowe), 54,038 (Jennings).

[109] *Ibid.*, qq. 51,965 ff.

[110] *Ibid.*, q. 51,681.

he was in effective day-to-day charge of the staff or, more commonly, because the registrar delegated many of his duties to him, as Norman's did.[111] W. H. Walter was the boldest exponent of the view that the chief clerk was in fact doing much of the registrar's work, and alarmed the Swift Committee by listing an impressive array of responsible functions before assuring them, 'you are shocked to hear it because you do not know how well it is done'.[112] Of course, what was true of Coventry was not necessarily true elsewhere, for Walter was uncommonly able; still, the unpleasant northern registrar under whom Bamford served was kept in line by his chief clerk and in his first court 'the office of registrar was practically a sinecure', the registrar living thirty miles away and barely able to alight from the cab on his rare visits; the office was run by an octogenarian clerk who styled himself 'assistant registrar'.[113]

Growing dissatisfaction among the clerks was not peculiar to the courts, for clerks everywhere felt themselves to be 'slipping down the status hierarchy',[114] unable to sustain the crucial difference between themselves and the skilled workers, threatened by the insidious competition from women and by the rising cost of living. It was deepened by the almost perfunctory treatment of county courts by the royal commission, which endorsed the Treasury line:

> The variety of conditions in the County Courts is such that it would be difficult to organise the staff on Civil Service lines with uniform scales of pay. Moreover, any such organisation would involve the cessation of the Registrar's pecuniary responsibility, which would entail a very large increase in the cost of audit, and a centralised administration which would be both expensive and probably unsatisfactory in its working.[115]

The only comfort was in the recommendation for a contributory pension scheme.

Though more than 300 able-bodied clerks joined the forces, business shrank faster than staff in most courts.[116] It was estimated

[111] *Swift Evidence*, 46P. Bridgeman agreed: *MacDonnell Evidence*, q. 51,575.

[112] *Swift Evidence*, 29H–K. Walter was the author of a practice work and became President of the CCOA in 1921 but his health gave way under the strain and he died on the last day of 1924: *CCO* 5 (1924–5), 6.

[113] I Remember, 17, 27.

[114] Anderson, *Victorian Clerks*, p. 131.

[115] *MacDonnell Commission*, p. 45.

[116] The *County Courts Gazette* published a Roll of Honour. See also Schuster to Keane, 9 Dec. 1915, in *County Courts Gazette* 2 (1914–16), 160.

that 250 of 350 CCOA members in the smaller courts were on less than £2 a week in 1917.[117] Most registrars were not ungenerous – many made financial sacrifices themselves to keep their clerks in a job and at a living wage – but the economics of the system were exploded by the fall in fees.

Threats of strikes, questions in Parliament and finally a deputation to the Prime Minister were evidence of the growing crisis, and enabled the Lord Chancellor to wring consent to a departmental committee from the Treasury.[118]

## *After the Swift Report*

Swift was trenchant on the plight of the clerks: 'in some instances clerks of several years' experience are paid less than the wage at the present day of an unskilled manual labourer. Such men cannot afford to retire, and are kept on from motives of charity after they have passed an age when they can render efficient service.'[119]

Once the Treasury accepted the principle of establishment in the '6,000 plaint courts', their complement of clerks had to be fixed. A 'unit scheme' allocating points for each clerical operation according to the labour it generated, was adopted and proved so successful that with modifications it endured until the end of the independent county court service.[120] One advantage was that it sheltered the county courts from the cold blast of civil service retrenchment;[121] another was that it prevented any bad blood between courts competing for staff.

The number of whole-timers in 1920 was 532 registrars' clerks and 280 high bailiffs', and as the number of established courts grew – from 255 out of 559 courts in 1925 to 385 out of 412 courts in 1950 – so did the number of established clerks, to 1,360 by 1939.[122] So much of the work was mundane that a flatter structure

117 *Ibid.*, 182–3; 3 (1916–17), 47, 64.

118 *Ibid.*, *passim.* In 1917 the Arbitration Board (see Humphreys, *Clerical Unions*, pp. 83–9) decided that county court staff were outside its remit. The deputation, accompanied by Judge Parry, two MPs, a registrar and a high bailiff, was intended as the last action before a strike.

119 *Swift Report*, p. 15 and see app. F.

120 *Ibid.*, app. H; PRO LCO 2/527, 8/32, 352; *CCO* 36 (1959), 79 (F. C. Yeomans).

121 A Short History, *CCO* 28 (1951–2), at 12.

122 *Ibid.*, 11; PRO LCO 8/57; *PP* 1938–9 [Cmd 6135] XXV: *Civil Judicial Statistics*.

than the 'Treasury gradings' was devised, with no place for the lowly writing assistants.[123] That was partly because the courts had created their own class of clerk-typists, entirely female and numbering 190 in 1939. Birmingham had pioneered their use before the Great War, but 'a good deal of persuasion had to be used at the outset to convince registrars of the utility of this class'.[124]

Women were also entering the offices through open recruitment to the general classes and by the mid-1930s there were enough of them to have a significant impact on office life.[125] Entrants via the civil service examination, beginning in 1927, also raised the overall standard. The older clerks were

> in the main the type of clerk found in solicitors' offices, narrow in outlook and experience but most of them whole-hearted and trustworthy and soaked in the innumerable details of county court procedure. A number of them, however, would never have gained appointment under competitive conditions and being appointed for family reasons under the old patronage system have never pulled their weight.[126]

With the introduction of compulsory retirement at sixty-five the age profile of the service gradually became younger. The 1920 median in the mid-forties was little different in 1930, one reason being that the department promised to keep on beyond sixty-five men still fit for duty and who would suffer hardship if retired, a practice not abandoned until 1937.[127] Newer entrants, who did not recall the bad old days, were apt to grumble that other parts of the civil service offered better promotion prospects, a more favourable salary scale (young clerks fared least well when salaries were renegotiated in 1936) and more generous holiday provision.[128]

Older clerks resented changes in bookkeeping, more elaborate statistical returns and the greater uniformity imposed on forms,

123 Humphreys, *Clerical Unions*, pp. 118–22; *CCO* 35 (1958), 79; Schuster's evidence to the Tomlin Commission and interview with the CCOA, PRO LCO 8/68; Establishment 1939, PRO LCO 8/61.

124 *MacDonnell Evidence*, qq. 53,357–62, 53,376–85; Martin's evidence, PRO LCO 4/121.

125 See e.g. *CCO* 16 (1935–6), pt 11; 15 (1934–5), pt 11.

126 PRO LCO 4/121 (F. Martin).

127 *Swift Report*, app. F; PRO LCO 8/68; *CCO* 8 (1927–8), pt 4; 15 (1934–5), pt 5; 17 (1936–7), pt 4.

128 Short History, *CCO* 28 (1951–2), 27–9, 43–4, 162–3; *CCO* 16 (1935–6), pt 8; 35 (1958), 79–80.

which lost some of their luxuriant local variety.[129] But change was slow. Coming from the notoriously conservative solicitors' profession, few registrars were disposed to organisational innovation and headquarters did not press them. There was virtually no mechanisation and the routine acceptance of cheques and use of the telephone lagged well behind business organisations.[130]

Through the pages of their journal the clerks themselves become more visible. W. D. Bremner rose from clerk to registrar of Blackburn, though he had to leave and qualify as a solicitor first. Others achieved a wider fame: T. W. Magnay quit the courts and went on to become a Labour MP, while Percy Harper of Stourbridge won more ephemeral renown by refereeing a cup final.[131] And some still managed to clock up immensely long periods of service: T. Glass of Cardiff died in the sixty-third year of his and in 1938 William Barnett of West Hartlepool and J. W. Farnsworth of Sheffield both reached fifty years in the same court.[132]

The Second World War brought all the petty inconveniences of paper shortages, blackouts and postal disruption to the court offices, and for some clerks it meant the call up or transfer to other departments.[133] But overall the clerks had a rather better war than the outdoor staff and this time they got a war bonus without a battle.[134]

The unit system continued to be the basis for fixing court complements but it was unpopular with the Treasury and in 1964 matters came to a head when the CCOA sought a revision of the scheme to accommodate a reduction in working hours from forty-four to forty-three which the Treasury insisted should be covered by increased productivity. Kewish wrote in alarm, 'they are seeking as a matter of policy first to undermine and finally to destroy the unit system as we know it'.[135] Coldstream, however,

[129] Circular 15/1924, PRO LCO 8/88; *CCO* 5 (1924–5), pt 3; 6 (1925–6), pt 8 (CHM); PRO LCO 8/6.

[130] Circular 12/1927, PRO LCO 8/88; circular 6/1939, PRO LCO 8/6.

[131] *CCO* 1 (1920–1), pt 3; 12 (1931–2), pts 4, 8.

[132] *CCO* 18 (1937–8), pt 3; 19 (1938–9), pt 4; 20 (1939–40), pt 2.

[133] Circular 2/1940, PRO LCO 8/6; *CCO* 20 (1939–40), pt 6; 21 (1940–1), pt 5.

[134] H. R. Kahn, *Salaries in the Public Services in England and Wales* (London, 1962), pp. 29–30.

[135] Kewish to Coldstream, 23 Sep. 1964, PRO LCO 4/545. For background see PRO LCO 8/50.

replied firmly that 'to adhere to well-tried formulae for job measurement simply because they have been in existence since 1920 and have become accepted by management and workers alike, seems to me the best possible recipe for ensuring that this country does not keep pace with its competitors',[136] and was quite amenable to a proper O & M inspection.

The main outcome was the long overdue introduction into the county courts of a grade of clerical assistants, hitherto resisted by branch and union alike. Given the essentially routine nature of so much court work the introduction of this grade was long overdue and after an experiment at Birmingham the grade was made national in 1966.[137] The new grade was an overdue response to a persistent problem of recruitment and retention. A generation less obsessed with job security found the civil service unattractive in an era of full employment and the county courts felt the full force of the change.[138] Because of the lapse of recruiting in wartime the quality of senior clerks was poor and the proportion of capable and experienced COs insufficient.[139] The rapid turnover among new entrants made things worse: 35 per cent of male and 55 per cent of female entrants left in their first year in 1963 – many simply bored by the routine tasks; the diversion of these to CAs might alleviate the problem.[140] A bad side-effect of the high staff turnover was that it encouraged the branch to maintain its opposition to any sort of training for new recruits beyond traditional 'desk training', and this was not overcome until 1961.[141]

Recruitment problems increased with the size of the service: by 1967 it was almost 3,000, concentrated in fewer offices.[142] Growth was accompanied by a striking alteration in the balance between the sexes. In 1953, 287 out of 1,059 clerks and typists were women (including all 147 typists), but girls were outperforming boys in

136 5 Oct. 1964, PRO LCO 4/545.

137 PRO LCO 8/50, 51.

138 Royal Commission on the Civil Service (the *Priestley Report*), *PP* 1955 (Cmd 9613) XI, paras. 482–5; *CCO* 40 (1967–8), 204.

139 Axmann's evidence to the Pugh Working Party, 21 Jan. 1960, PRO LCO 2/7161.

140 Note of 19 July 1963, PRO LCO 8/50. The annual turnover among established COs was 13 per cent for men and 22 per cent for women: *CCO* 40 (1967–8), 204.

141 PRO LCO 2/7161, evidence of Axmann and T. A. Riches' memo of 12 Jan. 1960; *CCO* 40 (1967–8), 291; 41 (1969–70), 428.

142 *Civil Judicial Statistics*.

the entrance examination to an extent which concerned the branch and by 1967, though still heavily outnumbered in the higher grades, they were a big majority among the COs.[143] The days of the essentially masculine county court office were gone, except of course among the bailiffs.

Pay continued to be a problem as the 'fair comparison' recommended by the Priestley Commission proved elusive, but once county court scales had become fairly close to the general civil service – including the introduction of provincial differentiation – complaints were muted[144] until the late 1960s, when talk of industrial action became widespread.[145] Promotion was another source of discontent. Until the characteristic civil service apparatus of annual reports, promotions boards and grievance procedures was introduced in 1941 it was complained that the auditors had too much influence and were prone to judge a man by his bookkeeping.[146] Subsequently it was alleged that the registrar of the court concerned usually got his way. Axmann retorted that many promotion candidates were unduly restrictive in their choice of district (some to the extent of awaiting a vacancy in their own court), hence the local bias found by critics.[147] Alterations in 1966 were not to the satisfaction of everyone, but the balance between accelerating the progress of the able and rewarding the diligently capable was always difficult and the officers eventually saw the creation of a national court service as the way to create better opportunities.[148]

Though most courts were still very small, a few had grown quite large – staff numbers at Liverpool grew from 45 to 130 during one clerk's career.[149] This, and their increasing concentration on their judicial duties, made registrars more remote from the supervision of their staff and it was inevitable that the chief clerk would, in most cases, become the real head of the office. The

143 *CCO* 30 (1953), 59; 40 (1967–8), 40.

144 Humphreys, *Clerical Unions*, pp. 212–22; Kahn, *Salaries*, pp. 25–58; *CCO* 37 (1961–2), 1 (D. F. Martin).

145 *CCO* 40 (1967–8), *passim*.

146 *CCO* 38 (1963–4), 10 (E. Slack). See also report of sub-committee on promotions, *CCO* 19 (1938–9), pt 8.

147 *CCO* 26 (1947–9), 119–20; 34 (1957), 96 ('Disgusted').

148 *CCO* 40 (1967–8), 371, and *cf.* p. 128 (D. Clark).

149 *CCO* 39 (1965–6), 262–4, 294–6; 40 (1967–8), 128–9; evidence to Beeching, PRO LCO 7/152.

CCOA pressed for some of the registrar's administrative functions to be formally transferred to the chief clerk, and many registrars agreed,[150] but Coldstream maintained a stout and successful resistance for twenty years and only Beeching overbore his objections.[151]

In 1947 Martin confessed that 'the county courts are not abreast of modern social ideas and modern administrative methods'.[152] The increasing diversity and complexity of county court actions needed a better-educated clerk and greater efficiency, but change was slow.[153] Gradually ledger cards displaced the primacy of the ledger book, adding machines became commonplace and the telephone was better utilised; even ball-point pens were eventually authorised.[154] Pressure for efficiency came rather from the staff than from headquarters. Upset by criticism from court users[155] and anxious about the impact of increasing business on their workloads, they became impatient with the LCD[156] and noted that Sutton's O&M report, however superficial, singled out the ledger card system and other familiar routines for criticism.[157] One of several union conference resolutions 'affirmed its belief that the present accounting and recording system in the county courts is antiquated and wasteful of time, money and energy'.[158] By the mid-1960s the courts in some areas were under heavy pressure and the level of service was dropping well below acceptable levels,[159] a new Rent Act and county court divorces threatening the effective functioning of the system.

Automation was coming to the rescue. Xerox machines made their first appearance in 1966 and Sheffield's experiment with mechanical accounting and a record card system was rapidly

150 *CCO* 36 (1959), 69.
151 Evidence of CCOA and D. Freeman Coutts to Austin Jones Committee, PRO LCO 2/3299, 3300; sub-committee report, *CCO* 35 (1958–60), 11; evidence to Wheatcroft Committee, PRO LCO 2/5064.
152 PRO LCO 2/3314.
153 A. J. Cole to F. Mayell, 22 May 1951, PRO LCO 8/61.
154 PRO LCO 8/17; evidence of CCOA, PRO LCO 2/3299; *CCO* 26 (1947–9), 124; 29 (1950–2), 130.
155 E.g. *CCO* 35 (1958–60), 62; 37 (1961–2), 262.
156 *CCO* 37 (1961–2), 1 (D. F. Martin).
157 PRO LCO 8/50. The outcome of the inspection ordered in 1964.
158 *CCO* 37 (1961–2), 206.
159 See e.g. correspondence in the *Solicitors' Journal*, 1966–7.

applied generally, at last doing away with minute books.[160] The new methods did not always please staff or users: automatic payments out had not been adequately publicised and the creation of a central typing pool at Haywards Heath was claimed to create more delays than it prevented.[161] Nevetherless, the last few years of the independent county court structure saw the pace of change in office life accelerate far beyond anything experienced before.

Staff felt themselves under pressure and unfairly criticised for their inability to cope with inadequate staffing levels[162] and it is not surprising that there was disharmony within their ranks. One division was between clerks and bailiffs over pay,[163] another over the allocation of manpower between the big courts and the rest.[164] There was a generally carping mood among the staff. The CCOA failed to win consultation about the closure of small courts; the ceiling increase of eighty-two posts announced in 1970 was denounced as inadequate and the executive was exploring forms of industrial action as the clerical staff impatiently awaited their turn at the trough;[165] then at the end of 1970 it was announced that 'with almost indecent haste' Treasury gradings were at last to be introduced and a major work measurement exercise undertaken.[166]

## BAILIFFS

### *Before the Swift Report*

The bailiffs were originally under the supervision of a high bailiff. This post was an afterthought, an office created for financial expediency, for by creating a high bailiff for each court and empowering him to appoint his assistants, they would be his servants, not officers of the court, and so, if the courts were a failure, not entitled to compensation.[167]

160 *CCO* 39 (1965–6), 380–1; 40 (1967–8), 244–5, 381; 41 (1969–70), 213, 238.

161 *CCO* 41 (1969–70), 348; *SJ* 114 (1970), 575.

162 It was widely agreed that staffing levels were too low: e.g. *MLR* 34 (1971), 61–70 (C. Glasser).

163 *CCO* 41 (1969–70), 207–8 and correspondence, e.g. at 233.

164 *Ibid.*, 209–10, 234.

165 *Ibid.*, 229, 269, 319–20, 395.

166 *Ibid.*, 367.

167 Evidence to the Judicature Commission, *Second Report*, q. 2615.

No qualifications were laid down for the office of high bailiff and, as with the registrars, a judge might either appoint one man to cover several courts[168] or several high bailiffs to the same court, presumably to secure the services of one in the courtroom without delaying the service of process and warrants. As a result, the national picture in 1850 shows great diversity.[169] In the south-west, for example, there were nine high bailiffs (including joint high bailiffs for one court) on circuit 59, while E. C. Coles of Taunton acted as high bailiff for all thirteen courts in district 57.

Diversity also marked the high bailiffs' occupations.[170] Many claimed to be full-time in the job, but in the smaller provincial courts the fees would scarcely have provided a living; hence in district 52 there was a builder, a clerk to the guardians, a baker, a writing clerk, a farmer and a coal and corn dealer. The number and quality of the men employed as under bailiffs, process servers, etc. was equally varied. Thus one of the high bailiffs in district 19 had as part-time assistants an assistant overseer of the poor, two tailors, a framework knitter, a labourer, an inspector of weights and measures and a schoolmaster – the range of social class presumably reflecting the different purposes for which they were employed. Generally the high bailiff employed full-timers only where he needed to and hired others as business required. At the bottom of the scale were 'possession men' hired by the day and not regarded as officers of the court.

The questionable honesty and efficiency of their bailiffs had been one of the most serious complaints against the courts of requests,[171] and the channelling of all county court process through its officers tied the success of the new courts closely to the efficiency of the bailiffs. Theirs was no easy task, for the pitfalls posed by a complicated and uncertain law surrounding executions were considerable,[172] and where high bailiffs were poorly rewarded they could not afford to pay their assistants enough to

168 County Courts Act 1846 s. 31.

169 *PP* 1850 (743) XLVI.

170 *Ibid. PP* 1861 (398) (LI) also gives the names, occupations and incomes of high bailiffs.

171 *LM* ns 5 (1846), 225, quoting the Commissioners' Report on Local Courts.

172 A writer in *LM* ns 12 (1850), 69 at 74 argued that because of their lack of legal qualifications the high bailiffs made many blunders in the first few years.

insure against the everyday temptation to try a little extortion on the side.[173]

Even the bigger, more efficient courts were not immune. In the early 1850s investigations were ordered into, *inter alia*, Dover, Bridgend, Newton Abbot, Hereford and Bristol, most resulting in dismissals or suspensions.[174] In addition there were persistent problems in getting bailiffs to handle summonses from other courts, for which they received no fees, and there were soon complaints about the slowness and indifference of bailiffs in serving process;[175] in Liverpool, one frustrated solicitor was driven to attempt bribery to get his business dealt with expeditiously.[176]

In 1866, over the protests of the judges, high bailiffs were prospectively abolished except where the Lord Chancellor, with Treasury concurrence, decided that the volume of business merited filling a vacancy.[177] Elsewhere his functions would be assumed by the registrar, though existing registrars could not be compelled to take on this role and some refused, claiming the remuneration was insufficient.[178] Responses to the Judicature Commissioners showed that most judges still hankered after a high bailiff but registrars presented more mixed views. Several emphasised that one was essential in busy courts[179] but it was claimed that in the more rural locations the high bailiff was 'an overpaid sinecure'.[180]

The number of high bailiffs dwindled steadily, to fifty-one in 1914 and thirty-six in 1920.[181] Some clung tenaciously to office; the high bailiff of Pontypridd, one of the first appointees, held out until 1892 and Charles Godfrey, in charge of six small Essex courts, did not retire until 1921, at the age of ninety-five.[182] Their

173 *Ibid.*, 76. The Home Secretary acknowledged as much: *Hansard* 1850 3rd s., vol. 109, cols. 816–17.

174 See e.g. PRO LCO 8/2 ff. 167, 269; 8/10, *passim*; PRO HO 86/2, f. 480.

175 New rules in 1851, the General Instructions of 1857 and a circular of 1864 all attempted to improve things: PRO LCO 8/2, ff. 107, 269, 311, 523.

176 *LT* 36 (1860–1), 383.

177 County Courts Act 1866 s. 11; *Second Report*, Nicol at q. 2619.

178 S. 12. *Second Report*, replies of T. Walker and G. L. Watson to q. 22.

179 *Second Report*, replies to q. 22.

180 J. J. Reynolds of Hereford. Cf. T. Meyler of Taunton.

181 *Childers Report,* Nicol at qq. 1767–79; *MacDonnell Commission*, p. 41; *Swift Report*, p. 11.

182 V. H. Thomas, *Swift Evidence*, 36A; *CCO* 3 (1922–3), pt 7.

disappearance eliminated one of the few promotion prospects open to clerks. Many high bailiffs had come up through the ranks; Edwin Ramsden, who had begun his working life in a factory aged nine and joined the Huddersfield county court as an office boy, and Walter Davey, high bailiff at Birmingham as the terminus of a sixty-seven year career in the courts, are instances.[183]

In the big courts it was a lucrative position. W. Young Hucks forsook his post as an examiner of county court accounts, having estimated that the high bailiff of Clerkenwell would clear £1,000 a year, though that was probably at the top end of the range.[184] In addition to their salary, high bailiffs got to keep certain other fees, most importantly those charged on taking possession of goods, which could be substantial: Young Hucks made £350 a year and the Pontypridd high bailiff nearly double that.[185]

Only the better-paid high bailiffs employed full-time clerks and their staffs varied widely. While Coombs of Oundle and Thrapston had a single full-time bailiff at one and a part-timer at the other, the biggest, Birmingham, had seven clerks and twenty-one bailiffs, divided between process servers and warrant officers.[186] In 1914 high bailiffs employed about 1,600 staff of all kinds.[187]

The importance of getting the right sort of bailiffs was always acknowledged by officialdom[188] and was underlined by the occasional scandals which surfaced. In the 1880s Judge Motteram at Birmingham had to investigate 'a grave and old-standing and oft-repeated scandal' involving charges against the chief bailiff, two of his underlings and a possession man. The abuses were of the commonest – extortion under the colour of 'expenses' and 'the habit of working for that side – the plaintiff's or defendant's – which paid best' – and the most difficult to eradicate.[189]

183 *County Courts Gazette* 2 (1915–16), 156; *MacDonnell Evidence*, qq. 53,638–9, 53,679.

184 *Swift Evidence*, 41E; *Swift Report*, app. E. Some earlier salaries are shown in *PP* 1883 (191) LV.

185 The high bailiff of Birmingham alone had a fixed salary: *Swift Evidence*, 36J, 40H. According to John Keane for the CCOA, possession fees were often not shared among his staff as they should have been: *ibid.*, 20K–L.

186 *Swift Evidence*, 36C, 40J; *MacDonnell Evidence*, q. 53,659. There are some earlier figures in *PP* 1883 (191) LV.

187 *MacDonnell Commission*, p. 41; *Swift Report*, app. F.

188 E.g. *Select Committee, 1878*, Nicol at q. 5190.

189 *LT* 75 (1883), 317–18. Motteram also referred to the possibility of further

Fifteen years later the *Daily Mail* investigated complaints against bailiffs in London, producing convincing testimony from solicitors and agents; 'if the bailiff is not "tipped" ', said one firm, 'there always appears to be some difficulty in the way of some, at least, of the summonses intrusted to him to serve'. By 'the judicious use of half-sovereigns' it was said that service could readily be evaded for months.[190] In the 1870s Nicol had admitted that 'the weak part of the county court system is the bailiff department'[191] but it was not an aspect later inquiries addressed.

Part of the problem lay in the low earnings bailiffs could expect for a job few would covet. The Treasury set an allowance for the largest courts which gave process servers 25s to 35s a week, a rate Davey said was scarcely a living wage; warrant officers did slightly better (35s to 45s) and the average earnings in these courts in 1914 was estimated at £80 a year.[192] In the smaller courts it was in the high bailiff's discretion.

These were not wages to attract good recruits. At risk of assaults[193] and with only the slenderest chance of promotion even to a clerkship (the clerks were hostile to this as threatening their 'respectable' status[194]), it is no wonder they sometimes succumbed to temptation. Yet higher wages would have meant higher fees, making the courts uneconomic for small claims.

One answer which appealed to the Treasury on several grounds

charges arising out of an interpleader action soon to be before the court and which had been the subject of allegations in the local press. The sections of the 1846 Act (116–17) empowering a judge to hold an inquiry and punish bailiffs did not extend to one of the accused who was only a possession man. For an investigation of less serious charges at Wandsworth see *Diedrich v. Rutland*, *LJ* 14 (1879), 113.

190 Quoted in *LT* 106 (1898–9), 39. Charges of corruption in London were not new, see e.g. *CCC* 31 (1888), 435.

191 *Second Report*, q. 2680. The judges' power to supervise the high bailiff was weakened by the decision in *Moore v. High Bailiff of Brompton CC* (*CCC* 34 (1893–4), 156), in which the divisional court held that misconduct within the terms of the County Courts Act did not extend to negligence.

192 *Hansard* 1913 5th s., vol. 55 (HC), col. 2042; *MacDonnell Evidence*, qq. 53660–5, 53708. A common wage was said to be 47s 6d, with many getting as little as 39s 9d: *CCO* 28 (1951), 44.

193 Nicol emphasised that assaults were frequent, (*Second Report*, q. 2425), and the departmental committee on staff in 1899 was shown an assortment of weapons used in assaulting process servers: Liddell, *Ordinary Mortal*, p. 318.

194 *MacDonnell Evidence*, qq. 52,146–8 (F. G. Hemans). According to 'Toothache' in *County Courts Gazette* 3 (1916–17), 36–7, registrars' clerks tried to maintain a superiority even over high bailiffs' clerks.

was to recruit retired policemen and servicemen who were already pensioned. Davey often found among ex-policemen the 'good, sharp, shrewd men who know their way about'[195] he needed as warrant officers, though Young Hucks felt that 'if you get a man who has only been a constable, his intelligence is not high'.[196] Thomas was unusual in preferring to recruit young men[197] for in 1920 only 21 out of 455 in the bigger courts were under thirty and 100 were over sixty; it is not surprising that the bailiffs sometimes lacked vigour.[198] At least however, there was a gradual rise in literacy among them.[199]

Like the clerks, the bailiffs were growing more and more discontented with their lot and though very much junior partners in the association, they were the only part of the court service actually to stage a strike, in Aberdare in 1917, and clearly could not be left out if the court staff became civil servants.[200] The high bailiffs also had their grievances, but their exigent demand that the state should bear the whole loss they had sustained through the war annoyed the Swift Committee and contributed to their own demise.[201] No more separate high bailiffs were to be appointed and one by one they faded into history.[202]

## *After the Swift Report*

It was more difficult to assimilate bailiffs into the civil service than clerks, none of the 'comparables' (Inland Revenue process servers, postmen, etc.) being really apposite.[203] The pay settlement – 33s a week rising slowly to 43s – was distinctly ungenerous[204] and the

195 *MacDonnell Evidence*, q. 53,696.

196 *Swift Evidence*, 41K.

197 *Ibid.*, 36B.

198 *Swift Report*, app. F. Even allowing for wartime distortions, it is hard to match these figures with the assertion in the 'Short History' that those recruited were mostly young men. Barker, Now When I Was a Young Man, said the recruitment of bailiffs 'left much to be desired'.

199 *MacDonnell Evidence*, Hemans at q. 52,147.

200 *County Courts Gazette* 1 (1913–14), 20; *Swift Evidence*, Thomas at 35L. Early complaints were noticed by Nicol in evidence to the *Select Committee, 1878*, q. 5188.

201 *Swift Report*, pp. 11–12; *Swift Evidence*, 35–41.

202 Five remained in 1938 and the County Courts Act 1934 had to include sections dealing with them. The last, at Bristol, retired in 1958.

203 PRO LCO 8/63, 8/57, 8/59; the union perspective is in the *CCO*.

204 PRO LCO 8/63: the scheme was dated 12 May 1923 but was not formally sanctioned until 21 Aug. 1924.

LCO supported an improvement, stressing that low pay was seen as a factor in most of the recent cases of bailiffs who had 'gone wrong' and that 'in many cases we have failed to secure a conviction apparently largely on this ground'.[205] Things slowly improved, with further rises in 1929 and in 1937, the latter after arbitration,[206] when the separate grades of process server and warrant officer were prospectively abolished.[207] Part-timers were still used but their numbers declined; in 1938 966 out of 1,193 bailiffs were full-time and with walking possession to be used 'to the utmost extent',[208] possession men also dwindled. Recruitment was still overwhelmingly from the ranks of the police, army and navy and a stereotype of the bailiff emerged: a stout middle-aged man, bowler-hatted, dark-suited and heavy-booted.[209]

This outward respectability seems to have been matched by a growing trustworthiness. In the 1920s circulars and instructions show a clear concern to stamp out doubtful practices and provide against them. Bailiffs were required to change districts frequently and at irregular intervals;[210] they were strictly enjoined from accepting payments of instalments and required to keep fuller records of service and hours.[211] There is less indication of concern in the 1930s. Assaults on bailiffs, which were vigorously prosecuted, seem to have been rarer too – indeed the bailiff was probably more seriously at risk from road accidents than irate debtors.[212]

The Second World War affected the outdoor staff more than the clerks. More than a hundred of the younger men went into the forces but the falling off in business led to eighty-seven being laid

205 Martin to J. Rae, 6 Aug. 1926, PRO LCO 8/67.

206 *CCO* 17 (1936–7). In 1929 the bailiffs also became entitled to protective clothing, circular 15a/1929, PRO LCO 8/88.

207 Arbitration decision, 27 July 1937, *CCO* 17 (1936–7), pt. 12.

208 This had been policy for some years: Martin to H. Parker, 1 July 1929, PRO LCO 8/67. Civil Judicial Statistics, *PP* 1938–9 [Cmd 6135] XXV, table XXI; circular 6/1929, PRO LCO 8/88. The oldest part-timer, H. Metcalfe of Beverley, retired at eighty-five in 1939.

209 PRO LCO 8/63; Short History, 44.

210 Circulars 2/1927, 15/1924, 8a/1929, PRO LCO 8/6 and 88 (the pieces overlap). The branch rejected criticism of this requirement (*CCO* 13 (1932–3), no. 5), which was also attacked by the registrars: ACCR Minutes, 4 Feb. 1927.

211 E.g. circulars 12/1925, 3a/1926, 2/1927, 8/1932.

212 Assaults were regularly reported in the *CCO* as providing support for pay claims, e.g. 16 (1935–6), pt. 3. For road accidents see *CCO* 19 (1938–9), pt 11 and PRO T 164/151/33.

off in 1942;[213] it would have been more, because postal service was introduced and courts heavily discouraged from sending men on unnecessary journeys, but the logistics of the rural circuits made it hard to economise on manpower.[214] By 1944 'there [was] a fed up feeling throughout the ranks of the outdoor staff'[215] and morale sank further with the failure of an inopportune pay claim and defeat at arbitration over car allowances.[216] It was not helped by an upsurge in possession cases in 1945, hated by bailiffs because of the lack of opportunity for judicious discretion and the potential for disturbance and violence.[217]

The Austin Jones Committee received conflicting testimony on the bailiffs. Martin called them 'an exceedingly fine body of men [who] do their work extraordinarily well'[218] and said he had a long waiting list.[219] Northern registrars on the other hand felt that many of the bailiffs were too old and passive and not always numerous enough.[220] The bailiffs naturally asserted that low pay militated against successful recruiting, but their biggest and abiding grievance was the Department's meanness in providing transport.[221] Bailiffs saw postmen and others cruising in vans while they struggled on foot or on bicycle and had no vehicles on call to transport men to prison or remove furniture.[222] Even for the few with vehicles the petrol allowance was kept low because, for all their virtues, 'this type of man, if you give him enough petrol, will never walk an inch'.[223]

Bailiff numbers quickly regained pre-war levels: the complement in 1955 was 690 but by 1968 there were 1,735, the great majority whole-time established civil servants. Many courts in the 1950s still had only one or two bailiffs and none more than fifteen;[224] even the

213 *CCO* 20 (1939–40), pt 11; 22 (1941–2), pt 7; departmental Whitley Council minute, *CCO* 23 (1943–5), pt 8.

214 See PRO LCO 8/6 *passim*, especially circular 2/1944, and *CCO* 23 (1943–5).

215 *CCO* 23 (1943–5), 32–3.

216 *Ibid*., 125 and pp. 209–10 above.

217 *CCO* 26 (1947–9), 49; Chief Clerk at Bow to J. A. Pugh, 20 Jan. 1948, PRO LCO 2/3302.

218 PRO LCO 2/3299. Cf. his earlier note on staff in PRO LCO 4/121.

219 PRO LCO 2/3299.

220 R. Cohen, W. R. Davies, D. Freeman Coutts, PRO LCO 2/3300.

221 PRO LCO 2/3299, 3300.

222 *CCO* 28 (1951–2), Whitley Council, 28 Sep. 1951; evidence to Wheatcroft Committee, *CCO* 33 (1956), 33–4.

223 Martin, PRO LCO 2/3299.

224 *Civil Judicial Statistics*; Wheatcroft papers, PRO LCO 2/5064.

union felt the formula reasonably generous; its replacement with a unit system was pronounced 'quite impossible'.[225]

Despite the contrary assertion of the Evershed Committee,[226] the LCD maintained that there was never a problem in recruiting or retaining bailiffs, invariably taken (usually on the recommendation of registrars) from the same sources as before.[227] On the scanty evidence available the turnover was well below that for the clerks, suggesting that the bailiff service was not entirely unattractive.[228]

Setting pay levels for the bailiffs was always difficult because of the lack of any analogues acceptable to both sides,[229] but technical difficulties were only partly responsible for the sometimes very dilatory progress of negotiations. The long delay in the 1965 pay round strained labour relations for several years[230] but on the whole the union was satisfied with the outcomes, though they failed to secure a change in title to 'warrant officer', a question in which Gardiner was said to have taken a personal interest.[231]

The bailiffs' lot was improved in some respects other than pay. They had complained about the non-existent promotion prospects, and following the recommendations of the Wheatcroft Committee, a new grade of supervisory bailiff was created in 1958,[232] with a further sub-grade in 1969.[233] And at last most bailiffs were motorised. They continued to complain of meanness over travel expenses[234] and the coveted vans were not forthcoming, but whereas in 1955 only 206 out of 694 had cars and 62 motorcycles, in 1962 1,118 were motorised out of 1,362.[235]

225 Report of inquiry, 20 Mar. 1963, PRO LCO 8/37. *CCO* 36 (1959–60), 246; 37 (1961–2), 7, 62; 38 (1963–4), 54.

226 *PP* 1952–3 [Cmd 8878] XIV, para. 384a, quoted in the CCOA submission to arbitration (*CCO* 32 (1955), 45–59) but rejected by the LCD: *CCO* 31 (1954), 9.

227 Axmann's evidence, PRO LCO 2/5063.

228 *Ibid*. This shows a turnover of *c*. 100 p. a. out of 700; most stayed for ten or eleven years and one or two a year were dismissed for financial irregularities.

229 The Pay Research Unit report (86 of 1963) confessed that the bailiffs posed an intractable problem: Lucas to Kewish, 9 Oct. 1963, PRO LCO 8/54.

230 PRO LCO 8/51, 54, 55.

231 *CCO* 41 (1969–70), 186.

232 Circular 5a/1958, PRO LCO 8/89.

233 *CCO* 41 (1969–70), 57. Training for supervisory and senior bailiffs had been introduced in 1964: *CCO* 38 (1963–4), 131.

234 PRO LCO 2/6064.

235 Evidence to Wheatcroft, PRO LCO 2/5063; *CCO* 37 (1961–2), 162–7.

However, they did not succeed in their campaign for a five-day week. In 1963 Saturday working occupied 8 per cent of their time with a further 2 per cent done before normal office hours and 17 per cent after,[236] though bailiffs probably exaggerated the number of times they rose at dawn or lingered till dark to ambush a wary debtor.[237] They still had to change districts every few months, a 'commonsense security measure'[238] which the Department would not waive and which one bailiff admitted was justified not so much because of the likelihood of corruption as the more insidious temptation to leniency.[239]

The bailiffs' work underwent changes after the war. Postal service reduced the time spent serving summonses, offset only in part by the rise in households with working wives.[240] In 1954 55 per cent of their work was summonses, 11 per cent judgment summonses and 32 per cent warrants of execution and committal; corresponding figures for 1963 are 37 per cent, 17 per cent and 45 per cent.[241] Most of the work was still 'routine and uneventful',[242] but in 1963 the bailiff was 'more than ever a debt collector rather than a Court officer'[243] and a further move in that direction was recommended: ending the use of bailiffs as ushers.[244] Apart from the peculiar case of Tom Lowe, coachman to Judge Caillard, who made him his usher and more or less bequeathed him to his successors,[245] only the biggest courts had ever had full-time ushers – there were just twenty-one in 1928 and forty-two in 1964 – and both indoor and outdoor staff had hitherto performed the role.[246]

It was their work as warrant officers which preoccupied the bailiffs interviewed by Paul Rock in the mid-1960s and he found them 'continually preoccupied with the dangers facing them ... aware that they may confront a violence which they feel singularly

236 *CCO* 39 (1965–6), 166; PRO LCO 8/54.

237 Cf. the differing emphasis of the submissions to the 1955 arbitration on this point: *CCO* 32 (1955), 45–59 and Loveday's account in *CCO* 40 (1967–8), 222.

238 *CCO* 29 (1952), 130; CCOA evidence, 7th meeting, PRO LCO 2/5063.

239 A. Duncan, The County Court Bailiff, *CCO* 40 (1967–8), 222–3 (the bailiff was Wilfred Loveday of Edmonton).

240 PRO LCO 2/5063 (Axmann).

241 *CCO* 37 (1961–2), 162–7.

242 P. Rock, *Making People Pay* (London, 1973), p. 197.

243 Report of branch investigation, 20 Mar. 1963, PRO LCO 8/37.

244 *Ibid.*, p. 9.

245 *CCO* 31 (1954), 107.

246 *CCO* 9 (1928–9), pt 3; 38 (1963–4), 191.

ill-prepared for'.[247] There are no figures to chart a rise in actual or threatened violence against bailiffs but in 1961 the branch received fifty reports of actual assaults,[248] some very serious. In 1960 William Walker was shot by a deranged tenant and others were attacked with spears, iron bars, etc.,[249] though ironically the worst incident was a shooting of clerical staff in the Liverpool courtroom.[250]

Evictions continued to be the most hated part of the job and a celebrated affair in St Pancras in which bailiffs of four London courts were met with bricks, poles and filthy oil was a forerunner of the battles with squatters which were to break out in the late 1960s.[251] At least in the St Pancras case the bailiffs had the active assistance of the police, but that was unusual.[252] The permissible limits of police assistance were unclear and a bid to clarify them was dropped as likely 'to result in a loss of elasticity and indeed that new doubts might be created as to the duty of the police'.[253]

When they were obstructed or assaulted bailiffs found that their own judges were usually willing to defend them vigorously but had powers that were too weak to be satisfactory, while magistrates were often unsympathetic.[254] They also faced a legal setback in *Vaughan v. McKenzie*, where the Court of Appeal[255] ruled that a bailiff had no authority to effect an entry against the expressed opposition of the householder. The LCD's proposal to change the law ran into such opposition from within the govern-

[247] Rock, *Making People Pay*, p. 198.

[248] *CCO* 38 (1963–4), 3. Naturally, it continued to receive emphasis in pay claims; the 1962 submission refers to the new dangers posed by 'teddy boys' and 'neurotic women': PRO LCO 8/54.

[249] Walker, whose assailant shot himself dead, was decorated for gallantry and lost an eye. Bailiff Heeks of Newcastle under Lyme became the first bailiff to be awarded compensation (£150) by the Criminal Injuries Compensation Board: *CCO* 40 (1967–8), 11.

[250] The victims were an official of the bankruptcy court and an official receiver; both recovered and, along with the two men who disarmed the gunman, received the British Empire Medal. There is a full account in PRO LCO 2/ 7066.

[251] *CCO* 35 (1958–60), 245.

[252] Rock, *Making People Pay*, pp. 202–5.

[253] *Ibid.*, p. 203, quoting a departmental letter to the CCOA.

[254] *Ibid.*, pp. 204–5. Serious cases could be taken to the divisional court, as in *James* (*CCO* 37 (1961–2), 137), but it was a slow and cumbersome course.

[255] [1969] 1 QB 557.

ment that it was withdrawn;[256] small wonder the bailiffs were aggrieved.

Actual violence was seen by many bailiffs as the most alarming symptom of a worrying social change, namely that 'people have no respect any more'.[257] The decline in deference to authority, leading to 'a growing tendency among the public to oppose an official', hit them hard, and was sometimes abetted by those who should have known better.[258] The growing publicity surrounding committals was also uncomfortable to those who did the dirty work of getting the debtors to prison.[259]

Since so much of the bailiff's work was unpleasant, it is perhaps surprising that the turnover was not higher. There must have been satisfactions and some of these probably derived from the distinctive sub-culture the bailiffs inhabited. Rock found that there were marked differences from court to court in how bailiffs were expected to meet their quotas, decidedly affecting their approach and the extent to which they could safely indulge in actions of doubtful (and more than doubtful) legality.[260] But wherever there were enough bailiffs to form a separate group it shared a common set of attitudes. Bailiffs pooled information about debtors, concerted strategies to take account of the particular views of their superiors, connived at each other's deceptions and stratagems. They also developed a camaraderie acquired in the police station or the barrack room.[261]

Above all, they cherished the relative autonomy they enjoyed in serving process or executing warrants, the entirely unofficial discretion with which Martin had astounded some members of the Austin Jones Committee.[262] Few registrars or chief clerks were really interested in keeping track of the progress of warrants provided that the bailiffs achieved their annual quota; indeed the bailiffs could be quite a formidable proposition, sleeping dogs better let lie. In Wheatcroft's view the ineffective supervision over

256 Dobson to Sir R. W. Payne, 8 Oct. 1968, PRO LCO 31/1. For the explanation given to the CCOA see F. Humphries, Assaults on Bailiffs, *CCO* 41 (1969–70), 12–13.

257 Duncan, County Court Bailiff.

258 *Ibid.* For an irresponsible article in the *Radio Times* see *CCO* 40 (1967–8), 360–1.

259 Rock, *Making People Pay*, pp. 210–18.

260 *Ibid.*, pp. 209–10.

261 Well evoked by Stan Hagan, *CCO* 40 (1967–8), 266.

262 PRO LCO 2/3299. See also the bailiffs' evidence in 2/3300.

executions was one of the biggest weaknesses;[263] for the bailiffs it made the job worthwhile.

## COURTHOUSES AND OFFICES

Since courts would be held only once a month in most places, no extensive building programme was envisaged. Treasurers were authorised to negotiate for the use of premises as courtrooms and offices and where nothing suitable was to be had they might, with the approval of the Secretary of State, have a courthouse built, the cost falling ultimately on the suitors using that particular court by way of a 'General Fund' levy on top of the normal fees. The arrangements for repairing and furnishing, cleaning, lighting and heating, supplying stationery and other necessaries were to be made by the registrars.[264]

It was evident however that new premises would be needed in London, where courts would be in permanent session and suitable accommodation hard to come by, and of eighteen early courthouses ten were in London and two more nearby.[265] Charles Reeves, the Police Surveyor, was appointed Surveyor of County Courts[266] and economy was the keynote: there would be no judges' lodgings, nor a convenient lock-up attached to the court;[267] outlays which were 'irregularly incurred and very extravagant' would be disallowed and before long a uniform set of furnishings was prescribed.[268] Offices were easier to hire even where the registrar could not simply use a room in his own premises, and treasurers rarely had to offer more than £10 or £20 a year.[269]

Changes were soon made in the light of experience. From 1850 boroughs were obliged to allow free use of the town hall,[270] and

263 The Committee noted that the tightening up required by circular 13/1949 had been ineffective: PRO LCO 2/5063, 5064.

264 County Courts Act 1846 ss. 58, 61–2, 65; *LR* 14 (1851), 130.

265 *PP* 1854–5 (350) XLIII. The others were Leeds, Dewsbury, Royston, Downham Market, Sheerness and Southampton.

266 PRO HO 86/1, f. 293 (10 July 1847).

267 J. M. Phillips to J. Trevor, 23 Mar. 1847, *Ibid.*, f. 256; H. Waddington to Reeves, 1 Dec. 1850, 86/2, f. 205.

268 Waddington to Mangles, 25 May, 3 June 1848, PRO HO 86/1 ff. 429, 431.

269 *PP* 1859 (3 sess. 2) XIX.

270 Waddington to G. Hayter, 20 Apr. 1850, PRO HO 86/2, f. 114; *HCJ* 82 (1850), 290, 307, 311; County Courts Act 1850 s. 24.

though some were unappealing, like Tonbridge, 'a huge ungainly building ... a tumbledown heterogeneous mass of stones and mortar',[271] this facility did help to reduce costs in an era of jealous parliamentary scrutiny.[272] Moreover in 1856 the government reluctantly assumed financial responsibility for the erection of new courts, though in reality this only transferred the burden from local litigants to litigants at large via court fees.[273]

Though there were justifiable grumbles about the courtrooms in small towns,[274] lawyers and judges had learned to be stoical at Westminster Hall and on assize and the most serious complaints were about the congestion in the busiest courts. Manchester was housed in a Georgian mansion in Quay Street and the growth of bankruptcy business forced hearings into the attic and the cellar, leading in 1873 to a petition from fifty-three firms.[275] Liverpool coped by utilising the old bankruptcy court, which left litigants and lawyers uncertain where they were to go.[276] But some Victorian cities made their courts an expression of civic pride. The new office suite Leeds provided to cope with the bankruptcy business was 'fitted up with exquisite taste and so contrived in its arrangements to afford every facility in expediting business'[277] and the *Wakefield Express* upbraided the corporation for failing to provide facilities equal to those in Dewsbury and Barnsley.[278]

London courts naturally attracted more attention.[279] By 1900 all the metropolitan courts bar Clerkenwell were claimed to need replacing,[280] but even where a new court was built it was not always satisfactory; the new flagship court of Westminster, for instance, was erected on the same cramped site in St Martin's Lane and was never spacious enough.[281]

In 1870 responsibility for buildings was ceded by the Home Office to the Office of Works, subject to the approval of the

271 *LJ* 3 (1868), 66.

272 See e.g. the questions in *Hansard* 1860 3rd s. vol. 160, cols. 1338–9 and 1863 3rd s., vol. 172, col. 1276.

273 County Courts Act 1856 s. 85, recommended by the *Romilly Report*, p. 42.

274 Wrexham town hall was so bad that Judge Lloyd paid out of his own pocket to use the Corn Exchange instead: *LJ* 12 (1877), 527.

275 Parry, *My Own Way*, p. 197; *SJ* 17 (1872–3), 923; *CCC* 21 (1869–70), 369; *LT* 55 (1873), 145.

276 *LJ* 6 (1871), 351.

277 *LJ* 5 (1870), 26.

278 *LJ* 12 (1877), 123.

279 See p. 98 above.

280 *LT* 120 (1905–6), 99.

281 *CCC* 40 (1905–6), 543. The court building is now Brown's Restaurant.

Treasury but omitting any reference to the Lord Chancellor,[282] a peculiar position which seems to have gone largely unremarked for many years.[283] The Office of Works also took over responsibility for supervising expenditure incurred by the registrars in running the courts and offices and caused friction, registrars resenting the close scrutiny of gas and water contracts and the Treasury's attempts to deprive them of their freedom to buy stationery from a supplier of their own choosing.[284] By and large, the Office of Works had little concern for the working conditions and the accommodation provided by some registrars was a disgrace; in one dark, musty building which had not been redecorated in many years the clerks had to improvise furniture out of old stationery boxes[285] and this was no isolated case.

Between the wars office conditions probably improved somewhat but many courtrooms were still unpleasant and unsuitable. Judge Crawford berated the 'parsimony and lack of vision of the Treasury and the Board of Works', and though his caustic comments persuaded Southend to provide a new building, at Edmonton he only got a decent chair when the old one collapsed beneath him.[286] The Board admitted that there was a serious backlog of rebuilding and replacement to do in such places as Warrington, a former Nonconformist chapel, 'foul smelling and pestilential', and Lambeth,[287] but these needs had to be balanced against the provision of entirely new courts for the outer London suburbs, in places such as Willesden, Ilford and Epsom. It was a marked improvement when the LCO secured a five-year programme from the Treasury, though it was immediately frozen because of the slump and had hardly got going properly again when stopped in its tracks by the war.[288]

Wartime brought court closures and bomb damage. The offices

282 County Courts Act 1870 s. 15.

283 The wording was altered in the 1934 Act (s. 34) by the inclusion of 'on the representation of the Lord Chancellor'.

284 *Lisgar Evidence* qq. 7537–9 (Nicol); Public Accounts Committee proceedings, *PP* 1874 (242) VI, pp. 70–97; *PP* 1903 (74) V, qq. 2873–89.

285 *CCO* 2 (1921–2), pt 2; the author may have been A. C. Barker.

286 *Reflections and Recollections*, pp. 172–7.

287 *Ibid.*, p. 174; *PP* 1928–9 (45, 113) IV, 662–71.

288 *PP* 1931–2 (42, 93) IV, 1974–6; 1933–4 (36, 97, 98) V, 24, 31; 1934–5 (93, 99) V, 1283. The programme was said to have produced fourteen new and 200 improved courts: *CCO* 26 (1947–9), 145.

at Coventry were an early casualty, followed by Cardiff, Portsmouth, Plymouth and Liverpool.[289] Surprisingly, Martin presented a cheerful picture to the Austin Jones Committee, pronouncing most of the offices acceptable; the courts were less good, but only Tredegar was truly awful.[290]

Not everyone was quite so satisfied. Judges grumbled at the disgraceful state of some country courts: Oakham offered nowhere to robe and in Chesham 'the place had been used for a whist drive the previous night, and it was full of cigarette ends and glasses, and I had to go and clear my room up, while my usher and the registrar meanwhile cleared the courtroom out, before the public could be admitted'.[291] Where bombing had necessitated makeshifts they were probably more forbearing, Armstrong resignedly dispensing justice between a piano and a beer barrel in the masonic hall at Plymouth instead of the luxurious guildhall.[292]

Coldstream spoke wistfully of the excellences of the pre-war programme which had produced courts like Lambeth, boasting an imposing facade and a marble hall,[293] though Epsom was probably more typical, 'a good modern example of the adaptation of the Georgian style to civic requirements'.[294] When the building programme resumed in the 1950s it was limited by Treasury control of budgets and could not respond quickly to the needs of places where business grew rapidly.[295] Nor did the new courts' design and facilities meet the standards demanded by users. Though denied advance consultation, the Bar Council and Law Society's complaints about Bow (1958) and Brentford (1963)[296] did bear some fruit; in particular, the GPO's refusal to provide public telephones inside new courts was overcome.[297] The other main complaint, the shortage of rooms for consultations, was

289 *CCO* 1939–45, *passim*.

290 27 Jan. 1948, PRO LCO 2/3299. He admitted that judges disliked having to use police courts.

291 *Ibid*., Judges Langman and Engelbach respectively.

292 J. W. S. Armstrong, *Yesterday* (London, 1955), p. 145.

293 PRO LCO 2/3299, p. 34.

294 *CCO* 27 (1949–50), 58; *LT* 220 (1955), 221.

295 J. D. Kewish to F. Humphries, 22 Jan. 1962, *CCO* 37 (1961–2), 175–6.

296 H. Boggis-Rolfe to F. Mayell, 3 Dec. 1958, R. Boulton to R. E. K. Thesiger, 24 Jan. 1963, PRO LCO 8/43.

297 D. M. Green to Kewish, 12 June 1963 and minute of 16 Sep. 1963, *ibid*.

much more difficult given the specifications to which the new courts were built.[298]

A programme formulated in 1955 envisaged nine directly funded courts by 1960 at an overall cost of £855,000 and two others – Plymouth and Windsor and Slough – built by the local authority to house criminal and civil courts with a contribution from government.[299] Offices were also causing problems. Growing workloads in the biggest, at Birmingham and Liverpool, had led the Treasury inspector to the rather desperate suggestion that they be divided.[300] The Lord Chancellor frowned on court officials sharing buildings with other government departments, 'since this tends to blur the distinction between the executive and the judiciary'.[301] The purpose built offices in Harlow, opened in 1961, were the first for many years.[302]

County courts seem never to have been noted for good architecture.[303] Though Marylebone's 'characterless Victorian style' and Liverpool's 'building of the most forbidding Dickensian gloom'[304] were out of favour, most of the new ones were undistinguished essays in plate glass and 'short of the dignity that one would like to see in a court of justice'.[305] The best that could be said was that they were completed on time and within budget.

With the rapid rise in business from the mid-1950s the shortage of courtrooms, especially overspill rooms, contributed to the worrying rise in adjournments. Pugh's working party initially aspired to have a crown building on every circuit but that was firmly squashed by the man from the Ministry of Works.[306] Pugh was also disquieted to learn that the ministry, despite its professed neutrality, 'regarded themselves as bound to question the demand [for a new court] if it felt it was not justified, and to report this fact to the Treasury'.[307] They had in fact done so with Hanley and

298 *Ibid.*

299 W. J. Gillmore to A. H. M. Hillis, 19 May 1955, PRO LCO 8/28.

300 Report, Sep. 1962, and note of meeting on 29 Nov. 1962, PRO LCO 8/50.

301 Gillmore to Hillis, 19 May 1955, PRO LCO 8/28.

302 *CCO* 37 (1961–2), 31.

303 Few are commended in N. Pevsner, *The Buildings of England*, though one was 'in the best Southampton tradition of solid Italianate austerity' (*Hampshire and the Isle of Wight* (London, 1967)), nor does any seem to be a listed building.

304 *LT* 230 (1960), 233; 218 (1954), 193.

305 Kewish to Thesiger, 28 Jan. 1963, PRO LCO 8/43.

306 12th meeting, PRO LCO 2/7161.

307 *Ibid.*

were about to do so for Leicester.[308] Pugh felt this was constitutionally improper but found the LCD indifferent.[309]

During the 1960s criticisms of the design and layout of courts became much more common. Judges aired them at their meeting with Gardiner in 1966 and he made his own sympathies clear by telling them of the blunders he had noticed when opening the new court at Croydon.[310] Before long the investigations of consumer bodies and scholars would underline the deficiencies.[311]

Courts adequate for the rapid processing of small debt cases lacked both the facilities for suits involving numerous lawyers and witnesses and the privacy essential for family matters. And it was no longer acceptable to ignore demands for basic facilities; the lavatories in some courts were anything but conveniences and the first tea vending machine, in Liverpool, did not appear until 1967.[312] These deficiencies were seized upon by critics of proposals to enlarge county court jurisdiction and improvements were made a precondition in the Winn Report.[313] In 1971, with responsibility now at the Department of the Environment, a joint working party was set up to report on the optimum design for courts dealing with the full range of civil and criminal matters, something that was long overdue.[314]

308 Mayell's evidence, PRO LCO 2/7159; notes by Hillis, 8/28.

309 This is evident from the response to the report, which condemned the buildings programme as extravagant: PRO LCO 2/7164–6.

310 First and fourth meetings, 14, 24 Oct. 1966, PRO LCO 12/90.

311 E.g. E. Elston, J. Fuller and M. Murch, Judicial Hearings of Undefended Divorce Petitions, *MLR* 38 (1975), 609–40.

312 *CCO* 41 (1969–70), 373–4; 40 (1967–8), 154.

313 *Hansard* 1968–9 5th s., vol. 777 (HC), cols. 408–78; *PP* 1967–8 [Cmnd 3691] XXX, para. 446.

314 A. Samuels, *NLJ* 122 (1972), 14. The growing interest is suggested by articles in *NLJ* 119 (1969), 509 and 953.

# APPENDIX 1

# THE MAYOR'S AND CITY OF LONDON COURTS

In the scheme for a nationwide network of county courts there was one glaring omission – the City of London.[1] Evidently the corporation had used its formidable political influence to secure the right to make its own arrangements.

Apart from the Palace Court, which was soon to be abolished, there were two ancient but active courts in the City, the Mayor's Court and the Sheriffs' Court. The Sheriffs' Court had jurisdiction over debt and personal actions at common law arising within the City and its liberties and adopted the pleadings and procedures of the superior courts.[2] In 1835 the City had also submitted to the fashion for courts of requests and in 1846 substituted a small debts court modelled on the new county courts.[3] In 1852, through a further local Act, this became the City of London Small Debts Court, presided over by the judge of the Sheriffs' Court, which remained in existence but ceased to perform any functions. The Small Debts Court obtained the same enlarged jurisdiction as the county courts and, perhaps due to the lack of effective scrutiny of local bills, it also obtained some powers which they did not possess.[4]

The judge was elected by the corporation and William Arabin, celebrated for his legal malapropisms, was followed first by the highly esteemed Russell Gurney and then by the mediocre Michael Prendergast.[5] On Prendergast's death in 1859 there was a stirring contest, finally won by Robert Malcolm Kerr on a vote of 102 to 100. It was a fateful decision, for the winner held onto his place for the rest of the century and was frequently in acrimonious public dispute with his paymasters.[6]

Kerr – 'an individuality' – insisted on being known as 'Commissioner Kerr' from the fact that he was *ex officio* in the commission for the Old

[1] County Courts Act 1846 s. 1.

[2] Mathew, The Mayor's Court, the Sheriffs' Court and the Palace Court; G. Pitt-Lewis, *Commissioner Kerr – an Individuality* (London, 1903), pp. 76–7; memo by H. Jenkyns, n.d., PRO LCO 2/14.

[3] 10 & 11 Vict. c. lxxi, 11 & 12 Vict. c. clii and 15 & 16 Vict. c. lxxvii.

[4] *LM & LR*, ns 28 (1870), 208–15 (G. M. Weatherfield).

[5] R. E. Megarry, *Arabinesque-at-Law* (London, 1969); *DNB*, vol. XXIII, p. 365; Pitt-Lewis, *Commissioner Kerr*, pp. 74–6.

[6] Pitt-Lewis, *Commissioner Kerr*, pp. 75–114.

Bailey. His manner on the bench was frequently rough and brutal, he was opinionated and stubborn, avaricious and self-righteous. Autocratic with juries, he quickly made clear his antipathy to moneylenders and became notorious for his abrasive attitude towards solicitors and in particular his meanness in the matter of their costs.[7] The Commissioner clashed repeatedly with the corporation and the judges of the superior courts.[8] Nevertheless when county courts received first equitable jurisdiction then admiralty, it was readily extended to the City Court, although in each case the question of Kerr's salary led to a dispute.[9]

The County Courts Act 1867 took things a stage further, providing (s. 35) that in that and future Acts the words county court 'include the "City of London Court" and the rules and orders in force for the time being for regulating the practice of and costs in the County Courts, and forms of proceedings therein, are to be in force in the said City of London Court, to the exclusion of any rules and orders then in force in that court'. The precise status of the City Court was left dismally unclear by this lazy piece of lawmaking, generating a series of disputes.[10]

Like many county court judges Kerr loathed appeals and abhorred the obligation to take notes when requested, leading him into an acrimonious and long-running row with the judges of the divisional court.[11] Nevertheless, under his aegis the City Court amply shared in the expansion of county court business and both he and the corporation benefited financially.[12]

Alongside the City Court there continued to operate the Lord Mayor's Court. Presided over by the recorder and the common serjeant, this was a court of great antiquity which had the status of an inferior court of record and possessed common law jurisdiction over all actions (except replevin) arising in whole or in part within the City.[13]

With both its courts handsomely in profit the corporation became ambitious. After several years of manoeuvring Kerr was at last bribed into retirement in 1901 by an extravagant pension of £3,000 p. a.[14] and the corporation sought two judges to replace him, hoping that one would be an admiralty specialist.[15] The patronage had however been removed to the Lord Chancellor by the Local Government Act 1888 and though Halsbury gave them one of the best county court judges, Lumley Smith

7 *Ibid.*, pp. 121–6, 227–8; *LT* 111 (1901), 491. His views on solicitors' costs were also marked by at least one error he refused to admit: *LT* 174 (1932), 90.

8 Pitt-Lewis, *Commissioner Kerr*, pp. 148–88. The legal press provides a corrective to this partisan account.

9 *Ibid.*, pp. 161–8.

10 *Ibid.*, pp. 159–61; *Osgood v. Nelson* (1871–2) 5 HL, 636; *Blades v. Lawrence* (1873–4) 9 QB 374.

11 'The battle of the notes', Pitt-Lewis, *Commissioner Kerr*, pp. 173–86.

12 *Ibid.*, appendixes A and B.

13 *Halsbury's Laws of England* (1st edn), vol. XX (1909), pp. 283–302; *London Corporation v. Cox* (1867) 2 HL 239.

14 *SJ* 47 (1902–3), 95; Pitt-Lewis, *Commissioner Kerr*, pp. 350–64.

15 Corporation memo of 1919, PRO LCO 2/461.

from Westminster, he also inflicted on them the man they were anxious to avoid, the hard-up Unionist MP J. A. Rentoul.[16] Though well intentioned and full of generous impulses Rentoul was a disaster,[17] and while Lumley Smith's good reputation ensured the court stayed in profit until he retired in 1913, another dreadful appointment, from the Liberals, the vain and self-regarding radical MP Atherley-Jones who 'had to be seen to be believed',[18] ruined the reputation of the court.

The Great War hit both City courts hard and the corporation became anxious to amalgamate them and reduce the number of judges.[19] Ideally both City Court judges would have departed, but though Rentoul did so, his position untenable after an unprecedentedly wounding rebuke from the Court of Appeal for a defective summing up at the Old Bailey, the ineffable Atherley-Jones stayed on[20] and the LCO wisely insisted on making provision for a fourth judge of the combined court.[21] In Lord Buckmaster's more elegant arrangement, substituted for the clumsy proposals in the corporation's bill,[22] the county court rules of the City Court would govern all actions save where either party, in an action outside the scope of the City Court's jurisdiction, insisted on the Mayor's Court procedure, once 'barbarous and severely technical'[23] but now based on the high court.[24]

The court regained some of its popularity thanks to the work of Showell Cooper as assistant judge from 1922 to 1936.[25] With nearly 60,000 suits p. a. in the 1920s, the vast majority within the county court limits, the extra judge was always needed and the two lesser judges probably did the bulk of the civil work, criminal business occupying the recorder and common serjeant.[26] The civil work fell off again in the Second World War and never came close to pre-war levels; from 9,314 in 1950, plaints rose only to 15,090 in 1960, the extended jurisdiction being

16 *LJ* 31 (1898), 421; *LT* 112 (1901–2), 1. The legality of making two City judges was very questionable: Schuster to Solicitor-General, 8 Jul. 1920, PRO LCO 2/461.

17 Obituaries, e.g. in *SJ* 63 (1918–19), 769, and his autobiography, *Stray Thoughts and Memories*.

18 G. D. Roberts, *Without My Wig* (London, 1957), p. 141. Atherley-Jones' autobiography, *Looking Back* (London, 1925), does not cover his judicial career. The corporation's annoyance with Haldane over this appointment is clear from the memo in PRO LCO 2/461.

19 PRO LCO 2/461; *SJ* 63 (1918–19), 769; Bosanquet, *Oxford Circuit*, p. 80.

20 *R v. Power (Joseph)*, [1919] 1 KB 572; *LJ* 54 (1919), 71; *Stray Thoughts and Memories*, p. 185; Schuster to Solicitor-General, 8 Jul 1920, PRO LCO 2/461.

21 Schuster to Col. S. Crawford, 22 May 1919, PRO LCO 2/461. The provisions governing appointments proved very confusing: PRO LCO 2/5731.

22 Hansard 1920 5th s., vol. 11 (HL), cols. 793–6, 1001–4.

23 *CCC* 26 (1878), 411.

24 *Halsbury's Laws of England* (4th edn), vol. XXV, p. 502.

25 C. Whiteley, *Brief Life* (London, 1942), p. 209.

26 H. C. Beazley in 1937 was the only county court judge after Lumley Smith to move to the City Court.

largely overlooked.[27] When the Courts Bill which was to sweep it away came before Parliament discussion focused almost exclusively on the consequences for the Old Bailey[28] and thenceforth the City of London Court was simply a county court with a fancy title.

27 *LJ* 107 (1957), 57.
28 *Hansard* 1970–1 5th s., vol. 312 (HL), cols. 654–66.

# APPENDIX 2

## COUNTY COURT TOWNS, 1847–1971

Unless otherwise shown these courts opened in 1847 and were still in use in 1971. The list is compiled from Orders published in the *London Gazette* and, from 1890 in *Statutory Orders and Instruments*, and from the annual *Law List*. It does not detail closures due to wartime conditions or rebuilding.

Aberavon 1900–22
Aberayron -1945
Aberdare -1856
Abergavenny
Abertillery -1919
Aberystwyth
Abingdon -1927
Accrington -1867
Alcester -1943
Aldershot -1874
Alfreton
Alnwick
Alston -1945
Alton -1928
Altrincham
Ambleside -1921
Amersham -1956
Ammanford -1918
Ampthill -1920
Andover
Appleby -1969
Arundel -1969
Ashbourne -1968
Ashby de la Zouch
Ashford (Kent)
Ashton-under-Lyne -1964
Atherstone -1950
Attleborough -1923
Axbridge 1848–1919
Axminster
Aylesbury
Aylsham -1930

Bacup 1859–1920
Bakewell -1960
Bala -1969
Banbury
Bangor
Bargoed 1925
Barnard Castle -1969
Barnet
Barnsley
Barnstaple
Barrow-in-Furness -1873
Barry 1899
Barton-upon-Humber -1967
Basingstoke
Bath
Beccles -1968
Bedford
Belford -1917
Bellingham -1934
Belper -1926
Berwick
Beverley
Bicester -1918
Bideford
Biggleswade

Bingham -1911
Birkenhead
Birmingham
Bishop Auckland
Bishop's Castle -1943
Bishop's Stortford
Bishop's Waltham -1953
Blackburn
Blackpool -1881
Blackwood -1950
Blaenau Ffestiniog 1883–1969
Blaenavon 1901–54
Blandford -1968
Bletchley -1929
Bloomsbury
Blyth 1897
Bodmin
Bolton
Boston (Lincs.)
Boston (Yorks.) -1854
Bourne -1940
Bournemouth -1875
Bow
Brackley -1920
Bradford
Bradford-on-Avon -1920
Braintree
Brampton 1851–1941
Brecknock
Brentford
Brentwood
Bridgend
Bridgnorth
Bridgwater
Bridlington
Bridport
Brigg -1967
Brighton
Bristol
Bromley
Brompton -1908
Bromsgrove
Bromyard -1962
Buckingham -1965
Builth Wells
Bungay 1859–1944
Burnley
Burslem 1858–1932
Burton upon Trent
Bury
Bury St Edmunds
Buxton -1871

Caerphilly -1965
Caistor -1958
Calne -1957
Cambridge
Camelford -1970
Canterbury
Cardiff
Cardigan
Carlisle
Carmarthen
Carnarvon
Chapel-en-le-frith -1931
Chard -1967
Cheadle -1917
Chelmsford
Cheltenham
Chepstow
Chertsey -1922
Chesham -1956
Chester
Chesterfield
Chichester
Chippenham
Chipping Norton -1969
Chipping Sodbury -1918
Chorley
Christchurch -1920
Churston Ferrers 1868–99
Cirencester -1970
Clacton 1908
Cleobury Mortimer -1927
Clerkenwell
Clitheroe -1944
Clutton -1854
Cockermouth -1970
Colchester
Colne -1948
Colwyn Bay -1910
Congleton
Consett -1882
Conway
Corby -1970
Corwen -1969

Coventry
Cowbridge 1848–76
Cranbrook -1859
Craven Arms 1933–50
Crediton -1927
Crewe -1859
Crewkerne -1929
Crickhowell -1929
Cromer 1949–69
Croydon
Cuckfield -1889

Darlington
Dartford
Daventry -1950
Deal
Denbigh
Derby
Devizes
Dewsbury
Didcot -1969
Diss 1859–1967
Dolgelly
Doncaster
Dorchester
Dorking
Dover
Downham Market -1969
Droitwich -1922
Dudley
Dunmow -1935
Durham
Dursley -1970

Easingwold -1937
East Dereham
East Grinstead
East Retford
East Stonehouse 1850–1911
Eastbourne -1878
Edmonton
Ellesmere Port -1964
Ely
Epsom
Evesham
Exeter
Eye -1962

Fakenham 1875–1969
Falmouth
Faringdon -1923
Farnham -1968
Faversham -1944
Felixstowe 1897–1950
Fishguard 1848–56
Fleetwood -1920
Flint -1927
Folkestone
Fordingbridge -1924
Framlingham -1924
Frodsham 1858–62
Frome

Gainsborough
Garstang -1920
Gateshead
Glossop -1958
Gloucester
Godalming -1924
Goole
Grantham
Gravesend
Grays Thurrock -1897
Great Driffield -1969
Great Grimsby
Great Malvern -1867
Great Yarmouth
Greenwich -1939
Guildford
Guisborough 1878–1955

Hadleigh -1927
Halesworth
Halifax
Halstead -1950
Haltwhistle -1964
Hanley -1967
Harleston -1949
Harlow -1961
Harrogate -1912
(West) Hartlepool
Harwich
Haslingden -1920
Hastings
Haverfordwest
Haverhill -1926

Hay -1960
Haywards Heath -1889
Hedon -1920
Helmsley -1941
Helston -1970
Hemel Hempstead -1967
Henley 1848–1943
Hereford
Hertford
Hexham
High Wycombe
Hinckley
Hitchin
Holbeach -1944
Holmfirth -1920
Holsworthy -1970
Holt -1947
Holyhead -1860
Holywell
Honiton -1970
Horncastle -1967
Horsham
Howden -1930
Huddersfield
Hungerford -1957
Huntingdon
Hyde
Hythe -1949

Ilford -1903
Ilkeston -1867
Ipswich

Jarrow 1900–37

Keighley
Kendal
Keswick -1934
Kettering
Kidderminster
King's Lynn
Kingsbridge
Kingston upon Hull
Kingston upon Thames
Kington -1970
Kirkby Lonsdale -1944
Kirkham -1925
Knaresborough -1912
Knighton -1852
Knutsford 1847–56

Lambeth
Lampeter
Lancaster
Langport -1953
Launceston
Ledbury -1959
Leeds
Leek
Leicester
Leigh
Leighton Buzzard
Leominster
Lewes
Leyburn -1953
Lichfield
Lincoln
Liskeard
Little Walsingham -1919
Liverpool
Llandovery
Llandrindod Wells -1897
Llandudno -1878
Llanelli
Llandilofawr -1944
Llanfyllin
Llangefni -1969
Llangollen 1867–1920
Llanidloes 1878–1970
Llanrwst -1969
Long Eaton 1898–1959
Longton 1863–1920
Loughborough
Louth
Lowestoft
Ludlow
Luton
Lutterworth -1924
Lymington

Macclesfield
Machynlleth
Madeley -1950
Maesteg 1906–13
Maidenhead 1901–18
Maidstone

Maldon
Malmesbury
Manchester
Mansfield
March
Margate
Market Bosworth -1925
Market Drayton
Market Harborough -1970
Market Rasen -1958
Marlborough -1970
Marylebone
Melksham -1969
Melton Mowbray
Menai Bridge 1883–1969
Merthyr Tydfil
Middlesbrough
Midhurst -1930
Midsomer Norton 1904–22
Mildenhall -1934
Millom 1899–1969
Minehead -1938
Mold
Monmouth
Morpeth
Mountain Ash 1897–1953

Nantwich -1961
Narberth -1956
Neath
New Malton
New Mills 1880–1955
Newark
Newbury
Newcastle in Emlyn -1947
Newcastle under Lyme -1970
Newcastle upon Tyne
Newent -1943
Newmarket
Newnham -1943
Newport (IOW)
Newport (Monm.)
Newport (Salop) -1922
Newport Pagnell -1929
Newquay 1917–70
Newton Abbot
North Shields
North Walsham -1947
Northallerton
Northampton
Northleach -1950
Northwich
Norwich

Oakham -1970
Okehampton
Oldbury -1889
Oldham
Ormskirk -1935
Oswestry
Otley
Oundle -1967
Oxford

Paignton 1900–28
Patrington 1923–5
Pembroke -1956 (as Pembroke Dock -1872)
Penrith
Penzance
Pershore
Peterborough
Petersfield
Petworth -1967
Plymouth 1847–50, -1911
Pocklington -1941
Pontefract
Pontypool
Pontypridd -1856
Poole
Port Talbot -1922
Porth 1896–1953
Portmadoc
Portsmouth
Poulton -1881 (as Poulton le Fylde -1872)
Presteigne -1942
Preston
Pwllheli -1969

Ramsgate
Rawtenstall 1901
Reading
Redditch
Redhill 1885–1953
Redruth

Reigate -1885, 1953-
Rhyader -1920
Rhyl 1867
Richmond (Yorks.) -1970
Ringwood 1882–1918, 1924–69
Ripon -1970
Rochdale
Rochester
Rochford -1888
Romford -1934
Romney -1908, New Romney - 1934
Romsey -1951
Ross -1970
Rothbury -1920
Rotherham
Royston -1968
Ruabon -1863
Rugby
Rugeley -1920
Runcorn
Ruthin
Ryde 1864–1967
Rye 1851–1923

Saddleworth -1922
Saffron Walden -1968
St Albans
St Asaph -1910
St Austell
St Colomb -1917
St Helens
St Neots -1930
Salford
Salisbury
Sandbach 1864–1939
Sandwich 1848–1920
Saxmundham 1861–1967
Scarborough
Scunthorpe -1900
Seaham Harbour 1859–1960
Selby -1968
Settle -1935
Sevenoaks
Shaftesbury
Sheerness
Sheffield
Shipston on Stour -1953
Shoreditch
Shotley Bridge -1881
Shrewsbury
Silloth 1920–32
Sittingbourne
Skegness 1934-
Skipton
Sleaford
Slough -1957
Soham -1918
Solihull -1920
South Molton -1969
South Shields
Southam -1927
Southampton
Southend -1878
Southport -1875
Southwark
Spalding
Spilsby
Stafford
Stalybridge -1881
Stamford
Stockport
Stockton-on-Tees
Stoke-on-Trent -1854
Stokesley -1953
Stone -1950
Stourbridge
Stow-on-the-Wold -1960
Stowmarket
Stratford-upon-Avon
Stroud
Sudbury
Sunderland
Swaffham -1969
Swanage
Swansea
Swindon

Tadcaster 1858–1961
Tamworth
Taunton
Tavistock -1970
Temple Cloud 1854–1922
Tenbury -1958
Tenterden -1967
Tewkesbury -1956

Thame
Thetford
Thirsk -1936
Thornbury
Thorne
Thrapstone 1847–1951
Tiverton
Todmorden
Tonbridge
Torquay -1863
Torrington -1944
Totnes -1967
Towcester -1928
Tredegar
Trowbridge
Truro
Tunbridge Wells
Tunstall 1858–1926

Ulverston
Uppingham -1924
Upton-upon-Severn -1867
Usk -1920
Uttoxeter
Uxbridge

Wakefield
Wallingford -1969
Walsall
Waltham Abbey -1939
Wandsworth
Wantage -1969
Wareham -1928
Warminster
Warrington
Warwick
Watford
Watton 1887–1920
Wellingborough
Wellington (Salop)
Wellington (Som.) -1953
Wells
Welshpool
Wem -1923
West Bromwich -1889
West London -1908
Westbury -1921
Westminster
Weston-super-Mare
Wetherby 1854–7
Weymouth
Whitby
Whitchurch
Whitechapel -1943
Whitehaven
Widnes -1886
Wigton -1967
Willesden -1930
Williton -1938
Wilmslow 1907–19
Wimborne Minster
Wincanton -1970
Winchcomb -1942
Winchester
Windermere 1921–69
Windsor -1957
Winsford 1895–1927
Wirkswirth -1895
Wisbech
Witney
Wolsingham -1920
Wolverhampton
Wood Green 1900–35
Woodbridge
Woodstock -1918
Wooler -1920
Woolwich 1848-
Worcester
Workington -1882
Worksop
Worthing
Wrexham
Wymondham -1944

Yatton 1919–29
Yeovil
York
Ystradyndwg -1886

# APPENDIX 3

## STATISTICAL TABLES[1]

These tables are drawn chiefly from the *County Court Returns* to 1921 inclusive and thereafter from the *Civil Judicial Statistics*. As noted in the bibliography, there are variations between these two series. A few other official publications have been used to supplement them and here again there are sometimes differences between sources.

Table 1 *Number of plaints in the county courts, 1847–1971*

| Year | Total plaints | Not above £20 | Above £20 | Above £20 but not above £50 | Above £50 | Not above £100 | Above £100 | Other proceedings |
|---|---|---|---|---|---|---|---|---|
| 1847 | 429,215 | | | | | | | |
| 1848 | 427,611 | | | | | | | |
| 1849 | 395,191 | | | | | | | |
| 1850 | 396,793 | | 4,297 | | | | | |
| 1851 | 441,584 | | 13,446 | | | | | |
| 1852 | 474,149 | | 12,567 | | | | | |
| 1853 | 484,496 | | 9,270 | | | | | |
| 1854 | 526,718 | | 9,395 | | | | | |
| 1855 | 538,168 | | 8,604 | | | | | |
| 1858 | 738,854 | | | | | | | |

[1] In the tables, where a column is blank either no return was made for the year(s) in question or the figures are not available.

Table 1 *Continued*

| Year | Total plaints | Not above £20 | Above £20 | Above £20 but not above£50 | Above £50 | Not above £100 | Above £100 | Other proceedings |
|---|---|---|---|---|---|---|---|---|
| 1856 | 581,053 | | 7,877 | | | | | |
| 1857 | 744,652 | | 10,491 | | | | | |
| 1859 | 714,562 | | | | | | | |
| 1860 | 782,326 | 773,415 | 8,911 | | | | | |
| 1861 | 903,875 | 893,433 | 10,442 | | | | | |
| 1862 | 847,169 | 838,783 | | 8,368 | 18 | | | |
| 1863 | 799,154 | 791,484 | | 7,662 | 8 | | | |
| 1864 | 738,362 | 730,079 | | 8,267 | 16 | | | |
| 1865 | 782,703 | 775,272 | | 7,414 | 17 | | | |
| 1866 | 872,446 | 864,193 | | 8,244 | 9 | | | |
| 1867 | 941,888 | 933,055 | | 8,822 | 11 | | | |
| 1868 | 975,373 | 964,146 | | 11,194 | 33 | | | |
| 1869 | 940,342 | 928,285 | | 12,029 | 28 | | | |
| 1870 | 912,298 | 898,810 | | 13,445 | 43 | | | |
| 1871 | 918,538 | 904,072 | | 14,431 | 35 | | | |
| 1872 | 900,775 | 886,951 | | 13,799 | 25 | | | |
| 1873 | 865,263 | 850,535 | | 14,695 | 33 | | | |
| 1874 | 865,040 | 849,816 | | 15,202 | 22 | | | |
| 1875 | 878,493 | 861,188 | | 17,273 | 32 | | | |
| 1876 | 946,705 | 929,159 | | 17,378 | 168 | | | |
| 1877 | 1,024,826 | 1,007,563 | | 16,879 | 384 | | | |
| 1878 | 1,031,041 | 1,014,631 | | 15,990 | 420 | | | |
| 1879 | 1,044,414 | 1,028,501 | | 15,584 | 329 | | | |
| 1880 | 1,095,269 | 1,081,879 | | 13,094 | 296 | | | |
| 1881 | 1,035,311 | 1,022,340 | | 12,689 | 282 | | | |
| 1882 | 1,021,226 | 1,009,185 | | 11,771 | 270 | | | |

Table 1 *Continued*

| Year | Total plaints | Not above £20 | Above £20 | Above £20 but not above£50 | Above £50 | Not above £100 | Above £100 | Other proceedings |
|---|---|---|---|---|---|---|---|---|
| 1883 | 1,002,948 | 991,002 | | 11,263 | 683 | | | |
| 1884 | 953,414 | 940,683 | | 12,066 | 665 | | | |
| 1885 | 961,413 | 948,480 | | 12,373 | 560 | | | |
| 1886 | 980,338 | 966,948 | | 12,716 | 674 | | | |
| 1887 | 1,013,727 | 1,000,729 | | 12,764 | 666 | | | |
| 1888 | 1,043,575 | 1,031,665 | | 11,178 | 732 | | | |
| 1889 | 1,034,686 | 1,022,295 | | 11,597 | 794 | | | |
| 1890 | 991,157 | 978,784 | | 11,573 | 800 | | | |
| 1891 | 1,031,608 | 1,019,053 | | 11,685 | 870 | | | |
| 1892 | 1,068,693 | 1,055,618 | | 12,139 | 936 | | | |
| 1893 | 1,069,211 | 1,055,611 | | 12,596 | 1,004 | | | |
| 1894 | 1,129,206 | 1,115,825 | | 12,489 | 892 | | | |
| 1895 | 1,082,857 | 1,068,908 | | 12,999 | 950 | | | |
| 1896 | 1,074,287 | 1,061,051 | | 12,226 | 1,010 | | | |
| 1897 | 1,085,654 | 1,072,922 | | 11,603 | 1,129 | | | |
| 1898 | 1,121,108 | 1,107,730 | | 11,996 | 1,382 | | | |
| 1899 | 1,117,596 | 1,104,334 | | 11,986 | 1,276 | | | |
| 1900 | 1,146,418 | 1,132,775 | | 12,353 | 1,290 | | | |
| 1901 | 1,193,895 | 1,179,886 | | 12,472 | 1,537 | | | |
| 1902 | 1,242,820 | 1,229,218 | | 12,509 | 1,093 | | | |
| 1903 | 1,284,772 | 1,271,101 | | 12,512 | 1,159 | | | |
| 1904 | 1,338,732 | 1,324,591 | | 13,052 | 1,089 | | | |
| 1905 | 1,300,437 | 1,284,637 | | 12,697 | 2,521 | | 582 | |
| 1906 | 1,281,446 | 1,265,908 | | 12,578 | 2,365 | | 595 | |
| 1907 | 1,272,480 | 1,256,415 | | 13,083 | 2,409 | | 573 | |
| 1908 | 1,305,175 | 1,288,872 | | 13,207 | 2,560 | | 536 | |

Table 1 *Continued*

| Year | Total plaints | Not above £20 | Above £20 | Above £20 but not above £50 | Above £50 | Not above £100 | Above £100 | Other proceedings |
|---|---|---|---|---|---|---|---|---|
| 1909 | 1,324,320 | 1,308,849 | | 12,586 | 2,450 | | 435 | |
| 1910 | 1,286,376 | 1,270,853 | | 12,763 | 2,376 | | 384 | |
| 1911 | 1,237,060 | 1,221,656 | | 12,718 | 2,326 | | 360 | |
| 1912 | 1,194,631 | 1,179,132 | | 12,806 | 2,337 | | 356 | |
| 1913 | 1,188,162 | 1,172,189 | | 13,121 | 2,490 | | 362 | |
| 1914 | 935,703 | 921,657 | | 11,622 | 2,151 | | 273 | |
| 1915 | 734,682 | 721,000 | | 11,176 | 2,213 | | 293 | |
| 1916 | 558,740 | 547,098 | | 9,404 | 2,002 | | 236 | |
| 1917 | 435,018 | 424,619 | | 8,421 | 1,750 | | 228 | |
| 1918 | 311,589 | 301,587 | | 7,986 | 1,839 | | 177 | |
| 1919 | 326,947 | 311,986 | | 11,476 | 3,221 | | 264 | |
| 1920 | 445,973 | 414,229 | | 25,108 | 6,254 | | 382 | |
| 1921 | 553,656 | 505,759 | | 38,727 | 8,848 | | 322 | |
| 1922 | 738,379 | 683,735 | | 44,953 | 9,378 | | 313 | |
| 1923 | 884,111 | 791,129 | | 41,410 | 8,274 | | 295 | 43,003 |
| 1924 | 926,664 | 839,257 | | 41,190 | 8,328 | | 289 | 37,600 |
| 1925 | 926,847 | 847,826 | | 38,520 | 7,226 | | 221 | 33,054 |
| 1926 | 869,769 | 792,797 | | 36,520 | 6,918 | | 179 | 33,355 |
| 1927 | 1,015,753 | 937,325 | | 36,111 | 7,221 | | 182 | 34,914 |
| 1928 | 1,092,478 | 1,013,242 | | 35,043 | 6,748 | | 184 | 37,261 |
| 1929 | 1,105,881 | 1,021,672 | | 38,040 | 6,876 | | 211 | 39,082 |
| 1930 | 1,169,048 | 1,085,377 | | 37,275 | 7,325 | | 209 | 38,862 |
| 1931 | 1,211,453 | 1,128,045 | | 37,512 | 7,173 | | 167 | 38,556 |
| 1932 | 1,281,003 | 1,192,367 | | 37,947 | 7,451 | | 192 | 43,046 |
| 1933 | 1,277,281 | 1,192,433 | | 36,963 | 7,190 | | 210 | 40,485 |
| 1934 | 1,199,421 | 1,115,395 | | 34,014 | 7,002 | | 175 | 42,835 |

Table 1 *Continued*

| Year | Total plaints | Not above £20 | Above £20 | Above £20 but not above£50 | Above £50 | Not above £100 | Above £100 | Other proceedings |
|---|---|---|---|---|---|---|---|---|
| 1935 | 1,201,335 | 1,121,952 | | 32,785 | 6,596 | | 168 | 39,834 |
| 1936 | 1,299,851 | 1,215,905 | | 34,859 | 7,462 | | 195 | 41,430 |
| 1937 | 1,137,409 | 1,052,210 | | 33,669 | 7,301 | | 196 | 44,033 |
| 1938 | 1,262,402 | 1,150,300 | | 34,696 | 7,652 | | 129 | 69,625 |
| 1939 | 1,094,770 | | | | | 1,044,873 | 1,632 | 48,265 |
| 1940 | 818,453 | | | | | 758,356 | 1,652 | 58,445 |
| 1941 | 510,879 | | | | | 456,832 | 2,826 | 51,221 |
| 1942 | 366,766 | | | | | 321,682 | 1,532 | 43,552 |
| 1943 | 263,466 | | | | | 222,530 | 1,346 | 39,590 |
| 1944 | 216,292 | | | | | 173,180 | 1,285 | 41,827 |
| 1945 | 212,483 | | | | | 158,177 | 1,444 | 52,862 |
| 1946 | 256,794 | | | | | 189,334 | 2,183 | 65,277 |
| 1947 | 312,275 | | | | | 238,891 | 3,142 | 70,242 |
| 1948 | 385,171 | | | | | 307,554 | 3,866 | 73,751 |
| 1949 | 434,510 | | | | | 358,756 | 4,760 | 70,994 |
| 1950 | 496,439 | | | | | 421,717 | 5,459 | 69,263 |
| 1951 | 528,355 | | | | | 457,288 | 4,431 | 66,636 |
| 1952 | 617,279 | | | | | 541,336 | 6,458 | 69,485 |
| 1953 | 642,423 | | | | | 571,397 | 4,990 | 66,036 |
| 1954 | 682,839 | | | | | 615,724 | 4,990 | 62,125 |
| 1955 | 727,154 | | | | | 659,157 | 6,089 | 61,908 |
| 1956 | 900,885 | | | | | 826,568 | 14,373 | 59,944 |
| 1957 | 1,078,097 | | | | | 1,011,740 | 16,730 | 49,627 |
| 1958 | 1,332,301 | | | | | 1,253,955 | 19,238 | 59,108 |
| 1959 | 1,322,117 | | | | | 1,244,476 | 22,437 | 55,204 |
| 1960 | 1,489,081 | | | | | 1,408,191 | 31,279 | 49,611 |

Table 1 *Continued*

| Year | Total plaints | Not above £20 | Above £20 | Above £20 but not above£50 | Above £50 | Not above £100 | Above £100 | Other proceedings |
|---|---|---|---|---|---|---|---|---|
| 1961 | 1,677,738 | | | | | 1,586,648 | 41,879 | 49,211 |
| 1962 | 1,676,609 | | | | | 1,579,869 | 45,108 | 51,632 |
| 1963 | 1,543,324 | | | | | 1,454,737 | 40,627 | 47,960 |
| 1964 | 1,510,324 | | | | | 1,416,060 | 43,655 | 50,609 |
| 1965 | 1,516,101 | | | | | 1,398,134 | 57,342 | 60,625 |
| 1966 | 1,548,021 | | | | | 1,397,538 | 83,030 | 67,453 |
| 1967 | 1,611,344 | | | | | 1,444,484 | 99,481 | 67,379 |
| 1968 | 1,509,658 | | | | | 1,340,197 | 100,882 | 68,579 |
| 1969 | 1,635,708 | | | | | 1,444,306 | 117,839 | 73,563 |
| 1970 | 1,791,870 | | | | | 1,565,029 | 146,845 | 79,996 |
| 1971 | 1,530,941 | | | | | 1,275,570 | 165,591 | 89,780 |

## Table 2a *Selected other business, 1858–1963*

| Year | Remitted from superior courts | Equity | Bankruptcy adjudications (to 1913) and receiving orders in bankruptcy (from 1921) | Administration orders (s. 122 Bankruptcy Act 1883) | Tithe applications | Workmen's compensation arbitrations | Workmen's compensation, memoranda registered |
|---|---|---|---|---|---|---|---|
| 1858 | 123 | | | | | | |
| 1859 | 61 | | | | | | |
| 1860 | 58 | | | | | | |
| 1861 | 82 | | | | | | |
| 1862 | 119 | | | | | | |
| 1863 | 100 | | 3,849 | | | | |
| 1864 | 119 | | 3,376 | | | | |
| 1865 | 146 | | 3,569 | | | | |
| 1866 | 244 | 814 | 3,544 | | | | |
| 1867 | 293 | 613 | 4,065 | | | | |
| 1868 | 583 | 679 | 4,161 | | | | |
| 1869 | 595 | 750 | 4,443 | | | | |
| 1870 | 597 | 668 | 1,032 | | | | |
| 1871 | 610 | 767 | 943 | | | | |
| 1872 | 554 | 683 | 684 | | | | |
| 1873 | 681 | 712 | 640 | | | | |
| 1874 | 655 | 722 | 656 | | | | |
| 1875 | 653 | 750 | 655 | | | | |
| 1876 | 655 | 655 | 682 | | | | |
| 1877 | 770 | 613 | 699 | | | | |
| 1878 | 764 | 633 | 829 | | | | |
| 1879 | 883 | 548 | 850 | | | | |
| 1880 | 924 | 640 | 715 | | | | |
| 1881 | 928 | 704 | 675 | | | | |

Table 2a *Continued*

| Year | Remitted from superior courts | Equity | Bankruptcy adjudications (to 1913) and receiving orders in bankruptcy (from 1921) | Administration orders (s. 122 Bankruptcy Act 1883) | Tithe applications | Workmen's compensation arbitrations | Workmen's compensation, memoranda registered |
|---|---|---|---|---|---|---|---|
| 1882 | 888 | 709 | 673 | | | | |
| 1883 | 886 | 698 | 700 | | | | |
| 1884 | 911 | 736 | 2,454 | 3,905 | | | |
| 1885 | 973 | 648 | 3,308 | | | | |
| 1886 | 901 | 811 | 3,833 | 4,005 | | | |
| 1887 | 884 | 693 | 3,867 | 3,635 | | | |
| 1888 | 865 | 728 | 3,901 | 3,425 | | | |
| 1889 | 1,579 | 792 | 3,632 | 2,905 | | | |
| 1890 | 1,575 | 798 | 3,177 | 2,304 | | | |
| 1891 | 1,707 | 758 | 3,355 | 2,411 | 242 | | |
| 1892 | 2,001 | 714 | 3,688 | 2,661 | 1,487 | | |
| 1893 | 1,807 | 850 | 3,923 | 3,351 | 3,264 | | |
| 1894 | 1,810 | 796 | 3,874 | 4,053 | 2,837 | | |
| 1895 | 1,350 | 760 | 3,652 | 4,203 | 3,783 | | |
| 1896 | 1,349 | 700 | 3,460 | 4,243 | 3,784 | | |
| 1897 | 1,328 | 842 | 3,369 | 4,164 | 3,309 | | |
| 1898 | 1,372 | 821 | 3,536 | 4,498 | 2,512 | 999 | 651 |
| 1899 | 1,420 | 761 | 3,332 | 4,071 | 2,534 | 1,145 | 1,188 |
| 1900 | 1,421 | 717 | 3,650 | 3,898 | 2,528 | 1,370 | 1,623 |
| 1901 | 1,445 | 785 | 3,491 | 3,878 | 2,531 | 1,269 | 2,152 |
| 1902 | 1,296 | 774 | 3,562 | 4,526 | 2,362 | 1,437 | 2,985 |
| 1903 | 1,291 | 703 | 3,571 | 6,214 | 2,249 | 2,435 | 3,625 |
| 1904 | 1,442 | 712 | 3,806 | 6,947 | 2,527 | 2,469 | 4,317 |
| 1905 | 1,127 | 733 | 3,943 | 6,368 | 2,481 | 2,532 | 5,171 |

Table 2a *Continued*

| Year | Remitted from superior courts | Equity | Bankruptcy adjudications (to 1913) and receiving orders in bankruptcy (from 1921) | Administration orders (s. 122 Bankruptcy Act 1883) | Tithe applications | Workmen's compensation arbitrations | Workmen's compensation, memoranda registered |
|---|---|---|---|---|---|---|---|
| 1906 | 1,074 | 751 | 3,706 | 6,219 | 2,506 | 3,330 | 9,349 |
| 1907 | 1,115 | 723 | 3,382 | 6,616 | 2,375 | 6,124 | 22,125 |
| 1908 | 1,109 | 744 | 3,531 | 6,030 | 2,730 | 6,509 | 18,763 |
| 1909 | 1,158 | 782 | 3,362 | 6,829 | 2,329 | 6,815 | 21,101 |
| 1910 | 1,118 | 671 | 3,139 | 6,896 | 2,677 | 8,120 | 23,101 |
| 1911 | 1,060 | 679 | 2,984 | 6,498 | 2,611 | 8,003 | 22,010 |
| 1912 | 1,156 | 723 | 2,837 | 5,673 | 2,867 | 7,576 | 19,162 |
| 1913 | 1,076 | 712 | 2,641 | 5,423 | 2,404 | 9,108 | 31,550 |
| 1914 | 938 | 566 | | 4,033 | 2,423 | 8,798 | 30,430 |
| 1915 | 982 | 530 | | 1,705 | 2,187 | 6,055 | 26,276 |
| 1916 | 718 | 421 | | 1,090 | | 5,431 | 24,187 |
| 1917 | 616 | 381 | | 727 | | 5,077 | 23,992 |
| 1918 | 520 | 342 | | 353 | | 5,041 | 23,087 |
| 1919 | 778 | 454 | | 330 | | 4,966 | 23,857 |
| 1920 | 1,133 | 597 | | 436 | | 4,668 | 24,631 |
| 1921 | | 653 | 2,632 | 752 | 2,099 | 4,664 | 23,685 |
| 1922 | 1,878 | 708 | 3,752 | 1,797 | | 5,343 | 25,580 |
| 1923 | 1,865 | 455 | 4,088 | 2,488 | | 4,959 | 17,365 |
| 1924 | 1,798 | 409 | 3,881 | 2,218 | 5,243 | 4,687 | 19,208 |
| 1925 | 1,693 | 424 | 3,810 | 2,241 | 5,512 | 4,600 | 19,182 |
| 1926 | 1,726 | 363 | 3,453 | 1,727 | 5,430 | 4,883 | 18,612 |
| 1927 | 1,893 | 361 | 3,552 | 1,925 | 7,217 | 4,891 | 18,869 |
| 1928 | 1,722 | 319 | 3,567 | 1,970 | 9,101 | 4,765 | 20,197 |
| 1929 | 1,743 | 350 | 3,252 | 1,641 | 11,570 | 4,626 | 19,642 |

Table 2a *Continued*

| Year | Remitted from superior courts | Equity | Bankruptcy adjudications (to 1913) and receiving orders in bankruptcy (from 1921) | Administration orders (s. 122 Bankruptcy Act 1883) | Tithe applications | Workmen's compensation arbitrations | Workmen's compensation, memoranda registered |
|---|---|---|---|---|---|---|---|
| 1930 | 1,982 | 327 | 3,443 | 1,700 | 11,294 | 4,717 | 21,328 |
| 1931 | 2,296 | 284 | 3,587 | 1,501 | 12,357 | 4,877 | 19,512 |
| 1932 | 2,469 | 360 | 3,809 | 1,688 | 15,193 | 4,754 | 15,193 |
| 1933 | 2,255 | 314 | 3,348 | 1,443 | 15,565 | 4,496 | 15,565 |
| 1934 | 1,804 | 322 | 2,896 | 1,363 | 21,640 | 4,755 | 18,803 |
| 1935 | 2,018 | 366 | 2,879 | 1,240 | 20,025 | 4,414 | 19,813 |
| 1936 | 1,871 | 328 | 2,619 | 1,155 | 21,084 | 4,482 | 20,815 |
| 1937 | 1,703 | 283 | 2,515 | 1,233 | 23,261 | 4,427 | 21,590 |
| 1938 | 1,747 | 283 | 2,460 | 1,147 | 48,932 | 4,572 | 22,454 |
| 1939 | | 300 | 2,110 | | | | 19,964 |
| 1940 | | 228 | 1,268 | | | | 19,249 |
| 1941 | | 258 | 470 | | | | 18,707 |
| 1942 | | 244 | 253 | | | | 20,687 |
| 1943 | | 250 | 165 | | | | 21,330 |
| 1944 | | 266 | 157 | | | | 20,967 |
| 1945 | | 313 | 152 | | | | 21,042 |
| 1946 | | 388 | 234 | | | | 24,329 |
| 1947 | | 467 | 444 | | | | 20,643 |
| 1948 | 1,436 | 283 | 850 | 29 | 28,526 | 2,422 | 20,341 |
| 1949 | 1,520 | 285 | 1,139 | 37 | 27,698 | 1,477 | 14,199 |
| 1950 | 1,736 | 249 | 1,390 | 40 | 25,054 | 781 | 7,340 |
| 1951 | 1,668 | 292 | 1,484 | 44 | 26,845 | 404 | 4,595 |
| 1952 | 1,725 | 245 | 1,623 | 31 | 27,717 | 298 | 2,866 |
| 1953 | 1,717 | 223 | 1,654 | 26 | 27,755 | 186 | 2,233 |

Table 2a *Continued*

| Year | Remitted from superior courts | Equity | Bankruptcy adjudications (to 1913) and receiving orders in bankruptcy (from 1921) | Administration orders (s. 122 Bankruptcy Act 1883) | Tithe applications | Workmen's compensation arbitrations | Workmen's compensation, memoranda registered |
|---|---|---|---|---|---|---|---|
| 1954 | 1,657 | 257 | 1,580 | 17 | 25,359 | 115 | 1,713 |
| 1955 | 1,622 | 252 | 1,630 | 18 | 25,426 | 49 | 1,305 |
| 1956 | 1,809 | 247 | 1,678 | 16 | 24,574 | | 1,073 |
| 1957 | 1,325 | 292 | 1,694 | 14 | 14,336 | | 807 |
| 1958 | 1,198 | 228 | 1,747 | 8 | 14,200 | | 672 |
| 1959 | 1,085 | 225 | 1,874 | 10 | 8,373 | | 623 |
| 1960 | 1,127 | 257 | 2,291 | 8 | 6,413 | | 573 |
| 1961 | 1,322 | 332 | 2,954 | 6 | 3,815 | | 421 |
| 1962 | 1,384 | 256 | 3,557 | 4 | 2,913 | | 384 |
| 1963 | 1,316 | 243 | 3,186 | 2 | 2,891 | | 323 |
| 1964 | 1,387 | 307 | 2,861 | 4 | 2,584 | | 357 |
| 1965 | 1,544 | 315 | 2,787 | 465 | 2,372 | | 329 |
| 1966 | 1,530 | 356 | 2,999 | 1,576 | 2,362 | | 224 |
| 1967 | 1,787 | 382 | 3,290 | 2,264 | 2,323 | | 183 |
| 1968 | 1,854 | 451 | 3,184 | 2,103 | 2,129 | | 144 |
| 1969 | 2,050 | 256 | 3,611 | 2,071 | 2,108 | | 93 |
| 1970 | 2,168 | 341 | 3,230 | 2,168 | | | 99 |
| 1971 | 2,426 | 678 | 3,773 | 4,230 | | | 104 |

Table 2b *Selected other business, 1923–1971*

| | Adoptions | Hire Purchase Act 1938 actions | Landlord and Tenant Act 1954: applications for new tenancies |
|---|---|---|---|
| 1923 | | | |
| 1924 | | | |
| 1925 | | | |
| 1926 | | | |
| 1927 | 235 | | |
| 1928 | 241 | | |
| 1929 | 250 | | |
| 1930 | 325 | | |
| 1931 | 288 | | |
| 1932 | 262 | | |
| 1933 | 287 | | |
| 1934 | 322 | | |
| 1935 | 350 | | |
| 1936 | 407 | | |
| 1937 | 402 | | |
| 1938 | 498 | 57 | |
| 1939 | | 10,904 | |
| 1940 | | 17,669 | |
| 1941 | | 19,992 | |
| 1942 | | 19,524 | |
| 1943 | | 13,123 | |
| 1944 | | 9,168 | |
| 1945 | | 7,971 | |
| 1946 | | 6,391 | |
| 1947 | | 7,028 | |
| 1948 | 4,186 | 10,186 | |
| 1949 | 4,383 | 11,639 | |
| 1950 | 3,594 | 16,410 | |
| 1951 | 4,048 | 17,614 | |
| 1952 | 4,192 | 25,121 | |
| 1953 | 4,354 | 27,540 | |
| 1954 | 4,275 | 26,735 | 8 [*sic*] |
| 1955 | 4,958 | 29,508 | 1,143 |
| 1956 | 5,239 | 37,068 | 1,367 |
| 1957 | 5,531 | 41,840 | 1,540 |
| 1958 | 6,043 | 40,234 | 2,364 |
| 1959 | 6,856 | 40,108 | 2,191 |
| 1960 | 7,701 | 59,855 | 2,148 |
| 1961 | 8,820 | 60,404 | 2,130 |
| 1962 | 10,129 | 57,043 | 2,220 |
| 1963 | 10,633 | 58,644 | 2,476 |
| 1964 | 12,917 | 58,877 | 2,563 |
| 1965 | 14,158 | 60,068 | 2,955 |
| 1966 | 15,087 | 83,972 | 3,962 |

Table 2b *Continued*

| | Adoptions | Hire Purchase Act 1938 actions | Landlord and Tenant Act 1954: applications for new tenancies |
|---|---|---|---|
| 1967 | 15,718 | 79,746 | 4,258 |
| 1968 | 16,401 | 64,705 | 3,651 |
| 1969 | 15,695 | 82,539 | 3,819 |
| 1970 | 14,834 | 84,770 | 3,820 |
| 1971 | 14,088 | 63,568 | 4,254 |

Table 3 *Sittings and trials, 1847–1971*

| Year | Total sitting days | Judges | Registrars | Trials before judges | Trials before registrars | Jury trials | Non-jury trials |
|---|---|---|---|---|---|---|---|
| 1847 | | | | | | 800 | |
| 1848 | | | | | | 884 | |
| 1849 | 7,565 | | | | | 802 | |
| 1850 | 8,153 | | | | | 769 | |
| 1851 | 8,236 | | | | | 879 | |
| 1852 | 8,570 | | | | | 796 | |
| 1853 | 8,615 | | | | | 863 | |
| 1854 | 9,283 | | | | | 715 | |
| 1855 | 9,085 | | | | | 685 | |
| 1856 | 9,209 | | | | | 741 | |
| 1857 | 9,591 | | | | | 1,068 | |
| 1858 | | | | | | 1,078 | 383,641 |
| 1859 | | | | | | 988 | 372,669 |
| 1860 | | | | | | 894 | 387,368 |
| 1861 | | | | | | 923 | 473,351 |
| 1862 | | | | | | 869 | 466,582 |
| 1863 | 7,931 | | | | | 877 | 441,428 |
| 1864 | 7,796 | | | | | 838 | 401,334 |
| 1865 | 7,592 | | | | | 823 | 433,160 |
| 1866 | 7,894 | | | | | 879 | 487,286 |
| 1867 | 7,893 | | | | | 856 | 541,704 |
| 1868 | 7,987 | | | | | 995 | 569,832 |
| 1869 | 7,969 | | | | | 1,063 | 544,910 |
| 1870 | 8,085 | | | | | 921 | 522,419 |
| 1871 | 8,041 | | | | | 953 | 520,991 |
| 1872 | 7,973 | | | | | 959 | 510,947 |

Table 3 *Continued*

| Year | Total sitting days | Judges | Registrars | Trials before judges | Trials before registrars | Jury trials | Non-jury trials |
|---|---|---|---|---|---|---|---|
| 1873 | 8,014 | | | | | 996 | 489,267 |
| 1874 | 8,028 | | | | | 991 | 494,483 |
| 1875 | 8,110 | | | | | 1,030 | 494,689 |
| 1876 | 8,212 | | | | | 1,143 | 545,829 |
| 1877 | 8,223 | | | | | 1,101 | 603,146 |
| 1878 | 8,271 | | | | | 993 | 615,497 |
| 1879 | 8,283 | | | | | 1,079 | 614,048 |
| 1880 | 8,268 | | | | | 995 | 657,695 |
| 1881 | 8,103 | | | | | 981 | 631,647 |
| 1882 | 8,125 | | | | | 952 | 624,493 |
| 1883 | 8,198 | | | | | 949 | 610,009 |
| 1884 | 8,252 | | | | | 1,196 | 576,394 |
| 1885 | 8,682 | | | | | 1,150 | 585,586 |
| 1886 | 8,714 | | | | | 1,076 | 603,299 |
| 1887 | 8,861 | | | | | 1,209 | 623,369 |
| 1888 | 9,224 | | | | | 1,181 | 654,784 |
| 1889 | 9,180 | | | | | 1,250 | 648,087 |
| 1890 | 9,184 | | | | | 1,270 | 616,660 |
| 1891 | 9,072 | | | | | 1,505 | 642,832 |
| 1892 | 9,241 | | | | | 1,487 | 671,413 |
| 1893 | 9,300 | | | | | 1,430 | 677,171 |
| 1894 | 9,445 | | | | | 1,237 | 712,321 |
| 1895 | 9,299 | | | | | 1,186 | 692,011 |
| 1896 | 9,174 | | | | | 1,150 | 700,562 |
| 1897 | 9,249 | | | | | 1,001 | 713,283 |
| 1898 | 9,090 | | | | | 1,068 | 724,256 |

Table 3 *Continued*

| Year | Total sitting days | Judges | Registrars | Trials before judges | Trials before registrars | Jury trials | Non-jury trials |
|---|---|---|---|---|---|---|---|
| 1899 | 9,244 | | | | | 1,018 | 732,094 |
| 1900 | 9,805 | | | | | 894 | 732,369 |
| 1901 | 9,766 | | | | | 1,001 | 782,654 |
| 1902 | 9,710 | | | | | 882 | 819,360 |
| 1903 | 10,024 | | | | | 889 | 857,136 |
| 1904 | 10,060 | | | 43,652 | 425,839 | 878 | 890,030 |
| 1905 | 10,071 | | | 39,747 | 412,112 | 843 | 874,437 |
| 1906 | 10,226 | | | 39,339 | 400,795 | 842 | 847,619 |
| 1907 | 10,230 | | | 38,347 | 394,879 | 887 | 835,642 |
| 1908 | 10,390 | | | 38,942 | 403,158 | 824 | 869,239 |
| 1909 | 10,384 | | | 40,121 | 405,570 | 725 | 896,217 |
| 1910 | 10,354 | | | 34,131 | 405,080 | 677 | 870,172 |
| 1911 | 10,342 | | | 34,881 | 385,509 | 735 | 821,889 |
| 1912 | 10,363 | | | 32,343 | 369,366 | 771 | 789,968 |
| 1913 | 9,299 | | | 30,970 | 373,591 | 762 | 784,692 |
| 1914 | 9,988 | | | 26,202 | 290,925 | 586 | 616,244 |
| 1915 | 9,654 | | | 23,309 | 196,105 | 529 | 448,010 |
| 1916 | 9,278 | | | 19,830 | 152,804 | 486 | 336,154 |
| 1917 | 8,865 | | | 17,834 | 119,355 | 319 | 257,886 |
| 1918 | 8,289 | | | 16,449 | 83,308 | 165 | 178,661 |
| 1919 | 8,315 | | | 22,573 | 80,013 | 14 | 177,640 |
| 1920 | 9,124 | | | 31,683 | 107,111 | 36 | 253,769 |
| 1921 | 9,819 | | | 36,094 | 116,495 | 34 | 319,909 |
| 1922 | 10,291 | | | 38,432 | 163,961 | | |
| 1923 | 10,400 | 8,199 | 2,141 | 46,123 | 203,026 | | |
| 1924 | 10,580 | 8,368 | 2,209 | 42,732 | 37,101 | | |

Table 3 *Continued*

| Year | Total sitting days | Judges | Registrars | Trials before judges | Trials before registrars | Jury trials | Non-jury trials |
|---|---|---|---|---|---|---|---|
| 1925 | 10,517 | 8,326 | 2,193 | 31,743 | 14,422 | | |
| 1926 | 10,388 | 8,222 | 2,165 | 29,600 | 9,548 | | |
| 1927 | 10,667 | 8,454 | 2,213 | 28,685 | 8,587 | | |
| 1928 | 10,664 | 8,511 | 2,153 | 26,951 | 7,115 | | |
| 1929 | 10,630 | 8,511 | 2,119 | 26,831 | 6,682 | | |
| 1930 | 10,760 | 8,507 | 2,253 | 26,328 | 7,403 | | |
| 1931 | 11,014 | 8,620 | 2,404 | 26,207 | 7,242 | | |
| 1932 | 11,175 | 8,714 | 2,461 | 26,022 | 7,391 | | |
| 1933 | 11,270 | 8,862 | 2,408 | 24,746 | 7,817 | | |
| 1934 | 11,280 | 8,765 | 2,515 | 23,376 | 8,040 | | |
| 1935 | 11,230 | 8,704 | 2,526 | 19,785 | 9,084 | | |
| 1936 | 11,224 | 8,651 | 2,753 | 18,742 | 9,486 | | |
| 1937 | 11,174 | 8,606 | 2,568 | 18,491 | 10,951 | | |
| 1938 | 11,387 | 8,671 | 2,716 | 19,414 | 11,407 | | |
| 1939 | | | | 16,262 | 10,568 | | |
| 1940 | | | | 13,557 | 6,961 | | |
| 1941 | | | | 12,876 | 4,447 | | |
| 1942 | | | | 11,913 | 3,864 | | |
| 1943 | | | | 11,844 | 3,358 | | |
| 1944 | | | | 13,710 | 2,760 | | |
| 1945 | | | | 16,431 | 2,525 | | |
| 1946 | | | | 24,437 | 3,274 | | |
| 1947 | | | | 23,166 | 3,182 | | |
| 1948 | 9,849 | 8,420 | 1,416 | 22,962 | 3,737 | | |
| 1949 | 10,283 | 8,630 | 1,652 | 20,512 | 3,693 | | |
| 1950 | 10,515 | 8,739 | 1,776 | 23,865 | 4,818 | | |

Table 3 *Continued*

| Year | Total sitting days | Judges | Registrars | Trials before judges | Trials before registrars | Jury trials | Non-jury trials |
|---|---|---|---|---|---|---|---|
| 1951 | 10,483 | 8,773 | 1,710 | 23,644 | 5,404 | | |
| 1952 | 10,610 | 8,789 | 1,821 | 24,377 | 5,750 | | |
| 1953 | 10,796 | 8,941 | 1,855 | 21,914 | 6,090 | | |
| 1954 | 14,889 | 8,936 | 5,953 | 20,623 | 5,898 | | |
| 1955 | 15,452 | 8,867 | 6,585 | 18,307 | 5,866 | | |
| 1956 | 16,467 | 9,302 | 7,165 | 16,290 | 7,664 | | |
| 1957 | 17,180 | 9,736 | 7,444 | 15,819 | 8,555 | | |
| 1958 | 17,857 | 10,142 | 7,715 | 17,110 | 9,822 | | |
| 1959 | 18,732 | 10,589 | 8,143 | 21,656 | 11,841 | | |
| 1960 | 19,554 | 11,025 | 8,529 | 19,103 | 12,586 | | |
| 1961 | 20,321 | 11,414 | 8,907 | 19,784 | 13,557 | | |
| 1962 | 20,290 | 11,375 | 8,915 | 19,865 | 14,492 | | |
| 1963 | 20,633 | 11,653 | 8,980 | 19,249 | 15,497 | | |
| 1964 | 20,657 | 11,450 | 8,807 | 18,091 | 16,569 | | |
| 1965 | 20,713 | 12,008 | 8,705 | 23,417 | 43,612 | | |
| 1966 | 21,208 | 12,350 | 8,858 | 29,898 | 97,301 | | |
| 1967 | 22,235 | 13,006 | 9,229 | 32,567 | 103,206 | | |
| 1968 | 22,500 | 13,292 | 9,208 | 33,978 | 106,336 | | |
| 1969 | 22,853 | 13,576 | 9,277 | 35,843 | 134,164 | | |
| 1970 | 23,406 | 13,724 | 9,082 | 43,239 | 149,757 | | |
| 1971 | 22,756 | 12,891 | 9,865 | 38,408 | 133,013 | | |

Table 4 *Outcomes, 1859–1921*

| Year | Judgment for the plaintiff | Judgment for the plaintiff by consent | Judgment for the plaintiff in default of appearance | Plaintiff non-suited | Judgment for the defendant |
|---|---|---|---|---|---|
| 1859 | 285,984 | 137,978 | 588 | 8,861 | 9,089 |
| 1860 | 296,719 | 151,851 | 814 | 8,867 | 9,089 |
| 1861 | 342,530 | 191,323 | 1,003 | 9,827 | 9,449 |
| 1862 | 259,400 | 187,646 | 1,128 | 10,170 | 9,107 |
| 1863 | 252,344 | 171,168 | 832 | 8,893 | 9,068 |
| 1864 | 236,758 | 147,855 | 464 | 8,440 | 8,655 |
| 1865 | 253,635 | 163,161 | 471 | 8,364 | 8,352 |
| 1866 | 285,791 | 184,147 | 470 | 8,883 | 8,874 |
| 1867 | 310,337 | 213,291 | 524 | 9,138 | 9,230 |
| 1868 | 334,675 | 215,732 | 2,466 | 8,844 | 9,110 |
| 1869 | 321,585 | 202,954 | 3,063 | 8,725 | 9,646 |
| 1870 | 306,272 | 195,749 | 3,723 | 8,185 | 9,411 |
| 1871 | 307,229 | 193,606 | 3,663 | 8,285 | 9,161 |
| 1872 | 305,354 | 185,896 | 3,463 | 8,339 | 8,854 |
| 1873 | 282,148 | 176,975 | 13,831 | 8,080 | 9,229 |
| 1874 | 288,788 | 178,352 | 11,183 | 7,975 | 9,176 |
| 1875 | 289,678 | 174,837 | 13,947 | 8,094 | 9,163 |
| 1876 | 304,818 | 189,102 | 35,435 | 7,028 | 10,589 |
| 1877 | 333,541 | 214,687 | 38,762 | 6,996 | 10,261 |
| 1878 | 336,024 | 223,312 | 40,547 | 6,567 | 10,040 |
| 1879 | 327,341 | 227,224 | 44,504 | 6,269 | 9,769 |
| 1880 | 354,196 | 245,637 | 42,210 | 6,334 | 10,313 |
| 1881 | 342,874 | 233,201 | 40,678 | 5,936 | 9,939 |
| 1882 | 342,525 | 228,789 | 37,228 | 6,023 | 9,880 |
| 1883 | 334,141 | 225,846 | 35,743 | 5,438 | 9,790 |
| 1884 | 313,004 | 213,481 | 36,324 | 5,164 | 9,617 |
| 1885 | 309,063 | 222,381 | 41,224 | 4,544 | 9,504 |
| 1886 | 316,070 | 231,917 | 42,829 | 4,133 | 9,426 |
| 1887 | 327,355 | 239,309 | 44,164 | 4,134 | 9,616 |
| 1888 | 350,849 | 249,871 | 42,064 | 3,691 | 9,490 |
| 1889 | 352,197 | 237,814 | 46,706 | 3,895 | 8,725 |
| 1890 | 342,024 | 220,480 | 43,303 | 3,460 | 8,663 |
| 1891 | 358,618 | 226,237 | 47,696 | 3,056 | 8,730 |
| 1892 | 367,942 | 241,848 | 51,071 | 3,195 | 8,844 |
| 1893 | 367,412 | 245,988 | 55,340 | 2,979 | 8,882 |
| 1894 | 383,065 | 259,727 | 59,299 | 2,637 | 8,828 |
| 1895 | 375,980 | 247,915 | 57,978 | 2,550 | 8,834 |
| 1896 | 373,480 | 261,281 | 55,531 | 2,562 | 8,858 |
| 1897 | 387,498 | 262,123 | 53,598 | 2,329 | 8,736 |
| 1898 | 383,727 | 274,509 | 56,452 | 2,109 | 8,678 |
| 1899 | 395,220 | 268,509 | 57,597 | 1,936 | 8,832 |
| 1900 | 395,855 | 267,757 | 59,827 | 1,625 | 8,219 |
| 1901 | 421,091 | 292,502 | 58,940 | 1,647 | 8,665 |
| 1902 | 436,068 | 308,796 | 65,112 | 1,719 | 8,547 |

Table 4 *Continued*

| Year | Judgment for the plaintiff | Judgment for the plaintiff by consent | Judgment for the plaintiff in default of appearance | Plaintiff non-suited | Judgment for the defendant |
|---|---|---|---|---|---|
| 1903 | 450,133 | 329,640 | 68,096 | 1,799 | 8,357 |
| 1904 | 459,435 | 345,112 | 76,412 | 1,821 | 8,235 |
| 1905 | 441,444 | 343,786 | 79,635 | 1,937 | 8,478 |
| 1906 | 430,555 | 329,655 | 78,662 | 1,697 | 7,882 |
| 1907 | 423,871 | 324,803 | 78,500 | 1,686 | 7,669 |
| 1908 | 433,052 | 341,413 | 86,550 | 1,605 | 7,443 |
| 1909 | 436,257 | 361,447 | 89,804 | 1,654 | 7,780 |
| 1910 | 430,868 | 345,533 | 86,086 | 1,356 | 6,987 |
| 1911 | 412,085 | 321,920 | 80,314 | 1,339 | 6,966 |
| 1912 | 393,675 | 308,212 | 80,818 | 1,221 | 6,813 |
| 1913 | 396,751 | 303,332 | 77,561 | 1,151 | 6,659 |
| 1914 | 310,641 | 232,499 | 67,204 | 972 | 5,514 |
| 1915 | 213,995 | 167,749 | 61,376 | 751 | 4,668 |
| 1916 | 167,901 | 123,979 | 40,027 | 656 | 4,077 |
| 1917 | 133,019 | 95,218 | 25,798 | 515 | 3,655 |
| 1918 | 95,939 | 62,429 | 16,640 | 479 | 3,339 |
| 1919 | 96,896 | 59,455 | 15,613 | 848 | 4,842 |
| 1920 | 129,586 | 85,301 | 29,710 | 936 | 8,272 |
| 1921 | 143,745 | 110,427 | 56,927 | 774 | 8,070 |

Table 5 *Enforcement proceedings 1847–1971*

| Year | Judgment summonses issued | Judgment summonses heard | Committal orders made | Committals enforced | Executions against goods issued | Sales made |
|---|---|---|---|---|---|---|
| 1847–1849 | | | 32,750 | 14,769 | 122,038 | |
| 1850 | | | 13,086 | 5,693 | | |
| 1851 | | | 9,839 | | | |
| 1852 | | | 11,044 | 5,231 | | |
| 1853 | 47,704 | 27,589 | 12,399 | 5,416 | | |
| 1854 | 56,046 | 28,781 | 14,211 | 5,977 | | |
| 1855 | 59,990 | 29,714 | 14,967 | 6,480 | | |
| 1856 | 72,467 | 35,141 | 17,252 | 7,011 | | |
| 1857 | 112,961 | 56,655 | 27,783 | 10,607 | | |
| 1858 | | | 30,756 | 10,748 | 98,709 | |
| 1859 | 118,878 | 55,082 | 27,284 | 9,003 | 98,589 | 3,766 |
| 1860 | 112,313 | 50,838 | 22,399 | 6,955 | 109,366 | 3,973 |
| 1861 | 130,254 | 59,388 | 26,696 | 8,635 | 129,140 | 4,913 |
| 1862 | 122,285 | 61,584 | 26,757 | 9,373 | 131,760 | 4,849 |
| 1863 | 119,713 | 62,363 | 27,861 | 8,588 | 129,922 | 4,075 |
| 1864 | 76,613 | 42,398 | 23,096 | 6,529 | 124,804 | 3,610 |
| 1865 | 88,835 | 47,226 | 24,428 | 6,346 | 133,589 | 3,739 |
| 1866 | 100,411 | 54,319 | 29,347 | 7,601 | 145,816 | 3,828 |
| 1867 | 107,674 | 59,277 | 30,684 | 8,362 | 159,784 | 4,523 |
| 1868 | 117,528 | 65,252 | 33,850 | 9,592 | 178,894 | 5,265 |
| 1869 | 120,062 | 67,367 | 34,299 | 9,709 | 179,791 | 4,927 |
| 1870 | 113,411 | 61,474 | 26,337 | 6,597 | 179,822 | 3,765 |

Table 5 *Continued*

| Year | Judgment summonses issued | Judgment summonses heard | Committal orders made | Committals enforced | Executions against goods issued | Sales made |
|---|---|---|---|---|---|---|
| 1871 | 123,928 | 66,606 | 33,704 | 7,969 | 181,123 | 4,435 |
| 1872 | 124,367 | 64,992 | 33,823 | 6,899 | 177,421 | 3,877 |
| 1873 | 106,534 | 54,111 | 27,637 | 5,199 | 174,682 | 3,441 |
| 1874 | 96,080 | 47,871 | 23,232 | 4,198 | 176,321 | 3,643 |
| 1875 | 94,553 | 47,195 | 23,062 | 4,063 | 176,078 | 3,690 |
| 1876 | 99,165 | 51,738 | 23,696 | 4,335 | 194,635 | 4,335 |
| 1877 | 108,948 | 58,335 | 25,543 | 5,020 | 216,609 | 5,341 |
| 1878 | 121,937 | 69,327 | 28,574 | 5,664 | 221,757 | 5,724 |
| 1879 | 135,137 | 76,886 | 31,201 | 6,246 | 223,203 | 5,535 |
| 1880 | 161,629 | 91,595 | 36,788 | 6,865 | 236,051 | 5,599 |
| 1881 | 127,138 | 74,827 | 35,113 | 5,544 | 240,709 | 5,409 |
| 1882 | 159,229 | 94,149 | 40,271 | 5,384 | 233,811 | 4,681 |
| 1883 | 161,186 | 96,213 | 43,344 | 5,370 | 231,682 | 4,808 |
| 1884 | 159,932 | 93,096 | 42,756 | 5,212 | 221,966 | 4,881 |
| 1885 | 163,422 | 96,640 | 43,475 | 5,483 | 227,082 | 4,649 |
| 1886 | 165,062 | 97,977 | 44,855 | 5,486 | 223,877 | 4,640 |
| 1887 | 180,286 | 113,947 | 46,869 | 5,277 | 232,876 | 4,811 |
| 1888 | 201,335 | 119,849 | 54,995 | 6,429 | 237,416 | 4,659 |
| 1889 | 213,811 | 127,619 | 68,836 | 6,554 | 233,478 | 4,220 |
| 1890 | 221,004 | 132,421 | 70,397 | 6,443 | 222,553 | 3,778 |
| 1891 | 229,686 | 135,421 | 74,108 | 5,852 | 228,538 | 3,854 |
| 1892 | 232,040 | 141,868 | 78,952 | 6,997 | 234,551 | 3,918 |
| 1893 | 227,711 | 138,042 | 75,834 | 6,889 | 240,199 | 4,393 |
| 1894 | 263,800 | 160,196 | 84,603 | 7,628 | 251,461 | 4,206 |

Table 5 *Continued*

| Year | Judgment summonses issued | Judgment summonses heard | Committal orders made | Committals enforced | Executions against goods issued | Sales made |
|---|---|---|---|---|---|---|
| 1895 | 275,423 | 166,875 | 93,041 | 8,375 | 225,591 | 3,968 |
| 1896 | 301,084 | 187,519 | 106,542 | 8,190 | 223,502 | 3,826 |
| 1897 | 307,635 | 189,107 | 112,096 | 7,727 | 225,589 | 3,885 |
| 1898 | 311,977 | 189,830 | 114,358 | 7,803 | 233,563 | 3,592 |
| 1899 | 325,343 | 203,054 | 121,608 | 7,864 | 233,771 | 3,539 |
| 1900 | 327,055 | 203,570 | 129,044 | 7,890 | 251,377 | 3,733 |
| 1901 | 333,091 | 204,746 | 129,976 | 8,490 | 268,204 | 3,961 |
| 1902 | 348,360 | 216,547 | 139,101 | 9,504 | 291,686 | 4,025 |
| 1903 | 358,251 | 227,061 | 145,251 | 10,527 | 314,572 | 4,218 |
| 1904 | 365,616 | 227,069 | 135,798 | 11,066 | 327,764 | 4,647 |
| 1905 | 390,305 | 249,845 | 146,682 | 11,405 | 328,363 | 4,299 |
| 1906 | 390,729 | 254,103 | 152,759 | 11,986 | 321,408 | 3,912 |
| 1907 | 373,100 | 238,445 | 146,075 | 9,214 | 325,007 | 3,613 |
| 1908 | 372,983 | 235,491 | 138,626 | 9,141 | 343,662 | 3,917 |
| 1909 | 375,254 | 234,753 | 136,630 | 8,904 | 352,308 | 3,805 |
| 1910 | 385,588 | 240,722 | 140,660 | 8,189 | 351,827 | 3,625 |
| 1911 | 387,644 | 242,301 | 142,899 | 7,681 | 342,219 | 3,300 |
| 1912 | 378,079 | 240,228 | 142,457 | 5,820 | 328,191 | 2,761 |
| 1913 | 404,260 | 258,007 | 157,827 | 5,711 | 326,341 | 2,678 |
| 1914 | 295,449 | 196,184 | 114,238 | 3,887 | 217,146 | 1,712 |
| 1915 | 223,386 | 138,564 | 70,331 | 1,542 | 125,829 | 1,029 |
| 1916 | 176,890 | 113,984 | 63,263 | 1,068 | 128,205 | 861 |
| 1917 | 131,297 | 83,902 | 46,433 | 559 | 104,298 | 608 |
| 1918 | 88,484 | 55,914 | 31,733 | 293 | 84,963 | 412 |

Table 5 *Continued*

| Year | Judgment summonses issued | Judgment summonses heard | Committal orders made | Committals enforced | Executions against goods issued | Sales made |
|---|---|---|---|---|---|---|
| 1919 | 74,815 | 44,761 | 21,647 | 206 | 83,236 | 274 |
| 1920 | 70,568 | 42,336 | 22,026 | 226 | 112,393 | 523 |
| 1921 | 62,430 | 37,688 | 18,511 | 424 | 142,387 | 1,084 |
| 1922 | 84,996 | 51,723 | 26,650 | 1,003 | 209,952 | 2,008 |
| 1923 | 117,307 | 74,042 | 39,697 | 1,635 | 271,694 | 2,471 |
| 1924 | 148,243 | 94,416 | 53,107 | 1,957 | 308,724 | 2,497 |
| 1925 | 174,356 | 112,855 | 67,489 | 2,632 | 339,429 | 2,500 |
| 1926 | 151,890 | 98,205 | 59,642 | 2,386 | 300,375 | 2,607 |
| 1927 | 200,686 | 127,883 | 75,330 | 2,894 | 330,283 | 3,767 |
| 1928 | 223,869 | 139,955 | 85,190 | 3,510 | 400,159 | 3,568 |
| 1929 | 240,301 | 146,883 | 87,581 | 3,484 | 409,039 | 2,734 |
| 1930 | 262,113 | 158,808 | 93,677 | 3,932 | 430,031 | 2,903 |
| 1931 | 267,354 | 160,785 | 93,927 | 3,554 | 442,675 | 3,091 |
| 1932 | 279,906 | 169,695 | 99,876 | 4,041 | 489,238 | 3,147 |
| 1933 | 285,236 | 170,127 | 100,015 | 3,542 | 501,576 | 2,894 |
| 1934 | 298,944 | 183,245 | 105,851 | 3,117 | 490,199 | 3,413 |
| 1935 | 302,803 | 185,538 | 113,965 | 3,087 | 474,091 | 3,434 |
| 1936 | 327,354 | 198,613 | 118,096 | 2,992 | 470,680 | 3,252 |
| 1937 | 348,349 | 216,079 | 125,042 | 2,597 | 460,929 | 2,601 |
| 1938 | 374,193 | 232,659 | 138,794 | 3,452 | 458,403 | 2,431 |
| 1939 | 351,580 | 204,176 | 107,002 | 2,593 | 334,579 | 1,669 |
| 1940 | 297,360 | 172,281 | 105,723 | 983 | 204,410 | 906 |
| 1941 | 219,979 | 132,015 | 88,177 | 864 | 161,860 | 653 |
| 1942 | 179,891 | 106,337 | 70,674 | 550 | 131,126 | 576 |

Table 5 *Continued*

| Year | Judgment summonses issued | Judgment summonses heard | Committal orders made | Committals enforced | Executions against goods issued | Sales made |
|---|---|---|---|---|---|---|
| 1943 | 122,762 | 71,185 | 53,821 | 367 | 98,814 | 440 |
| 1944 | 74,388 | 45,712 | 34,096 | 271 | 74,549 | 356 |
| 1945 | 61,144 | 39,304 | 26,872 | 221 | 65,046 | 253 |
| 1946 | 60,744 | 37,472 | 22,915 | 243 | 80,923 | 301 |
| 1947 | 60,027 | 37,613 | 23,911 | 254 | 98,598 | 457 |
| 1948 | 61,270 | 39,015 | 23,045 | 349 | 122,515 | 838 |
| 1949 | 66,430 | 40,970 | 22,208 | 445 | 139,580 | 1,137 |
| 1950 | 78,628 | 48,859 | 23,737 | 489 | 188,325 | 1,403 |
| 1951 | 91,720 | 56,741 | 27,151 | 628 | 242,502 | 1,736 |
| 1952 | 106,065 | 65,054 | 32,320 | 810 | 283,419 | 1,980 |
| 1953 | 122,395 | 76,175 | 35,824 | 1,061 | 316,628 | 1,971 |
| 1954 | 134,698 | 84,076 | 39,267 | 1,187 | 363,459 | 2,235 |
| 1955 | 147,296 | 93,519 | 46,883 | 1,215 | 393,323 | 2,635 |
| 1956 | 170,425 | 104,837 | 53,712 | 1,668 | 452,977 | 2,680 |
| 1957 | 212,786 | 126,601 | 63,570 | 2,539 | 591,101 | 4,899 |
| 1958 | 259,227 | 158,536 | 76,714 | 4,160 | 813,689 | 8,906 |
| 1959 | 317,655 | 201,468 | 93,018 | 5,355 | 1,026,631 | 12,442 |
| 1960 | 434,481 | 263,544 | 118,304 | 5,675 | 1,200,739 | 10,539 |
| 1961 | 491,381 | 321,400 | 159,600 | 6,323 | 1,349,280 | 7,656 |
| 1962 | 547,557 | 361,801 | 178,304 | 7,913 | 1,607,585 | 7,314 |
| 1963 | 572,729 | 378,585 | 181,505 | 7,551 | 1,650,685 | 5,505 |
| 1964 | 579,725 | 396,140 | 199,159 | 5,948 | 1,757,615 | 4,113 |
| 1965 | 558,652 | 385,096 | 199,214 | 3,669 | 1,788,710 | 3,269 |
| 1966 | 539,026 | 370,847 | 182,857 | 3,155 | 1,654,848 | 3,206 |

Table 5 *Continued*

| Year | Judgment summonses issued | Judgment summonses heard | Committal orders made | Committals enforced | Executions against goods issued | Sales made |
|---|---|---|---|---|---|---|
| 1967 | 531,370 | 360,511 | 177,946 | 3,329 | 1,608,332 | 3,445 |
| 1968 | 539,797 | 366,847 | 173,852 | 2,789 | 1,621,383 | 3,065 |
| 1969 | 520,347 | 353,389 | 175,634 | 2,364 | 1,599,198 | 3,204 |
| 1970 | 496,447 | 331,286 | 172,262 | 2,252 | 1,776,625 | 3,125 |
| 1971 | 163,782 | 129,938 | 88,594 | 1,200 | 1,611,614 | 3,920 |

# BIBLIOGRAPHY

## PRIMARY SOURCES

### MANUSCRIPT SOURCES


*Public Record Office, London*
Lord Chancellor's Department
PRO LCO 1 and 2: General series
4: Establishments
7: Royal Commission on Assizes and Quarter Sessions
8: County Courts, headquarters files
12: County Courts Branch
26: Registry of County Court Judgments
29: Reports of Committees
31: Committee on Judgment Debts
33: Personal Files
49: County Court Rule Committee minutes

Home Office
HO 86: County Courts, out letters

Treasury
T 10: County Courts, out letters, 1849–1913
15: General Law Letter Books
164 Superannuations

Board of Trade
BT 37/22: Report of Select Committee on Debtors, 1909

Ministry of Pensions and Social Security
PIN 12/1: Workmen's Compensation inquiry, 1903

Cairns MSS
PRO 30/8

*British Library*
BL Add. MSS 56,370–5: Halsbury MSS

*Association of County Court Registrars*
Minute Books and other papers

PARLIAMENTARY AND OFFICIAL PUBLICATIONS

Annual series
*Parliamentary Debates* (*Hansard*), 1820 to 1980
*House of Lords Journals*, 1820 to 1980
*House of Commons Journals* 1820 to 1980
*Returns from County Courts*: these began with *PP* 1847–8 (271) LI, initially providing for each court details of the plaints (grouped by amount), sittings, trials, receipts and execution. They ceased with the inception of the annual series of civil judicial statistics in 1858 but were revived in 1867 with *PP* 1867 (244) LVII and continued to be requested and produced in parallel with the main series. Though much of the information is duplicated and the two returns are not always in agreement, the county court series contains some not available elsewhere, though without much in the way of a commentary. The last in the *Parliamentary Papers* is 1914–16 (319) LIV, but from 1916 to 1922 (covering 1915–21), they were published as non-Parliamentary papers. Following the report of the Chitty Committee they were discontinued.
*Civil Judicial Statistics*: in 1859 (*PP* 1859 (C 3) XXVI sess. 1) the annual series of Civil Judicial Statistics was begun, compiled in the Home Office but with county court information supplied by the Treasury's County Courts Department. They were redesigned and greatly improved from *PP* 1896 [C 8263] XCIV (covering 1894) under Sir John MacDonnell's auspices and continued in this style until 1922 and thereafter in greatly reduced and skimpy fashion. Following the report of the Adams Committee in 1968 they were modestly expanded. Between 1940 and 1948 (covering 1939–47) only an annual summary was issued, as a non-parliamentary publication.
*Annual Reports from the Public Accounts Committee*, 1865–1972.
*Annual Reports of the Comptroller and Auditor-General on the County Court Accounts*: these were instituted after changes to the treatment of funds in court in the mid-1930s, see *PP* 1936–7 (85) XXI. They contain little of interest.
*Annual Reports of the Comptroller on the Legal Aid Fund*: these began in the 1950–1 session but only became important for the county courts from 1956 onwards.

*Bills*
*HLSP* 1820 CXIV (18, 97): For the more convenient recovery of small debts . . .
*PP* 1821 (85, 233) I: To regulate the proceedings of county courts as to small debts.
*HLSP* 1824 CLIX (76); *PP* 1824 (49, 117, 213) and *HLSP* 1825

CLXXV (108); *PP* 1825 (14, 261) I: For preventing delays and expenses in the proceedings of county courts.

*PP* 1826–7 (535) II: For the more easy recovery of small debts in county courts.

*HLSP* 1830–1 CCLXXXIII and *PP* 1830 (568, 569) I and *HLSP* 1833 CCXIV (16, 79, 86, 95, 100): For establishing courts of local jurisdiction.

*PP* 1837 (363) IV: To enable recorders ... to hold court ... for the recovery of small debts.

*PP* 1837–8 (296) III: For the improvement of the criminal and civil jurisdiction of the county courts.

*PP* 1839 (71, 387–I), II: For improving the county courts.

*HLSP* 1841 (180) II; *PP* 1841 (43, 153) I: To improve the practice of the county courts.

*PP* 1841 (85, 535, 1827) I: For the more easy recovery of small debts.

*HLSP* 1841 (186) II and *HLSP* 1842 (22) II: To enable ... certain proceedings in chancery, bankruptcy, insolvency and lunacy ... to be carried on in county courts.

*HLSP* 1842 (139, 215) II and *PP* 1842 (498, 531, 550) I: For regulating the practice of county courts (also as *PP* 1843 (198) I).

*PP* 1842 (364) II: To encourage the establishment of district courts.

*PP* 1843 (214) I: For altering and improving the proceedings in the superior courts.

*PP* 1843 (232) IV and *PP* 1844 (9, 161, 216) I: For the more easy recovery of small debts and demands.

*HLSP* 1845 (153) V; *PP* 1845 (374, 414, 526, 566) VI: For the more easy recovery of small debts.

*HLSP* 1845 (180, 192, 198, 214, 346, 363) V: For better securing the payment of small debts.

*HLSP* 1846 (187, 259, 321) V; *PP* 1846 (587, 609, 644, 678) IV: For the more easy recovery of small debts. *County Courts Act 1846*, 9 & 10 Vict. c. 95.

*PP* 1847–8 (265) VI; *PP* 1848–9 (433, 470) VI: *County Courts Act 1849*, 12 & 13 Vict. c. 101.

*PP* 1849–50 (92, 298, 449, 608) I; *HLSP* (214, 259, 265, 307) III; (214a, 259a 306): *County Courts Extension Act 1850*, 13 & 14 Vict. c. 61.

*HLSP* 1849–50 (312) III: County Courts Extension Act Amendment Bill.

*HLSP* 1850–1 (7, 12, 137) IV: To give county courts jurisdiction in bankruptcy; also *HLSP* 1852 (62, 62a) IV, 1852–3 (12) III.

*HLSP* 1850–1 (71) IV: County courts Equitable Jurisdiction Bill; also 1852–3 (11) IV.

*HLSP* 1850–1 (41, 53, 55, 58, 58a, 68, 70, 304) IV; *PP* 1851 (257, 364, 461, 636) I: County Courts Further Extension Bill.

*HLSP* 1852 (5, 44, 192) III; *PP* 1852 (178, 251, 455) I: *County Courts Act 1852*, 15 & 16 Vict. c. 54.

*HLSP* 1854 (34) III; *PP* 1854 (38) II: *County Courts Act 1854*, 17 & 18 Vict. c. 16.

*HLSP* 1856 (52, 100, 153) IV; *PP* 1856 (179, 252, 256) II: *County Courts Act 1856*, 19 & 20 Vict. c. 108.
*HLSP* 1857 (151 sess. 2) III; *PP* 1857 (143) I: *County Courts (Salaries) Act 1857*, 20 & 21 Vict. c. 36.
*HLSP* 1858 (171, 171a, 191) III; *PP* (195) I: *County Courts (Districts) Act 1858*, 21 & 22 Vict. c. 74.
*HLSP* 1859 (57) II; *PP* 1859 (58) I (51 sess. 2) I: *Small Debts Imprisonment Act 1859*, 22 & 23 Vict. c. 57.
*PP* 1860–1 (117) I; also *PP* 1861–2 (19) I: County Courts Procedure Bill.
*HLSP* 1864 (70, 76a) III: County Courts Amendment Bill.
*HLSP* 1864–5 (9, 82, 94, 98, 210) III; *PP* 1864–5 (150, 236) I: *County Courts (Equitable Jurisdiction) Act 1865*, 28 & 29 Vict. c. 99.
*PP* 1865–6 (47) II; *HLSP* 1865–6 (55) III: *County Courts Act 1866*, 29 & 30 Vict. c. 14.
*PP* 1866–7 (212) II; *HLSP* 1866–7 (108a, 140a, 156a, 169, 344) III: *County Courts Act 1867*, 30 & 31 Vict. c. 142.
*HLSP* 1866–7 (348) III: County Court Proceedings Bill.
*PP* 1866–7 (28) I: County Courts (Admiralty Jurisdiction) Bill
*PP* 1867–8 (33, 94) I; *HLSP*, (108a, b, c, 219) III: *County Courts (Admiralty Jurisdiction) Act 1868*, 31 & 32 Vict. c. 71.
*PP* 1868–9 (2) I: Admiralty Jurisdiction (County Courts) Bill.
*PP* 1868–9 (121) II; *HLSP* 1868–9 (173) IV: *County Courts (Admiralty Jurisdiction) Act (1868) Amendment Act 1869*, 32 & 33 Vict. c. 51.
*PP* 1868–9 (9) II: County Court Proceedings Bill.
*PP* 1868–9 (61, 98, 179, 252) III: *Debtors Act 1869*, 32 & 33 Vict. c. 62.
*PP* 1869–70 (91) I; *HLSP* (70, 80, 83) III: *County Court (Buildings) Act 1870*, 33 & 34 Vict. c. 15.
*PP* 1870–1 (91) I: County Courts (Jurisdiction and Procedure) Bill.
*PP* 1871–2 (85, 121) I: County Courts (Small Debts) Bill.
*HLSP* 1873–4 (117, 129) III; *PP* 1873–4 (175) I: County Courts Bill.
*HLSP* 1874–5 (57, 57a, 212) III; *PP* 1874–5 (156, 225) I: *County Courts Act 1875*, 38 & 39 Vict. c. 50.
*PP* 1875 (134) III; 1876 (33) III: Abolition of Imprisonment for Debt; also 1877 (49) II; 1881 (309) II; 1882 (102) II; 1883 (79) VI.
*PP* 1877 (71) and 1878 (10) I: To amend the law relating to the jurisdiction of county courts.
*PP* 1877 (110) I; 1878 (102) I: To further extend the jurisdiction of county courts.
*PP* 1877 (330) II: Abolition of imprisonment for debt . . . in certain cases.
*PP* 1878 (125) I: To amend the jurisdiction and procedure of county courts.
*PP* 1878 (100, 241) I: To extend the jurisdiction of county courts.
*PP* 1878–9 (40) I; 1880 (6), 1881 (34) II: To extend the jurisdiction of county courts.
*PP* 1878 (239) I: County Courts Jurisdiction Bill.
*PP* 1878–9 (191) I: County Courts Bill.
*PP* 1882 (146) I: To amend the County Courts Act 1867.
*PP* 1882 (188) I: *County Courts (Costs and Salaries) Act 1882*, 45 & 46 Vict. c. 57.

*PP* 1883 (103) II: To extend the jurisdiction of county courts.

*PP* 1883 (112) II: To enable county court judges to render assistance ... at the assizes.

*PP* 1884 (118) I: Bill to amend the laws as to appeals in bankruptcy.

*PP* 1884–5 (77) I: County Courts (Divorce) Bill.

*PP* 1887 (177) I: *County Courts (Expenses) Act 1887*, 50 & 51 Vict. c. 3.

*PP* 1887 (294) I: County Courts (Consolidation) Bill.

*PP* 1888 (173, 263) II: *County Courts Act 1888*, 51 & 52 Vict. c. 43.

*PP* 1889 (362) I; *PP* 1890 (344) I: County Courts Act (1888) Amendment Bill.

*HLSP* 1895 (134); *PP* 1898 (126) I: County Courts (Rights of Audience Bill).

*PP* 1897 (42) I; 1898 (41) I; 1900 (99) I: County Courts Jurisdiction Bill.

*PP* 1900 (216) I: *County Courts (Investments) Act 1900*, 63 & 64 Vict. c. 47.

*PP* 1900 (301) II: To amend the law regarding the imitation of county court process.

*PP* 1902 (82) I; 1903 (96) I: To extend the jurisdiction of county courts.

*PP* 1902 (26) I; 1903 (33, 122, 319) I: *County Courts Act 1903*, 3 Edw. VII c. 42.

*PP* 1904 (291) I: County Courts Bill.

*PP* 1904 (221) I: County Courts (Admiralty Jurisdiction) Amendment Bill.

*PP* 1905 (150, 180) I: County Courts Amendment Bill.

*PP* 1908 (269) I: County Courts Amendment Bill.

*PP* 1911 (91) I, 1912 (48) I: County Courts Bill.

*PP* 1911 (28) I: To abolish imprisonment for debt.

*PP* 1919 (230) I: *County Courts Act 1919*, 9 & 10 Geo. V c. 73.

*PP* 1919 (173) I: *County Court Judges (Retirement and Pensions) Act 1919*, 9 & 10 Geo. V c. 70.

*PP* 1922 (182) I: Economy (Miscellaneous Provisions) Bill.

*PP* 1923 (130) I; 1924 (62) I, *PP* 1924–5 (HL 91) I: *Administration of Justice Act 1925*, 15 & 16 Geo. V c. 28.

*PP* 1923 (211) I; *PP* 1924 (96) I: *County Courts Act 1924*, 14 & 15 Geo. V c. 17.

*PP* 1933–4 (158) I: *Administration of Justice (Appeals) Act 1934*, 24 & 25 Geo. V c. 40.

*PP* 1933–4 (65) I: *County Courts (Amendment) Act 1934*, 24 & 25 Geo. V c. 17.

*PP* 1933–4 (180) I: *County Courts Act 1934*, 24 & 25 Geo. V c. 53.

*PP* 1935–6 (40) I: County Courts Bill.

*PP* 1937–8 (124) I: *Administration of Justice (Miscellaneous Provisions) Act 1938*, 1 & 2 Geo. VI c. 63.

*PP* 1937–8 (14, 92, 221) II: *Hire Purchase Act 1938*, 1 & 2 Geo. VI c. 53.

*PP* 1940–1 (21) I: *Liabilities (War-time Adjustment) Act 1941*, 4 & 5 Geo. VI c. 24.

*PP* 1943–4 (46) I: *Liabilities (War-time Adjustment) Act 1944*, 7 & 8 Geo. VI c. 40.

*PP* 1950 (18) I: *High Court etc. Judges Act 1950*, 14 Geo. VI c. 4.

*PP* 1950–1 (13) I: *Administration of Justice (Pensions) Act 1950*, 14 & 15 Geo. VI c. 11.
*PP* 1954–5 (74) II: *County Courts Act 1955*, 4 Eliz. II c. 8.
*PP* 1955–6 (87) I: *Administration of Justice Act 1956*, 4 & 5 Eliz. II c. 46.
*PP* 1958–9 (70) I: *County Courts Act 1959*, 7 & 8 Eliz. II c. 22.
*PP* 1962–3 (39) I: *County Courts (Jurisdiction) Act 1963*, 11 & 12 Eliz. II c. 53
*PP* 1963–4 (62) I: *Administration of Justice Act 1964*, 12 & 13 Eliz. II c. 42.
*PP* 1963–4 (59) I: *Administration of Justice Act 1965*, 13 & 14 Eliz. II c. 21.
*PP* 1963–4 (165) I: County Courts (Non-Suit) Bill.
*PP* 1966–7 (217) III: *Matrimonial Causes Act 1967*, 15 & 16 Eliz. II c. 56.
*PP* 1968–9 (60) I: *Administration of Justice Act 1969*, 17 & 18 Eliz. II c. 58.
*PP* 1969–70 (85) I: *Administration of Justice Act 1970*, 18 & 19 Eliz. II c. 31.
*PP* 1970–71 (HL85) II: Courts Act 1971, 19 & 20 Eliz. II c. 23.

REPORTS OF COMMISSIONS, COMMITTEES ETC

*House of Commons series*

*PP* 1823 (386) IV: *Report of the Select Committee on County Courts.*
*PP* 1825 (276) V: *Minutes of Evidence to the Select Committee on County Courts.*
*PP* 1829 (46) IX: *First Report of the Royal Commission on the Courts of Common Law.*
*PP* 1831–2 (239) XXV: *Second Report of the Royal Commission on the Courts of Common Law.*
*PP* 1833 (247) XXII: *Fifth Report of the Commissioners on the Courts of Common Law.*
*PP* 1839 (387 II) XIII: *Report from the Select Committee on the County Courts Bill.*
*PP* 1854 [1731] XXIV: *Second Report of the Royal Commission on the Court of Chancery.*
*PP* 1854–5 [1914] XVIII: *Report of the Royal Commission on County Courts.*
*PP* 1858 (413) XVI: *Report from the Select Committee on Tribunals of Commerce.*
*PP* 1871 (409) XII: *Report from the Select Committee on Tribunals of Commerce.*
*PP* 1872 [C 631] XX: *Second Report of the Judicature Commissioners.*
*PP* 1873 (248) VII: *Report from the Select Committee on Civil Service Expenditure.*
*PP* 1873 (348) XV: *Report from the Select Committee on Imprisonment for Debt.*
*PP* 1874 (C 949, C 1107), XXIV: *First and Second Reports of the Royal Commission on the Legal Departments.*

*PP* 1875 (C 1245) XXX: *Minutes of Evidence etc. to the Royal Commission on the Legal Departments.*

*PP* 1878 (267) XI: *Report from the Select Committee on the County Courts (no. 2) Bill.*

*PP* 1887 [C 1539] XXVII: *Report of a Committee on s. 122 Bankruptcy Act 1883.*

*PP* 1888 (172) X: *Report from the Standing Committee on Law and Courts of Justice on the County Courts Bill.*

*PP* 1897 (364) XI; 1898 (260) XI: *First and Second Reports from the Select Committee on Moneylending.*

*PP* 1903 (97) V: *Report from the Standing Committee on Law etc. on the County Courts Jurisdiction Extension Bill.*

*PP* 1904 [Cd 2208] LXXXVIII; 1905 [Cd 2334]: *Report of the Departmental Committee into the Law relating to Compensation for Injuries to Workmen.*

*PP* 1908 (344) VII; 1909 (239) VII: *Report from the Select Committee on Debtors (Imprisonment).*

*PP* 1908 [Cd 4068, 4069] XXXIV: *Report of the Departmental Committee on Bankruptcy Law.*

*PP* 1909 (71) LXXII: *Report of the Departmental Committee into County Court Procedure.*

*PP* 1912–13 [Cd 6478] XVIII: *Report of the Royal Commission on Divorce and Matrimonial Causes.*

*PP* 1913 [Cd 6817] XXX: *Report of the Departmental Committee on Jury Law and Practice.*

*PP* 1913 [Cd 6761] XXX; *PP* 1914 [Cd 7177, 7178] XXXVII: *First and Second Reports of the Royal Commission on Delays in the King's Bench Division.*

*PP* 1914–16 [Cd 7832, 8130] XII: *Sixth Report of and Evidence to the Royal Commission on the Civil Service.*

*PP* 1916 [Cd 8200] XV: *Final Report of the Committee on Retrenchment.*

*PP* 1918 [Cd 9230] XII: *Report of the Machinery of Government Committee.*

*PP* 1919 [Cmd 431] XIIIa: *Report of the Lord Chancellor's Committee on County Courts.*

*PP* 1920 [Cmd 816, 908, 909], XXVI: *Report of and Evidence to the Departmental Committee on Workmen's Compensation.*

*PP* 1920 [Cmd 1049] XIII: *Report of the Lord Chancellor's County Court Staff Committee.*

*PP* 1922 [Cmd 1589] IX: *Third Report of the Public Expenditure Committee.*

*PP* 1923 [Cmd 1856] X: *Report of the Committee on County Court Fees.*

*PP* 1924 (88) VI: *Report of Standing Committee C on the County Courts Bill.*

*PP* 1924–5 (153) VIII: *Report of the Joint Select Committee on the Moneylenders Bill.*

*PP* 1928 [Cmd 3016] XI: *Report of the Committee on Legal Aid for the Poor.*

*PP* 1929–30 [Cmd 3375] XVII: *Report of the Poor Persons (Divorce Jurisdiction) Committee.*

*PP* 1930–1 [Cmd 3911] XVII: *Report of the Inter-Departmental Committee on the Rent Restrictions Acts.*

*PP* 1931–2 [Cmd 4152] VII: *Report of the Committee on Dormant Funds.*

*PP* 1932–3 [Cmd 4265] X: *First Interim Report of the Business of the Courts Committee.*

*PP* 1933–4 (68) V: *Report of Standing Committee A on the County Courts Amendment Bill.*

*PP* 1933–4 [Cmd 4471] XI: *Second Interim Report of the Business of the Courts Committee.*

*PP* 1935–6 [Cmd 5065] VIII: *Report of the Royal Commission on the Despatch of Business at Common Law.*

*PP* 1937–8 (157) V: *Report of Standing Committee C on the Administration of Justice (Miscellaneous Provisions) Bill.*

*PP* 1942–3 [Cmd 6480] V: *Report of the Committee on Matrimonial Causes (Trial in the Provinces).*

*PP* 1944–5 [Cmd 6641] V: *Report of the Committee on Legal Aid and Legal Advice.*

*PP* 1945–6 [Cmd 6945] XIII: *Second Interim Report of the Committee on Procedure in Matrimonial Causes.*

*PP* 1946–7 [Cmd 7024] XIII: *Final Report of the Committee on Procedure in Matrimonial Causes.*

*PP* 1947–8 [Cmd 7468] XI; 1948–9 [Cmd 7668] XIII: *Interim and Final Reports of the Committee on County Court Procedure.*

*PP* 1948 [Cmd 7536] I: *Report of the Committee on the Law of Defamation.*

*PP* 1948–9 [Cmd 7706] XII; 1950 [Cmd 7982] XII: *Interim and Final Reports of the Committee on Tenure and Rents of Business Premises.*

*PP* 1948–9 [Cmd 7764] XIV: *Interim Report of the Committee on Supreme Court Practice and Procedure.*

*PP* 1950–1 [Cmd 8364] XI: *Report of the Departmental Committee on the Court of Record for the Hundred of Salford.*

*PP* 1952–3 [Cmd 8746] XIV: *Final Report of the Committee on Supreme Court Practice and Procedure.*

*PP* 1953–4 [Cmd 9248] VIII: *Report of the Committee on Adoption of Children.*

*PP* 1955 (Cmd 9613) XI: *Report of the Royal Commission on the Civil Service.*

*PP* 1955–6 (259) VI: *Report of Standing Committee A on the Administration of Justice Bill.*

*PP* 1955–6 [Cmd 9678] XXIII: *Report of the Royal Commission on Marriage and Divorce.*

*PP* 1958–9 [Cmnd 818] XIII: *Report of the Committee on Funds in Court.*

*PP* 1961–2 [Cmnd 1781] XII: *Final Report of the Committee on Consumer Protection.*

*PP* 1964–5 [Cmnd 2785] XIII: *Report of the Committee on the Legal Status of the Welsh Language.*
*PP* 1966–7 [Cmnd 3084] XXXIX: *Report of the Committee on Legal Records.*
*PP* 1966–7 [Cmnd 3096] XXVI: *Final Report of the Committee on Mechanical Recording of Court Proceedings.*
*PP* 1967–8 [Cmnd 3684] XVIII: *Report of the Committee on Civil Judicial Statistics.*
*PP* 1967–8 [Cmnd 3691] XXX: *Report of the Committee on Personal Injury Litigation.*
*PP* 1967–8 [Cmnd 3529] XXVII: *Report of the Prices and Incomes Board on the Remuneration of Solicitors.*
*PP* 1968–9 (253) V: *Report from Standing Committee D on the Administration of Justice Bill.*
*PP* 1968–9 [Cmnd 4153] XXVIII: *Report of the Royal Commission on Assizes and Quarter Sessions.*
*PP* 1968–9 [Cmnd 3909] XXXVI: *Report of the Committee on the Enforcement of Judgment Debts.*
*PP* 1969–70 [Cmnd 4217] XXV: *First Report of the Prices and Incomes Board on the standing reference on Solicitors' Remuneration.*
*PP* 1970–1 [Cmnd 4596] IX: *Report of the Committee on Consumer Credit.*
*PP* 1970–1 [Cmnd 4609] XXXIII: *Report of the Committee on the Rent Acts.*
*PP* 1971–2 [Cmnd 5107] XXXVIII: *Report of the Departmental Committee on the Adoption of Children.*
*PP* 1974–5 [Cmnd 5794] XV: *Report of the Committee on Contempt of Court.*
*PP* 1974–5 [Cmnd 5909] XV: *Report of the Committee on Defamation.*
*PP* 1975–6 [Cmnd 6385] XX: *Report of the Law Commission on the Jurisdiction of Certain Ancient Courts.*
*PP* 1979–80 [Cmnd 7648] XVIII: *Report of the Royal Commission on Legal Services.*
*PP* 1981–2 [Cmnd 8558]: *Report of the Committee on Insolvency Law and Practice.*

*House of Lords papers*
*HLSP* 1865 (81): *Report from the Select Committee on the County Courts Equitable Jurisdiction Bill.*
*HLSP* 1878–9 (61): *Report from the Select Committee on the County Courts Bill.*
*HLSP* 1882 (189): *Report from the Select Committee on the Bills of Sale Act.*
*HLSP* 1893–4 (156): *Report from the Select Committee on Imprisonment for Debt.* The report is also in HLJ 125.

*House of Lords Journals*
1934–5 vol. 167: *Reports of the Select Committee on the Road Traffic (Compensation for Accidents) Bill.*

*Non-parliamentary publications*

1922: *Minutes of Evidence to the Committee on County Court Staff* (BL 24/30).

ACCOUNTS AND RETURNS

*House of Commons papers (PP series)*

1839 (338–1) XLIII: *Returns of officers, fees, business etc. from each court of request and county court.*

1847 (608) XLVI: *Summonses, causes, sittings etc. from Liverpool and Manchester.*

1849 (265) XLV: *Names, occupations, residences etc. of treasurers.*

1850 (241) XLVI: *Receipts from treasurers to 1 Mar. 1850.*

1850 (743) XLVI: *Judges' sittings and deputies; clerks and high bailiffs' fees, occupations, assistants etc.*

1851 (503) XLVII: *Abstract of general rules and orders.*

1851 (654) XLVII: *Fees, residences, assistants etc. of clerks and high bailiffs.*

1852 (550) XLII: *Warrants granted by Courts of Bankruptcy and county court judges under 14 & 15 Vict. c. 61 s. 52.*

1854–5 (350) XLIII: *Judges, clerks and high bailiffs' fees, allowances etc. and court houses built.*

1854–5 (434) XLIII: *Arbitrations under the Common Law Procedure Act 1854 ss. 3, 6 since 24 Oct. 1854.*

1856 (119) L: *Returns relating to the Registry of County Court Judgments.*

1856 (340) L: *New charges on the exchequer through the County Courts Bill.*

1857 (90 sess. 1) XIV: *Imprisonments in metropolitan gaols; sums due, times imprisoned, grounds etc.*

1857–8 (245) XLVII: *Registrars holding a plurality of courts.*

1857–8 (446) XLVII: *Names, salaries, allowances of treasurers.*

1859 (3 sess. 2) XIX: *Expenses in providing courthouses etc.*

1860 (310) LVII: *Plaints etc. in Stockton and Stokesley.*

1860 (322) LVII: *Proceedings in Liverpool and Manchester.*

1861 (398) LI: *Names, salaries etc. of registrars and high bailiffs.*

1862 (351) XLIV: *Imprisonments under s. 99 for six months to 30 Apr. 1862.*

1864 (536) XLVIII:*Number of days each county court judge sat, 1861–4.*

1865 (160) XXX: *Expenses of the county courts in year ending 31 Mar. 1864.*

1866 (236) LVIII: *Plaints etc. at Stockton and Middlesbrough issued by residents and others.*

1867 (209) LVII: *Answers of the judges to questions on commitments, 1859.*

1867 (294) LVII: *Total plaints, causes, judgments, executions, imprisonments etc. 1859–66.*

1868–9 (391) LI: *Committals to prison 1866–7 from each court.*

1871 (254) LVIII: *Deputy judges' sittings, 1869–70.*

1871 (477) LVIII: *Judges' sittings and hearings.*

1872 (18) L: *Plaints and executions.*

1872 (246) L: *Judges' travelling expenses for year ending 31 Mar. 1871.*
1873 (329) LIV: *Imprisonments, analysed by size of debt.*
1874 (137) LIV: *Correspondence relating to the appointment of Homersham Cox in 1871.*
1874 (346) LIV: *Continuation of no. 329 of 1873.*
1874 (347) LIV: *Imprisonments from each court, previous record, time served etc.*
1875 (45) LXI: *Imprisonments for debts exceeding £50.*
1875 (375) LXI: *Continuation of no. 329 of 1873.*
1876 (19) LXI: *Fees and remuneration of registrars with bankruptcy jurisdiction.*
1877 (22) and (434) LXIX: *Imprisonments from each court, 1875 and 1876, with summary comparisons with 1871–4.*
1877 (451) LXIX: *Continuation of no. 19 of 1876.*
1878 (172) LXIII: *Arbitrations by county court judges, 1875–7.*
1878 (371) LXIII: *Continuation of no. 22 of 1877.*
1878–9 (377) LIX: *Continuation of no. 22 of 1877.*
1880 (384–sess. 2) LXIX: *Continuation of no. 22 of 1877.*
1881 [C 2859] LXXVI: *Replies of judges and registrars to circular letter on the operation of the Bills of Sale Act 1878.*
1883 (322) LV: *Registrars in courts with at least 4,000 plaints; fees, salaries, other appointments etc.; information on high bailiffs.*
1884 (207) LXIII: *Sittings of each county court.*
1887 (300) LXVII: *Deputy judges, with qualifications.*
1888 (148) LXXXIII: *Registrars' earnings.*
1889 (341) LXI: *Judges' number of sitting days and use of deputies.*
1890–1 (362) LXIV: *Continuation of no. 341 of 1889.*
1893–4 (74) LXXIV pt 1: *Persons imprisoned for contempt of court.*
1896 (346) LXIX: *Treasury minute granting retiring allowance to Henry Nicol.*
1899 [C 9251] LXXIX: *Proceedings under the Workmen's Compensation Act 1897 and Employers' Liability Act 1880.*
1900 [Cd 281] LXIX: *Continuation of C 9251.*
1919 [Cmd 939] XLII: *Financial memorandum on the Judges Bill.*
1924 [Cmd 2110] XIX: *Proceedings for the recovery of dwellings under s. 139 County Courts Act 1888.*
1924 [Cmd 2118] XIX: *Possession warrants issued and executed.*
1924 [Cmd 2140] XIX: *Financial memorandum on the County Courts Bill.*

*House of Lords Sessional Papers*

1847–8 (262) XVIII: *Returns of plaints, fees etc. from circuit 38.*
1850 (96) IV: *Return of actions in 1848 . . . for the recovery of debts . . . for the supply of beer.*
1851 (21) I: *Answers of the county court judges on examination of parties.*
1851 (25) I: *Number of writs of* certiorari, *1847–51.*
1851 (64) III: *Number of* prohibitions *in the Queen's Bench, 1846–1851.*

1851 (67) III: *Sums paid to the Treasury and to Treasurers to 1 March 1851.*

1851 (161) XI: *Writs of* certiorari, *1849–51.*

1851 (176) XI: *Returns of fees and their application, 1848–50.*

1851 (224) XI: *Return of costs in undefended suits and judgments by default.*

1851 (239) XI: *Writs of* certiorari, *1849–51.*

1851 (271) XI: *Costs allowed in Edmonton CC in actions of various causes.*

1852 (260) VII: *Names of clerks and their remuneration.*

1852 (261) VII: *Insolvency causes in county courts.*

1852 (262) VII: *Plaints in 1851, divided by amount and number heard by jury.*

1852–3 (139) XIII: *Number of summonses and application of fees to 1851.*

1852–3 (257) XVIII: *Costs awarded in relation to judgments.*

1852–3 (268) XIX: *Plaints etc. in Uxbridge CC in 1851.*

1854 (2) I: *Return of plaints etc. from each court for 1852.*

1854 (3) I: *Return of county court judges.*

1854–5 (38) I: *Copies of letters on judges' salaries.*

1856 (85) III: *Returns of commitments, showing the debt, costs etc.*

1856 (91) III: *Commitments issued by Loughborough CC, 1847–55.*

1859 (sess. 1) (3) I: *Returns of plaints etc., 1857.*

1860 (405) VII: *Returns of plaints etc., 1858–9.*

1873 (277) XVIII: *Return of judges' sitting days, 1873.*

1875 (103) XIV: *Judgment summonses etc. from each court.*

1893–4 *HLJ* 125, 260: *Report of Select Committee on the Debtors Act*; minutes of evidence in *HLSP* 1893–4 (156) II.

1932–3 *HLJ* 165, 119 (no. 52): *Select Committee on the Road Traffic Bill; First report, p. 260; Second Report no. 169, pp. 334–5.*

1933–4 *HLJ* 166, 298: *Report on the County Courts Bill.*

## SECONDARY SOURCES

### WORKS OF REFERENCE

Boase F. R., *Modern English Biography* 6 vols., Truro, 1892–1903.

Butchaell G. D. and Sadleir T. U. (eds.), *Alumni Dublinienses, 1593–1860.* New edn, Dublin, 1935.

Collinge J. M. (ed.). *Officials of Royal Commissions of Inquiry.* London, 1984.

*Debrett's House of Commons and the Judicial Bench.* Edns of 1868 and 1890

*The Dictionary of Welsh Biography.* Oxford, 1959.

Foster J. *Alumni Oxonienses, 1715–1886.* Oxford, 1888.

*Men At The Bar.* 2nd edn, London, 1885.

Foster J. (ed.). *Register of Admissions to Gray's Inn, 1521–1889.* London, 1889.

*Halsbury's Laws of England.* 1st and 4th edns, various years, London.

*Law List.* London, various years from 1835.

*Lincoln's Inn Admissions, 1800–1893.* London, 1896.

McGeagh H. F. and Sturgess H. A. C.. *The Middle Temple Register*, vols. II–IV, London, 1949–77.

Simpson A. W. B. (ed.). *A Biographical Dictionary of the Common Law*. London, 1984.

Stephen L. and Lee S. (eds.). *The Dictionary of National Biography and Supplements*. London, 1885–1959.

Venn J. and J. A. *Alumni Cantabrigienses 1752–1900*. Cambridge, 1954.

*Walford's County Families of the United Kingdom*. Edn of 1865, London.

*Who's Who* and *Who Was Who*. London, 1897–1998.

## PERIODICALS, NEWSPAPERS AND ANNUAL PUBLICATIONS

*Anglo-American Law Review*
*Annual County Courts Practice*
*Cambridge Law Journal*
*Civil Justice Quarterly*
*Conveyancer and Property Lawyer*
*County Court Officer*
*County Court Practice*
*County Courts Chronicle*
*County Courts Gazatte*
*Current Legal Problems*
*Family Law*
*Graya*
*Journal of Legal History*
*Jurist* (1837–66)
*Jurist* (1877–90)
*LAG Bulletin* (*Legal Action* from 1984)
*The Law*
*Law Chronicle*
*Law Gazette*
*Law Guardian*
*Law Journal* (including the *County Court Reporter*, 1912–33)
*Law Magazine* (1828–56), thereafter the *Law Magazine and Law Review* (1856–71) and the *Law Magazine and Review*
*Low Notes*
*Law Quarterly Review*
*Law Review*
*Law Society's Gazette*
*Law Times*
*The Lawyer*
*Legal Observer*
*Legal Practitioner and Solicitor's Journal*
*Modern Law Review*
*Monthly Law Magazine*
*New County Court Practice*
*New Law Journal*
*Pump Court*

*Solicitor* (1934–61), thereafter the *Solicitor Quarterly*
*Solicitors' Journal*
*The Times*
*Transactions of the National Association for the Promotion of Social Science*
*Yearly County Court Practice*

BOOKS, ARTICLES, ETC.

Abel R. *The Legal Profession in England and Wales*. Oxford, 1988.
Abel-Smith R. and R. Stevens. *Lawyers and the Courts*. London, 1967.
Aberdare Lord. *The Letters of H. A. Bruce, Lord Aberdare of Druffyn*. Oxford, 1902.
Abinger E. *Forty Years at the Bar*. London, 1930.
Alexander D. *Retailing in England during the Industrial Revolution*. London, 1970.
Alexander G. *After Court Hours*. London, 1950.
Allen C. J. W. *The Law of Evidence in Victorian England*. Cambridge, 1997.
Alverstone Lord. *Recollections of Bar and Bench*. London, 1914.
Amos A. *On the Expediency of Admitting the Testimony of Parties to Suits* ... Cambridge and London, 1850.
Anderson G. *Victorian Clerks*. Manchester, 1976.
Anderson J. S. *Lawyers and the Making of English Land Law*. Oxford, 1992.
Anon. Bentham, Brougham and Law Reform. *Westminster Review* 11 (1829), 447–71.
Law Reform – District Courts. *Edinburgh Review* 51 (1830), 478–95.
Lord Brougham and Local Judicatories. *Westminster Review* 13 (1830), 420–57.
Lords Brougham, Lyndhurst and Local Courts. *Blackwood's Magazine*, 35 (1834), 562–86.
Fifth Report of the Common Law Commissioners. *British and Foreign Review* 3 (1836), 400–45.
Local Courts. *Monthly Law Magazine*, 10 (1841), 90 ff.
The New Local Court Bill. *LM* 25 (1841), 310–44.
The Local Courts Bill. *LO* 24 (1842), 193 ff.
The County Court Bill. *LM* ns 5 (1846), 152–60.
The New County Courts. *LR* 5 (1846–7), 194–213.
County Courts. *LM* ns 7 (1847), 1–20.
The Small Debts Act. *LM* ns 6 (1847), 120–9.
New County Courts. *LM* ns 7 (1847) 201–16.
The County and Superior Courts. *LR* 7 (1847–8), 246–58.
County Court Extension. *Westminster Review* 54 (1850), 104–17.
County Courts. *LR* 14 (1851), 124–42.
Equity Jurisdiction in County Courts. *LR* 15 (1851–2), 63–74.
County Courts. *LR* 18 (1853), 394–400.
A Practitioner's Experiences of the County Courts. *LT* 20 (1853), 211 ff., vol. 21, 38 ff.
The Amendment of the County Courts. *LM* ns 22 (1855), 114–25.

The County Courts Commission. *LM* ns 23 (1855), 129–41.
Local Judicature. *LM & LR* 5 (1858), 307–14.
Lord Brougham and Law Reform. *Quarterly Review* 105 (1859), 504–26.
Lives of Lord Lyndhurst and Lord Campbell. *Quarterly Review* 126 (1860), 1–61.
County Court Legislation. *LM & LR* 13 (1862), 262–83.
Law Reform and Local Jurisdiction. *LM & LR* 24 (1867–8), 248–65.
Imprisonment for Debt. *LM & LR* 28 (1870), 29–48.
The Future of the County Courts. *The Law.* 1 (1874), 16–24.
*Public Men of Ipswich and East Suffolk.* Ipswich, 1875.
County Courts – Past, Present and Future. *LT* 83 (1887), 242 ff.
*The County Court Handbook.* London. *c.* 1890.
The County Court. *Strand Magazine,* 1 (1891), 531–8.
The County Court Rules (March 1897). *SJ* 41 (1896–7), 324–6.
The Progress and Procedure of the Civil Courts in England. *Edinburgh Review* 185 (1897), 156–82.
Economy in Law. *Edinburgh Review* 225 (1917), 319–42.
Where Are We Going? *CCO* 24 (1945–7), 183.
A Short History. *CCO* 27 (1949–50), 162–4; 28 (1951–2), 11 ff.
County Court Appeals. *LT* 220 (1955), 185 ff.; 221 (1956), 3 ff.
The Liverpool Court of Passage. *LT* 220 (1955), 236–7.
Archbold J. F. *The Practice of the New County Courts.* London, 1847 and subsequent editions to 1886.
Armstrong J. W. S. *Yesterday.* London, 1955.
Arthurs H. W. 'Without the Law': Courts of Local and Special Jurisdiction in Nineteenth Century England. *JLH* 5 (1984), 130–49.
*'Without the Law': Administrative Justice and Legal Pluralism in Nineteenth Century England.* Toronto, 1985.
Askwith Lord. *Lord James of Hereford.* London, 1930.
Aspinall A. *Lord Brougham and the Whig Party.* Manchester, 1927.
Atherley-Jones L. A. *Looking Back.* London, 1925.
Atiyah P. S. *The Rise and Fall of Freedom of Contract.* Oxford, 1979.
Atkinson C. Imprisonment for Debt. *LM & R* 5th s., 31 (1905–6), 129–47.
Atkinson C. J. F. *Recollections from a Yorkshire Dale.* London, 1936.
Atkinson S. *The Law and Practice of the New County Courts . . .* London, 1850.
Atlay J. B. *The Victorian Chancellors.* 2 vols., London, 1908.
'B. B.' The County Courts Bill. *Westminster Review,* 36 (1841), 58–68.
'G. M. B.' County Court Procedure. *SJ* 93 (1949), 275–6, 293–4, 309–11; 94 (1950), 543–6.
Bahlman D. W. R. (ed.) *The Diary of Sir Edward Walter Hamilton.* 2 vols., Oxford, 1972.
Baker J. H. *An Introduction to English Legal History.* 3rd edn, London, 1990.
Ball W. V. Pages from an Autobiography. *LT* 189 (1940), 309 ff.
A Master's Memories. *LT* 211 (1951), 4 ff.

Bamford G. F. I Remember. *CCO* 33 (1956), 17, 27–8, 95–6, 100–1.
Barker A. C. 'Now When I Was a Young Man'. *CCO* 26 (1947–9), 154–5.
Barnett M. J. *The Politics of Legislation*. London, 1969.
'Barrister'. Letters to the Lord Chancellor on his Project for Establishing Local Courts. *LO* 1 (1830–1), 145 ff.; 3 (1831–2), pp. 469 ff.
*A Plain Guide for Suitors in the County Court*. London, 1868.
*Justice in England*. London, 1938.
Bartrip P. W. J. County Court and Superior Court Registrars, 1820–1875: the Making of a Judicial Official, in Sugarman and Rubin, *Law, Economy and Society*, pp. 349–79.
*Workmen's Compensation in Twentieth Century Britain*. Aldershot, 1987.
Bartrip P. W. J. and S. B. Burman *The Wounded Soldiers of Industry*. Oxford, 1983.
Batten E. C. and H. Ludlow *A Treatise on the Jurisdiction ... of the County Courts in Equity*. London, 1866.
Batzel V. M. Parliament, Businessmen and Bankruptcy, 1825–1883: a Study in Middle-Class Alienation. *Canadian Journal of History*, 18 (1983), 171–86.
Beard M. *English Landed Society in the Twentieth Century*. London, 1989.
Becke G. *A Letter ... on the County Courts Extension Bill* ... London, 1850.
Beckett J. C. *The Aristocracy in England, 1660–1914*. Oxford, 1986.
Beirne P. *Fair Rent and Legal Fiction*. London, 1977.
Beresford M. W. *The Leeds Chamber of Commerce*. Leeds, 1951.
Birks M. *Gentlemen of the Law*. London, 1960.
The Recovery of Small Debts. *LSG* 59 (1962), 590–2.
Biron Sir C. *Without Prejudice*. London, 1936.
Bitner H. Inexpensive Justice, the English Experience. *University of Kansas City Law Review* 11 (1943), 86–108.
Blackstone Sir W. *Commentaries on the Laws of England*. 1979 edn, Chicago.
Blom-Cooper, L. Judicial Promotion. *Solicitor*, 25 (1958), 81.
Bolling C. H. *Hire Purchase Trading*. 5th edn, London, 1939.
Borrie G. The Courts Act 1971. *NLJ* 121 (1971), 474–6, 505–6.
Borrie G. and J. Pyke. The Administration of Justice Act 1969. *NLJ* 119 (1969), 1012–13.
The Administration of Justice Act 1970. *NLJ* 120 (1970), 540–2, 564–6.
Bosanquet Sir F. A. *The Oxford Circuit*. London, 1951.
Bowen C. S. Progress in the Administration of Justice in the Victorian Period, in *Select Essays in Anglo-American Legal History*, compiled and edited by a committee of the Association of American Law Schools, vol. I. pp. 516–57. Cambridge, 1907.
Bowley A. L. *Prices and Wages in the United Kingdom, 1914–20*. Oxford, 1921.
Bowley M. *Housing and the Welfare State*. London, 1945.

Box M. *Rebel Advocate*. London, 1983.
Bradley (Judge) F. H. The County Court II: the Equitable Jurisdiction. *LJ* 58 (1923), 537–8.
Rent Restriction in the County Court. *LQR* 39 (1923), 441–57.
Broadgate F. W. *County Court Costs*. London, 1931.
Brooks C. W. Interpersonal Conflict and Social Tension: Civil Litigation in England, 1640–1830, in A. L. Beier (ed.), *The First Modern Society*, pp. 357–400. Cambridge, 1989.
Brooks C. W. and M. Lobban (eds.). *Communities and Courts in Britain, 1150–1900*. London, 1997.
Broom H. *The Practice of the County Courts*. 2nd edn, London, 1857.
Brougham H. (Lord) *The Life and Times of Henry, Lord Brougham*. 3 vols., London, 1871.
Browne J. H. Balfour *Forty Years at the Bar*. London, 1916.
Burke P. *The Complete Book of the New County Courts*. 2nd edn, London, 1847.
Burn W. L. *The Age of Equipoise*. London, 1964.
Butts G. M. *Modern County Court Procedure*. London, 1937.
Cairns A. *The County Court Pleader*. London, 1937.
Campbell J. (Lord) *Lives of Lord Lyndhurst and Lord Brougham* (vol. VIII of *Lives of the Lord Chancellors*). London, 1869.
Campbell J. *F. E. Smith*. London, 1983.
Cannadine D. *The Decline and Fall of the British Aristocracy*. Rev. edn, London, 1996.
Carr C. T. *A Victorian Law Reformer's Correspondence*. London, 1955.
Cautherley C. *Costs in the County Courts*. London, 1886.
The County Court System. *LQR* 7 (1891), pp. 346–53.
Cecil Lady G. *The Life of Lord Salisbury*. 4 vols., London, 1921–32.
Cecil H. (Judge H. C. Leon) *Not Such an Ass*. London, 1961.
*Tipping the Scales*. London, 1964.
*The English Judge*. London, 1970.
*Just Within the Law*. London, 1975.
Chalmers M. D. The County Court System. *LQR* 3 (1887), 1–13.
Imprisonment for Debt. *Fortnightly Review* 50 (1888), 337–46.
The County Courts Consolidation Act 1888. *LQR* 5 (1889), 1–10.
Petty Perjury. *LQR* 11 (1895), 217–22.
Chambers R. C. Some Aspects of Workmen's Compensation. *MLR* 5 (1941–2), 113–17.
Chamier D. *The Law and Practice Relating to County Court Appeals*. London, 1896.
Chapman F. H. B. *A Guide to County Court Procedure*. 2nd edn of *The Trader's Guide* . . ., revised by B. S. Hills, London, 1930.
Chorley Lord. The Report of the Royal Commission on Assizes and Quarter Sessions. *MLR* 33 (1970), 184–90.
Clark D. The County Courts: What can be done for the Future? *CCO* 40 (1967–8), 128–9.
Clarke Sir E. *The Story of My Life*. London, 1918.
Cocks R. *Foundations of the Modern Bar*. London, 1983.

Cohn E. J. The Political Parties and Legal Aid. *MLR* 8 (1945), 97–117.

Coldstream G. P. Judicial Appointments in England. *Journal of the American Judicature Society*, 43 (1959), 41–55.

The Lord Chancellor's Office. *Graya*, 55 (1962), 13–21.

Collinge C. J. One Hundred Years of the County Courts. *Fortnightly Law Journal* 16 (1946), 151–2.

Colombine D. E. *The Handbook to the County Courts*. London, 1851.

Colyer J. S. The Rent Act 1965. *Conv.* ns 29 (1965), 429–63.

Comyn J. *Summing It Up*. Dublin, 1991.

Consumer Council. *Justice Out of Reach*. London, 1970.

Cookson M. The New Judicature. *Fortnightly Review*, ns 19 (1876), 277–94.

Corfield P. *The Impact of English Towns*. Oxford, 1982.

Cornish W. R. and G. de N. Clark. *Law and Society in England, 1750–1950*. London, 1989.

'County Court Judge'. The Reform of the Courts. *LJ* 75 (1933), 109–10, 127–8.

Coutts D. Freeman Mr Registrar. *LSG* 54 (1957), 65–7.

Cowburn J. *The Suitor's Guide to the New County Courts*. London, 1847.

Cox E. W. and M. Lloyd *The Law and Practice of the County Courts*. London, 1848 and six edns to 1854.

Craven J. *A Handbook for the High Bailiffs of the County Court*. London, 1887.

Crawford (Judge) J. D. *Reflections and Recollections*. London, 1936.

Cretney S. M. The Administration of Justice Act 1969. *SJ* 113 (1969), 951–3.

The Administration of Justice Act 1970. *SJ* 114 (1970), 596–9.

'Tell Me the Old, Old Story' – the Denning Report 50 Years On. *Child and Family Law Quarterly* 7 (1995), 163–79.

Crispe T. E. *Reminiscences of a KC*. London, 2nd edn, 1909.

Cross A. L. Old English Local Courts and the Movement for their Reform. *Michigan Law Review*, 30 (1942), 369–85.

Dale R. A. *A County Court Formulist*. London, 1887.

Davis J. E. *A Manual of the Law of Evidence on Trial of Actions in County Courts*. London, 1848.

*The County Courts Equitable Jurisdiction Act 1865*. London, 1865.

*The County Courts Act 1867*. London, 1867.

Dawson J. I. *Reminiscences of a Rascally Lawyer*. Kendal, 1949.

Dawson J. P. *A History of Lay Judges*. Cambridge, Mass., 1960.

Deane P. and W. A. Cole *British Economic Growth, 1688–1959*. 2nd edn, Cambridge, 1962.

de Colyar H. A. *Reports of Cases in the County Courts Included in Circuits 45 and 46*. London, 1883.

de Montmorency J. E. G. *John Gorell Barnes, 1st Lord Gorell*. London, 1920.

Denning A. T. (Lord). *The Due Process of Law*. London, 1980.

Derriman J. *The Pageantry of the Law*. London, 1955.

Dillon J. F. Bentham's Influence on the Reforms of the Nineteenth Century, in *Select Essays in Anglo-American Legal History*, compiled and edited by a committee of the Association of American Law Schools, vol. I, pp. 492–515.

Donagrodski A. P. New Roles for Old: the Northcote–Trevelyan Report and the Clerks of the Home Office, 1832–48, in G. Sutherland (ed.), *Studies in the Growth of Nineteenth Century Government*, pp. 82–109. London, 1972.

Drewry G. How Vital Statistics? *NLJ* 119 (1969), p. 771.

Lord Haldane's Ministry of Justice – Stillborn or Strangled at Birth?. *Public Administration* 61 (1983), 396–414.

Lawyers and Statutory Reform in Victorian Government, in R. McLeod (ed.), *Government and Expertise*. Cambridge, 1988.

Duff F. E. B. (ed.), *Reports of Cases in the Hampshire County Courts, 1917–20*. 1920.

Duman D. *The Judicial Bench in England, 1727–1875*. London, 1982.

*The English and Colonial Bars in the Nineteenth Century*. London, 1983.

Duncan A. The County Court Bailiff. *CCO* 40 (1967–8), 222–3.

Dunn Sir R. *Sword and Wig*. London, 1993.

Eardley Wilmot Sir J. *Lord Brougham's Acts and Bills, from 1811 to the Present Time*. London, 1957.

Edwards J. L. *The Law Officers of the Crown*. London, 1964.

Egerton R. Historical Aspects of Legal Aid. *LQR* 61 (1945), 87–94.

*Legal Aid*. London, 1945.

The Birth and Death of the London Small Claims Court. *NLJ* 130 (1980), 488–90.

Elston E., J. Fuller and M. Murch. Judicial Hearings of Undefended Divorce Petitions. *MLR* 38 (1975), 609–40.

Elwyn Jones, Lord *In My Time*. London, 1983.

Engelbach A. *Anecdotes of Bench and Bar*. London, 1913.

Englander D. *Landlord and Tenant in Urban Britain, 1838–1918*. Oxford, 1983.

Ensor R. C. K. *Courts and Judges in France, Germany and England*. Oxford, 1933.

'J. F.' The County Courts. *LM* ns 12 (1850), 69–78.

Falconer T. F. Notes on County Courts. *CCC* 20 (1867), 290–5.

*On County Courts, Local Courts of Record, etc*. London, 1873.

Salford and Other Local Courts. *LT* 65 (1878), 245–7, 261–2.

Farries T. F. *Precedents of Bills of Costs in the Superior Courts of Equity and on the Equity Side of the County Courts*. London, 1869.

Faulks N. *No Mitigating Circumstances*. London, 1977.

Fay E. S. *A Life of Mr Justice Swift*. London, 1939.

Finer M. The Liabilities (War-time Adjustment) Act 1941. *MLR* 5 (1941–2), 120–5, continued by M. Harnik at 125–8.

Finlason C. E. The Reform of our Civil Procedure. *Westminster Review* ns 34 (1868), 313–34.

Finn M. Debtors and Creditors in Bath's Court of Requests, 1829–39. *Urban History* 21 (1994), 211–36.

Foot M. R. D. and H. C. G. Matthew (eds.). *The Gladstone Diaries*. 14 vols., Oxford 1968–94.

Foote J. A. *Pie-Powder*. London, 1911.

Ford T. H. Brougham as Lord Chancellor. *AALR* 9 (1980), 365–91.

Truro, Brougham and Law Reform during Russell's Administration. *Revue Historique de Droit* 52 (1984), 1–43.

Henry Brougham on the Northern Circuit: Even his Own Solicitor, paper given to the 10th British Legal History Conference, Oxford, 1991.

*Henry Brougham and his World*. Chichester, 1995.

Fowler E. H. *A Life of Lord Wolverhampton*. London, 1912.

Fradley S. County Court Registrars, Brunel University LL B dissertation, 1975.

Francillon J. *Judgments in Causes . . . in the County Court of Gloucestershire and Wiltshire, 1847–52*. 2 vols., Cheltenham, 1850, 1852.

Francis C. W. Practice, Strategy and Institution: Debt Collection in the English Common Law Courts, 1740–1840. *North-Western University Law Review* 80 (1986), 808–954.

Freeman S. *A Guide to County Court Costs*. London, 1909.

Gardiner Lord. Two Lawyers or One? *Current Legal Problems* 23 (1970), 1–22.

The Role of the Lord Chancellor in the Field of Law Reform. *LQR* 87 (1971), 326–37.

Garnham J. and D. Templeman. Operation Divorce. *CCO* 40 (1967–8), 274.

Gash N. *Mr Secretary Peel*. London, 1961.

Gaskell E. *Cheshire Leaders, Social and Political*. Exeter, 1896.

Gibbons H. F. *Equity in the County Courts*. London, 1866.

Gifford T. *Where's the Justice?* London, 1986.

Gilchrist A. *The Temple in the 'Nineties*. London, 1938.

Gilmour J. *The County Courts Act 1867*. London, 1868.

Glasser C. The Pearson Report on Civil Judicial Statistics. *MLR* 32 (1969), 193–7.

The First Prices and Incomes Board Report. *MLR* 33 (1970), 547–51.

The Administration of Justice Act 1970. *MLR* 34 (1971), 61–70.

Goddard Lord. Politics and the British Bench. *Journal of the American Judicature Society*, 43 (1959), 124–33.

Goldman L. The Social Science Association, 1857–1886: a Context for mid-Victorian Liberalism. *English Historical Review* 101 (1986), 95–134.

Gower L. C. B. The Cost of Litigation. *MLR* 17 (1954), 1–23.

Graham E. *Fifty Years of Famous Judges*. London, 1930.

Grant J. *The Bench and the Bar*. 2nd edn, London, 1838.

Gregory R. C. L. The Genesis of the New County Court Rules. *Civil Justice Quarterly* 2 (1983), 1–6.

Grimmer W. H. *Anecdotes of the Bench and Bar*. 2nd edn, London, 1858.

Guest A. G. *The Law of Hire Purchase*. London, 1966.
Gurney-Champion F. C. G. *Justice and the Poor in England*. London, 1926.
'H'. Lord Brougham's Local Court Bill. *LM* 5 (1831), 1–49.
Fifth Report of the Common Law Commissioners – Local Courts. *LM* 8 (1833), 162–8.
Lord Brougham's New Local Court Bill. *LM* 9 (1833), 392–413.
The Local Court Bill. *LM* 31 (1844), 364–74.
Hagan S. A Beginner's Guide to the Bailiff. *CCO* 40 (1967–8), p. 266.
Hailsham Lord. *The Door Wherein I Went*. London, 1975.
*A Sparrow's Flight*. London, 1990.
Haldane Lord *An Autobiography*. London, 1929.
Haly W. T. and H. W. Wills. Law at a Low Price. *Household Words*, 18 May 1850, 176–80.
Hammond J. L. and B. *James Stansfeld, a Victorian Champion of Sex Equality*. London, 1932.
Hammond L. E. The Administration of the Workmen's Compensation Acts. *MLR* 5 (1941–2), 215–18.
Hanham H. J. Political Patronage at the Treasury, 1870–1912. *Historical Journal* 3 (1960), pp. 75–84.
Hardcastle M. S. *The Life of Lord Campbell*. 2 vols., London, 1881.
Harding R. W. The Hire Purchase Act 1964. *Journal of Business Law* (1965), 15–21.
Hardman W. S. The Evolution of the County Courts Officers' Association. *CCO* 3 (1922–3), pts 7, 8.
Harley H. The Courts of Birmingham. *Journal of the American Judicature Society*, 11 (1928), 166–77.
Harper J. C. Personal Injuries Litigation. *MLR* 34 (1971), 70–4.
Harper J. C. and P. R. Kimber. The Winn Committee. *MLR* 32 (1969), pp. 67–75.
Harris G. *The Autobiography of George Harris*. London, 1888.
Harris R. and A. Seldon (eds.). *Hire Purchase in a Free Society*. London, 1958.
Hart H. L. *The Way to Justice*. London, 1941.
Harvey C. P. Law Reform after the War. *MLR* 6 (1943), 39–46.
Hastings Sir P. *Autobiography*. London, 1948.
Hawes F. *Henry Brougham*. London, 1957.
Hawkes C. P. *Bar and Bench in the Saddle*. London, 1928.
Heighton J. *Legal Life and Humour*. London, 1917.
Heuston R. F. V. *Lives of the Lord Chancellors, 1885–1940*. Oxford, 1964.
*Lives of the Lord Chancellors, 1940–70*. Oxford, 1987.
Heywood G. W. *The Common Law and Equity Practice of the County Courts*. London, 1870. 4th edn, retitled *The Jurisdiction and Practice of the County Courts*, London, 1886.
Holdsworth W. S. *The County Court Guide*. London, 1862.
*A History of English Law*. 17 vols., London, 1903–66.
*Charles Dickens as a Legal Historian*. Yale, 1928.
Hollams Sir J. *Jottings of an Old Solicitor*. London, 1906.

Honey J. R. de S. *Tom Brown's Universe*. London, 1977.

Hough P. A. *A Handy Guide to County Court Costs*. 3rd edn, London, 1903.

Howe M. D. (ed.). *The Holmes–Laski Letters, 1916–1935*. Oxford, 1953.

Huch R. K. *Henry, Lord Brougham. The Later Years, 1830–1868*. Lewiston, 1993.

Huebner M. Outline of the New System. *NLJ* 122 (1972), 4–5.

Humphreys B. V. *Clerical Unions in the Civil Service*. Oxford, 1958.

Humphries F. Memorandum on Treasury Gradings. *CCO* 35 (1958), 79–82.

Assaults on Bailiffs. *CCO* 41 (1969–70), 12–13.

Hurst G. B. *Closed Chapters*. Manchester, 1942.

*Lincoln's Inn Essays*. London, 1949.

Hyde L. *County Court Costs*. London, 1904.

Ilbert Sir C. *Legislative Forms and Methods*. Oxford, 1901.

Ilersic A. R and P. F. B. Liddle. *The Parliament of Commerce*. London, 1960.

Impey, H. *Debt Recovery and County Court Procedure, a Practical and Easy Guide for Business Men*. 2nd edn, London, 1909.

Ison T. G. Small Claims. *MLR* 35 (1972), 18–37.

'J'. A Chapter of Discussions on County Court Matters. *LM* 17 (1852), 21–37.

Jackson R. *The Chief*. London, 1957.

Jackson R. M. The Incidence of Jury Trial During the Past Century. *MLR* 1 (1937–8), 132–44

*The Machinery of Justice in England*. Cambridge, 1940 and 6th edn, 1972.

Jacob I. H. The Present Importance of Pleadings. *CLP* 13 (1960), 171–92.

The Inherent Jurisdiction of the Court. *CLP* 23 (1970), 23–52.

Civil Procedure since 1800, in A. Alsop (ed.), *Then and Now, 1799–1974*. London, 1974.

Jagoe J. *The Practice of the County Courts*. 3rd edn, London, 1847.

Jay C. *The Law*. London, 1868.

Jeaffreson J. C. *A Book About Lawyers*. 2 vols., London, 1867.

Johnes A. J. On the Union of Law and Equity in Relation to the County Courts. *LR* 15 (1851–2), 313–26.

County Courts and their Claims. *LR* 17 (1853), 265–78.

The County Courts. *LR* 19 (1853–4), 257–71.

Johnson N. E. (ed.). *The Diary of Gathorne Hardy, later Lord Cranbrook*. Oxford, 1981.

Johnson P. Class Law in Victorian England. *Past and Present* 141 (1993), 147–69.

Small Debts and Economic Distress in England and Wales, 1857–1913. *Economic History Review* 46 (1993), 67–87.

Jones C. *The Business Man's County Court Guide*. London, 1893.

Jones H. Kay *Butterworths, History of a Publishing House*. London, 1980.

Jones M. *Justice and Journalism*. London, 1974.
Jones (Judge) T. A. *Without My Wig*. Liverpool, 1944.
Joyce S. *Remarks on the Operation of the County Courts Act*. London, 1850.
Kahn H. R. *Salaries in the Public Services in England and Wales*. London, 1962.
Kent H. S. *In on the Act: Memoirs of a Lawmaker*. London, 1979.
Kerchner B. The Transformation of Imprisonment for Debt in England, 1828–38. *Australian Journal of Law and Society* 2 (1984), 61–109.
Kilmuir Lord. *Political Adventure*. London, 1964.
Kirk H. *Portrait of a Profession*. London, 1976.
Knafla L. *Kent at Law*. London, 1994.
Kostal R. W. *Law and English Railway Capitalism*. Oxford, 1994.
Lailey (Judge) B. Agricultural Holdings in the Courts. *LJ* 58 (1923), 607–9.
*Jottings from a Fee Book of a Man of All Work*. Portsmouth, 1932.
Lane E. *Hear the Other Side*. London, 1985.
Laski H. *Studies in Law and Politics*. London, 1928.
Leevers M. *et al. A Fair Hearing? Possession Cases in the County Court*. London, 1977.
Le Marchant Sir D. *A Memoir of John Charles, Viscount Althorp*. London, 1876.
Leonard P. M. *Precedents of Pleading in Equity in the County Courts*. London, 1869.
Lester V. M. *Victorian Insolvency*. Oxford, 1995.
Lewis, G. *Lord Hailsham*. London, 1997.
Lewis J. R. *The Victorian Bar*. London, 1982.
Liddell A. G. C. *Notes from the Life of an Ordinary Mortal*. London, 1911.
Lloyd C. E. *The County Courts Act 1888*. London, 1888.
Lloyd D. The Final Report of the County Courts Committee. *MLR* 12 (1949), 354–9.
The Cost of Litigation. *CLP* 7 (1954), 55–74.
Lobban M. *The Common Law and English Jurisprudence, 1760–1850*. Oxford, 1991.
London Chamber of Commerce *Memorandum on the Expense of Litigation*. London, 1930.
Lowe R. Have We Abolished Imprisonment for Debt? *Fortnightly Review* 27 (1877), 307–16.
Lowry J. P. Register of County Court Judgments. *CCO* 40 (1967–8), 113.
MacDonagh O. *Early Victorian Government, 1830–1870*. London, 1977.
Maguire J. M. Poverty and Civil Litigation. *Harvard Law Review*, 36 (1923), 361.
Manchester A. H. Law Reform in England and Wales, 1840–1880. *Acta Juridica* (1977), 189–202.
*A Modern Legal History of England and Wales, 1750–1950*. London, 1979.

Manisty H. *A Letter to Sir Frederick Pollock ... on Local Courts*. London, 1843.

Manning C. A. *Durham Lives*. London, 1897.

Martin T. B. *The Life of Lord Lyndhurst*. London, 1883.

Mathew T. The Mayor's Court, the Sheriffs' Courts and the Palace Court. *Juridical Review* 31 (1919), 139–51.

Mathias P. *The First Industrial Nation*. 2nd edn, London, 1983.

Matthews H. C. *The Gladstone Diaries*. Vol. 7. Oxford, 1982.

Mayer S. *Reminiscences of a KC, Theatrical and Legal*. London, 1924.

Mayhall J. *A Tradesman's Guide to the Practice of County Courts*. 3rd edn, London, 1881.

McGregor O. R. *Divorce in England*. London, 1957.

McKendrick N., J. Brewer and J. H. Plumb. *The Birth of a Consumer Society*. London, 1982.

McLeary (Judge) R. E. *Precedents of Claims in the County Courts*. London, 1929.

*Precedents of Proceedings in the County Courts Subsequent to Claims*. London, 1930.

*The County Courts Consolidation Act 1934*. London, 1935.

McManus J. J. The Emergence and Non-Emergence of Legislation. *BJLS* 5 (1978), 185–201.

Megarry Sir R. E. *The Rent Acts*. 10th edn, 3 vols., London, 1967.

*Arabinesque-at-Law*. London, 1969.

Mellors R. *Men of Nottingham and Nottinghamshire*. Nottingham, 1924.

Milward C. *The County Courts Act 1850*. London, 1850.

Morgan R. I. The Introduction of Civil Legal Aid in England and Wales, 1914–1949. *Twentieth Century British History*, 5 (1994), 38–76.

Moseley B. L. The Proposed Extension of County Court Jurisdiction. *LM* 4 4th s. (1878–9), 345–72.

Moseley J. *A Treatise on the New County Courts*. London, 1846, *Part Two*, London, 1847.

Muir C. *Justice in a Depressed Area*. London, 1936.

Mullins C. *In Quest of Justice*. London, 1930.

The Poor Man's Court of Justice. *The Nineteenth Century and After*, 113 (1933), 207–19.

Legal Aid ad infinitum. *LJ* 95 (1945), 215–16.

*Fifteen Years Hard Labour*. London, 1948.

Munday R. The Judge who Answered his Critics. *CLJ* (1987), 303–14.

Munton F. K. County Court Reform. *LQR* 5 (1889), 134–9.

Ought the County Court to be Made a Branch of the High Court? *LM* 5th s., 31 (1905–6), 328–36.

Murch M. *et al. The Overlapping Family Jurisdiction of the Magistrates' Courts and the County Courts*. Bristol, 1977.

Myers E. *Lord Althorp*. London, 1890.

New C. *A Life of Henry Brougham to 1830*. Oxford, 1961.

Nield Sir B. *Farewell to the Assizes*. London, 1972.

Odgers W.B. Changes in Procedure and the Law of Evidence, in *A Century of Law Reform*. London, 1901.
Owen W. H. The Reorganization of Provincial Courts. *LQR* 9 (1893), 321–30.
Page R. G. The Conveyancer in the County Court. *Conveyancer* ns 5 (1940–1), 84–102.
Palmer G. H. The County Courts and Imprisonment for Debt. *LT* 38 (1862–3), 27–8.
Parker C. S. *The Life and Letters of Sir James Graham*. London, 1907.
Parris H. *Staff Relations in the Civil Service*. London, 1973.
Parris J. *Under My Wig*. London, 1961.
Parrott V. *A Route to Respectability; Solicitors and their Changing Image, 1830–1910*. Salford University Occasional Papers in Politics, 26, 1991.
Parry E. A. The Insolvent Poor. *Fortnightly Review* os 69 (1898), 797–804
A Day of My Life in the County Court. *Cornhill Magazine* ns 16 (1904), 343–56.
*What the Judge Saw*. London, 1912.
*The Gospel and the Law*. London, 1928.
*My Own Way*. London, 1932.
Parsons A. and R. Allen. *The Workmen's Compensation Act 1906*. London, 1906.
Passingham B. *Gibson's County Court Practice*. London, 1938.
Paterson, A. The Infirm Judge. *British Journal of Law and Society* 1 (1974), 83–9.
Judges: a Political Elite? *Ibid.*, 118–35.
Paterson W. *The County Courts Act* .... 3rd edn, London, 1847.
Payne D. Appeals on Fact. *CLP* 11 (1958), 185–207.
Pearson F. *Memories of a KC's Clerk*. London, 1935.
Pellew J. *The Home Office, 1848–1914*. London, 1982.
Law and Order: Expertise and the Victorian Home Office, in R. McLeod (ed.). *Government and Expertise*, pp. 59–72. Cambridge, 1988.
Pickles J. *Judge for Yourselves*. London, 1992.
Pickstone C. H. The Extension of the County Courts. *LJ* 42 (1907), 643–5.
Pitt-Lewis G. *A Complete Practice of the County Courts*. London, 1880 and 4th edn, 1890.
*The County Courts Act 1888*. London, 1888.
The Development of the County Court System. *LT* 105 (1898), 196–7.
*Commissioner Kerr – an Individuality*. London, 1903.
Pitt Taylor J. A New County Court Act. *LT* 49 (1870), 219 ff.
Polden P. *A Guide to the Records of the Lord Chancellor's Department*. London, 1988.
The Public Trustee in England, 1906–1986: the Failure of an Experiment? *JLH* 10 (1989), 228–55.

Judicial Independence and Executive Responsibilities. *AALR* 25 (1996), part one at pp. 1–38, part two pp. 133–62.

Safety First: the Appointment of Metropolitan Stipendiary Magistrates, 1950–61. *Cambrian Law Review* 27 (1996), 57–74.

Judicial Selkirks: the County Court Judges and the Press, 1847–1880, in C. W. Brooks and M. Lobban (eds.). *Communities and Courts in Britain, 1150–1900*, pp. 245–62. London, 1997.

'Oiling the Machinery': the Lord Chancellor's Office and the County Court Bench, 1927–1944. *JLH* 19 (1998), 224–44.

The Strange Death of County Court Nonsuit. *Cambrian Law Review* 30 (1999).

Pollock C. E. *The Practice of the County Courts*. London, 1851 and subsequent editions, including 9th, 1880, by H. Nicol and H. C. Pollock.

Pollock C. E. and H. Nicol. *The Practice of the County Courts in Respect of Probate and Administration*. London, 1857.

Pollock E. *County Court Notebook*. London, 1933.

Powell-Smith V. The Rights and Duties of Bailiffs. *NLJ* 119 (1969), 393–4.

'Practising Solicitor'. County Court Defects. *LT* 118 (1904–5), 297–8.

Prest W. Law Reform in Eighteenth Century England, in P. Birks (ed.). *The Life of the Law*, London, 1993, pp. 113–24.

Pritchard M. J. Non-Suit: a Premature Obituary. *CLJ* 18 (1960), 88–96.

Pue W. W. Rebels at the Bar. *AALR* 16 (1987), pp. 303–52.

Pulling A. Local Courts and the Bounds of Their Jurisdiction. *LM & LR* 32 (1871), 156–67.

Purcell E. D. *Forty Years at the Criminal Bar*. London, 1916.

Radcliffe (Judge) F.R.Y. County Courts IV: Circuits and Districts. *LJ* 58 (1923), 582–3.

Radcliffe G. R. Y. and G. Cross *The English Legal System*. 6th edn, by G. J. Hand and D. J. Bentley, London, 1977.

Rees (Judge) J.Tudor. *Reserved Judgment*. London, 1956.

Rentoul J. A. *Stray Thoughts and Memories*. London, 1921.

Rider D. *Ten Years' Adventures among Landlords and Tenants*. London, 1927.

Riley H. L. *The Consolidated County Court Orders and Rules, 1875–7*. London, 1880.

Roberts G. D. *Without My Wig*. London, 1957.

Robson W. A. *Justice and Administrative Law*. London, edns of 1931, 1947.

Rock P. *Making People Pay*. London, 1973.

Roe R. (Lord Bessborough). *Straws from my Wig*. London, 1954.

Rogers J. W. *The County Courts Extension Act*. London, 1850.

Rogers P. H. Thorold. Hire Purchase and the Emergency Legislation. *Conv*., ns 4 (1939–40), 348–60.

The Courts (Emergency Powers) Acts 1939 and 1940: a View in Retrospect. *Conv*. ns 5 (1940–1), 4–23.

The Liabilities (War-time Adjustment) Act 1941. *Conv.* ns 6 (1941–2), 31–49.

Rosenbaum S. Rule Making in the County Courts. *LQR* 31 (1915), 304–13.

Roseveare H. *The Treasury*. London, 1969.

Routh G. *Occupation and Pay in Great Britain, 1906–60*. Cambridge, 1965.

Rowlands E. Bowen. County Court Judges and their Jurisdiction. *LQR* 18 (1902), 237–46.

*In the Light of the Law*. London, 1931.

Rubin G. R. Law, Poverty and Imprisonment for Debt, 1869–1914, in Sugarman and Rubin, *Law, Economy and Society*, pp. 241–99.

The County Courts and the Tally Trade, 1846–1914, *Ibid.*, pp. 321–48.

Debtors, Creditors and the County Courts. *JLH* 17 (1996), 74–82.

Ruegg (Judge) A. H. *The Law Regulating the Relations of Employers and Workmen in England*. London, 1905.

The County Court I: its Foundation and Progress. *LJ* 58 (1923), 506–8.

Russell R. (ed.). *The Early Correspondence of Lord John Russell, 1805–40*. London, 1913.

Russell-Jones, A. The Administration of the Workmen's Compensation Acts. *MLR* 6 (1943), 157.

'S'. Small Debts Act. *LM* ns 3 (1845), 309–15.

Schuster Sir C. Lord Birkenhead, in W. R. Inge (ed.). *The Post-Victorians*, London, 1933, pp. 83–100.

Selborne Lord. *Memorials, Part II: Personal and Political*. 2 vols., London, 1898.

Shawcross Lord. *Life Sentence*. London, 1996.

Shetreet S. *Judges on Trial*. Amsterdam, 1976.

Simpson J. H. Our County Courts. *The Lawyer*, 1900, 102–3, 136–8.

Slatter M. The Norwich Court of Requests – a Tradition Continued. *JLH* 5 (1984), 97–107.

Smith H. The Resurgent County Court in Victorian Britain. *American Journal of Legal History* 13 (1969), 126–37.

Snagge T. W. *The Evolution of the County Court*. London, 1904.

Snow T. The Near Future of Law Reform, II: the High Court and the County Court. *LQR* 16 (1900), 229–36.

The Consolidation of the High Court and the County Courts. *LQR* 22 (1906), 127–35.

'Solicitor'. *County Court Practice Made Easy*. London, edns of 1902 and 8th, 1937.

*English Justice*. London, 1932.

Southgate D. *The Passing of the Whigs*. London, 1965.

Spickett J .E. *The Practice of the County Courts*. London, 1928.

Stephen Sir G. *A Digest of County Court Cases* . . . London, 1855.

Stephen H. and R. A. Stephen *County Courts Acts, Orders and Practice*. London, 1889.

Stevens R. *Law and Politics: the House of Lords as a Judicial Body, 1800–1976*. London, 1979.

*The Independence of the Judiciary*. Oxford, 1993.

Stewart R. *Henry Brougham, 1778–1868*. London, 1985.

Sugarman D. Who Colonized Whom?, in Y. Dezalay and D. Sugarman (eds.). *Professional Competition and Professional Power*, London, 1995, pp. 227–36.

Bourgeois Collectivism, Professional Power and the Boundaries of the State. The Private and Public Life of the Law Society, 1825 to 1914. *International Journal of the Legal Profession* 3 (1996), 81–135.

Sugarman D. and G. R. Rubin (eds.). *Law, Economy and Society, 1750–1914*. Abingdon, 1984.

Taylor G. Appeals from the County Courts to the Superior Courts of Law. *CCC* 15 (1862), 167 ff.

Thomas P. A. and G. Mungham. The Lay Advocate. *AALR* 3 (1974), 7–28.

Thorneley J. W. A. and J. S. Ziegel. Hire Purchase Reformed. *CLJ* 23 (1965), 59–92.

*Transactions of the National Association for the Promotion of Social Science*, 1858: G. W. Hastings (135–44, 160–3), E. Heath (153–9); 1865: A. J. Williams (143–5); 1867: R. M. Pankhurst (198–204); 1868: Williams (205–16), W. T. S. Daniel (225–37) and discussion at 272–5; 1869: T. Sherwood-Smith (204–5); 1870: Daniel and W. S. Daglish (191–208); 1871: discussion (208–37); 1882: J. Motteram (184–95), Pankhurst (195–202) and discussion (203–6).

Treherne J. T. *A Practical Treatise on the Bankruptcy Act and Debtors Act 1869*. London, 1870.

Turberville A. S. *The House of Lords in the Age of Reform, 1784–1837*. London, 1958.

Turner J. N. Small Claims and the County Court in England. *AALR* 9 (1980), 150–76.

Turner R. W. Our Archaic Forms of Execution. *MLR* 4 (1940–1), 210–13.

Tyler E. L. G. Possession by a Mortgagee. *NLJ* 120 (1970), 808.

Udall H. *The New County Courts*. London, 1846.

Veale W. V. The Bristol Tolzey Court. *Journal of the Society of Public Teachers of Law*, (1936), 20–9.

Veall D. *The Popular Movement for Law Reform, 1640–1660*. Oxford, 1970.

Wade J. *The Extraordinary Black Book*. London, 1830 edn.

Walpole S. *A History of England from 1815*. London, 1878–86.

Walsh N. Whitleyism in the County Courts. *CCO* 41 (1969–70), 156 ff.

Warren, S. *Miscellanies*. London, 1855.

Watson E. A. *Whig Renaissance: Lord Althorp and the Whig Party, 1782–1845*. New York and London, 1987.

Weatherfield G. M. The City Courts. *LM & LR* 28 (1870), 208–15.

County Court Commitments. *LM & LR* 31 (1871), 236–43.

Amalgamation of the City Courts. *LM* ns 2, (1873), 13–24.

Weiss B. *The Hell of the English*. Lewisburg, 1986.

Whiteley C. *Brief Life*. London, 1942.

Whitelock W. H. County Courts VI: Claims and Defences. *LJ* 59 (1924), 29–30.

Will J. S. *Changes in the Jurisdiction and Practice of the County Courts ... Effected by the County Courts Act 1867*. London, 1868.

Wilson Sir A. and H. Levy. *Workmen's Compensation*. 2 vols., Oxford, 1941.

Winder W. H. D. The Courts of Requests. *LQR* 52 (1936), 369–94.

Wright M. *Treasury Control of the Civil Service, 1854–74*. Oxford, 1969.

Treasury Control, 1854–1914, in G. Sutherland (ed.). *Studies in the Growth of Nineteenth Century Government*, pp. 195–227. London, 1972.

Yate-Lee L. A Practical Scheme for the Extension of the Jurisdiction of the County Courts. *LM* 5th s., 24 (1898), 257–71.

Yeomans F. C. Units. *CCO* 36 (1959–60), 79–81.

# INDEX